An Era of Value Change

An Era of Value Change

The Long 1970s in Europe

EDITED BY

FIAMMETTA BALESTRACCI,
CHRISTINA VON HODENBERG,
AND ISABEL RICHTER,

GERMAN HISTORICAL INSTITUTE LONDON

OXFORD
UNIVERSITY PRESS

OXFORD
UNIVERSITY PRESS

Great Clarendon Street, Oxford, OX2 6DP,
United Kingdom

Oxford University Press is a department of the University of Oxford.
It furthers the University's objective of excellence in research, scholarship,
and education by publishing worldwide. Oxford is a registered trade mark of
Oxford University Press in the UK and in certain other countries

Published in the United States
by Oxford University Press Inc., New York

First published 2024

British Library Cataloguing in Publication Data

Data available

Library of Congress Cataloging in Publication Data

Data available

Library of Congress Control Number: 2024930961

ISBN 978-0-19-892899-7

1 3 5 7 9 10 8 6 4 2

Typeset by John Waś, Oxford
Printed in Great Britain
on acid-free paper by
Biddles Ltd, King's Lynn

Foreword

In the historian's imagination, the decade of the 'long' 1970s occupies a strange place, with images oscillating between bleak economic stagnation and crisis on the one hand, and the rise of democratization, social movements, and a new type of politics on the other. More and more often, the 1970s appear as the starting point for our present, or at least as a key period of transformation within a continuum spanning the long twentieth century. The decade stands for the emergence of new subjectivities and new modes of activism and self-expression; for changing attitudes towards gender, sexuality, family, work, and leisure; and for new configurations of expert knowledge. As the editors of this volume, we have therefore set out to reassess and compare the developments of this tumultuous decade across Europe—west and east, north and south. We put forward an explanative model for the rapid socio-cultural changes of the period which seeks to test the theory of 'value change', and in particular our hypothesis of 'post-rational' value experimentation. We explain our approach, and the conceptual challenges associated with it, in more detail in the introduction. But more importantly, we have also gathered contributions by specialists from different countries who throw light on the long 1970s from a range of angles and perspectives. The twelve essays collected here are authored by academics based at universities in five European and North American countries. They reflect an international research community that spans different specializations, notably political and gender history, intellectual history and the history of knowledge, social and cultural history, the history of the family and of sexuality, feminism, and youth.

This volume grew out of an international conference titled 'An Era of Value Change: The Seventies in Europe' and held in March 2019 at the German Historical Institute London. The conference itself was the outcome of a long-standing research collaboration between Fiammetta Balestracci, then Marie Skłodowska-Curie Fellow at Queen Mary University of London, and the GHIL director Christina von Hodenberg. Martin Baumeister joined as co-convener for the German Historical Institute Rome, and additional funds were contributed by the Deutsche Forschungsgemeinschaft and the European programme Horizon 2020. These funds, for which we are grateful, enabled us to invite historians from across the continent, both to present in panels and to comment on the state of the field in their respective national communities. A wide range of papers were given on the Soviet Union, Poland, East and West Germany, the Netherlands, Britain, Spain, Scandinavia, Italy, the Mediterranean region, Portugal, and Greece, of which this volume only includes a selection. Our thanks go to the scholars who enriched our discussions at the conference but did not join the publication: James Mark, Claudia Kraft, Gerd-Rainer Horn, Detlef Siegfried, Ekaterina Emeliantseva Koller, Tobias Becker, Emily Robinson, Johan van Merriënboer, Barbara Klich-Kluczewska, Isabel Heinemann, Corrado Tornimbeni, Aline Maldener, Florian Schui, Fernando Esposito, Jan-Henrik Friedrichs, and Ulf Brunnbauer. We were fortunate, too, that Juliane Fürst and Kinga Bloch agreed to contribute their research when we approached them after the workshop.

Many people helped to make this volume a reality. First of all, I thank my co-editors, Fiammetta Balestracci and Isabel Richter, for their dedication and team spirit. I want to express my particular gratitude to Angela Davies and Jozef van der Voort for their expert help in making the pieces come together as a publication. I thank Carole Sterckx and Anita Bellamy for their support in organizing the conference. My thanks also go to the Delegates and staff at Oxford University Press, particularly Bethany Williams, and to the two anonymous reviewers whose suggestions helped to improve the volume.

The making of this book was overshadowed by the tragic death of one of our contributors, Dr Lisa Dittrich (University of Munich). With Lisa, we lost not only a friend, but also a deeply original researcher and an important voice in the field of European history. Her essay in this volume, on marriage counselling and partnership ideals in the German Democratic Republic, represents a major outcome of her last research project, which promised a history of love and marriage in the two German states between 1945 and 1990 but was cut short in a cruel manner. We miss Lisa Dittrich, as a colleague and as a person, and want to dedicate this book to her memory.

Christina von Hodenberg

London
May 2024

Contents

Introduction

1

The Long 1970s in Europe as a Transformational Period towards Post-Rational Values

FIAMMETTA BALESTRACCI,
CHRISTINA VON HODENBERG,
AND ISABEL RICHTER

Recently, the long 1970s have emerged more and more clearly as the beginning of a new epoch in which we still live, a watershed moment in the history of Europe. Disagreements and uncertainty prevail, however, about the contours of the new forces, the factors driving change, and geographical and chronological parallels and differences. The historiographies on Western, Central, Eastern, and Southern Europe, particularly for the Cold War period, are often less connected than the processes of change back then, which were already intertwined to a considerable extent. With this volume we want to advance the international historiographical debate on the history of the 1970s as the beginnings of our present society, to conduct a historical evaluation of theories of 'value change', and to approach the history of the present from a long-term interpretative perspective, reconnecting it to the history of the long twentieth century in highly industrialized Europe.[1]

Different societal sectors and factors have been identified as responsible for fundamental transformations during the last third of the twentieth century. Scholarship has often pointed to socio-economic ruptures: to deindustrialization, globalization, and deregulation, the rise of digital finance capitalism, and the decline of trade unions and working-class milieux. Other factors variously credited with the emergence and proliferation of new values are rising affluence, mass consumerism, new mass media, widened access to higher education,

---

[1] For the 'long' twentieth century see Ulrich Herbert, 'The Short and the Long Twentieth Century: German and European Perspectives', *German Historical Institute London Bulletin*, 42/2 (2020), 9–24; Christoph Cornelißen, *Europa im 20. Jahrhundert* (Berlin, 2021).

as well as changing gender roles, ideas of family, and sexual mores. Lastly, new ideas of the political, the future, modernity, and progress have been identified and at times tied to specific intellectual groups or political generations challenging 'the establishment'. This volume seeks to advance a joined-up assessment of these phenomena. We want to differentiate between triggers, causal factors, and outcomes, and attempt to develop comparative answers across Western, Central, Eastern, and Southern Europe. Our comparison extends geographically, across the Iron Curtain and including 'smaller' countries, as well as chronologically, seeking to place the 1970s as a key decade of transformation into a continuum spanning the long twentieth century. We shall ask how the transformations of the 1970s were linked to the legacy of the two world wars, but also how they were related to the period of the 1960s (which has been presented by some scholars as the key window of change, rather than the 1970s).[2]

We propose to understand the sea change represented by the period within the framework of 'value change'. The theory of value change goes back to Clyde Kluckhohn's 1951 understanding of values as 'conception(s) . . . of the desirable'[3] and was popularized by Ronald Inglehart from the early 1970s onwards (on which more below). It had a powerful impact on the social sciences and historiography, especially—but not only—in Germany; and the latter fact explains why many of the case studies presented here include a German component or involve German scholars.[4] By bringing historians from Germany into discussion with their colleagues from across Europe, this volume seeks to test the wider

---

[2] Arthur Marwick, *The Sixties: Cultural Revolution in Britain, France, Italy, and the United States*, c.*1958*–c.*1974* (New York, 1998), 3–7; Axel Schildt, Detlef Siegfried, and Karl Christian Lammers, 'Einleitung', in eid. (eds.), *Dynamische Zeiten: Die 60er Jahre in den beiden deutschen Gesellschaften* (Hamburg, 2000), 11–20, at 13, 16; Gerd-Rainer Horn, *The Spirit of Vatican II: Western European Progressive Catholicism in the Long Sixties* (Oxford, 2015), 1; Richard Vinen, *The Long '68: Radical Protest and its Enemies* (London, 2018), p. xiii; Lawrence Black, *Redefining British Politics: Culture, Consumerism and Participation 1954–70* (Basingstoke, 2010).

[3] Clyde Kluckhohn et al., 'Values and Value-Orientations in the Theory of Action: An Exploration in Definition and Classification', in Talcott Parsons and Edward Shils (eds.), *Toward a General Theory of Action: Theoretical Foundations for the Social Sciences* (Cambridge, Mass., 1951), 388–433, at 395.

[4] See Helmut Thome, 'Wandel gesellschaftlicher Wertvorstellungen aus der Sicht der empirischen Sozialforschung', in Bernhard Dietz, Christopher Neumaier, and Andreas Rödder (eds.), *Gab es den Wertewandel? Neue Forschungen zum gesellschaftlich-kulturellen Wandel seit den 1960er Jahren* (Munich, 2014), 41–68, at 42–3.

applicability and usefulness of the concepts of values and value change. It also experiments with our hypothesis of the rise of 'post-rational values' (an ideal-type concept which should not be mistaken for irrationality or spirituality) during the long 1970s.

In the following, we shall first discuss the question of periodization and 'post-rationalism'. Section I of our introduction will ask: when did the changes of the 1970s begin and end? How did they relate to the world wars and the 1960s, and to long-term processes of modernization and rationalization? In section II we shall delve into theories of value change put forward by contemporary social scientists, political scientists, and historians, before we expand on the more recent historiography of the 1970s (section III) and on the actors and areas of change (section IV). We then conclude with an overview of the contributions in this volume, all of which grapple with the concepts of value change and post-rationality in multiple arenas of transformation.

I. *Post-War and Post-Rationalism*

While the local timings of value transformation varied across Europe, we shall take the 'long 1970s' to mean a period of change which in most countries began in the last third of the 1960s and lasted until the late 1970s or early 1980s. Thus, when we speak of the 'long 1970s', we do not mean the numerical decade, but rather the localized chronological boundaries of the period in which value change had its breakthrough. The period of the long 1970s, with its transition towards the spread of 'post-rational' values, therefore sits between the postwar decades of economic growth and the rise of the neo-liberal, individualist paradigm from the 1980s onwards.

The ferocity of value change experienced during the long 1970s was a result of arrested societal developments following the world wars. After the Second World War, most European peoples were exhausted and craved cultural stability; majorities across Europe tended to reject proposals for value experiments for almost two decades. This tendency can most clearly be observed in post-fascist, defeated Italy and West Germany. Gender roles, sexual mores, and political values were temporarily all but 'frozen' in an attempt to integrate societies which were still unstable. Other postwar European states also had to cope with multiple instabilities, navigating the war's economic fallout, upheaval of gender roles, forced population movements, and often new and untested international alliances, national borders, and constitutions. Where a legacy of fascism or collaboration persisted, tensions between victims, bystanders, and perpetrators of Nazi mass crimes added to the often overwhelming desire for stability. In the most extreme cases, these societies even harked back to 1920s values, gender roles, and morals in an attempt to avoid any association with the era of fascism and war.[5] An increasingly stark disconnect between publicly promoted values and contradictory everyday practices sometimes followed, as in late 1950s and 1960s Italy and West Germany. Societal resistance to change was widespread, but at the same time small subgroups began to experiment with new ideas which grew out of increasing prosperity, the economic upswing, and the entrenchment of mass consumerism.[6] When the long 1970s began, these arrested postwar value developments then gave way to an almost explosive, rapid, contested, and conflictual transformation touching all sectors of society.

We want to test whether the value change of the long 1970s across Europe—and the social, cultural, and political transformations that accompanied it—had common characteristics going back to 'post-rational' roots. Instead of focusing on individualism or post-materialism, as Ronald Inglehart's much-discussed theory has long advocated, we emphasize experiments with new norms and practices that challenged the centuries-old Western rationalism which, in its different forms, dominated the industrialized world. Following Western philosophy from Kant onwards, Western rationalism understands the organization of modern Western society as

[5] For Italy see Stephen Gundle, 'Feminine Beauty, National Identity and Political Conflict in Postwar Italy 1945–1954', *Contemporary European History*, 8/3 (1999), 359–78; Anna Treves, *Le nascite e la politica nell'Italia del Novecento* (Milan, 2001); and Liliosa Azara, *I sensi e il pudore: l'Italia e la rivoluzione dei costumi (1958–68)* (Rome, 2018). For Germany see Ulrich Herbert, 'Liberalisierung als Lernprozeß: Die Bundesrepublik in der deutschen Geschichte. Eine Skizze', in id. (ed.), *Wandlungsprozesse in Westdeutschland: Belastung, Integration, Liberalisierung 1945–1980* (Göttingen, 2002), 7–49, at 35–40; Elisabeth Heineman, 'Sexuality in West Germany: Post-Fascist, Post-War, Post-Weimar, or Post-Wilhelmine?', in Friedrich Kiessling and Bernhard Rieger (eds.), *Mit dem Wandel leben: Neuorientierung und Tradition in der Bundesrepublik der 1950er und 60er Jahre* (Cologne, 2011), 229–45; and Dagmar Herzog, 'Desperately Seeking Normality: Sex and Marriage in the Wake of the War', in Richard Bessel and Dirk Schumann (eds.), *Life after Death: Approaches to a Cultural and Social History of Europe during the 1940s and 1950s* (Cambridge, 2003), 161–92.

[6] David Forgacs and Stephen Gundle, *Mass Culture and Italian Society from Fascism to the Cold War* (Bloomington, Ind., 2007).

the product of a multilayered process of rationalization. In Max Weber's perspective, the rise of modern capitalism went along with an increasingly rational organization of life and a reconfiguration of people's world-views. Referring to the loss of religious and metaphysical meaning, Weber describes rationalization as 'Entzauberung der Welt'—the disenchantment of the world.[7] Not only Weber's but also Karl Marx's theory is based on the idea of advancing rationalization and its links with capitalist production. Sigmund Freud emphasizes the rationalization of the individual's instincts and sexuality too. Lastly, the idea of the rationalization of society is also at the centre of the theories of the Frankfurt School. In their *Dialektik der Aufklärung*,[8] Theodor Adorno and Max Horkheimer argue that civilization is underpinned by an instrumental rationalization whose goal is to dominate nature as a precondition of human self-preservation. Adorno and Horkheimer present the scientific revolution of the seventeenth century and the atemporal, enduring process of the Enlightenment as the decisive turn towards the reduction and rationalist reorganization of the world. Another representative of the Frankfurt School, Herbert Marcuse, combines Marx and Freud to posit the rationalization of society and the ideology of rationalism as fundamental characteristics of late industrialized Western society. Recalling Freud's theory of individual instincts, Marcuse argues that in this kind of society the 'reality principle', which he calls the 'performance principle', conflicts with the 'pleasure principle', repressing 'Eros' through work and productivity. Unlike Marx, Marcuse understood work not as the origin of human emancipation but as the cause of human unhappiness. Although the late industrialized Soviet and American societies aim to promote happiness, Marcuse holds, they are destined to produce unhappiness. For Marcuse, this represented the 'irrational rationality' of advanced industrialized societies in the East and West.[9]

Taken together, these theories of rationalized, industrialized society follow a peculiar trajectory. The early authors—Marx,

[7] Max Weber, *Wirtschaft und Gesellschaft: Grundriss der verstehenden Soziologie* (Tübingen, 1922), first published in English as *Economy and Society: An Outline of Interpretive Sociology* (New York, 1968).

[8] Theodor W. Adorno and Max Horkheimer, *Die Dialektik der Aufklärung: Philosophische Fragmente* (Amsterdam, 1947), first published in English as *Dialectic of Enlightenment*, trans. John Cumming (New York, 1972).

[9] Herbert Marcuse, *Eros and Civilization: A Philosophical Inquiry into Freud* (Boston, 1955); id., *One-Dimensional Man: Studies in the Ideology of Advanced Industrial Society* (Boston, 1964); and id., *Soviet Marxism: A Critical Analysis* (New York, 1958).

Freud, and Weber—all witnessed the growing rationalization of society during the nineteenth and early twentieth centuries. We can therefore assume that their theories, which gained global influence, became part of this very process.[10] During the nineteenth century, as tensions between the Enlightenment and Christianity mounted and national states gingerly detached themselves from religious authorities, ideas of industrialism and advancement began to transform. Ideals of progress and the Enlightenment were driven by the notion of an autonomous, rational, male subject. This link between agency and masculinity and between progress and patriarchy sheds a light on the gender organization of European societies. All these elements characterized the structure and development of European societies until the fractures of the two world wars and the social upheavals of reconstruction and the economic boom, when groups started to test new values that questioned many of the certainties on which modernity had been built.

Around this time, the Frankfurt School described the process of societal rationalization with an emphasis on its fallout for individual behaviour, taking a different approach from both Marx and the contemporary American sociologist Talcott Parsons. Marcuse in particular, writing on the cusp of the transformation of late industrialized society, began to demand a change in 'desirable conceptions' or values. From the time of the Second World War onwards, these theories revealed a perception, expressed in words and complex social theories, that people were living in a society based on outdated social structures and overly rigid norms. We hold that perception to be the very premiss of the epochal value change under discussion here.

The search for 'post-rationalism' was not an escape into irrationalism or into an 'irrational rationality', to use Marcuse's formulation. Nor did it manage to disentangle itself fully from the Western, Eurocentric outlook of modernity. Instead, this search was a slow, contradictory, and at times painful quest to shape a new form of rationalism which would fit societal realities across Europe as the Continent emerged from the long aftermath of the two world wars. This new form of rationalism had to do with the search for new forms of social organization based on a different understanding of

---

[10] Christof Dipper, 'Moderne, Version: 2.0', in *Docupedia-Zeitgeschichte: Begriffe, Methoden und Debatten der zeithistorischen Forschung*, 17 Jan. 2018 ⟨https://doi.org/10.14765/zzf.dok.2.1114.v2⟩.

gender, class, and race relationships, and with a new kind of politics far removed from the battles between nationalisms and imperialisms. In short, it involved searching for the happiness that Marcuse believed to be lost.

We suggest that the new 'post-rational' values were meant to fit a world where traditional authorities and institutions such as unions, churches, class milieux, catch-all political parties, and reformist politics were in decline but not yet obsolete. There were several preconditions for this change. Postwar economic growth was one, but others were the rise of mass consumerism; the spread of secularization; the increasingly common self-fashioning of identities; the demands raised by women, young people, and sexual minorities; and the advancement of concepts of human and basic rights on both sides of the Iron Curtain. The rise and popularization of 'post-rational' values were accompanied by an intensification of transnational and global contacts and communications. In different contexts, the move towards 'post-rationalism' enabled challenges to class, gender, and generational hierarchies, family models, sexual mores, political norms, and political institutions that had developed during the nineteenth and twentieth centuries. Even in areas which are not always understood to be value-led, such as politics, statehood, and the economy, the expansion of post-rational ideas left its mark.

'Post-rationalism' in our view does not refer to a rise in emotionality, spirituality, or irrationalism. Instead, the concept is meant to indicate a world-view and lifestyle that built on older, Eurocentric, imperialist, and productivist rationalisms, but selectively inserted into them more liberal and individualist takes on personal agency, social cohesion, and politics. The concept of the 'post-rational' retains much of the content of its 'rational' predecessor, in a manner similar to terms such as 'postmodern' or 'post-industrial'. To a certain extent, this coexistence of the old and the new was also mirrored in the contemporary debate in the social sciences when they began to grapple with understanding the changing values of their times.

II. *Contemporary Theories of Value Change*

As far back as the early 1970s, the American and European social science debate highlighted an ongoing, unprecedented change in values in the industrialized Western countries. Based on empirical surveys, social scientists argued that the long 1970s embodied a move towards post-materialism, individualism, and ethical pluralization as a result of the preceding economic boom. As the decade unfolded, journalists, pollsters, and social scientists started to discuss their time as one of fundamental transformation. Step by step, their debates moved away from patterns of growth and potentials of the nation state and instead centred on terms such as individualism, pluralism, and secularization.

As the American social sciences turned their focus from promoting economic growth to understanding the subjective, individualist factors underpinning such growth, the term 'quality of life' and the concept of lifestyles became important for empirical social research (as Pascal Germann's contribution to this volume shows). Coming from this context, the political scientist Ronald Inglehart argued that knowledge about people's subjective attitudes was the key to successfully predicting their political leanings. Inglehart's hypothesis of a 'silent revolution', a fundamental transformation from 'materialist' to 'post-materialist' values in highly industrialized Western countries starting in the 1970s, informed much of the ensuing debate. In Inglehart's view, values shifted from an overwhelming emphasis on material well-being and physical security towards a greater emphasis on quality of life, political participation, and freedom of speech.[11] Analysing public opinion surveys, Inglehart referred to two pivotal theoretical concepts. On the one hand he highlighted Abraham Maslow's theory of the hierarchy of needs which have to be satisfied before moving to the next, post-material level. On the other, Inglehart's socialization hypothesis holds that the basic values held by adults reflect the socio-economic conditions present during their youth and are retained throughout the individual's life. Inglehart analysed France, West Germany, Belgium, the Netherlands, Italy, and Britain using data from the founding group of the European Values Study. These societies revealed large differences between the value priorities of older and younger generations. Among the older cohorts, 'materialist' values, emphasizing economic and physical security, were overwhelmingly predominant—but when moving from older to younger birth cohorts, 'post-materialist' values, emphasizing autonomy and self-expression, became increasingly

[11] See Ronald Inglehart, *The Silent Revolution: Changing Values and Political Styles among Western Publics* (Princeton, 1977), 3.

widespread. Inglehart attributed this value shift to socio-economic changes, the rising level of education, and shifts in occupational structures.[12]

Inglehart's study triggered a multilayered response in the social sciences, provoking critique but also inspiring a wealth of empirical research. Political scientists of the 1970s, embroiled in a debate about the crisis of the democratic nation state, worried about the ungovernability brought on by social groups who were no longer loyal to their nation, their church, or their class, but mainly sought 'self-fulfilment' (as Martin Deuerlein shows in this volume with regard to North America and West Germany). In Italy, the sociologist and anthropologist Carlo Tullio Altan joined the debate in 1974, coining the term 'difficult values' (*valori difficili*), which he traced to the younger generations and their demands for political participation and a new politics based on different values. Altan advised Italian parties that they should respond by introducing new political programmes. Although Altan's empirical research went back to 1964, his interpretation was partially inspired by Inglehart's theory and validated the latter's idea of a generational move from materialism to post-materialism.[13]

In the German-language social and political sciences, Inglehart's intervention served to establish an enduring focus on values and value change which persists to this day. Opinion polls by the West German Allensbach Institute, founded in 1947 and close to the conservative CDU party, had already found evidence of a supposed weakening of bourgeois virtues and a hesitancy to engage politically during the 1950s and 1960s. But during the 1970s, under the influence of Inglehart's interpretation, polling results were reread and surveys redesigned to confirm generational divides in values and a supposedly dangerous decline of traditional morals. The head of Allensbach, Elisabeth Noelle-Neumann, sounded the alarm, suggesting that 'we all might end up proletarians' and that the loss of Catholic and German educated middle-class (*bürgerlich*) values

---

[12] Ibid., ch. 2: 'The Nature of Value Change', 21–71; see also id., 'Changing Values among Western Publics from 1970 to 2006', *West European Politics*, 31/1–2 (2008), 130–46.

[13] Altan quoted Inglehart's first publication on the topic (1971), as well as Maslow's theory of needs. He was also influenced by Israeli and German social scientists, such as Shmuel N. Eisenstadt's *From Generation to Generation: Age Groups and Social Structure* (Glencoe, Ill., 1956); Ludwig von Friedeburg's survey on German intimacy, *Die Umfrage in der Intimsphäre* (Stuttgart, 1953); Erich Fromm; and Jürgen Habermas. See Carlo Tullio Altan, *I valori difficili: inchiesta sulle tendenze ideologiche e politiche dei giovani in Italia* (Milan, 1974).

should be met by a conservative counter-offensive.[14] While Noelle-Neumann took value change as evidence of a general moral decline, other scholars concentrated on critiques of Inglehart's empirical method and conceptual framework. They argued, for example, that there was not a linear trend of 'new' post-materialist values replacing 'old' materialist ones, but rather that many materialist orientations survived the rise of certain post-materialist attitudes.[15] The social scientist Helmut Klages went one step further in the 1980s, developing his own method of diagnosing fundamental value shifts and positing the theory of *Wertesynthese* (value synthesis). He agreed with Inglehart that traditional values were being replaced at an unprecedented pace, but doubted the linear direction of the 1960s and 1970s as depicted by Inglehart and suggested that value change could manifest in multiple patterns simultaneously. In particular, Klages argued that 'active realists'—one of several population groups he defined—adapted most successfully to ongoing changes by merging older and newer values.[16] It thus appears that the contemporary social science debate was already grappling with the Janus face of what we propose to call the move to 'post-rational' values.

While the German social sciences and humanities were deeply influenced by Inglehart's theory, it made less of an impression on contemporary American, British, and French research. In the United States the long 1970s were often understood, without explicit reference to value change, as 'the great shift', the beginning of the 'culture wars', or, following Daniel Bell, as the 'coming of post-industrial society'.[17] In Britain the social sciences remained focused on class and social mobility rather than values, a tradition which continued in British historiography.[18] In French academia

[14] See Elisabeth Noelle-Neumann, *Werden wir alle Proletarier? Wertewandel in unserer Gesellschaft* (Zurich, 1978); Norbert Grube, 'Seines Glückes Schmied? Entstehungs- und Verwendungskontexte von Allensbacher Umfragen zum Wertewandel 1947–2001', in Dietz, Neumaier, and Rödder (eds.), *Gab es den Wertewandel?*, 95–119.

[15] Thome, 'Wandel gesellschaftlicher Wertvorstellungen', 49–51. See also id., 'Wandel zu postmaterialistischen Werten? Theoretische und empirische Einwände gegen Ingleharts Theorie-Versuch', *Soziale Welt*, 36/1 (1985), 27–59.

[16] Helmut Klages, *Wertorientierungen im Wandel: Rückblick, Gegenwartsanalyse, Prognosen* (Frankfurt a.M., 1984). On Klages see Isabel Heinemann, 'Wertewandel', *Docupedia-Zeitgeschichte*, 22 Oct. 2012 〈https://doi.org/10.14765/zzf.dok.2.261.v1〉; Thome, 'Wandel gesellschaftlicher Wertvorstellungen', 54–7.

[17] Heinemann, 'Wertewandel'.

[18] Mike Savage, *Identities and Social Change in Britain since 1940: The Politics of Method*

the long 1970s remained in the shadow of the controversies over the rebellious year of 1968 and its relationship to the French revolutionary tradition. The sociologist Henri Mendras called the period between 1965 and 1985 'a second French revolution', a silent structural transformation towards individualism, secularism, decentralization, and liberalization, but he did so without relying on Inglehart.[19] After that, the rise of Pierre Bourdieu's sociological theories on 'distinction' overshadowed the debate on Inglehart's theses in France.[20]

III. *Historiography on the Long 1970s*

From the turn of the 2000s onwards, historical research on the long 1970s intensified as a result of the opening of state archives, the end of the Cold War, and the acceleration of European integration. Historians at that point advanced several master narratives for the decade and for the broader period of the long 1970s. Some of them conceptualized the era as one of value change, but these were mostly by German historians. As the prolific debate about Inglehart, Klages, and Noelle-Neumann's theses had been conducted in German, it was rarely taken up outside the confines of German-language historiography.

In surveys of European history the long 1970s appear with markedly different accents. With reference to Eastern Europe, the decade is identified as a sea change or great shift (*Umbruchzeit*).[21] The period is often interpreted in the light of the civic revolutions from below which connected the decade to the global history of the years 1989–91, highlighting how activists in Czechoslovakia, East

(Oxford, 2010); Jon Lawrence, *Me, Me, Me? The Search for Community in Post-War England* (Oxford, 2019); Florence Sutcliffe-Braithwaite, *Class, Politics, and the Decline of Deference in England, 1968–2000* (Oxford, 2018). Sutcliffe-Braithwaite writes about changing attitudes in the British working class since 1968, but uses the term 'cultural change' rather than 'value change'.

[19] Henri Mendras, *La Seconde Révolution française: 1965–1984* (Paris, 1988).

[20] See Pierre Bourdieu, *La Distinction: critique sociale du jugement* (Paris, 1979), first published in English as *Distinction: A Social Critique of the Judgement of Taste*, trans. Richard Nice (Cambridge, Mass., 1979). See also Jean-François Lyotard, *La Condition postmoderne: rapport sur le savoir* (Paris, 1979), first published in English as *The Postmodern Condition: A Report on Knowledge*, trans. Geoff Bennington and Brian Massumi (Minneapolis, 1984).

[21] Claudia Kraft, 'Paradoxien der Emanzipation: Regime, Opposition und Geschlechterordnungen im Staatssozialismus seit den späten 1960er-Jahren', *Zeithistorische Forschungen/Studies in Contemporary History*, 3/3 (2006), 381–400, at 383.

Germany, Poland, and Hungary fought for counter-public spheres and more respect for autonomous political agency and human rights. In the process, they invoked alternative values to challenge the socialist systems of the Eastern bloc.[22] As for Western Europe, most narratives prioritize the far-reaching changes in economic structures. In the foreground are usually the beginnings of a more globalized[23] or financialized capitalism, the advent of fundamental economic or 'structural' changes 'after the boom',[24] the 'crisis of the labour society', the shift from an 'industrial to a services society', or the rise of large-scale unemployment and neo-liberal economic theories. Often such interpretations are then linked to the notion of 'transition' or 'crisis'.[25]

Where historians emphasize the transitional character of the period, they occasionally go so far as to avoid its complexities by stating that these years represent a contradictory epoch defying clear definition, a 'decade of complexity' or 'decade of plurality'.[26]

[22] Mark James, Bogdan C. Iacob, Tobias Rupprecht, and Ljubica Spaskovska (eds.), *1989: A Global History of Eastern Europe* (Cambridge, 2019).

[23] In recent social science the 1970s are also characterized as the precursor of a redeployment of global capitalism, which developed refined, more subtle forms of exploitation as a response to challenges from active unionism. In France, for instance, this decade features as a social movement on the offensive, extending significantly beyond the boundaries of the working class, beyond a highly active trade unionism, and shifting the distribution of value added in favour of wage earners. Workers and other wage earners still benefited from legislation affording greater social security in the 1970s. This decade is then contrasted with the years 1985 to 1995, which were marked by a disoriented trade unionism that lost the initiative for action; growth in income inequality; a distribution of value added that was once again favourable to capital; and a more subtle and successful form of exploitation. See Luc Boltanski and Eve Chiapello, *The New Spirit of Capitalism*, trans. Gregory Elliott (London, 2018; 1st pub. 2005); originally published in French as *Nouvel esprit du capitalisme* (Paris, 1999).

[24] Anselm Doering-Manteuffel and Lutz Raphael, *Nach dem Boom: Perspektiven auf die Zeitgeschichte seit 1970*, 2nd edn. (Göttingen, 2008); Konrad H. Jarausch (ed.), *Das Ende der Zuversicht? Die Siebziger Jahre als Geschichte* (Göttingen, 2008); and Edgar Wolfrum, *Die 70er Jahre: Republik im Aufbruch* (Darmstadt, 2007). See also Anselm Doering-Manteuffel, Lutz Raphael, and Thomas Schlemmer (eds.), *Vorgeschichte der Gegenwart: Dimensionen des Strukturbruchs nach dem Boom* (Göttingen, 2016).

[25] Barbara Keys, Jack Davies, and Elliott Bannan, 'The Post-Traumatic Decade: New Histories of the 1970s', *Australasian Journal of American Studies*, 33/1 (2014), 1–17; Sonja Levsen, 'Einführung: Die 70er Jahre in Westeuropa — un dialogue manqué?', *Geschichte und Gesellschaft*, 42 (2016), 213–42; Giovanni Gozzini and Tommaso Detti, *L'età del disordine: storia del mondo attuale 1968–2017* (Rome, 2018); Frank Bösch, *Zeitenwende 1979: Als die Welt von heute begann* (Munich, 2020).

[26] Konrad H. Jarausch, 'Krise oder Aufbruch? Historische Annäherungen an die 1970er-Jahre', *Zeithistorische Forschungen/Studies in Contemporary History*, 3/3 (2006), 334–41, at 339; Laurel Forster and Sue Harper, 'Introduction', in eaed. (eds.), *British Culture and Society in the 1970s: The Lost Decade* (Newcastle, 2010), 1–12.

But most accounts, whether on a global or a European scale, define the long 1970s as a time of far-reaching transformations during a transition towards a new era.[27] At times this transition is identified as a move from modernity to postmodernity.[28] At other times authors insist that transition-related terms such as the 'post-industrial society', the 'postmodern society', and 'value change' can capture only segments of the great shift in the 1970s, as none of them suits the far-reaching changes of the decade in all their complexity.[29] For the French case, historians see this time as a transitional shift between *les trente glorieuses* and *la nouvelle société* (the new society) of the present. French historiography suggests that the 'thirty glorious years' of affluence and stability ended in the wake of the social changes produced by recessions and the workers' and students' protests that erupted in 1968, and that what came afterwards was structurally different from before. This pattern also seems to suit the Italian case.[30]

The other label most commonly used for the era is 'crisis'. Frequently the period is termed a crisis of capitalist democracies in Western Europe, picking up the debate where political and social scientists left off.[31] Jürgen Habermas in particular raised the alarm for the crisis of advanced capitalism in Europe, followed by the report of the Trilateral Commission, a North American think tank founded in 1973, on the political situation of the United

[27] Antonio Varsori (ed.), *Alle origini del tempo presente: l'Europa occidentale nella crisi degli anni Settanta* (Milan, 2007); Akira Iriye, *Global and Transnational History: The Past, Present, and Future* (Basingstoke, 2013); Cornelißen, *Europa im 20. Jahrhundert*; Bösch, *Zeitenwende 1979*; Lawrence Black, Hugh Pemberton, and Pat Thane (eds.), *Reassessing 1970s Britain* (Manchester, 2013).

[28] See the reference to Jean-François Lyotard's criticism of the European Enlightenment and its advocacy of master narratives, firm conviction in progress and telos, and rational mapping of the world in Andreas Rödder, *Wertewandel und Postmoderne: Gesellschaft und Kultur der Bundesrepublik Deutschland 1965–1990* (Stuttgart, 2004). See also Thomas Großbölting, Massimiliano Livi, and Carlo Spagnolo (eds.), *Jenseits der Moderne? Die Siebziger Jahre als Gegenstand der deutschen und italienischen Geschichtswissenschaft* (Berlin, 2014).

[29] Jarausch, 'Krise oder Aufbruch?'; Keys, Davies, and Bannan, 'The Post-Traumatic Decade'; Levsen, 'Einführung'.

[30] Philippe Chassaignes, *Les Années 1970: fin d'un monde et origine de notre modernité* (Paris, 2012); Vittorio Vidotto, *Italiani/e: dal miracolo economico a oggi* (Rome, 2005).

[31] On the origin of the debate see Jürgen Habermas, *Legitimationsprobleme im Spätkapitalismus* (Berlin, 1973), first published in English as *Legitimation Crisis*, trans. Thomas McCarthy (Boston, 1975); James O'Connor, *The Fiscal Crisis of the State* (New York, 1973); Joyce Kolko, *America and the Crisis of World Capitalism* (Boston, 1974); Michel J. Crozier, Samuel P. Huntington, and Joji Watanuki, *The Crisis of Democracy: Report on the Governability of Democracies to the Trilateral Commission* (New York, 1975).

States, Europe, and Japan. In this shared document the three major capitalist states outlined the danger of an excess of democracy as the reason for the current ungovernability of industrialized societies. In line with these ideas, there is still a body of literature that conceives of the 1970s as a phase of political and economic crisis and that sees the main concerns of the decade as, first, the economic and financial crisis heralded internationally by the so-called 'shock of the global' in 1973 and at a national level by unemployment, stagflation, and the failure of many industrial branches; and, second, in the 'system crisis' of Western democracies, which saw social and political movements and even new forms of terrorism demanding solutions for the unsolved problems of inequality and representation.[32] These interpretations tend to share the perspectives of the grand narratives of the twentieth century, from Marxist theory to the functionalist narratives of modernization and neo-liberalism.[33]

The crisis narrative resonated strongly in Italy until recently. The emotional reaction to the failure of the so-called 'First Republic' (1945–92) during the 1990s, when major parties splintered and corruption scandals shook Italy, led scholars to comparisons with the challenges experienced two decades earlier.[34] Italian historians even found the roots of the 'First' Italian Republic's downfall in the political crises of the long 1970s. This thesis, however, has been refuted by Agostino Giovagnoli. He argues that in its narrative of the 'crisis of the long 1970s', Italian historiography has created a metaphorical screen onto which all the problems of the First Italian Republic can be projected.[35] This may explain why Italian historians have largely sidestepped theories of value change and

---

[32] Eric Hobsbawm, *The Age of Extremes: The Short Twentieth Century, 1914–1991* (London, 1994), 403.

[33] On Marxist interpretations of the crisis of the 1970s see Ernest Mandel, *La Crise 1974–1982: les faits, leur interprétation marxiste* (Paris, 1982); Liliana Baculo (ed.), *La crisi degli anni '70 nel dibattito marxista: saggi di analisi e teoria economica* (Bari, 1976). For a current bibliography see Andreas Wirsching, 'European Responses to the Crisis of the 1970s and 1980s: Introductory Remarks', *Journal of Modern European History*, 9/2 (2011), 167–9; Simon Reid-Henry, *Empire of Democracy: The Remaking of the West since the Cold War, 1971–2017* (New York, 2019), 58–9; Niall Ferguson, Charles S. Maier, Erez Manela, and Daniel J. Sargent (eds.), *The Shock of the Global: The Seventies in Perspective* (Cambridge, Mass., 2011); Duco Hellema, *The Global 1970s: Radicalism, Reform, and Crisis* (London, 2018).

[34] See Luca Baldissara (ed.), *Le radici della crisi: l'Italia tra gli anni Sessanta e Settanta* (Rome, 2001).

[35] Agostino Giovagnoli, 'Gli anni Settanta e la storiografia sull'Italia repubblicana', *Contemporanea*, 13/1 (2010), 183–95.

why Tullio Altan's intervention on 'difficult values' did not spark much public debate when the long 1970s became a subject of intense research.[36] Another strong current in the historical literature sees the 1970s as a time of crisis and transformation of the labour society.[37] Workers' biographies in West Germany, Britain, France, and Italy saw radical changes from the 1970s onwards resulting from the dramatic decline of the industrial labour market. This process hit male workers hard, but young adults and women even more so. While the economic crises of the decade had deep impacts on the lives and careers of industrial workers, recent studies also highlight that notions of good work, quality, and competence persisted in the 1970s. Recent research on industrial workers in the 1970s underlines processes of erosion in working-class milieux, but also sheds light on enduring traditional values such as class consciousness, ideals of solidarity, notions of good work, and competence. Doubtless, experiments with changing values in the 1970s did not simply replace but went side by side with and complicated traditional values. Furthermore, processes of cultural erosion and the simultaneity of processes of change in industrialized postwar societies also remind us of the large contingent of people who did not yet benefit from educational expansion, mass consumption, and value change experiments: groups such as unskilled workers, young people entering the shrinking job market, migrant workers, and rural people. A swift and uncomplicated transition to 'post-material values' thus cannot be taken for granted.[38]

---

[36] Exceptions that do discuss the value change of the 1960s and 1970s include Enrica Asquer, *Storia intima dei ceti medi: una capitale e una periferia nell'Italia del miracolo economico* (Rome, 2011); Giovanni Gozzini, *La mutazione individualista: gli italiani e la televisione 1954–2011* (Rome, 2011); and Paul Ginsborg, *Storia d'Italia dal dopoguerra ad oggi: società e politica 1943–1988* (Turin, 1989).

[37] Pietro Causarano, 'Storia del lavoro e della conflittualità sindacale', in Fiammetta Balestracci and Catia Papa (eds.), *L'Italia degli anni Settanta: narrazioni e interpretazioni a confronto* (Soveria Mannelli, 2019), 103–23; Lutz Raphael, 'Arbeitsbiografien und Strukturwandel "nach dem Boom": Lebensläufe und Berufserfahrungen britischer, französischer und Westdeutscher Industriearbeiter und -arbeiterinnen von 1970 bis 2000', *Geschichte und Gesellschaft*, 43/1 (2017), 32–67; Manfredi Alberti, *Senza lavoro: la disoccupazione in Italia dall'Unità a oggi* (Rome, 2016).

[38] Alberti, *Senza lavoro*; Lutz Raphael, *Jenseits von Kohle und Stahl: Eine Gesellschaftsgeschichte Westeuropas nach dem Boom* (Berlin, 2019); Boltanski and Chiapello, *The New Spirit of Capitalism*; Massimiliano Livi (ed.), *Migration—Region—Integration/Migrazione—Regione—Integrazione*, special issue of *Geschichte und Region/Storia e regione*, 2/28 (2019); Jörg Neuheiser, 'Der "Wertewandel" zwischen Diskurs und Praxis: Die Untersuchung von Wertvorstellungen zur Arbeit mit Hilfe von betrieblichen Fallstudien', in Dietz, Neumaier, and Rödder (eds.), *Gab es den Wertewandel?*, 141–68. On the discussion of

Only in German-language historiography has the theory of value change been used extensively to explain the social and cultural changes in pre-1990 West Germany and the reunified Germany.[39] However, the theory was only rarely applied to the GDR or other former Eastern bloc countries.[40] Value shifts in Western Europe and the United States during the long 1970s have been explored by German scholars with a strong focus on the interrelation of cultural values, social practices, and institutions, and have been theorized as non-linear, multifaceted, and open processes with multiple intersections between milieu, age, gender, political preference, religious denomination, and citizenship.[41] More recently, a critical discussion about the historicization of social science-generated concepts has emerged in Germany, in part focusing explicitly on debates about 'value change'. While the economic historians Rüdiger Graf and Kim Christian Priemel stress the need to deconstruct contemporary postwar social science terms such as 'value change', 'post-industrial society', 'globalization', and 'structural transformation' (of the economy), and take the discipline to task for making these the unquestioned basis of historical narratives, the social historians Bernhard Dietz and Christopher Neumaier defend their approach of writing the history of value change in a manner which critiques and historicizes the social sciences.[42] As a result of this

how far value change affected working environments see also Bernhard Dietz and Jörg Neuheiser (eds.), *Wertewandel in der Wirtschaft und Arbeitswelt: Arbeit, Leistung und Führung in den 1970er und 1980er Jahren in der Bundesrepublik Deutschland* (Berlin, 2017); on the decline of deference among male workers see Sutcliffe-Braithwaite, *Class, Politics, and the Decline of Deference*.

[39] On the German debate on values after national reunification see Hans Joas, *Die Entstehung der Werte* (Frankfurt a.M., 1997), published in English as *The Genesis of Values*, trans. Gregory Moore (Chicago, 2001); Rödder, *Wertewandel und Postmoderne*; Ernest Albert, *Wandel schweizerischer Arbeitswerte: Eine theoriegeleitete empirische Untersuchung* (Wiesbaden, 2011); Döring-Manteuffel and Raphael, *Nach dem Boom*; Dietz, Neumaier, and Rödder (eds.), *Gab es den Wertewandel?*; Großbölting, Livi, and Spagnolo (eds.), *Jenseits der Moderne?*.

[40] Research on value change in the GDR and Eastern European countries is in its early stages. For a recent quantitative overview see Horaţiu Rusu and Mircea Comşa, 'Value Change in Eastern Europe: What is Happening There?', *Studia Universitatis Babes-Bolyai—Sociologia*, 56/1 (2011), 33–61.

[41] Dietz, Neumaier, and Rödder (eds.), *Gab es den Wertewandel?*; Isabel Heinemann, *Wert der Familie: Ehescheidung, Frauenarbeit und Reproduktion in den USA des 20. Jahrhunderts* (Berlin, 2018); Christopher Neumaier, *Familie im 20. Jahrhundert: Konflikte um Ideale, Politiken und Praktiken* (Berlin, 2019); Bernhard Dietz, *Der Aufstieg der Manager: Wertewandel in den Führungsetagen der Westdeutschen Wirtschaft, 1949–1989* (Berlin, 2020).

[42] See Rüdiger Graf and Kim Christian Priemel, 'Zeitgeschichte in der Welt

debate, present-day historians are called upon not only to familiarize themselves more than before with the genesis of these concepts, but also to reanalyse the data collected and the empirical methods used by contemporary social research.[43]

If we free the concept of value change from its German-centric confines, it can be fruitfully linked to the above-mentioned narratives of 'transition' and 'crisis'. What appears to be a period of transition can be analysed in greater depth once we add 'values' to the mix in order to identify the direction of travel, the factors driving change, and the areas and actors involved. The 'crisis' narrative, too, relies mainly on the contemporary perception of economic decline and stagnation; this may appear different from today's vantage point. In this volume, we set out to test whether the long 1970s were an age of value transformation regardless of economic downturns and challenges. Did countries which experienced relative stability undergo trends in value change similar to those in countries which went through recessions and bouts of political instability?

IV. Actors and Areas of Change

While value change certainly affected the world of work, schooling, and the political sphere, private life-worlds were arguably its most important arena. Some of the best-researched value changes happened in the parts of their lives that people defined as largely private: mass consumerism, sexual mores, relationships, parenting, going on holiday, media usage, and 'doing gender'. In these areas the specialized historical literature claims a 'revolutionary' character for the era of the long 1970s more often than it does in regard to politics and the economy. This volume brings together the different areas that contemporaries defined as public and as private in order to test the timing of value change in these arenas and how 'private' and 'public' developments were interrelated. This is where

der Sozialwissenschaften: Legitimität und Originalität einer Disziplin', *Vierteljahrshefte für Zeitgeschichte* (hereafter *VfZ*), 59/4 (2011), 479–508, at 488; Bernhard Dietz and Christopher Neumaier, 'Vom Nutzen der Sozialwissenschaften für die Zeitgeschichte: Werte und Wertewandel als Gegenstand historischer Forschung', *VfZ*, 60/2 (2012), 293–304, at 294.

[43] See Jenny Pleinen and Lutz Raphael, 'Zeithistoriker in den Archiven der Sozialwissenschaften: Erkenntnispotenziale und Relevanzgewinne für die Disziplin', *VfZ* 62/2 (2014), 173–95, at 195; Kerstin Brückweh et al., 'Sozialdaten als Quellen der Zeitgeschichte: Zur Einführung', *Geschichte und Gesellschaft*, 48/1 (2022), 5–27.

contemporary 'vanguards' of value change come in, particularly those which aimed to make the private political.

Some of the most intensely explored fields of value change are alternative youth milieux in Western and Northern Europe and changing forms of political participation in Western and Eastern Europe from the late 1960s onwards.[44] There were different, often fluid factions within the counter-cultural milieux and the student movements of the 1960s and 1970s. Nevertheless, two distinct tendencies were prominent: activists who engaged in developing a critical academic analysis of late capitalism on the one hand, and those who sought to find ways to live a meaningful life in what they perceived as the spiritually empty and boring world of consumer capitalism on the other. The personal that became political in the civil rights, anti-war, and women's movements in the long 1970s was widespread in many countries, including the USA, France, Italy, Denmark, and West Germany, to mention just a few, and fuelled new technologies of the self and new forms of self-exploration and self-reflection.[45] Such developments also extended far into Eastern Europe, as Juliane Fürst's contribution to this volume shows. Explorations and reinterpretations of body–mind practices saw a revival in the late 1960s and played a crucial role for new forms of subjectivation in the 1970s. The ideal of an embodied subject

---

[44] See Sven Reichardt and Detlef Siegfried (eds.), *Das alternative Milieu: Antibürgerlicher Lebensstil und linke Politik in der Bundesrepublik und Europa 1968–1983* (Göttingen, 2010); Sven Reichardt, *Authentizität und Gemeinschaft: Linksalternatives Leben in den siebziger und frühen achtziger Jahren* (Berlin, 2014); Joachim C. Häberlen, *The Emotional Politics of the Alternative Left: West Germany, 1968–1984* (Cambridge, 2018); Detlef Siegfried, *1968: Protest, Revolte, Gegenkultur* (Ditzingen, 2018); Thomas Etzemüller, 'A Struggle for Radical Change? Swedish Students in the 1960s', in Axel Schildt and Detlef Siegfried (eds.), *Between Marx and Coca-Cola: Youth Cultures in Changing European Societies, 1960–1980* (New York, 2006), 239–57. On changing forms of political participation in Eastern Europe see Kraft, 'Paradoxien der Emanzipation'; and Raluca Maria Popa, 'Translating Equality between Women and Men across Cold War Divides: Women Activists from Hungary and Romania and the Creation of International Women's Year', in Shana Penn and Jill Massino (eds.), *Gender Politics and Everyday Life in State Socialist Eastern and Central Europe* (New York, 2009), 59–74.

[45] See Pascal Eitler, '"Alternative" Religion: Subjektivierungspraktiken und Politisierungsstrategien im "New Age" (Westdeutschland 1970–1990)', in Reichardt and Siegfried (eds.) *Das Alternative Milieu*, 335–52; Maik Tändler, *Das therapeutische Jahrzehnt: Der Psychoboom in den siebziger Jahren* (Göttingen, 2016); Isabel Richter, 'Die Osterweiterung des Bewußtseins: Techniken der Selbstentgrenzung in den langen 1960er Jahren', *Mittelweg 36*, 4–5 (2016), 107–26; ead., 'Psychonauts and Seekers: West German Entanglements in the Spiritual Turn of the Global 1960s and 1970s', *Contemporary European History*, 4 May 2022 (FirstView) ⟨https://doi.org/10.1017/s0960777322000121⟩.

allowed practitioners in the 1970s to question what they perceived as the cold and detached rationality of efficiency-driven societies.

While minority groups were often first in experimenting with such new practices of the self both before and during the long 1970s, such forays were quickly taken up in wider society. The actors involved in value change go far beyond the small elite groups often addressed as alternative or bohemian vanguards. Popular culture and mass media served to widen the reach of value experiments, shortening the transmission time between the rise of counter-cultures and the broad entrenchment (and indeed often commercialization) of new values.[46] Historians have highlighted the particular role that youth and women played in this process. In postwar Europe these population groups were not only more numerous, after the decimation of the male population caused by the wars, but also central addressees of the mass-consumerist, mass-mediated economy of the 1960s and 1970s. In most European countries it took until the 1970s for the majority of the population to overcome postwar hardship, to engage in high-value consumerism (such as the purchase of private cars, travel abroad, and eating out), and to be able to choose between a variety of pluralized market options, highlighting their individual distinction and self-fashioning their identities in the process.[47]

Whereas the elite counter-cultures harked back to older ideas from the early twentieth and even late nineteenth centuries, so that the values they promoted were often not entirely new, many actors were unaware of the long historical trajectory in which they were rooted. Feminist groups in the long 1970s, for example, often had only shadowy memories of feminist struggles which had played out

[46] See Christina von Hodenberg, *Television's Moment: Sitcom Audiences and the Sixties Cultural Revolution* (New York, 2015); Fiammetta Balestracci, 'The Invention of Female Sexuality in West Germany and in Italy in the Long Seventies: An Essay on Media and Value Change in Europe', *Themenportal europäische Geschichte*, 2022 ⟨www.europa.clio-online.de/essay/id/fdae-29029⟩ [accessed 12 Dec. 2023]; and Detlef Siegfried, *Time is on my Side: Konsum und Politik in der Westdeutschen Jugendkultur der 60er Jahre* (Göttingen, 2006).

[47] Schildt and Siegfried (eds.), *Between Marx and Coca-Cola*; Paolo Capuzzo, 'Crisi e trasformazione della società dei consumi negli anni Settanta', in Balestracci and Papa (eds.), *L'Italia degli anni Settanta*, 189–203; Frank Trentmann, *Empire of Things: How We Became a World of Consumers, from the Fifteenth Century to the Twenty-First* (London, 2016); Sina Fabian, 'Individualisierung, Pluralisierung und Massenkonsum: Wandel von Konsummustern im 20. Jahrhundert', in Christian Kleinschmidt and Jan Logemann (eds.), *Konsum im 19. und 20. Jahrhundert* (Berlin, 2020), 337–61.

decades ago in their respective countries.[48] The elites who engaged in the 'sexual revolution' of the long 1970s in Germany and Italy also tended to dissociate themselves from the legacies of the 1950s and the Nazi and fascist era, and instead looked back to the cultural heritage left by intellectuals such as Wilhelm Reich and Herbert Marcuse, who from the late 1920s onwards criticized the repression of individual instincts by fascist and totalitarian societies.[49] One rather widespread misunderstanding among counter-cultural actors at the time was a view of 1950s Europe as a stiflingly immobile place of stability—a view that conveniently allowed them to contrast the progressive present with the straitjacket of the past, but which conflicted with the widespread instability that 1950s societies had laboured under, and often responded to creatively, across Europe (see also the essay by Martin Deuerlein in this volume).

Another group of actors driving the value change of the long 1970s were the very experts observing it. Social scientists were more than mere bystanders, because their interpretations and the terms they coined were picked up by contemporaries and the mass media, shaping perceptions of and responses to changing values. Expert semantics, surveys, and debates made a difference, as the essays in this volume by Lisa Dittrich, Pascal Germann, and Martin Deuerlein show.[50] It has also become increasingly clear how great an impact those social scientists had who studied private behaviours such as sexual intimacy, only to become best-selling authors exploited by the popular mass media—Alfred Kinsey being only one of many such examples during the so-called 'sexual revolution' of the time.[51]

While the long 1970s are often still understood as a time of 'sexual revolution', scholarship has shown that sexual mores began to change earlier and that gaps between practices and debates persisted. Indeed, in many Western and Southern countries, and in

[48] Lucy Delap, *Feminisms: A Global History* (London, 2020), 137–8, 154–5; Christina von Hodenberg, 'Writing Women's Agency into the History of the Federal Republic: "1968", Historians, and Gender', *Central European History*, 52/1 (2019), 87–106, at 98–9; Molly Tambor, *The Lost Wave: Women and Democracy in Postwar Italy* (New York, 2014).

[49] Dagmar Herzog, *Sex after Fascism: Memory and Morality in Twentieth-Century Germany* (Princeton, 2005). On the influence of Marcuse, Reich, and Weimar culture on postwar Italian society see Fiammetta Balestracci, *La sessualità degli italiani: politiche, consumi e culture dal 1945 ad oggi* (Rome, 2020), 210–14.

[50] See also Heinemann, *Wert der Familie*.

[51] Sybille Steinbacher, *Wie der Sex nach Deutschland kam: Der Kampf um Sittlichkeit und Anstand in der frühen Bundesrepublik* (Munich, 2011); Balestracci, *La sessualità degli italiani*.

some Eastern European ones, the long 1970s were the starting point for a pluralization of sexual morality, but traditional ideals of family and sexuality were not abandoned.[52] Individual sexual freedoms now became a political issue, especially in relation to women's rights and female bodies, and were increasingly enshrined in law. Across Europe, legal provisions which separated gendered spheres and regulated family relations were subject to challenges. Women's equal rights in private and public life, traditionally in tension with ideas of familial and social stability, had been theorized since the late nineteenth century but only now became central political issues which could command majorities in legislation and public opinion.[53] In popular culture, the 'unisex' fashion wave of the 1970s gave sartorial expression to this social and moral development.[54] Not only women's but also children's rights were now increasingly used to challenge the traditions of the patriarchal family. The 1970s were the key decade in which, for example, West German parents and schools turned away from corporal punishment and parenting became mostly 'child-centred'.[55]

Consumerism, already mentioned above and the subject of several essays in this volume, was another area in which 1970s value change transformed private life-worlds. The growing affluence of consumers enabled them to engage in new forms of exploration and fashioning of the self, for example by embracing travel, drugs, fashion, or religious beliefs (see the essays by Isabel Richter, Kristoff

[52] On the transformation of sexuality in the 1970s see Gert Hekma and Alain Giami (eds.), *Sexual Revolutions* (Basingstoke, 2014); David Allyn, *Make Love, Not War: The Sexual Revolution. An Unfettered History* (London, 2001); Fiammetta Balestracci, 'Le rivoluzioni sessuali degli anni Settanta in Italia: storia, narrazioni e metodologie', in Balestracci and Papa (eds.), *L'Italia degli anni Settanta*, 165–87; Eric Schaefer (ed.), *Sex Scene: Media and the Sexual Revolution* (Durham, NC, 2014). For a contextualization of the decade within twentieth-century history see Dagmar Herzog, *Sexuality in Europe: A Twentieth-Century History* (Cambridge, 2011).

[53] See Marzio Barbagli and David I. Kertzer (eds.), *Family Life in the Twentieth Century* (New Haven, 2004); Christopher Neumaier, *Familien im 20. Jahrhundert: Konflikte um Ideale, Politiken und Praktiken* (Berlin, 2019); Chiara Saraceno, 'The Italian Family from the Sixties to the Present', *Modern Italy*, 9/1 (2004), 47–57; Fiammetta Balestracci, 'Prozesse der Re-Normativierung in Italien: Normative Vorstellungen von der Familie in der Kommunistischen Partei Italiens (1964–1974)', in Dietz, Neumaier, and Rödder (eds.), *Gab es den Wertewandel?*, 247–68.

[54] Jo Barraclough Paoletti, *Sex and Unisex: Fashion, Feminism, and the Sexual Revolution* (Bloomington, Ind., 2015).

[55] Miriam Gebhardt, *Die Angst vor dem kindlichen Tyrannen: Eine Geschichte der Erziehung im 20. Jahrhundert* (Munich, 2009); Sonja Levsen, *Autorität und Demokratie: Eine Kulturgeschichte des Erziehungswandels in Westdeutschland und Frankreich, 1945–1975* (Göttingen, 2019).

Kerl, and Patricia Hertel in this volume).[56] Historiographical case studies of these new mass trends often highlight the ways in which pop culture and consumption fuelled value change and popularized new world-views and lifestyles, but simultaneously deradicalized the initial, far-reaching impetus of the late 1960s.[57] Television's role in this process has received particular attention.[58]

Given the fields of change outlined above, we have organized the essays in this volume around pivotal arenas of change and transformation. Four Parts will deal in turn with the role of the social sciences, of counter-cultural activists, of consumers, and of negotiations about sexuality.

V. Conclusion

The essays in this volume grapple with our hypothesis of the advent of the 'post-rational' in the long 1970s without always explicitly referring to it as such. They come at the subject from different perspectives, use different terminology, arrive at different conclusions, and at times they productively disagree. We hope to advance the debate on the subject by showcasing the different approaches to the problem adopted in recent scholarship.

The first Part historicizes the role of the social sciences in processes of value change. Martin Deuerlein explores how scientific observers interpreted the current and future importance of the nation state and analyses the contemporary diagnosis of a profound crisis in the 1960s and 1970s. He links the increasing irrelevance

[56] On new forms of travelling and consumerism since the late 1960s see Axel Schildt, 'Across the Border: West German Youth Travel to Western Europe', in Schildt and Siegfried (eds.), *Between Marx and Coca-Cola*, 149–60; Isabel Richter, 'Alternativer Tourismus in den 1960er und 1970er Jahren: Transkulturelle Flows und Resonanzen im 20. Jahrhundert', in Detlef Siegfried, Axel Schildt, and Alexander Gallus (eds.), *Deutsche Zeitgeschichte — transnational* (Göttingen, 2015), 155–78; Richard Ivan Jobs, *Backpack Ambassadors: How Youth Travel Integrated Europe* (Chicago, 2017).

[57] See Uta G. Poiger, 'Imperialism and Consumption: Two Tropes in West German Radicalism', in Schildt and Siegfried (eds.), *Between Marx and Coca-Cola*, 161–72; Detlef Siegfried, 'Protest am Markt: Gegenkultur in der Konsumgesellschaft um 1968', in id. and Christina von Hodenberg (eds.), *Wo '1968' liegt: Reform und Revolte in der Geschichte der Bundesrepublik* (Göttingen, 2006), 48–78. In *Storia intima dei ceti medi*, Enrica Asquer insists on the role played by materialist consumption in building new values and normative behaviours in the Italian middle-class family, which, however, generally remained modelled on unequal and conservative gender relations.

[58] Hodenberg, *Television's Moment*. In *La mutazione individualista* Giovanni Gozzini discusses Inglehart's theory and points out that the individualistic turn of the baby boomers in Italian society was accompanied by the rise of television.

of nationalism in the eyes of contemporary observers in the USA and West Germany to fundamental changes in social values. Intellectuals and social movements whose criticisms were fuelled by 'changes in social values', especially among the younger generation, questioned authority by engaging in contemporary debates. In a similar vein, Pascal Germann illustrates how social science experts shaped social knowledge and influenced mentalities and changing values in the long 1970s. The emerging fields of the social indicators movement and quality of life studies created a new realm of knowledge about 'social reality' which interacted in many ways with the public and political spheres. With Lisa Dittrich's essay on socialist East Germany, the focus then shifts to the impact of social scientists and advisers on ordinary people's lives. Dittrich follows the debates among marriage counsellors and legal experts about the 'proper' management of marriage, and also reconstructs exchanges between unhappy couples and counsellors. She questions whether 'post-rational', emotional behaviour and ideals replaced rational principles in everyday marriage management over time, constructing a nuanced argument. While the GDR codified love as the guiding principle of marriage as early as 1955 in a move towards post-rationality which met grass-roots demand, other models of partnership persisted which remained closer to rationalized values.

The essays in Part II explore experiments with the self and the notion of the embodied subject during the long 1970s. Isabel Richter assesses the meditation boom and spiritual practices introduced by Maharishi Mahesh Yogi and Bhagwan Shree Rajneesh, who both gained a large following of young adults in the 1960s and 1970s in Western industrialized countries. Meditation and spiritual practices were a popular arena of transformation, especially in alternative milieux. These practices could be group-oriented, like the Rajneesh movement, but were always related primarily to the body–mind nexus, to action, and, above all, to the experiences of the practitioners. Their followers questioned not authority and rationality as such, but the authority of detached rationality. A similarly playful attitude towards rationality is described by Juliane Fürst in her essay on the Soviet Union. She traces a paradigm change by which intellectual dissent gave way to a rise in personal emotionality that was outwardly apolitical but still challenged the system. Fürst juxtaposes official rhetoric and tropes with those used by people who wanted to position themselves against or outside Soviet norms, highlighting that from the mid 1960s onwards the entire discursive field of the USSR moved towards a more subjective, sensual, and affective rhetoric emphasizing well-being and the mind. The Part closes with Kristoff Kerl's analysis of the intersections between drug use and sexual politics in West Germany. Kerl shows that activists combined substances such as psychedelics and cannabis with erotic experiences to achieve states of ecstasy which were then politically charged. For them, an ecstatic body was a pivotal factor in the struggle for social and cultural change because it underpinned the alternative politics of 'liberating' the subject and thereby creating a new society. Again, these counter-culturalists did not reject rationality per se, but rather saw the mind and the body as entangled in a 'body–mind complex', which had a political role to play.

Part III, on consumerism and politics, collects contributions on travel and humanitarian aid practices. With holidays abroad becoming more and more affordable in postwar consumer societies, Patricia Hertel writes about the dictatorial countries Spain, Greece, and Portugal as the most popular European travel destinations in the long 1970s. Her case study of boycott appeals by British, Swedish, and German activists offers an early example of how tourism became connected to political awareness and to the idea of 'conscious consumerism'. Like Hertel, Norbert Götz also places social movement activists at the forefront of his analysis. He explores the Biafran War of 1967–70 as a transformative media event in Western societies such as the UK, Sweden, Ireland, and West Germany. Instead of depoliticizing non-governmental organizations and the voluntary sector as neutral agents in great power games, Götz highlights the power of civil society. Aid agencies took value-based decisions which served to shape knowledge and create contemporary notions of 'authentic witnessing' and post-rational forms of engagement.

Part IV is devoted to rethinking sexualities, tracing value transformations in the arenas of reproductive rights and mediated sexual policies. In her analysis of French feminists' political discourse Maud Anne Bracke emphasizes how feminism as theory and as political activism advocated new forms of embodied (post-)rationalism. French activists fought for fundamentally new legal frameworks in the realms of family and reproductive rights, but also for different sexual practices, moral values, gender roles, and consumer cultures. Rejecting the disembodied subject of the Enlightenment, the feminists of the long 1970s introduced the idea of the gendered citizen and embodied political subject, driven by rationality and individual will as well as by desires and emotions emanating from the body. As we can see from Roseanna Webster's oral history of working-class towns and neighbourhoods in Spain, such value changes were demanded not only by feminist elites, but also by the grass roots. Webster focuses on value changes relating to sex, childbirth, and the body. Starting in the early 1970s and before the official transition to democracy in Spain, the edges of the metropolitan heartlands, such as towns in Asturias and the outskirts of Seville, were key to shaping new attitudes towards reproductive politics. Last but not least, Kinga S. Bloch investigates the Polish 'sexual revolution' through the lens of the audio-visual mass media. Her focus on television entertainment series reveals the long 1970s in Poland to be a transitional phase, a period during which restrictions on discourses about sexuality gradually loosened. At the same time, however, the only stories about the sexual revolution worth telling on national television under socialism were still those coming from a male perspective.

Taken together, all these essays describe how institutional cultures, national experts, new media, mass consumption, and grassroots activists engaged in a far-reaching reconceptualization of the world and the self. Politics was redefined through the emergence of new national and international actors, shifting the boundaries between the personal and the political and politicizing individual behaviour in both private and public settings. Experiments with new values and new concepts of the subject resulted in practices which overstepped traditional boundaries and therefore challenged the centuries-old primacy of Western rationalism. We conceptualize these experiments and ideas as 'post-rational' inasmuch as they combined old elements of Enlightenment rationality with attempts to introduce new forms of the rational subject, foregrounding variously the body, emotion, spirituality, or self-fulfilment. At the same time, the meaning of the rational subject was fundamentally expanded by gendering it, and by consequently conceiving of the public and the private together, thus arriving at a new political morality emphasizing the impact of everyday individual behaviour in arenas such as relationships, sexuality, religiosity, consumerism, and humanitarianism, while de-emphasizing national belonging and duty. As experimental as they were, many of the new practices and theories remained Janus-faced, rejecting certain aspects of Western rationality while holding on to others.

The essays in this volume show that the debates and practices through which new values were negotiated had deep impacts on countries across Western, Central, Eastern, and Southern Europe, albeit with slightly different timings and meanings. Regardless of economic boom and bust cycles—in other words, structural changes—and despite the ideological fractures dividing Europe, each of the countries considered here saw a transformation of collective 'conceptions of the desirable' between the late 1960s and the early 1980s. The acceleration of value change expressed itself in different arenas, such as scholarly debates and the mass media, commercial and political consumerism, religious and lay counter-cultures, social and political movements, and sexuality and relationships. The Iron Curtain was a permeable boundary in this respect. It could only slow down value transformations in Soviet-dominated Eastern European countries, not prevent them altogether. Value change was driven as much by grass-roots trends (as shown in the case studies by Webster and Dittrich) as by mass-mediated popularization (see Bloch, Götz, and Hertel) and a growing global political and intellectual interdependency (see Deuerlein and Germann).

What united the different regions across Europe was a pattern of growing scepticism towards the old order of society and politics, connected with a new assertion of the importance of individual rights, choices, bodies, and emotions. New visions of the socio-political order developed which strengthened the role of the individual and represented attempts to disconnect society from the rationalizing tendencies brought about by the historical macro processes of industrialization, nation-state formation, and androcentrism. The new-found emphasis on the individual was a response to the history of capitalism, with its disregard for the needs of individual souls and bodies, as well as to the history of Marxism and of socialist dictatorships, with their similar disregard for individual choices and liberties. It is therefore unsurprising that the 1960s and 1970s saw the rediscovery of authors such as Reich and Marcuse, who had applied these ideas critically to fascist and, in Marcuse's case, postwar society, implying a direct link between the past dictatorships and the present democracies. At the centre of these critics' thought was the necessity to rediscover the needs of the individual in their multiple meanings and everyday life applications as a way to redefine how to build individual identities and the world around them. Existing means of identity-building had been shaped by the two world wars, which radicalized the political battle among the nations and at the same time interrupted older social patterns and broke human ethical boundaries. The world wars were thus a fundamental precondition for value change. But this period of value transformation could only take off once the necessary stability had been achieved. The ensuing, at times ferocious, eruptions of change during the long 1970s were in part the result of vanguard action by feminists, young activists, intellectuals, and experts; in part the product of agency at the grass-roots level through consumption, mass media, and social and civil movements; and in part triggered by underlying social and economic processes of the *longue durée*. This explains the diversity of outcomes in the arenas and countries under consideration. The different shades of 'post-rational' orientations, debated by the essays in this volume, embody the varied forms and dynamics assumed by cultural change.

The key part of this process was mainly situated in the 1970s, not the 1960s, as this was when popularization and mass dissemination took off. While the 1960s saw the first stirrings of vanguard experiments, during the 1970s the search for new values broadened its social reach and transferred to new sectors of society. The era of the long 1970s became the first high point of a process of post-rationalization that knew many nuances and ambivalences, and which continues via many different strands into our present. The move towards 'post-rational values' triggered decades-long conflicts and negotiations. While these values were successfully adopted in their original forms in some areas, they were deradicalized and commercialized in others. In many ways, value change in the long 1970s meant a lasting reorganization of European societies and politics, often accompanied by a backlash against these outcomes. We are still grappling with the ambivalent responses to post-rational value change today.

PART I

Social Scientists and Theories of Value Change

2

Modernization and the Fate of the Nation State: Expert Debates in West Germany and the United States during the Long 1970s

MARTIN DEUERLEIN

During the last decade of the twentieth century, observers in the social sciences, as well as journalists and politicians, believed that the world was entering a new 'global age' that questioned existing modes of social and political organization. This especially applied to the sovereign nation state, which was coming under pressure from two different directions. First, observers believed that states were losing authority due to the growing influence of global corporations and other aspects of globalization. Commentators such as the Japanese management consultant Kenichi Ohmae assumed that the forces of the global market had made territoriality meaningless and were heralding 'the end of the nation state' in a 'borderless world'.[1] Second, the loyalties of citizens—at least in the Western world—appeared to be shifting from nations to more cosmopolitan outlooks.[2] Overall, the process of 'denationalization' seemed to be spurring the transition of the world into a 'postnational age'.[3]

While contemporaries in the 1990s believed that these developments were a fundamentally new feature of their globalized present, a closer look reveals that the debate about the decline of the nation state can be traced back much further: in parts to the early twentieth century, but especially to the long 1970s. Current historiography

---

[1] Kenichi Ohmae, *The Borderless World: Power and Strategy in the Interlinked Economy* (New York, 1990), and id., *The End of the Nation State: The Rise of Regional Economies* (New York, 1995). For the debate on 'deterritorialization' see Gearóid Ó Tuathail, 'Borderless Worlds? Problematising Discourses of Deterritorialisation', *Geopolitics*, 4/2 (1999), 139–54.

[2] On this question see the contributions to Martha Nussbaum et al., *For Love of Country: Debating the Limits of Patriotism*, ed. Joshua Cohen (Boston, 1996).

[3] See Saskia Sassen, 'Globalization or Denationalization?', *Review of International Political Economy*, 10/1 (2003), 1–22.

portrays the years between the mid 1960s and the early 1980s as a time of profound change, not only in the realm of economic structures, but also as regards values, ideas, and world-views. The growth of world trade and financial exchange, the beginnings of deregulation and liberalization, and the rise of neo-liberalism have prompted historians to locate the beginning of our current phase of globalization in this decade.[4] Contemporary observers debated such developments as features of a new 'age of interdependence'.[5]

This essay will show how, from the late 1960s onwards, the interaction between these processes of change led contemporaries to question the sovereign nation state as the dominant actor in politics and economics, and as the main object of citizen loyalties. It will analyse how observers assessed the current and future importance of the nation state, what arguments they used to substantiate their findings, and how preconceived assumptions and contemporary political and economic conditions influenced such interpretations. The analysis will focus on political scientists, historians, and a number of other intellectual observers of current events in West Germany and the United States. While their interpretations were usually based on a limited number of cases and influenced by specific local or national circumstances, they were engaged in a transnational debate, and their conclusions were often universalized to allegedly speak for all 'advanced societies' or even wider parts of the globe.

The main challenge for the historicization of such debates is the profound ambiguity and imprecision of the term 'nation state', both in the sources and in historical studies. In English, especially, 'the nation' denotes both the 'nation state' and 'national society'.[6] While writers in the interwar years distinguished between statehood and nationhood and included empires among states,[7] the nation state was increasingly naturalized until it had become the only

---

[4] On the concept of the 'long 1970s' see Poul Villaume, Rasmus Mariager, and Helle Porsdam (eds.), *The 'Long 1970s': Human Rights, East–West Détente and Transnational Relations* (Abingdon, 2016). On 'globalization' in the 1970s see Niall Ferguson, Charles S. Maier, Erez Manela, et al. (eds.), *The Shock of the Global: The 1970s in Perspective* (Cambridge, Mass., 2011).

[5] See Martin Deuerlein, *Das Zeitalter der Interdependenz: Globales Denken und internationale Politik in den langen 1970er Jahren* (Göttingen, 2020).

[6] See John Breuilly, 'Introduction: Concepts, Approaches, Theories', in id. (ed.), *The Oxford Handbook of the History of Nationalism* (Oxford, 2013), 1–20, at 16 n. 10.

[7] See Tomohito Baji, 'Zionist Internationalism? Alfred Zimmern's Post-Racial Commonwealth', *Modern Intellectual History*, 13/3 (2016), 623–51. In contrast, see

imaginable form of statehood after 1945. The term was now used as shorthand for the 'as-is state', a state that was not—or no longer—a colony or colonial empire, without reflecting on the precise meaning of this classification.[8] To this day, not only the 'state' but also 'sovereignty' are terms that are frequently used, yet rarely defined and only sparsely theorized, in social sciences and historical research.[9] Research on nationalism after 1945 is still far less differentiated in terms of definitions, typologies, and explanations than the work that has been done on the nineteenth and early twentieth centuries, and the precise relationship of nationalism to the state and its various forms has not been studied in much detail for the second half of the twentieth century.[10]

Charles Maier's distinction between 'decision space' and 'identity space' is helpful in examining this nexus with more precision. Nationalistic movements aspired to establish a congruence between these two categories—between the polity of the territorial state and the imagined community of the nation.[11] The term 'nation state' thus describes a specific form of relationship between an assumed social group and a political order. Despite the limitations of social realities, the nationalist imagination—that is, the idea that the world was divided into nations and that the political division of the world ideally corresponded to this division—is still highly influential. Conversely, when either the authority of the national state (decision space) or the persuasive power of the nation (identity space) was undermined in

formulations such as the 'transition from empire to statehood', in Or Rosenboim, 'State, Power and Global Order', *International Relations*, 33/2 (2019), 229–45, at 232.

[8] For example, John H. Herz used the terms 'territorial state', 'nation-state', and 'nation' interchangeably. See his 'The Territorial State Revisited: Reflections on the Future of the Nation-State', *Polity*, 1/1 (1968), 11–34, at 12; id., 'Introduction', in id., *The Nation-State and the Crisis of World Politics: Essays on International Politics in the Twentieth Century* (New York, 1976), 1–56, at 13.

[9] See Peter M. R. Stirk, 'Introduction: The Concept of the State in International Relations', in id. and Robert Schuett (eds.), *The Concept of the State in International Relations: Philosophy, Sovereignty, Cosmopolitanism* (Edinburgh, 2015), 1–22, at 1.

[10] On nationalism after 1945 see Heiner Timmermann (ed.), *Nationalismus in Europa nach 1945* (Berlin, 2001). For an overview see Umut Özkırımlı, *Theories of Nationalism: A Critical Introduction*, 2nd edn. (Basingstoke, 2010). Aleida Assmann, *Die Wiedererfindung der Nation: Warum wir sie fürchten und warum wir sie brauchen* (Munich, 2020), 23, and Siniša Malešević, *Grounded Nationalisms: A Sociological Analysis* (Cambridge, 2019), 1–5, criticize the belief still held by many social scientists that with the advent of a postnational era, research on nationalism became a task for historians only.

[11] Charles S. Maier, 'Consigning the Twentieth Century to History: Alternative Narratives for the Modern Era', *American Historical Review*, 105/3 (2000), 807–31, esp. 816.

the perception of contemporary observers, or when the two categories were decoupled, this led to assumptions of a general crisis of the
nation state on several occasions in the twentieth century.

This essay will briefly look at a number of such instances between
the 1910s and 1940s that set the tone for later debates, before
focusing on diagnoses of a profound crisis of the nation state in
the 1960s and 1970s. By this time, the challenge was coming from
various directions at once: the authority and autonomy of the state
as the central actor in politics and economics were challenged by the
growing interdependence and increasing influence of multinational
corporations and other transnational actors. At the same time, rising
demands from citizens of Western states led to perceptions of a deep
crisis of governability and democracy. The national character of
nation states was simultaneously undermined by a perceived decline
in national loyalties during the general process of 'value change'.

I. The 'Obsolescence of the Sovereign
National State': Debates before the 1960s

The significance—or even continued existence—of the nation state
was not challenged for the first time in the 1970s. In the years before
the First World War, observers concluded from multiplying cross-
border contacts that in a shrinking world states could no longer be
completely independent units. In 1911 British liberal sociologist L. T.
Hobhouse assumed this meant that the 'old doctrine of sovereignty'
was dead.[12] At this time, most observers expected smaller states
to be transformed or absorbed into larger empires uniting several
nations.[13] However, the dissolution of multinational empires in
Europe and the dynamics of anti-colonialism soon changed this
equation. The doctrine of national self-determination became a key
principle of international politics and the future appeared to belong
to nation states.[14] Liberal observers in Europe and North America

---

[12] Leonard T. Hobhouse, *Liberalism* (London, 1911), 228. Cf. Brian C. Schmidt, *The Political Discourse of Anarchy: A Disciplinary History of International Relations* (Albany, NY, 1998), 109–19.

[13] e.g. John A. Hobson, *Imperialism: A Study* (London, 1902), 281; Alfred E. Zimmern, 'German Culture and the British Commonwealth', in id., R. W. Seton Watson, J. Dover Wilson, et al., *The War and Democracy* (London, 1914), 348–84, esp. 369.

[14] For a new perspective on self-determination as a universalist concept of global world-making see Adom Getachew, *Worldmaking after Empire: The Rise and Fall of Self-Determination* (Princeton, 2019).

still believed that the independent, sovereign, and self-sufficient state was a mythical concept that corresponded less and less to the realities of an interconnected world.[15] Yet despite the apparent irrationality of this construct, extreme forms of nationalism were on the rise among populations in Europe and Asia during the 1920s and 1930s. In 1922 US philosopher William Ogburn coined the term 'cultural lag' to describe the growing gap between the ever-increasing interdependence of the world and popular mentalities that still clung to small units such as the nation, and to warn of the dangers inherent in that development.[16]

It took the horrors of fascism and the Second World War, however, to bring about a widespread disillusionment with all forms of nationalism. While National Socialism itself can be considered a break with the nineteenth-century concept of the nation state,[17] observers in Europe held this very idea responsible for the violence they had experienced. This interpretation was strongest in Germany, where even conservatives and national liberals believed that the 'ideal of the autonomous nation state' had become an 'apparent absurdity', and that a revision of traditional notions of statehood and sovereignty was inevitable.[18] In order to overcome this crisis of the nation state and to adapt the political order to a new era of global politics, intellectuals in Europe and North America devised new forms of political organization ranging from European or transatlantic federation to world government.[19]

[15] Francis Delaisi, *Political Myths and Economic Realities* (London, 1925); Leonard S. Woolf, *The Way of Peace* (London, 1928); Alfred E. Zimmern, *Internationale Politik als Wissenschaft* (Leipzig, 1933). On these debates in the interwar years see Deuerlein, *Das Zeitalter der Interdependenz*, 38–54.

[16] William F. Ogburn, *Social Change with Respect to Culture and Original Nature* (New York, 1922), 200–13.

[17] Hannah Arendt, *The Origins of Totalitarianism*, new edn. (New York, 1973), 124, believed that National Socialism had 'destroyed' the nation state. On Nazi statehood see Rüdiger Hachtmann, 'Elastisch, dynamisch und von katastrophaler Effizienz: Zur Struktur der Neuen Staatlichkeit im Nationalsozialismus', in Sven Reichardt and Wolfgang Seibel (eds.), *Der prekäre Staat: Herrschen und Verwalten im Nationalsozialismus* (Frankfurt a.M., 2011), 29–73.

[18] Hans Rothfels, 'Zur Krise des Nationalstaats', *Vierteljahrshefte für Zeitgeschichte*, 1/2 (1953), 138–52, at 138. For a more differentiated view see Jörg Echternkamp, '"Verwirrung im Vaterländischen"? Nationalismus in der deutschen Nachkriegsgesellschaft 1945–1960', in id. and Sven Oliver Müller (eds.), *Die Politik der Nation: Deutscher Nationalismus in Krieg und Krisen 1760–1960* (Munich, 2002), 219–46.

[19] e.g. Wolfgang Friedmann, *The Crisis of the National State* (London, 1943), or the sources in Walter Lipgens (ed.), *Europa-Föderationspläne der Widerstandsbewegungen, 1940–1945: Eine Dokumentation* (Munich, 1968). On a global level, see Joseph P. Baratta,

Such projects were based not only on a normative condemnation of nationalism and the nation state, but also on a strengthened conviction that these concepts were anachronistic and irrational. In addition to the further growth of entanglements of all kinds, there was now an entirely new factor contributing to the 'obsolescence of the sovereign national state':[20] nuclear weapons. In 1957 John H. Herz, an émigré scholar from Germany who taught political science in the United States, argued that this new technology was able to penetrate the 'hard shell' of the sovereign nation state and had thus eliminated its basic source of legitimacy—the ability to protect its citizens from external attack. For Herz, therefore, traditional notions of territoriality and sovereignty had become obsolete, and a fundamental transformation of statehood into new forms of global rule was required to guarantee the survival of mankind.[21] However, ordinary citizens might not yet have realized how dramatically circumstances had changed, and this insight had to be actively promoted. The sociologist David Mitrany believed that the idea of nationality was still strong and therefore proposed to break the link between authority and territory. He argued that instead of global or regional federation, functional co-operation in technical areas and international planning by elites would leave sovereignty intact, while at the same time gradually overcoming 'irrational' ideologies of nationalism.[22]

But a number of countervailing developments also had to be taken into account. While fascism and war had profoundly discredited the nation state for some, for others it was precisely the (re-)establishment of a state with a fixed territory and a means of defending itself that would provide protection from attack and racial persecution. This was one of the reasons why the United Nations so strongly

The Politics of World Federation, 2 vols. (Westport, Conn., 2004); Or Rosenboim, *The Emergence of Globalism: Visions of World Order in Britain and the United States, 1939–1950* (Princeton, 2017).

[20] Hans J. Morgenthau, *Politics among Nations: The Struggle for Power and Peace*, 2nd edn. (New York, 1954), p. vii.

[21] John H. Herz, 'Rise and Demise of the Territorial State', *World Politics*, 9/4 (1957), 473–93 (for 'hard shell' see esp. 474, 485). In his *International Politics in the Atomic Age* (New York, 1959), Herz further elaborated on the 'decline of the territorial state'. Similar views are found in E. H. Carr, *Nationalism and After* (London, 1945), 38.

[22] See esp. David Mitrany, *A Working Peace System: An Argument for the Functional Development of International Organization* (London, 1943), and id., 'The Functional Approach to World Organization', *International Affairs*, 24/3 (1948), 350–63. Cf. Rosenboim, *The Emergence of Globalism*, 27–53.

enshrined the principles of 'self-determination', 'sovereign equality', 'territorial integrity', and non-interference in its Charter.[23]

These principles were soon adopted by anti-colonial nationalists. By the 1950s, proposals for imperial or world federation appeared as thinly veiled attempts to continue colonialism by other means, and the sovereign nation state had become the dominant vision for the future of newly independent countries.[24] While observers in the West had initially discarded nationalism in Asia, the Near East, and Africa as 'outmoded' and deeply irrational in an 'age when . . . traditional nation statehood has become incapable of providing populations' with two basic needs—economic well-being and military protection—they had to take it more seriously by the 1960s.[25] They might still believe that the nation state was 'dangerous for peace and illogical for welfare' and that Third World nationalism in particular was fuelled by uncontrollable passions that would lead to a dangerous 'balkanization' of the world, but could not deny that both the nation and the national territorial state were on the rise in developing countries.[26]

Meanwhile, in Europe and the United States the nation state also remained strong. The New Deal, the war economies, and the expansion of the welfare state had significantly extended the reach of states into society and economy between the 1930s and the 1960s. While this process had also been the result of transnational interactions, social policy had been conceptualized within the boundaries of nation states and could be interpreted as a consequence of left nationalist projects, based on state control of economic exchange and migration.[27] The institutions of the Bretton Woods system were

---

[23] Articles 1.2, 2.1, 2.4, and 2.7 of the UN Charter, available online at ⟨https://www.un.org/en/about-us/un-charter/full-text⟩ [accessed 15 Oct. 2021]. Cf. Mark Mazower, *No Enchanted Palace: The End of Empire and the Ideological Origins of the United Nations* (Princeton, 2013), 25, 124.

[24] Cf. Mazower, *No Enchanted Palace*, chs. 1 and 4; on imperial federation see Michael Collins, 'Decolonisation and the "Federal Moment"', *Diplomacy and Statecraft*, 24/1 (2013), 21–40.   [25] Herz, *International Politics in the Atomic Age*, 340–1.

[26] Stanley Hoffmann, 'Obstinate or Obsolete? The Fate of the Nation-State and the Case of Western Europe', *Daedalus*, 95/3 (1966), 862–915, at 862. For examples from Britain and references to 'balkanization' see Ian Hall, 'The Revolt against the West: Decolonisation and its Repercussions in British International Thought, 1945–75', *International History Review*, 33/1 (2011), 43–64.

[27] See Sandrine Kott, 'L'État social et la nation allemande', in Hans Günter Hockerts (ed.), *Koordinaten deutscher Geschichte in der Epoche des Ost-West-Konflikts* (Munich, 2004), 79–102. For Britain see David Edgerton, *The Rise and Fall of the British Nation: A Twentieth-Century History* (London, 2018), p. xx.

therefore designed not only to foster free trade, but also to 'shelter nation states from globalization's disruptive effects'.[28] Instead of turning to federation, European governments founded institutions such as the European Economic Community (1957), which was primarily based on intergovernmental co-operation. Arguably, this did not hasten the demise of nation states, but helped to stabilize them against the disruptive effects of war and economic entanglements.[29] Instead of heralding the end of the sovereign nation state, the 1950s thus witnessed an unprecedented heyday of this form of social organization.[30]

These developments also had an impact on the social sciences, where methodological nationalism was gaining ground. Sociology now studied classes and groups *within* national societies, and behaviouralistic approaches conceptualized a world of nation states as political systems. Nation states—not empires or private actors—were considered to be the central players in international relations, while earlier works that had questioned the concept of the sovereign nation state were now viewed as idealistic musings, far removed from the reality of power politics.[31]

By the end of the 1950s, the nation state had become the dominant paradigm for the interpretation of contemporary developments. In 1954 historian and political scientist Karl Deutsch, like many of his colleagues, believed that the nation state was becoming an outdated mode of government.[32] Only a few years later he argued that the growth of international trade in the 1950s was an exception caused by postwar reconstruction, and that European integration had

---

[28] Daniel Sargent, 'The Cold War and the International Political Economy in the 1970s', *Cold War History*, 13/3 (2013), 393–425, at 399.

[29] Alan S. Milward, *The European Rescue of the Nation-State* (Berkeley, 1992). On the current state of the debate see Anthony B. Atkinson, Peter M. Huber, Harold James, et al. (eds.), *Nationalstaat und Europäische Union: Eine Bestandsaufnahme* (Baden-Baden, 2016).

[30] Cf. Frederick Cooper, 'States, Empires, and Political Imagination', in id., *Colonialism in Question: Theory, Knowledge, History* (Berkeley, 2005), 153–203, at 190.

[31] This interpretation was first put forward by E. H. Carr in 1939 against authors such as Alfred Zimmern. See E. H. Carr, *The Twenty Years' Crisis 1919–1939: An Introduction to the Study of International Relations* (London, 1939). Cf. Deuerlein, *Das Zeitalter der Interdependenz*, 66–73.

[32] Karl W. Deutsch, *Nationalism and Social Communication: An Inquiry into the Foundations of Nationality* (Cambridge, Mass., 1953); id., *Political Community at the International Level: Problems of Definition and Measurement* (Garden City, NY, 1954), 25; id., Sidney A. Burrell, Robert A. Kann, et al., *Political Community and the North Atlantic Area: International Organization in the Light of Historical Experience* (Princeton, 1957).

reached a plateau and might tip over into growing nationalism and increasingly isolated states. As the need for political control grew in modern industrial economies, Deutsch expected the relevance of nation states and the importance of nationalism to increase in domestic politics as well.[33] By the end of the 1960s, John Herz had also changed his mind. In *The Territorial State Revisited* he conceded that he had underestimated the impact of decolonization, the power of nationalism, and the stability of the nuclear balance. Instead of bringing about the replacement of the nation state by new forms of political organization, current trends pointed in the direction of retrenchment, new self-sufficiency, and a 'new territoriality' in a world of multiple 'nationally defined and delimited units'.[34]

II. *Sovereignty at Bay? Multinational Corporations and Transnational Actors*

But at this very moment, when the continued dominance of the sovereign nation state had been widely accepted, it was, in fact, facing a triple threat: the autonomy of the state in international politics and economics was being challenged by new types of non-state actors; the governability of democracies was threatened by rising complexity and demands from domestic audiences; and the nation appeared to be losing relevance as the focal point of the identity and loyalty of citizens in democratic societies as a result of a fundamental change in basic values.

In 1968 US economist Richard Cooper published *The Economics of Interdependence*, in which he described a world economy that was composed not of interactions between national economies, but

[33] Karl W. Deutsch, 'Shifts in the Balance of Communication Flows: A Problem of Measurement in International Relations', *Public Opinion Quarterly*, 20/1 (1956), 143–60; id. and Alexander Eckstein, 'National Industrialization and the Declining Share of the International Economic Sector, 1890–1959', *World Politics*, 13/2 (1961), 267–99; Karl W. Deutsch, 'The Impact of Communications upon International Relations', in Abdul A. Said (ed.), *Theory of International Relations: The Crisis of Relevance* (Englewood Cliffs, NJ, 1968), 74–92, esp. 88–92. Edward L. Morse, 'The Politics of Interdependence', *International Organization*, 23/2 (1969), 311–26, criticized Deutsch for neglecting capital flows, which had become more important than trade. More than a decade later, Deutsch observed gradual advances in European integration, but still believed that nation states would remain the 'main arenas and instruments of political action' for the rest of the century. See Karl W. Deutsch, *Tides among Nations* (New York, 1979), 235.

[34] Herz, *The Territorial State Revisited*, 22–3. In similar vein, Stanley Hoffmann, 'Report of the Conference on Conditions of World Order, June 12–19, 1965, Villa Serbelloni, Bellagio, Italy', *Daedalus*, 95/2 (1966), 455–78, esp. 457–8.

of multiple types of actors and of 'flows' of funds and goods.[35] Cooper's work was an early example of a veritable avalanche of books that appeared in the following decade dealing with the growth of international trade and financial transactions. Unlike Deutsch, most observers now assumed that this was not an exceptional phenomenon of postwar recovery, but part of a general trend towards an increasingly interdependent world.

A central aspect of this trend was the growth of foreign direct investment by a supposedly new type of actor in international economics: multinational corporations. The political and social consequences of their business activities had first been debated in France in the early 1960s. Economists initially assumed that negative effects would be felt only in newly independent countries, where business interests competed with national development goals.[36] In the United States such firms—mostly headquartered in the country—were first seen as an asset to US foreign and economic policy. By the end of the 1960s, however, they increasingly appeared as independent actors who cared little for state borders or national interests. Instead of working towards the goals of their home state, multinationals pursued their own interests, transcending national markets, relocating jobs to countries with a cheaper labour force, disregarding state regulation and taxation, and forcing states to enter into new forms of economic competition.[37] These firms were now considered not only a threat to development efforts in the Global South or to the economic autonomy of Western Europe, but a challenge to the very sovereignty of nation states, and perhaps even to their continued existence as social units. In his book *Sovereignty at Bay*, published in 1971, economist Raymond Vernon argued that the concept of the sovereign nation state seemed increasingly outdated, while his colleague Charles Kindleberger had declared two years earlier that the nation state was 'just about through as an economic unit'.[38]

---

[35] Richard N. Cooper, *The Economics of Interdependence: Economic Policy in the Atlantic Community* (New York, 1968).

[36] e.g. Roger Demonts and François Perroux, 'Grande firme — Petite nation', *Présence Africaine*, 38/3 (1961), 3–19.

[37] On the threat to Europe see Jean-Jacques Servan-Schreiber, *Le Défi américain* (Paris, 1967). On the early outsourcing debate see e.g. Richard J. Barnet and Ronald E. Müller, 'Companies Go Abroad and Jobs Go Along', *New York Times*, 22 Dec. 1974, 3.

[38] Charles P. Kindleberger, *American Business Abroad: Six Lectures on Direct Investment* (New Haven, 1969), 207; Raymond Vernon, *Sovereignty at Bay: The Multinational Spread*

Multinational corporations were not the only type of non-state actor that engaged in cross-border activities. Such 'transnational' actors, as German political scientist Karl Kaiser described them in 1969, ranged from NGOs to terrorist groups. They often evoked expectations of solidarity and international civil society, but were also a cause for concern: Kaiser worried that the detrimental effect of 'transnational politics' on the autonomy of nation states could challenge democratic legitimacy and lead to new conflicts and new forms of neocolonial dependence.[39]

Contemporary observers assessed the scenario of weakening state authority in international politics and the global economy in different ways. For some, it was a cause for concern. They believed that the nation state played an important role in securing social peace, and that nationalism was an important means to resolve persistent class conflicts.[40] Others pointed out that what was actually at stake was not the sovereignty of nation states, but their autonomy. On closer inspection, concerns about the loss of state control resulted less from a crisis of sovereignty than from a growing 'control gap' between states' rising aspirations to plan and steer societies and economies, and the real chances of exercising such control in the face of interdependence and transnational actors.[41]

Yet another group of observers assumed that the decline of the nation state held great promise. They included Marxists, who still expected the state to finally wither away, and a group of people who could be called 'evolutionists'. US sociologist Frank Tannenbaum and former US Under-Secretary of State George Ball interpreted the assumed decline of the state as an inevitable consequence of modernization. While the nation state was a 'very old fashioned idea', Ball described the multinational corporation as 'a modern

of U.S. Enterprises (New York, 1971). For more details on this debate see Deuerlein, *Das Zeitalter der Interdependenz*, 123–38.

[39] Karl Kaiser, 'Transnationale Politik: Zu einer Theorie multinationaler Politik', in Ernst-Otto Czempiel (ed.), *Die anachronistische Souveränität: Zum Verhältnis von Innen- und Außenpolitik* (Cologne, 1969), 82–119, at 104; and id., 'Transnational Relations as a Threat to the Democratic Process', *International Organization*, 25/3 (1971), 706–20.

[40] Stephen Hymer and Robert Rowthorn, 'Multinational Corporations and International Oligopoly: The Non-American Challenge', in Charles P. Kindleberger (ed.), *The International Corporation: A Symposium* (Cambridge, Mass., 1970), 57–91, at 89.

[41] Cooper, *The Economics of Interdependence*, 151–3; Joseph S. Nye and Robert O. Keohane, 'Transnational Relations and World Politics: A Conclusion', *International Organization*, 25/3 (1971), 721–48, at 743–4.

concept designed to meet the requirements of a modern age'.[42] The sovereign state, by contrast, Tannenbaum claimed in 1968, led only to conflict and war. In an article with the telling title 'The Survival of the Fittest', he argued that its current crisis held great promise, as supranational enterprises would lead to a more prosperous and peaceful world.[43] This might not have been a majority position in the 1960s or 1970s, but Tannenbaum's and Ball's arguments are important indicators of an intellectual shift. While it was widely accepted by the 1960s that the nation state was a central feature of modernity and the main driver of modernization, it now increasingly appeared as an outdated relic, while multinational corporations seemed ideally suited to the requirements of a new era of global interdependence.

III. *Ungovernability and the Crisis of Democracy*

While evolutionists believed that giant corporations would gradually replace states as drivers of prosperity and providers of security, the general tone of the 1970s debate about the role of states in the domestic politics of Western democracies was less optimistic. Governments in various countries of Western Europe, in the United States, and in Japan were increasingly unable to deal with the economic disruptions of the 1970s and to fulfil the ambitious promises of social reform they had made in the preceding decade. The state seemed to be failing and no other type of actor was ready to take over. The 'disintegration of civil order, the breakdown of social discipline . . . and the alienation of citizens' that intellectuals had observed in the civil rights movement, the protests against the Vietnam war, the student revolts, and the general unrest of 1968 in North America and Western Europe deepened such concerns.[44] In West Germany, this aspect of the challenge to the nation state in the 1970s was debated under the heading of 'ungovernability' (*Unregierbarkeit*); in the United States, it fed into a debate on the crisis of democracy.[45]

[42] George W. Ball, 'The Promise of the Multinational Corporation', *Fortune*, 75/6 (1967), 80.

[43] Frank Tannenbaum, 'The Survival of the Fittest', *Columbia Journal of World Business*, 3/2 (1968), 13–20.

[44] The quotation is from Michel Crozier, Samuel P. Huntington, and Joji Watanuki, *The Crisis of Democracy: Report on the Governability of Democracies to the Trilateral Commission* (New York, 1975), 2.

[45] On these debates see Gabriele Metzler, 'Staatsversagen und Unregierbarkeit in

Contemporary observers identified mostly endogenous factors feeding into this situation. With the New Deal, the war economies, and the expansion of the welfare state in many countries after 1945, state institutions had started to plan and intervene in more and more areas of social activity. The 'increasing complexity of the social order' produced by the modernization process, however, made it 'more and more difficult for governments' to achieve their social planning goals. At the same time, the expansion of state activity had increased the need to secure democratic legitimization that, according to contemporary observers, was becoming ever harder to obtain. Promises of reform and social planning had resulted in higher expectations among populations about what a state could and should do. When these rising expectations and demands were confronted with the limits of state influence, the resulting gap appeared all the more dramatic.[46]

Moreover, international and domestic challenges appeared closely linked. The 1975 *Report on the Governability of Democracies* that coined the buzzword 'crisis of democracy' was presented to the Trilateral Commission—an organization founded by David Rockefeller and Zbigniew Brzezinski in 1973 in order to foster co-operation among elites from North America, Western Europe, and Japan. In their report, Michel Crozier, Samuel P. Huntington, and Joji Watanuki identified three types of challenges to the future of democracy. 'Contextual challenges' stemmed from international relations or the world economy and included inflation, growing economic interdependence, and North–South issues. 'Intrinsic challenges' resulted from the functioning of democracy itself, while changes in the 'social structure and social trends' could also destabilize a country's social order. These included a 'challenge to authority' by intellectuals and social movements whose criticisms were fuelled by 'changes in social values', especially among the younger generation, by a shift from 'materialistic... public-spirited values' towards 'private satisfaction' and 'self-fulfillment'.[47] Consequently, while in the past people had found 'their purposes in religion, in nationalism, and in ideology', in the present 'neither church, nor state, nor class' commanded

---

den siebziger Jahren?', in Konrad H. Jarausch (ed.), *Das Ende der Zuversicht? Die siebziger Jahre als Geschichte* (Göttingen, 2008), 243–61.

[46] In summary: 'The demands on democratic government grow, while the capacity of democratic government stagnates' (Crozier, Huntington, and Watanuki, *The Crisis of Democracy*, 9, 163–4).   [47] Ibid. 7.

people's loyalties.[48] This quotation shows how challenges to the capacity of states to steer social developments, brought about by rising expectations and declining autonomy, were closely linked to the increasing irrelevance of nationalism in the eyes of contemporary observers. They traced this development back to fundamental and wide-ranging changes in social values that therefore constituted an inherent aspect of the notion of a general crisis of the nation state in the 1970s.

IV. Value Change

The authors of *The Crisis of Democracy* had taken this argument from the work of Ronald Inglehart.[49] In the late 1960s the American political scientist had engaged with Karl Deutsch's thesis that European integration had reached a plateau in the late 1950s and that nationalism was on the rise in Europe. According to Inglehart, Deutsch had focused too exclusively on structural integration, elite attitudes, and the policies of de Gaulle. In contrast, Inglehart emphasized the significance of political culture and values in democratic states. 'Europeanness' was on the rise among the younger generation, who had been socialized in the anti-nationalist and pro-European environment of the postwar years and increasingly considered nationalism to be 'archaic and dangerous'.[50] In 1971 Inglehart expanded this observation into the broader argument of a general shift in the 'political cultures of advanced industrial societies' from materialist to post-materialist values, which included a declining adherence to nationalism and the nation state.[51]

In 1977 he dedicated a chapter of his study *The Silent Revolution* to 'Parochialism, Nationalism, and Supra-Nationalism' and argued that in virtually all 'post-industrial societies', nationalistic sentiments were losing support while both 'super-national' and 'tribal' loyalties

[48] Ibid. 159, 166–8.

[49] Especially from Ronald Inglehart, 'The Silent Revolution in Europe: Intergenerational Change in Post-Industrial Societies', *American Political Science Review*, 65/4 (1971), 991–1017.

[50] Id., 'An End to European Integration?', *American Political Science Review*, 61/1 (1967), 91–105, at 94.

[51] Id., 'Changing Value Priorities and European Integration', *Journal of Common Market Studies*, 10/1 (1971), 1–36, at 2. Here, Inglehart used the terms 'acquisitive' and 'post-acquisitive' value priorities; in 'The Silent Revolution in Europe' he spoke of 'acquisitive' and 'post-bourgeois' value priorities. Later he used the terms 'materialist' and 'post-materialist'.

were on the rise. This could happen simultaneously, as Inglehart observed that the same individuals often supported supranational integration while at the same time emphasizing regional identities or ethnic ties.[52] This assumed shift of citizens' loyalties from nations to larger and smaller identity spaces constituted an important aspect of the supposed crisis of the nation state in the 1970s. If we follow Ernest Gellner's idea that nations do not occur naturally, but that nationalisms are constitutive for their existence, the decline in support for nationalist positions found in surveys meant a challenge to the stability of nation states in general.[53]

In Western Europe this triple challenge to the autonomy, stability, and national character of states during the 1970s was expressed less in debates about European integration, which seemed to be stagnating during a time of 'Eurosclerosis',[54] than in an increasing focus on various regionalisms.[55] From today's perspective, multilayered loyalties had always existed, and regional identifications appear more as new forms of nationalism than as indicators for post-materialist values. For Inglehart and most of his contemporaries, however, loyalties to smaller or larger social units constituted a profound challenge to the legitimacy and integrative function of nations and states in general. In the United States, the debate on the national character of the state was less territorially framed, but revolved around the limits of an assimilationist understanding of the 'American nation' and the observation that ethnicity and other forms of group identity had gained political importance since the 1960s.[56]

Just a few years earlier, most observers had marvelled at the enduring power of nationalism and the capacity of the nation state to flourish not only in developing countries, but also in the West. But

[52] Ronald Inglehart, *The Silent Revolution: Changing Values and Political Styles among Western Publics* (Princeton, 1977), 5, 14–16, 322–62.

[53] Ernest Gellner, *Nations and Nationalism* (Oxford, 1983).

[54] Herbert Giersch, *Eurosclerosis* (Kiel, 1985).

[55] Ayn Rand, *Global Balkanization* (Palo Alto, Calif., 1977), treats both European regionalisms and the new focus on ethnicity in the USA as aspects of a general trend.

[56] e.g. Philip Gleason, 'American Identity and Americanization', in Stephan Thernstrom, Ann Orlov, and Oscar Handlin (eds.), *Harvard Encyclopedia of American Ethnic Groups* (Cambridge, Mass., 1980), 31–58. Cf. Stanley A. Renshon (ed.), *One America? Political Leadership, National Identity, and the Dilemmas of Diversity* (Washington, DC, 2001). Attempts by Black separatists or Native American groups to form independent, sovereign territorial states in North America hardly figured in these more general debates.

by the mid 1970s their decline had once again been diagnosed. John Herz, for example, modified his assessment one more time in 1976. In the eight years since *The Territorial State Revisited* he had become sceptical about the 'ability of nations—both new and old—to fulfil their minimum functions'. Factors such as environmental pollution and population growth now imperilled the functioning of states, respecting neither their boundaries nor their sovereignty. But Herz was still unsure where these new developments might lead. While 'global survival problems' challenged concepts of state sovereignty, he mused, using the 'idea of nationhood' to solve them might bestow new legitimacy upon 'nations'.[57]

V. *Nationalism, the State, and Modernization Thinking*

As we have seen in the debate on the consequences of the rise of multinational corporations, these developments were contradictory and hard to place. The 'withering away of nationalism', a central assumption of many intellectuals after the Second World War, made them uneasy by the mid 1970s. With nationalism, democracy was losing one of the binding 'forces and commitments' that had shaped its institutions and inspired its citizens to espouse a common purpose.[58]

But was this a process that could be influenced by human action, or did it occur almost naturally? For several decades, the nation state and nationalistic attitudes had repeatedly been described as atavistic remnants of an earlier age. Since the 1960s, their weakening had been attributed to the further progress of modernization in Western Europe and North America. This view was foreshadowed by typologies of nationalism developed from the 1950s within the mental framework of the Cold War. Based on the work of Hans Kohn and Louis L. Snyder, historians and social scientists differentiated between 'typical Western', 'typical Eastern', and 'non-European' forms of nationalism. The first could be found in Britain, France, and the United States and were supposedly liberal, democratic, pluralistic, rational, and based on political community. Non-Western forms, by contrast, comprising Central and Eastern European as well as Asian and other Third World nationalisms, were generally

---

[57] Herz, *The Nation-State and the Crisis of World Politics*, 18–19, 47.
[58] Crozier, Huntington, and Watanuki, *The Crisis of Democracy*, 4–9, 159–60.

conceived of as illiberal, irrational, cultural, mystical, and based on ethnic community.[59]

Types of nationalism, territorial spaces, historical periods, and ideas about 'progress' and 'backwardness' now converged in the eyes of observers. In 1966, for example, German historian Theodor Schieder identified three general types: 'Western', that is, French and British nationalism originating in the seventeenth and eighteenth centuries; 'Central', dating from the early nineteenth century; and 'Eastern' European nationalism from the early twentieth century.[60] From Europe, he argued, nationalism had spread to the rest of the world. This view allowed different regions of the world to be allocated to different stages of development. In nineteenth-century Europe and North America, according to such modernist research, nationalism had played an important role in fulfilling the need for homogenization that had arisen from the emergence of industrial societies and the resulting differentiation and social fragmentation.[61] Eastern Europe had followed suit, while from the perspective of the 1960s and 1970s, the decolonized world had only recently entered this stage of development. Just as in Europe's past, modernization theorists such as Walt W. Rostow believed, 'reactive nationalism' was once again the primary spur to modernization—in the case of developing countries against 'intrusion from more advanced nations'.[62] They were trying to catch up, not only by accelerating industrialization, but also through the heightened importance that anti-colonial and postcolonial actors ascribed to nationalism and the sovereign nation state.[63] However, Third World nationalisms were believed to rely on 'primordial' communities of blood and land, while the West had moved ahead once again and had already entered a new stage. There, nationalism had not only been more

---

[59] Louis L. Snyder, *The Meaning of Nationalism* (New Brunswick, NJ, 1954); Hans Kohn, *The Idea of Nationalism: A Study in its Origins and Background* (New York, 1944); id., *Nationalism, its Meaning and History* (Princeton, 1965).

[60] Theodor Schieder, 'Typologie und Erscheinungsformen des Nationalstaats in Europa', *Historische Zeitschrift*, 202/1 (1966), 58–82. While the title mentions 'nation states', Schieder actually offers a typology of 'nationalisms'—yet another example of the ambiguous use of these terms.

[61] See e.g. Gellner, *Nations and Nationalism*.

[62] Walt W. Rostow, *The Stages of Economic Growth: A Non-Communist Manifesto* (Cambridge, 1960), 26.

[63] In *The Nation and its Fragments: Colonial and Postcolonial Histories* (Princeton, 1993), 3–4, Partha Chatterjee laments that this view obscures the emancipatory aspects of nationalism and portrays it as the main source of conflict in the Third World.

'progressive' from the outset, but was now supposedly based on 'routine allegiance to a civil state' that was gradually making nationalism obsolete altogether.[64] Once again, the West believed itself at the forefront of history while the rest of the world was supposedly lagging behind.[65]

Aspects of this thinking can be observed most clearly in the Federal Republic of Germany, where intellectuals went to great lengths to emphasize that their country was entering not only a new time, but also a new space as a result of its profound 'Westernization'. A central aspect of this development was the shift from an ethnically to a politically defined nation, and from emotional attachments to a rational legitimization of the state. For some observers, the state now existed primarily to provide services to a society that for rational reasons had decided to adopt this form of political organization. 'The state', once so revered in German thought, had become nothing more than the 'self-description of social systems'.[66] Thus, in the 1970s and 1980s, when social scientists in North America and Western Europe tried to assess the character and scope of 'value change' in the wake of Inglehart, they rarely dealt with attitudes towards nationalism or the nation when talking about the state, but focused on the shift from 'values of duty and acceptance' to 'values of self-fulfilment', and on the relationship between individuals and government.[67]

Behind this approach lay the conviction that large sections of the general population were finally subscribing to the idea that nationalism was irrational and obsolete. Surveys during the 1970s and early 1980s showed that fewer people expressed explicit pride in being German.[68] In 1987 philosopher Jürgen Habermas recapi-

---

[64] Clifford Geertz, 'The Integrative Revolution: Primordial Sentiments and Civil Politics in the New States [1963]', in id., *The Interpretation of Cultures: Selected Essays* (New York, 1973), 255–310, at 260. Ten years later, Geertz also saw such 'primordial sentiments' at work in 'modern' areas of the world such as 'Canada, Belgium, Ulster'.

[65] Hedley Bull, 'The State's Positive Role in World Affairs', *Daedalus*, 108/4 (1979), 111–23, at 122, noted that only the West could assume that its own way of life would be universally adopted once the barriers separating states had vanished.

[66] Niklas Luhmann, 'The "State" of the Political System', in id., *Essays on Self-Reference* (New York, 1990), 165–74. Cf. Gabriele Metzler, *Der Staat der Historiker: Staatsvorstellungen deutscher Historiker seit 1945* (Berlin, 2018), 184–97.

[67] e.g. Helmut Klages and Willi Herbert, *Wertorientierung und Staatsbezug: Untersuchungen zur politischen Kultur in der Bundesrepublik Deutschland* (Frankfurt a.M., 1983); 'Pflicht- und Akzeptanzwerte' vs. 'Selbstentfaltungswerte', in Helmut Klages, *Wertorientierungen im Wandel: Rückblick, Gegenwartsanalyse, Prognosen*, 2nd edn. (Frankfurt a.M., 1985), 39–41.

[68] Summarized in Thomas Gensicke, 'Wertewandel und Nationalbewußtsein: Über

tulated that a majority of West Germans now equated nationalism with National Socialism and had developed a 'postnational identity' since 1945.[69] (West) German national consciousness finally appeared to be 'modernized' because it was oriented towards the West, relied on cultural values instead of ethnicity, and drew pride from the economic strength and welfare system of the country.[70] To provide new forms of positive identification with the polity, West German intellectuals focused on allegiance to liberal values and democratic institutions—an attitude that political scientist Dolf Sternberger termed 'constitutional patriotism' (*Verfassungspatriotismus*) and that Habermas in the 1980s advocated as the only permissible form of rational and reflective political identification for West Germans.[71] This allowed intellectuals to believe not only that their country was finally approaching 'normal' Western ways, but also that for the first time in history it was at the forefront of political modernization. In 1990 historian Thomas Nipperdey felt compelled to warn against the 'arrogance of the seemingly noble rejection of the national' and the 'fatal inclination' to lecture the rest of the world that it had to adopt these 'postnational' German ways.[72]

Discarding nationalism did not, however, mean discarding the national framework. The older focus on the nation and the state had been replaced by a focus on society among West German intellectuals. But they still perceived this object of study through the lens of methodological nationalism. Habermas's public sphere was framed within the boundaries of the West German state, which also provided the legal and social security that was required for such a rational and reflective discourse to function. Nor was the concept of 'constitutional patriotism' suitable for including immigrants, as it relied on an 'inherited' responsibility for the German past.

die Modernisierung des Nationalgefühls in Westdeutschland', in Bernd Estel and Tilman Mayer (eds.), *Das Prinzip Nation in modernen Gesellschaften: Länderdiagnosen und theoretische Perspektiven* (Opladen, 1994), 197–218, at 199.

[69] Jürgen Habermas, 'Geschichtsbewusstsein und posttraditionale Identität: Die Westorientierung der Bundesrepublik', in id., *Kleine politische Schriften*, 12 vols. (Frankfurt a.M., 1981–2013), vi: *Eine Art Schadensabwicklung* (1987), 161–79, at 169.

[70] Gensicke, 'Wertewandel und Nationalbewußtsein', 198.

[71] Dolf Sternberger, 'Verfassungspatriotismus', *Frankfurter Allgemeine Zeitung*, 23 May 1979; Jürgen Habermas, 'Heinrich Heine und die Rolle des Intellektuellen in Deutschland', in id., *Eine Art Schadensabwicklung*, 25–54, at 40. Cf. Jan-Werner Müller, *Constitutional Patriotism* (Princeton, 2007), 15–45.

[72] Thomas Nipperdey, 'Die Deutschen wollen und dürfen eine Nation sein: Wider die Arroganz der Post-Nationalen', *Frankfurter Allgemeine Zeitung*, 13 July 1990, 10.

West Germany was a special case, not only because ideas of nationalism and nation statehood had been so profoundly discredited
there by the crimes of National Socialism, but also because the congruence between nation, society, and state, and between identity
space and decision space, had been disassembled by partition.[73]
Nevertheless, the German case illustrates a broader transnational
trend. During the 1960s, intellectuals in the West increasingly viewed
nationalism as an irrational remnant of the past, because 'modern
societies' had allegedly developed more rational ways to legitimize
their polity. Whether this state of affairs could still be called a
nation state was hardly debated, however, as this type of political
organization had become the only imaginable form of statehood
after 1945. Conversely, the uncertainty surrounding concepts such
as the nation, the state, and the nation state meant that a variety of
developments were counted as features of an overarching crisis of
the nation state during the long 1970s—be they the rising influence
of multinational corporations that interfered with state control of
the economy, the perceived crisis of democracy, or the decline in
nationalist feelings among the people.

VI. *The 1980s and 1990s*

After the 1970s, the debate about the 'ungovernability' of Western democracies abated as its most pessimistic scenarios had not
materialized. The same was true—at least temporarily—for the
controversy about the challenges to the nation state from growing
interdependence and multinational corporations. This debate had
been conditional on détente in East–West relations. With the Second
Cold War setting in, other issues were coming to the fore. During
the 1980s the state began to be reaffirmed in the social sciences.
While Kenneth Waltz's 'neorealism' restored the state as the central
actor in international relations, British political scientist Hedley Bull
argued that the sovereign state was not the opposite of, but a central
precondition for, the growth of transnational relations.[74]
    When it came to questions of nationalism, teleological forecasts

---

[73] On this unique situation see Jürgen Habermas, 'Grenzen des Neohistorismus', in
id., *Kleine politische Schriften*, vii: *Die nachholende Revolution* (1990), 149–56.
[74] Kenneth N. Waltz, *Theory of International Politics* (New York, 1979); Bull, 'The
State's Positive Role in World Affairs'. On the revived interest in the state in general
see Peter B. Evans, Dietrich Rueschemeyer, and Theda Skocpol (eds.), *Bringing the State
Back In* (Cambridge, 1985).

of the decline of the state in the West were on shaky ground, and criticism of modernization thinking intensified.[75] At the same time, attention to a potential transformation of nationalisms increased. Regionalisms in Europe, for example, were now interpreted as new forms of 'peripheral' nationalism or 'subnationalism', rather than as indicators for the decline of the idea of nationalism altogether.[76] Regardless of these shifts, most observers in West Germany held on to the diagnosis of a postnational state during the 1980s and considered the consolidated nation state to be an exceptional phenomenon of an era that was coming to a close.[77]

Everything changed around 1989–90. This does not necessarily mean that the end of the Cold War, the transition in Eastern Europe, or German reunification were significant turning points in every aspect of the history of nationalism or the nation state. But the events of these years had a profound impact on how observers interpreted contemporary trends and shaped their predictions for the future. In Germany, reunification had for some solved the question of the nation and its relationship to the state, and created a post-classical German nation state.[78] But it also brought the perceived dangers of nationalism back into view—concerned observers now wrote about the 'return' of a phenomenon they had already consigned to the past.[79] While the German case was atypical, it now appeared as one instance in a more extensive resurgence of nationalism, especially in Central and Eastern Europe and in post-Soviet Central Asia.[80]

During the 1990s, the continuing advance of regionalization and decentralization in Western Europe was believed to undermine both

[75] In the German case this was mainly the result of the debate on the 'modern' aspects of National Socialism. See Riccardo Bavaj, *Die Ambivalenz der Moderne im Nationalsozialismus: Eine Bilanz der Forschung* (Munich, 2003).

[76] See Stein Rokkan and Derek W. Urwin, 'Introduction: Centres and Peripheries in Western Europe', in eid. (eds.), *The Politics of Territorial Identity: Studies in European Regionalism* (London, 1982), 1–17, at 16. The new emphasis on the 'imagined' character of national communities since the 1980s also reflected the perception of their renewed importance, especially in Britain. See Benedict R. Anderson, *Imagined Communities: Reflections on the Origin and Spread of Nationalism* (London, 1983).

[77] Wolfgang J. Mommsen, 'Wandlungen der nationalen Identität', in Werner Weidenfeld (ed.), *Die Identität der Deutschen* (Bonn, 1983), 170–82.

[78] e.g. Heinrich A. Winkler, 'Nationalismus, Nationalstaat und nationale Frage in Deutschland seit 1945', *Aus Politik und Zeitgeschichte*, 40 (1991), 12–24.

[79] e.g. Jürgen Habermas, 'Der DM-Nationalismus', *Die Zeit*, 30 Mar. 1990.

[80] For contemporary assessments see the contributions in Heinrich Winkler and Hartmut Kaelble (eds.), *Nationalismus — Nationalitäten — Supranationalität* (Stuttgart, 1993); and Rogers Brubaker, *Nationalism Reframed: Nationhood and the National Question in the New Europe* (Cambridge, 1996).

national identities and the nation state 'from below'.[81] In Europe state sovereignty was challenged 'from above' by further advances in the process of European integration, while on a worldwide scale the strengthening clout of global corporations made it harder for states to manage their economies and forced them to compete for investment by offering low tax rates and deregulation. Just as in the 1970s, policy decisions were now based on the assumption that the influence of nation states was declining, and sometimes brought about the very processes they believed they were reacting to.[82]

For contemporaries, these developments often appeared to be a consequence of an overarching process of globalization that they could not influence but had to adapt to. Globalization, as it was now understood, meant not only a challenge to state autonomy or even sovereignty, but also a perceived weakening of national loyalties, as cosmopolitan identities seemed on the rise throughout the Western world.[83] This trend could lead to a new global culture and global citizenship, but also to new forms of fragmentation and conflict. Samuel Huntington famously wrote about an impending 'clash of civilizations' as the most likely consequence of the weakening of both state authority and national loyalties.[84] Ronald Inglehart, for his part, played a leading role in the World Values Survey from the 1980s, an ambitious project investigating the cultural, moral, religious, and political values of people in more than 121 countries (as of 2020). Since the 1990s, this research has resulted in multiple versions of a map of up to nine cultural zones, arranged along the axes of 'traditional' versus 'secular–rational' and 'survival' versus 'self-expression' values.[85]

Again, contemporary observers were trying to make sense of such contradictory developments by arranging them within the framework of modernization thinking. The resurgence of nationalism in

---

[81] See Tony Judt, *Postwar: A History of Europe Since 1945* (New York, 2005), 701–13.

[82] This included an active attack on state planning and intervention by neo-liberals whose ideas had gained political influence during the 1970s and 1980s, along with aspects of a voluntary retreat by the state after the limits of social planning had become apparent during the 1970s. Strengthening the market seemed to be a way to avoid the excessive demands confronting national governments.

[83] e.g. Ulrich Beck, 'The Cosmopolitan Perspective: Sociology of the Second Age of Modernity', *British Journal of Sociology*, 51/1 (2000), 79–105.

[84] Samuel P. Huntington, *The Clash of Civilizations and the Remaking of World Order* (New York, 1996).

[85] The Inglehart–Welzel Cultural Map of the World, available online at ⟨www.worldvaluessurvey.org/WVSContents.jsp⟩ [accessed 28 Oct. 2021].

some areas of the world appeared as a temporary aberration— part of another process of delayed development. This time it was the post-socialist countries in particular that had to 'catch up' because socialist dictatorships had earlier denied them a 'normal' national development.[86] The future, however, seemed to belong to postnational and cosmopolitan identities and new forms of global governance beyond the state.[87]

VII. *Conclusion*

Studying the debate on modernization and the fate of the nation state during the long 1970s and embedding it into a longer time frame can help us not only to historicize contemporary assumptions, but also to scrutinize predictions of the 'inevitable' decline or return of nation states. Looking back, the 'era of value change' does indeed appear to have been a time of fundamental change. It is debatable whether the role of the state in international politics and economics really changed, whether its capacity to fulfil the ambitious promises of social reform diminished, or whether there was a profound and enduring decline in nationalist orientations as part of a process of value change. As so often, such interpretations were also a matter of perspective.

Most observers of contemporary events during the 1970s were not aware of developments or debates before 1945, but looked mainly at the 1950s when comparing their own present with the past. Yet the 1950s were not only the heyday of the nation state as an analytical concept, but also a time of unusually successful state control and planning. While some perceptive observers, such as the two political scientists Robert Keohane and Joseph Nye, noted that 'it was the 1950s that were exceptional, not the present', most of their colleagues took the situation of the 1950s as 'normal' for the form of nation states and their political role.[88] Any changes

[86] This view included a resurgence of ideas of Western 'rational' nationalism vs. its 'emotional' and 'mythical' counterpart in Central and Eastern Europe. For a counterargument, see Ulrike von Hirschhausen and Jörn Leonhard, 'Europäische Nationalismen im West-Ost-Vergleich: Von der Typologie zur Differenzbestimmung', in eid. (eds.), *Nationalismen in Europa: West- und Osteuropa im Vergleich* (Göttingen, 2001), 11–45, esp. 37.

[87] On this thinking see Nina Glick Schiller and Andreas Wimmer, 'Methodological Nationalism and Beyond: Nation-State Building, Migration and the Social Sciences', *Global Networks*, 2/4 (2002), 301–34.

[88] Joseph S. Nye and Robert O. Keohane, 'Transnational Relations and World Politics: An Introduction', *International Organization*, 25/3 (1971), 329–49, at 343.

made their own present look crisis-prone, leading social scientists to diagnose the long-term decline of the nation state and treat the 'nation' as an obsolete nineteenth-century concept. In reality, these experts were mostly referring to a situation that had taken shape from the 1930s and had become dominant in the 1950s. What had changed was the social scientists' basic outlook, such as their reliance on modernization thinking or methodological nationalism. These paradigms strongly impacted on the interpretation of developments during the 1970s, but were starting to unravel at the same time.[89] In a longer perspective, this marks the 1970s as the beginning of a process of reconfiguration whose consequences we still feel today.

The 1990s saw a resurgence of the debate on modernization and the fate of the nation state that began in the 1960s. Again, observers were often unaware of earlier works and perceived their own present as a new era of globalization and denationalization. They often oversimplified the past as the age of national sovereignty in order to emphasize the novelty of their own present. When Kenichi Ohmae wrote in 1995 that nation states were 'dinosaurs waiting to die', he alleged that this form of social organization had been around from time immemorial, but had now been rendered obsolete by social evolution.[90] From today's perspective, such assumptions appear overly teleological. Responses to the financial crisis of 2007–8 demonstrated that reports of the death of the nation state had been greatly exaggerated and showed that states still performed essential functions in maintaining the stability of the global economy.[91] Today, 'the national' and 'the global' are no longer seen as a contradiction, but as interacting modes of social organization.[92]

We are back at the insights of the 1960s and 1990s: the state and its various forms are not fixed entities in social reality, but a

[89] See e.g. Robert A. Nisbet, *Social Change and History: Aspects of the Western Theory of Development* (New York, 1969).

[90] Kenichi, *The End of the Nation State*, blurb. Stuart Hall criticized the assumption 'that just because we are thinking about an idea it has only just started', in 'The Local and the Global: Globalization and Ethnicity', in Anthony D. King (ed.), *Culture, Globalization and the World-System: Contemporary Conditions for the Representation of Identity* (Binghamton, NY, 1991), 19–39, at 20.

[91] See Ran Hirschl and Ayelet Shachar, 'Spatial Statism', *International Journal of Constitutional Law*, 17/2 (2019), 387–438, at 389; Graeme Turner, 'The Nation-State and Media Globalisation: Has the Nation-State Returned—or Did it Never Leave?', in Terry Flew, Petros Iosifidis, and Jeanette Steemers (eds.), *Global Media and National Policies: The Return of the State* (Basingstoke, 2016), 92–105.

[92] Saskia Sassen, *Territory, Authority, Rights: From Medieval to Global Assemblages* (Princeton, 2006).

process, constantly in transformation.[93] In general, the nation state often serves as a straw man. Commentators who want to emphasize the revolutionary character of globalization portray a form of social organization that has not changed for centuries—the Westphalian type of sovereign nation state—and has only recently been challenged. In contrast, those who take a 'long-term perspective in which the state continuously evolves' are much more sceptical about the idea of fundamental ruptures within a short period of time.[94]

Similarly, any notion that there was a clear-cut process of nationalism rising and declining in importance that could be identified with specific world regions and imbued with normative connotations has been shattered in recent years. The rise of populist movements in Europe, North America, and elsewhere made observers realize that nationalism had not staged a short-lived comeback in the 1990s, but had, in truth, never gone away. It can certainly no longer be interpreted as a problem of 'backward' regions outside the Western world.[95] At a time when some commentators lament that identity politics is destroying the foundations of larger communities, the search for new inclusive and democratic forms of national consciousness continues.[96]

[93] Similar observations had been made by Hoffmann, 'Obstinate or Obsolete?', 889, 910–11, and Michael Mann, 'Nation-States in Europe and Other Continents: Diversifying, Developing, Not Dying', in Gopal Balakrishnan (ed.), *Mapping the Nation* (London, 1996), 295–316. For the state as a process see Gunnar Folke Schuppert, *Staat als Prozess: Eine staatstheoretische Skizze in sieben Aufzügen* (Frankfurt a.M., 2010).

[94] Michiel S. de Vries, 'The Attack on the State: A Comparison of the Arguments', *International Review of Administrative Sciences*, 67/3 (2001), 389–414, at 406. Cf. also Stirk, 'Introduction', 8–11.

[95] For this argument see Malešević, *Grounded Nationalisms*, esp. 1–16.

[96] For the United States see Jill Lepore, *This America: The Case for the Nation* (New York, 2019); for Germany see Assmann, *Die Wiedererfindung der Nation*.

3

Changing Values and Social Knowledge: The Social Indicators Movement, Quality of Life Studies, and the 'Silent Revolution' in the 1970s

PASCAL GERMANN

In 1977 the political scientist Ronald Inglehart published his book *The Silent Revolution*, triggering a long-lasting debate on 'value change'. His main thesis is in the book's first and probably most cited sentence: 'The values of Western publics have been shifting from an overwhelming emphasis on material well-being and physical security toward greater emphasis on the quality of life.'[1] Inglehart thus used the term 'quality of life' to capture the essence of the value change he suggested was taking place in the 1970s; however, he did not mention that this term was of very recent origin. It was hardly heard before the mid 1960s, at which point its usage increased spectacularly. This rise was not at all a silent revolution; rather, media reports frequently discussed the popularity of this new term. In January 1970, for example, a *New York Post* columnist forecast: 'The quality of life . . . That's the phrase most likely to dominate the 1970s.'[2]

Translated into many languages and widely received as a new key goal of Western societies and a challenge to the postwar era's focus on material well-being and economic growth, the phrase 'quality of life' evolved into a pivotal reference point in debates on such divergent issues as the environment, work satisfaction, social welfare, health care, leisure culture, family life, and urban development. From the late 1960s, quality of life became a key term of the so-called social indicators movement, whose proponents—governmental officials, statisticians, and academics—campaigned

---

[1] Ronald Inglehart, *The Silent Revolution: Changing Values and Political Styles among Western Publics* (Princeton, 1977), 3.
[2] Harriet Van Horne, 'The Dominant Theme', *New York Post*, 12 Jan. 1970.

for the development of new measures of social progress beyond GNP.[3] Measuring quality of life subsequently became a priority for international organizations, government agencies, and social science research centres. Endeavours to monitor people's quality of life created a new world of ideas, concepts, numbers, graphs, and facts which circulated between universities, state agencies, NGOs, the media, and social movements, and affected how social issues were perceived and discussed in public.

This brings me to the starting point of my essay. The social indicators movement and quality of life studies produced a new realm of knowledge about 'social reality' which interacted in many ways with the public and political spheres. I will show how quality of life emerged as an object of knowledge, how it changed its meaning in the 1970s, and how it circulated between social contexts. In the process, I aim to highlight interrelations between social scientists' quality of life endeavours and those cultural shifts that were labelled 'value change'. From a history of knowledge perspective, I argue that changing value orientations of the 1970s were not merely an expression of changing mentalities, but were enabled and shaped by newly accessible social knowledge.

'Social knowledge' is used here in a broad sense, with three meanings. First, it describes all forms of information and evidence, as well as theories and analytical statements, pertaining to what is usually called 'social reality'.[4] Second, the word 'social' refers to the shaping of this knowledge through interactions between various actors, institutions, and discourses. And third, the phrase points to the potential of knowledge to change social relations.

---

[3] The history of the social indicators movement has not yet been written. Aspects of it are discussed in Jean-Baptiste Fleury, 'Drawing New Lines: Economists and Other Social Scientists on Society in the 1960s', *History of Political Economy*, 42, suppl. 1 (2010), 315–42; Matthias Schmelzer, *The Hegemony of Growth: The OECD and the Making of the Economic Growth Paradigm* (Cambridge, 2016), 300–312; Stephen Macekura, 'Whither Growth? International Development, Social Indicators, and the Politics of Measurement, 1920s–1970s', *Journal of Global History*, 14/2 (2019), 261–79; and Pascal Germann, 'The Quality of Life Turn: The Measurement and Politics of Well-Being in the 1970s', *KNOW: A Journal on the Formation of Knowledge*, 4/2 (2020), 295–324. There are also some historical accounts of key protagonists: Kenneth C. Land and Alex C. Michalos, 'Fifty Years after the Social Indicators Movement: Has the Promise Been Fulfilled?', *Social Indicators Research*, 135/3 (2018), 835–68; Heinz-Herbert Noll, 'Social Indicators and Quality of Life Research: Background, Achievements and Current Trends', in Nikolai Genov (ed.), *Advances in Sociological Knowledge: Over Half a Century* (Wiesbaden, 2004), 151–81.

[4] For a similar understanding of 'social knowledge' see Charles Camic, Neil Gross, and Michèle Lamont (eds.), *Social Knowledge in the Making* (Chicago, 2011), 3.

In what follows, I will deal with all three meanings of 'social knowledge' by examining the emergence of quality of life as a new object of knowledge; the shaping of this knowledge by various actors, institutions, and discourses; and finally, its effects on value orientations and new subjectivities in the 1970s.

I. *Beyond GNP: The Rise of 'Quality of Life' and the Social Indicators Movement*

The term 'quality of life' was crucially shaped in the US liberal era of the 1960s.[5] If anyone could claim to have coined the phrase, that person would be the Harvard economist John Kenneth Galbraith. Author of the best-selling book *The Affluent Society*,[6] political adviser to Presidents Kennedy and Johnson, and arguably the most famous economist of the 1960s, Galbraith wielded significant influence on the public debates and the mindset of liberal Americans.[7] On 27 December 1963 Galbraith gave a lecture at the annual meeting of the American Association for the Advancement of Science in which the term 'quality of life' probably first took centre stage in an intellectual argument.[8] In this lecture he made a case for nothing less than a fundamental paradigm shift in economics. He argued that the 'affluent society' of the postwar era faced new problems, and so economics should abandon its preoccupation with economic growth. Rather, in all societies 'with a relatively advanced state of economic development', Galbraith contended, the new goal should be 'what may broadly be called the quality of life'.[9] Under this new umbrella term, Galbraith addressed issues such as education, regional development, racial equality, health care, cultural opportunities, leisure facilities, the advertising industry, the aesthetics of cities, and air pollution, and he clarified that progress in all these domains was possible only by improving and expanding the public sector.

The lecture was published in *Science*, in revised form in the British literary magazine *The Encounter*, and in French translation in the

---

[5] On the rise of the term see also Germann, 'The Quality of Life Turn', 300–2.

[6] John Kenneth Galbraith, *The Affluent Society* (New York, 1958).

[7] On Galbraith see in particular Richard Parker, *John Kenneth Galbraith: His Life, his Politics, his Economics* (New York, 2005).

[8] JFK Presidential Library, Boston, Galbraith Papers, Ser. 9.3, Box 864, 'Economics and the Quality of Life', 27 Dec. 1963.　　　　　　　　　　　　　　　[9] Ibid.

magazine *Citoyens 60*.[10] Galbraith's arguments received broad public attention and 'quality of life' swiftly became a key political phrase in the context of Lyndon B. Johnson's Great Society programme. Picking up his adviser's term, President Johnson announced in his State of the Union Address of 1965 that he would 'improve the quality of life for all' by expanding education, social security, and health care.[11] In the late 1960s references to quality of life as a new key goal became widespread. Five years after Johnson's speech, Richard Nixon promised in his State of the Union Address of 1970 to shift priorities from an exclusive focus on material prosperity towards a new quest for 'quality of life' by putting environmental issues high on the agenda and by waging an intensified 'war on crime'.[12] Around the same time, debates on quality of life crossed the Atlantic, and social movements, political parties, and governments increasingly adopted the popular phrase in Western Europe. In West Germany, for example, trade unions played a pioneering role in discussing quality of life as a crucial task for the future, and the Social Democrats widely deployed the term in Willy Brandt's successful election campaign in 1972.[13] In France, by contrast, it was the centre-right government of Valéry Giscard d'Estaing that jumped on the bandwagon by announcing the creation of a new Ministry for Quality of Life in 1974.[14]

To be sure, the new phrase was attractive both to liberals and social democrats who advocated an expansion of public services and social welfare, and to members of the New Left who argued that capitalism was unable to satisfy human needs.[15] As these examples illustrate, references to quality of life as a new key concern cut across

[10] JFK Presidential Library, Boston, Galbraith Papers, Ser. 9.2, Box 797, Articles, 'Economics and the Quality of Life'.

[11] Lyndon B. Johnson, 'Annual Message to the Congress on the State of the Union, January 4, 1965' ⟨http://www.lbjlibrary.net/collections/selected-speeches/1965/01-04-1965.html⟩ [accessed 29 Oct. 2021].

[12] Richard Nixon, 'Annual Message to the Congress on the State of the Union', 22 Jan. 1970 ⟨https://www.presidency.ucsb.edu/documents/annual-message-the-congress-the-state-the-union-2⟩ [accessed 29 Oct. 2021].

[13] Bernd Faulenbach, *Das sozialdemokratische Jahrzehnt: Von der Reformeuphorie zur neuen Unübersichtlichkeit. Die SPD 1969–1982* (Bonn, 2011), 224–9; Günther Friedrichs, *Aufgabe Zukunft: Qualität des Lebens*, vol. i (Frankfurt a.M., 1972).

[14] *Journal officiel de la République française*, Lois et décrets (version papier numérisée), No. 0133, 7 June 1974, 6119.

[15] That is why some conservatives denounced quality of life as a new buzzword from the left. See Hermann Lübbe, 'Lebensqualität oder Fortschrittskritik von links', *Schweizer Monatshefte*, 53 (1973/74), 606–20.

political divides. Thus, the term was also adopted by policymakers who were eager to address conservative concerns such as surges in crime, urban decay, or a perceived decline of moral values.

These political discourses interacted with a new field of statistics and social science that was dubbed 'quality of life' or 'social indicators' research. A crucial driver of this new realm of knowledge production was the so-called social indicators movement, a network of academics, government officials, and representatives of international organizations who called into question the dominance of GNP and its widespread use as a welfare measure. They argued that because a nation's social progress and its citizens' well-being could not be appropriately measured by purely economic indicators, state administrations and the social sciences had to develop new social statistics that would assess progress or regression in areas such as health, education, working life, the environment, safety, and social participation.[16] In order to define a common goal in all these areas of concern, the movement used 'quality of life' as a key term serving as an alternative benchmark for assessing a nation's advancement beyond GNP growth. One of the movement's key demands was the establishment of comprehensive social information systems that would let governments and the public know how the nation was faring with respect to its citizens' quality of life. As proponents of the movement emphasized, this knowledge was supposed to be directly relevant to policymaking. The regular measurement of the people's quality of life would enable governments to set social policy goals, make resource allocation decisions, and assess welfare programmes. Moreover, it was hoped that it would provide a basis for rationalizing public debate.[17]

Like the term 'quality of life,' the social indicators movement emerged in the United States during the Johnson era. In contrast to what the word 'movement' suggests, the social indicators endeavour was initiated by a small group of renowned social scientists, officials in the Johnson administration, and prominent policymakers. 'Movement' is a term of self-description adopted by its protagonists, who were anxious to project an image of democratic bottom-up activism for what was actually an establishment project with a distinctly

---

[16] A founding text of the movement was Raymond Augustine Bauer (ed.), *Social Indicators* (Cambridge, Mass., 1966).

[17] See e.g. Wilbur J. Cohen, 'Social Indicators: Statistics for Public Policy', *American Statistician*, 22/4 (1968), 14–16, and Wolfgang Zapf, 'Social Indicators: Prospects for Social Accounting Systems', *Social Science Information*, 11/3–4 (1972), 243–77.

top-down approach. Many of the project's key actors looked back on double careers as social scientists at universities and as civil servants at governmental institutions. Among them were some of the most influential figures in US politics at the time, such as the statistician Wilbur Cohen, one of the key architects of Johnson's welfare programme, or the sociologist and senator Daniel P. Moynihan, who as a conservative-leaning Democrat became an adviser to Richard Nixon. Overall, the movement's political mindset tended towards what one of its protagonists called 'liberal incrementalism', which endorsed gradual social reforms within the established institutions.[18] In the United States the movement encountered fierce opposition from conservatives who disparaged the social indicators and quality of life projects as blatant examples of the 'great research boondoggle'.[19] At the end of the 1960s, the movement's ambitious plans to establish a comprehensive reporting system on social progress had to be downsized as they were unable to win a majority in the US Congress. Such setbacks, however, did not impede the rapid growth and increasing institutionalization of social indicators and quality of life programmes in the following years.

The 1970s were shaped by transatlantic crossings of the social indicators movement and by the extended production and global dissemination of quality of life knowledge. Within the social sciences, quality of life and social indicators studies became a booming research field around the world.[20] Sociologists, psychologists, political scientists, and economists launched large-scale projects and worked together in cross-disciplinary ventures that aimed to quantify quality of life at the levels of social groups, communities, cities, regions, nation states, and beyond. The measurement of quality of life also climbed the political agenda. As a consequence, social indicator programmes were increasingly incorporated into the routines of statistical agencies and bureaucracies, and these routines accelerated, widened, and stabilized the communication of quality of life knowledge. International organizations had a huge impact on this development. In particular, the OECD, UNESCO, and the United Nations Research Institute for Social Development

[18] Zapf, 'Social Indicators', 249.

[19] Baker Library Special Collections, Harvard Business School, Raymond A. Bauer Papers, b. 4, f. 4-2, Congressional Record—House, 2 March 1967.

[20] The most important journal in the field was founded in 1974 with the title *Social Indicators Research: An International and Interdisciplinary Journal for Quality-of-Life Measurement*, which it still retains today.

launched international programmes of work on social indicators and the measurement of quality of life.[21] These endeavours fostered the production of internationally comparable data and fuelled a trend of social reporting at the national level. Starting with the UK in 1970, an increasing number of nation states (nearly all of them OECD members) began to publish regular social reports that informed policymakers and the public of the nation's social progress and its citizens' well-being.[22]

In the 1970s quality of life was frequently regarded as a condensed expression of new feelings and value orientations at a time of accelerated social change. These feelings and values, however, were articulated and mediated through newly produced social knowledge. The rise of the term 'quality of life' was essentially driven by the emergence and growth of a broadly received research field that produced huge amounts of papers, reports, and statistics on people's well-being. Importantly, it is not possible to separate this realm of knowledge from the realm of values. Activists of the social indicators movement were fully aware that the new quality of life knowledge had a distinctly normative dimension. From the movement's outset, its main proponents argued that the omnipresence of purely economic indicators such as GNP or the cost of living index entailed what they called 'a new philistinism'—a spiritless materialistic view that uses 'monetary units as the common denominator of all that is important in human life'.[23] Conversely, it was hoped that new quality of life indicators would change people's values in a positive way, as they would measure all the achievements of a society that could not be expressed in monetary units. Thus, social scientists involved in the social indicators movement not only offered a new description of changing value preferences in the 1970s, but were also active proponents of the new value orientations towards quality of life.

[21] Wolfgang Glatzer, 'International Actors in Social Indicators Research', *Social Indicators Newsletter*, 16 (1981), 1–12.

[22] Heinz-Herbert Noll, 'Social Monitoring and Reporting: A Success Story in Applied Research on Social Indicators and Quality of Life', *Social Indicators Research*, 135/3 (2018), 951–64.

[23] Bertram M. Gross, 'The State of the Nation: Social Systems Accounting', in Bauer (ed.), *Social Indicators*, 154–271, at 167.

II. *Rival Notions of Quality of Life*

Although quality of life measurement developed into a burgeoning research field in the early 1970s, there was hardly a consensus on what was meant by the new phrase. Accordingly, the large-scale projects conducted by international organizations, government agencies, and social science research centres revealed considerable disagreements about how to define quality of life and how to measure it. Some of these conflicts were political in essence. Within the OECD, for example, governmental officials in Scandinavian countries insisted that the OECD programme should factor in social inequality as a major quality of life concern, while other delegates argued that distributional issues were of no direct importance for determining people's quality of life.[24] Political divisions of this kind were interwoven with turf conflicts and methodological differences between different disciplines of the social sciences. Economists argued that if the goal of social indicator programmes was to enable rational policymaking, then social indicators would have to be moulded as normative measures of progress in order to be used for cost–utility analysis.[25] Sociologists, in contrast, argued that such a one-sided economic view of social issues was exactly what the social indicators movement sought to critique. That is why sociologists preferred purely descriptive social indicators in order to measure social change.[26]

The disagreements also related to rival notions of quality of life. Sociological studies often used statistical data on living conditions to gauge quality of life. Psychologists, in turn, were sceptical when quality of life was measured only by 'objective' conditions such as statistics on crime, employment, housing, or air quality. Instead, they preferred survey techniques because these emphasized that quality of life was always determined by the people's *perception* of their living conditions and their *sense* of well-being. This psychological approach to measuring quality of life was also fostered by a rhetoric of 'democratizing' the social indicators undertaking. Accordingly, media reports claimed that traditional social statistics represented

[24] Germann, 'The Quality of Life Turn', 309.

[25] Fleury, 'Drawing New Lines'.

[26] Eleanor Bernert Sheldon and Howard E. Freeman, 'Notes on Social Indicators: Promises and Potential', *Policy Sciences*, 1/1 (1970), 97–111.

the view of 'government planners', whereas psychological survey techniques revealed the 'people's view'.[27]

Overall, psychological notions of subjective well-being acquired greater importance within quality of life research as many of its proponents agreed that their measurements had to factor in the activities, perceptions, and feelings of individuals. By attributing to quality of life a less materialistic and more subjective meaning, social scientists generally demarcated the concept from the prevalent welfare measures of the postwar era, such as 'standards of living' or 'levels of living'. The meaning of 'quality of life' remained controversial in the 1970s, but in an increasing body of research literature the term was semantically shifting towards subjective well-being. This change was accompanied by a remarkable upswing of subjective measures, which were supposed to quantify people's life experiences, feelings, aspirations, and attitudes.

The measurement of subjective well-being had a long history, emerging from various fields such as marital success studies and educational psychology in the 1920s, or mental health research and gerontology in the postwar era, among others.[28] But the social indicators movement and quality of life studies were what decisively propelled the establishment of subjective measures within mainstream social science and within the statistical programmes of governments and international organizations. Overall, the quality of life programmes of the 1970s helped turn contested measures of subjective well-being into accepted variables for the study and governance of human well-being. By doing this, they set the stage for the upswing in the science and politics of happiness two decades later.[29] In the 1970s there was one research institution that did more than any other to foster the turn towards subjective well-being and the psychological reframing of the quality of life concept: the University of Michigan Institute for Social Research (ISR) in Ann Arbor. This was the same institution where Ronald Inglehart studied the changing value orientations of Western societies and developed his theory on value change.

[27] See e.g. 'Quality of Life Surveys Show Different Results', *Tulsa Daily World*, 28 Mar. 1976.

[28] Erik Angner, 'The Evolution of Eupathics: The Historical Roots of Subjective Measures of Wellbeing', *International Journal of Wellbeing*, 1/1 (2011), 4–41.

[29] On the history of this happiness movement see in particular Daniel Horowitz, *Happier? The History of a Cultural Movement that Aspired to Transform America* (New York, 2017).

III. *The University of Michigan, the OECD, and the Turn towards Subjective Well-Being*

In 1970 the social psychologist Angus Campbell and the political scientist Philip Converse from the ISR launched a large-scale survey project called 'Monitoring the Quality of American Life'.[30] The project's beginning was timely: the successful research proposal was submitted to the Russell Sage Foundation on 26 January 1970, four days after Richard Nixon's aforementioned call in his State of the Union Address for 'a new quest—a quest not for a greater quantity of what we have, but for a new quality of life in America'.[31] Echoing the President's words, the Michigan social scientists stated in their proposal that the USA 'takes pride in the fact that in material achievements it leads the world but it is disturbed by the possibility that as its population is growing larger and richer the human experience of living in America may be deteriorating'.[32] With references to the new national quest proclaimed by the government, the social scientists were confident that Michigan's 'program of study of the quality of American life' would become 'one of the most important social science research undertakings in the United States'.[33]

The project was characterized by a pronounced psychological understanding of quality of life. According to the Michigan social scientists, indicators of the nation's economic status, its social condition, or its demographic trends would say little about the quality of American life as they would fail to assess how people experienced and perceived their lives. Following this line of reasoning, Angus Campbell argued that 'the quality of life is always in the eye of the beholder, and it is there we seek ways to evaluate it'.[34] Guided by this frequently cited dictum and accompanied by several other projects on perceived quality of life, the Michigan project was based on interviewing people by means of standardized questionnaires and

---

[30] Bentley Historical Library, Angus Campbell Papers, Box 4, Russell Sage Foundation, 1970–7, Monitoring the Quality of American Life, A Proposal to the Russell Sage Foundation, Jan. 1970.   [31] Nixon, 'State of the Union'.
[32] Bentley Historical Library, Angus Campbell Papers, Box 4, Russell Sage Foundation, 1970–7, Monitoring the Quality of American Life, A Proposal to the Russell Sage Foundation, Jan. 1970.   [33] Ibid.
[34] Angus Campbell, 'Aspiration, Satisfaction, and Fulfillment', in id. and Philip E. Converse (eds.), *The Human Meaning of Social Change* (New York, 1972), 441–66, at 442.

drew heavily on so-called subjective indicators measuring people's satisfaction and their evaluations of various life concerns.[35] By setting methodological standards for survey-based quality of life studies around the world, the Michigan social scientists aimed to take the lead in this burgeoning field of research.

The Quality of American Life project exemplified the Michigan institute's ability to adjust its research agenda to highly topical issues and new political priorities, as well as its ambition to serve as the United States' social observatory and provide data on the social health of the nation.[36] Since its foundation in 1949, the ISR had become one of the world's largest academic survey research centres and was renowned for its cutting-edge survey sampling methods and its use of quantitative data to analyse social changes. Although the institute's research programmes brought together a range of social sciences, the Michigan approach was characterized by a socio-psychological orientation and a focus on individual behaviour and motivation.[37] Angus Campbell and Philip Converse, for instance, had become famous for developing a socio-psychological approach to the study of voting behaviour.[38] Following this research tradition, Michigan's quality of life programme drew on methodologies that were developed and cultivated at the institute in the 1950s and 1960s. This meant that the importance of subjective indicators was already emphasized in the institute's research on political attitudes, consumer sentiments, and mental health. From the mid 1960s, Michigan researchers became involved in the social indicators movement, arguing from the beginning that social indicator projects should factor in the psychological meanings of social change.[39] Thus, both the institute's research traditions and its sheer capacity (with 457 full-time equivalent salaried employees by 1970)[40] provided the ideal stage for the ambitious quality of life programme.

The programme proved to be remarkably successful. Indeed, by the early 1970s the ISR had already assumed a world-leading role in quality of life research. The Michigan social scientists advised international organizations such as the OECD on their quality

[35] Angus Campbell, Philip E. Converse, and Willard L. Rodgers, *The Quality of American Life: Perceptions, Evaluations, and Satisfactions* (New York, 1976).

[36] Anne Frantilla, *Social Science in the Public Interest: A Fiftieth-Year History of the Institute for Social Research* (Ann Arbor, 1998), 55.   [37] Ibid. 29–35.

[38] Angus Campbell et al., *The American Voter* (New York, 1960).

[39] Campbell and Converse, *The Human Meaning of Social Change*.

[40] Frantilla, *Social Science in the Public Interest*, 26.

of life programmes, prominent exponents of the social indicators movement travelled to Ann Arbor from Western Europe (and beyond) to learn from the Michigan approach, and the Quality of American Life project served as a blueprint for survey-based quality of life studies around the globe. There was arguably no other academic institution worldwide that wielded similar influence on the study of quality of life in the 1970s.

While the institute's quality of life programme was thriving, Ronald Inglehart, who had joined the University of Michigan in 1966 and risen from assistant professor to associate professor to professor in the following twelve years, was engaged at the ISR in his long-term research project on changing values in Western countries. Not only did the two research undertakings emerge and develop in the same place, but they also shared common ground. Most importantly, both projects relied on the use of subjective measures. Both Angus Campbell and Ronald Inglehart argued that psychological data on people's attitudes, values, perceptions, aspirations, and feelings were in principle as valid and meaningful as 'hard data' on the economy or social conditions, and they regarded the measurement of this psychological reality as essential for monitoring social change and informing policymakers.[41] This viewpoint drew on methodological preferences in the tradition of Michigan's socio-psychological approach, and was also a product of Campbell's and Inglehart's framing of contemporary conflicts, challenges, and transformations in Western societies. In their eyes, many of the ongoing social and political changes in the 1970s were psychological in essence and 'occurring within individuals', as Inglehart put it, and thus became visible only through subjective measures.[42]

On the basis of this shared vision, the Michigan researchers acted in concert to exert influence on the social indicators movement and international quality of life endeavours. A welcome opportunity was offered by the OECD's social indicators development programme, which was launched in 1970 and became a major benchmark for social reporting and quality of life measurement around the world.[43] The OECD's engagement in this field reflected a salient

---

[41] Campbell, Converse, and Rodgers, *The Quality of American Life*, 1–13; Inglehart, *The Silent Revolution*, 12.   [42] Inglehart, *The Silent Revolution*, 12.

[43] On the OECD's social indicator programme see Germann, 'The Quality of Life Turn', and Schmelzer, *The Hegemony of Growth*, 300–12.

reorientation of the organization's key goals. In 1961 its declared task was to promote policies to encourage the highest achievable economic growth rates. In contrast, ten years later an official declaration stressed that 'growth is not an end in itself, but rather an instrument for creating better conditions of life'.[44] In the early 1970s the OECD saw the social indicator programme 'as a key element' in their efforts 'to turn this organization toward more concentration on "quality of life" issues'.[45]

The ambition of OECD officials was that their social indicator programme should draw on cutting-edge social science, and so they sought to involve renowned experts in the field. The social scientists from the University of Michigan were able to play a privileged role in this regard. In 1972 the OECD invited them to organize a conference on 'subjective elements of well-being'[46] in Paris, where they met with delegates from member countries and top-level OECD officials. After the conference, Michigan researchers continued to advise the OECD project on social indicators.[47] Among these Michigan experts were Angus Campbell and Philip Converse, as well as Ronald Inglehart. Thus, in the 1970s Inglehart not only observed value transformations towards quality of life, but was also personally involved in these transformations as an adviser to a large-scale programme that aimed to shift policy goals in this direction.

Invited as experts by the OECD, the Michigan researchers took the opportunity to campaign for their socio-psychological approach by postulating that 'subjective indicators of individual well-being' should be considered indispensable elements of contemporary social indicator efforts and ought to become 'components of regular governmental statistical reporting'.[48] In his statements at the OECD, Ronald Inglehart claimed that quantifications of people's attitudes were as meaningful as those of economic phenomena, since they would better predict subjective decisions by the mass public. With reference to his own research, he asserted that individuals' value priorities were a much better predictor of political behaviour,

[44] OECD, *List of Social Concerns Common to Most OECD Countries* (Paris, 1973), 3.

[45] Bentley Historical Library, Angus Campbell Papers, Box 8, OECD 1971–5, Christian to Campbell, 7 Feb. 1972.

[46] Burkhard Strumpel (ed.), *Subjective Elements of Well-Being* (Paris, 1974).

[47] Germann, 'The Quality of Life Turn', 310–11.

[48] Angus Campbell and Burkhard Strumpel, 'Summary of the Seminar Proceedings and Proposals', in Strumpel (ed.), *Subjective Elements of Well-Being*, 185–97, at 187.

including voting decisions and protest activities, than economic indicators.[49]

Pointing to the global increase in protest movements at the time—in particular the student revolts of 1968, race riots, labour conflicts, and environmental protests—Inglehart and his Michigan colleagues emphasized the political importance of psychological data and their potential usefulness for governments. In their eyes, these protests were increasingly motivated not by poverty or social inequalities, but by feelings of alienation, distrust of institutions, negative perceptions of social change, and unsatisfied 'post-material' needs for participation and self-fulfilment—in short, by problems of subjective well-being that could be monitored only by routinely conducted surveys on attitudes, values, and feelings, and not by social statistics.[50] At the OECD conference in Paris, the Michigan researchers explained the relevance of this socio-psychological perspective for policymakers by discussing, for example, the possibility of tackling social problems through 'motivation programmes' (specific training courses for employees, students, and so on to increase their motivation),[51] and they envisioned new forms of collective bargaining which would focus more on making jobs more interesting than on higher wages and shorter working hours.[52]

However, the Michigan researchers' focus on subjective elements of quality of life was also met with scepticism within the OECD. Sociologists objected that the focus on individuals would disregard structures of power and social inequality, and some national delegates and OECD officials were not convinced of the usefulness of subjective measures for governments.[53] However, after the conference with the Michigan social scientists, the OECD concluded that individual perceptions of well-being ought to be a necessary com-

---

[49] OECD Archives, SI/39, Ronald Inglehart: 'A Commentary on Social Environment', 4 July 1972; Samuel H. Barnes and Ronald Inglehart, 'Affluence, Individual Values, and Social Change', in Strumpel (ed.), *Subjective Elements of Well-Being*, 153–84.

[50] See in particular OECD Archives, SI/39, Ronald Inglehart: 'A Commentary on Social Environment', 4 July 1972.

[51] OECD Archives, SI/20, Preparatory Discussion Paper, 10 Apr. 1972.

[52] Angus Campbell, 'Quality of Life as a Psychological Phenomenon', in Strumpel (ed.), *Subjective Elements of Well-Being*, 9–20, at 13.

[53] Hans-Joachim Hoffmann-Novotny, 'Poverty and Disadvantaged Minorities: Some Considerations concerning Social-Psychological Indicators and Social Structure', in Strumpel (ed.), *Subjective Elements of Well-Being*, 123–40; OECD Archives, SI/51, Annex 1, Mr Eldin's opening speech, 9 Oct. 1972.

ponent of any social indicator programme.[54] Overall, the Michigan researchers made a crucial contribution to the acceptance of psychological indicators for measuring quality of life and analysing social change.

The Michigan quality of life studies and Inglehart's studies on changing values also reflected wider epistemic shifts in the 1970s, which meant that psychological framings of social reality, notions of individual choice, and subjective measures all gained in attractiveness and authority. The common framing of the era's transformations as a value change and a move towards quality of life were thus embedded in contested developments in the 1970s through which psychological representations and understandings of the social world became more persuasive. These developments within the social sciences and their interaction with political discourses and institutions were one of the reasons why quality of life knowledge became more related to individual attitudes, feelings, and perceptions of well-being. However, it was also shaped by discussions in the public sphere, where the results of quality of life studies were adopted, evaluated, and transformed. The ISR's Quality of American Life project, for instance, interacted with the activities of social movements and with public discussions of family values and lifestyle choices in the 1970s.

IV. From Childless to Child-Free: Quality of Life Knowledge and Changing Family Values

The ISR's Quality of American Life project was ambitious in several respects. Its goal was to bring forward the social sciences by exploring new avenues of quality of life measurement. Yet it was also designed from the beginning to reach a broad public and to enlighten public policy. Public outreach, however, proved to be a tricky task, as Angus Campbell and his colleagues frequently stated. Major difficulties included the project's advanced methodology, its elaborate design, and the variety of topics it was dealing with. Unlike other studies, which hoped to imitate the success of GNP as an indicator, the Michigan project refrained from representing people's quality of life by one single measure. Indeed, though the survey included questions on general satisfaction with life, its core

---

[54] OECD Archives, SI/47, Conclusions, 4 Oct. 1972.

interest was to study how satisfied people were in relation to a variety of specific life domains, which ranged from working life, housing, and education to more personal aspects such as health, family life, and marriage. Accordingly, the results of the study were multifaceted, sometimes ambiguous, and they referred to many different issues. One result was, for example, that in all measured life domains except education, Black women were less satisfied than Black men and White people.[55] Another not easily interpretable finding was that income was not a good predictor of housing satisfaction.[56] Less surprising was the result that unemployment had deleterious effects on perceived quality of life.[57]

Despite difficulties in communicating this broad array of issues and results, the Quality of American Life project received considerable media attention. However, this largely focused on one rather marginal aspect of the study: the life satisfaction of married couples over 30 without children. In an interim report, released in 1974, the social scientists stated that these couples tended to be more satisfied, or at least equally satisfied, with life than married Americans with children. The press—including leading newspapers such as the *New York Times*, the *Chicago Tribune*, and the *Los Angeles Times*—reported widely on this finding, which was summed up in headlines such as 'Couples Found Happiest with No Children' or "Childlessness Breeds Happiness, Says Survey'.[58] The news on 'happy childlessness' also crossed the Atlantic, with the German news magazine *Der Spiegel* devoting an article to the topic.[59] While the Michigan social scientists used 'satisfaction' as the basic concept of their study, the media preferred the word 'happiness', thus giving quality of life a more subjective meaning related to a short-term emotional state.

The media interest in the reported happiness of childless couples resonated in ongoing debates in which 'voluntary childlessness' became a contested issue. In 1972 a group of activists founded the National Organization for Non-Parents (NON), which campaigned for the social acceptance of being 'childless by choice'. The historian Jenna Healey has examined how the organization's activism intervened in, but was also shaped by, pivotal controversies on

---

[55] Campbell, Converse, and Rodgers, *The Quality of American Life*, 465.
[56] Ibid. 252.   [57] Ibid. 318.
[58] Bentley Historical Library, Angus Campbell Papers, Box 3, Quality of Life: Correspondence 1974 and 1975, newspaper clippings.
[59] 'Mehr Glück ohne Kinder', *Der Spiegel*, 49 (1974), 180.

gender, family, and reproduction in the 1970s.[60] Although rather small in size, it was successful in achieving publicity and support; however, it also faced hostility. While the NON had close ties to the population control movement, its crusade for individual reproductive decision-making was also inspired by the sexual revolution, the upsurge of identity politics, and the women's movement. In particular, it was encouraged by the recent successes of the abortion movement, which was fighting for reproductive rights and against mandatory motherhood.[61] However, the 1970s were not simply an era of liberalization in which obstacles to sexual and reproductive freedom were overcome.[62] The decade also experienced an upswing of the religious right, and in the light of rising divorce rates, economic turbulence, and expectations of a dawning 'me decade',[63] voicing anxieties about moral permissiveness, the erosion of family values, and alleged female selfishness became mainstream.[64] In the context of such fears, social conservatives turned voluntary childlessness into a symbol of moral and economic decline. In the face of such antagonizing discourses, mass media seemed eager to cover the findings on 'happy childlessness' as such reports were liable to generate attention, trigger emotions, and attract highly polarized views. Moreover, the issues of voluntary childlessness and the challenged norm of motherhood were also addressed at the very beginning of the debates on value change. In an OECD expert's report, Ronald Inglehart claimed that one important reason for declining fertility rates in Western countries was 'an increasing concern among women for self-fulfillment in other roles than that of mother'.[65] In his eyes, even demographic trends depended on individual value

[60] Jenna Healey, 'Rejecting Reproduction: The National Organization for Non-Parents and Childfree Activism in 1970s America', *Journal of Women's History*, 28/1 (2016), 131–56.

[61] Ibid.

[62] Dagmar Herzog, *Sexuality in Europe: A Twentieth-Century History* (Cambridge, 2011), 133–75; Isabel Heinemann, 'Vom "Kindersegen" zur "Familienplanung"? Eine Wissensgeschichte reproduktiven Entscheidens in der Moderne 1890–1990', *Historische Zeitschrift*, 310/1 (2020), 23–51, at 38–43.

[63] Tom Wolfe, 'The Me Decade and the Third Great Awakening', in id., *Mauve Gloves & Madmen, Clutter & Vine* (New York, 1976), 126–67.

[64] Matthew D. Lassiter, 'Inventing Family Values', in Bruce J. Schulman and Julian E. Zelizer: *Rightward Bound: Making America Conservative in the 1970s* (Cambridge, Mass., 2008), 13–28; Melinda Cooper, *Family Values: Between Neoliberalism and the New Conservatism* (New York, 2017).

[65] OECD Archives, SI/39, Ronald Inglehart: 'A Commentary on Social Environment', 4 July 1972.

orientations and lifestyle choices—an argument that was meant to prove the importance of attitudinal and psychological data once again. Thus, owing to different overlapping discourses, opposing cultural and social movements, and heated debates on family values, the role of motherhood, and reproductive rights, the issue of voluntarily childless marriages was highly topical and fiercely contested in the 1970s.

In the media coverage, the results of the Quality of American Life survey were perceived in the context of these contested debates. Conservative viewpoints on family values and motherhood clashed with new claims of second-wave feminists, environmentalists, and non-parent activists, who criticized the social pressure on women to bear children or urged action against population growth.[66] While, for instance, a conservative columnist in the *Daily Telegram* attacked the study as biased,[67] an article in the popular fashion magazine *Harper's Bazaar* used the results to argue against the 'stereotypes' of blissful parents and 'unfulfilled' childless couples.[68] Although Angus Campbell referred to the media reports on childless couples 'as quite exaggerated and not altogether accurate',[69] he nonetheless contributed to this popularization of his quality of life study. In 1975 he published an article in *Psychology Today*—a highly popular social science magazine that sold around a million copies per year in the mid 1970s[70]—in which he highlighted the 'mixed experience' of having children.[71] The article attracted a remarkable response among readers and the author received dozens of letters on the subject of childless couples.

To be sure, some of the letters were also critical. For instance, one member of the clergy accused Angus Campbell of bias and spoke in

---

[66] See e.g. Isabel Heinemann, 'American Family Values and Social Change: Gab es den Wertewandel in den USA?', in Bernhard Dietz, Christopher Neumaier, and Andreas Rödder (eds.), *Gab es den Wertewandel? Neue Forschungen zum gesellschaftlich-kulturellen Wandel seit den 1960er Jahren* (Munich, 2014), 269–84.

[67] Bentley Historical Library, Angus Campbell Papers, Box 3, Quality of Life: Correspondence, Dec. 1974, 'Happiness Survey', *Daily Telegram*, 26 Nov. 1974.

[68] Bentley Historical Library, Angus Campbell Papers, Box 8, Publications: Childless or Child-Free (1975), Jane Shapiro, 'Childless Marriage', *Harper's Bazaar*, June 1975.

[69] Bentley Historical Library, Angus Campbell Papers, Box 3, Quality of Life: Correspondence, Dec. 1974, Campbell to *Daily Telegram*, 20 Dec. 1974.

[70] Bruce V. Lewenstein, 'Was There Really a Popular Science "Boom"?', *Science, Technology, & Human Values*, 12/2 (1987), 29–41, at 32.

[71] Angus Campbell, 'The American Way of Mating: Marriage *Si*, Children Only Maybe', *Psychology Today*, May 1975, 37–43.

favour of the deeper 'fulfilment' that came from having children.[72] Most of the letters, however, ranged from positive to enthusiastic. Some of them were from representatives of non-governmental organizations which regarded the results of the quality of life study as an affirmation of their own agendas. For instance, the NON, which frequently tried to enlist the support of social scientists, invited Angus Campbell to speak at its convention.[73] Moreover, Campbell's article received a positive response from the organization Zero Population Growth, which had been founded by radical ecologists in 1968 and played an important role in the population control movement. The organization's executive director saw Campbell's article as a welcome political statement: 'I hope you will continue to include articles on the subject of non-parenthood as an acceptable lifestyle, and continue to combat pronatalism when you were [*sic*] able.'[74] The letter echoed a new strategy of the population control movement— namely, to respond to increasing criticism of coercive population control measures in the 1970s by adopting more individualistic messages strengthening reproductive choices.[75]

Most of the letters, though, were written by women who commented on the article as private individuals. Of course, they were not at all a representative sample of the population, as the readership of popular science magazines was overwhelmingly well educated, White, and middle to upper class.[76] Beyond that, the article predominantly attracted the attention of women who were sympathetic to the causes of the non-parent movement. However, the letters give an insight into how quality of life knowledge was used to challenge family norms and to shape new forms of subjectivity.

The letter writers saw the article as empowering them to make free reproductive choices and as promoting the case for accepting childlessness as a normal lifestyle. One woman wrote: 'In the past

---

[72] Bentley Historical Library, Angus Campbell Papers, Box 8, Publications: The American Way of Mating, collected letters.

[73] Bentley Historical Library, Angus Campbell Papers, Box 3, Quality of Life: Correspondence, letter, 24 Mar. 1975.

[74] Bentley Historical Library, Angus Campbell Papers, Box 8, Publications: The American Way of Mating, collected letters.

[75] Roman Birke, *Geburtenkontrolle als Menschenrecht: Die Diskussion um globale Überbevölkerung seit den 1940er Jahren* (Göttingen, 2020), 241–75; Matthew Connelly, *Fatal Misconception: The Struggle to Control World Population* (Cambridge, Mass., 2009), 327–69; Paige Whaley Eager, *Global Population Policy: From Population Control to Reproductive Rights* (London, 2017).

[76] Lewenstein, 'Was There Really a Popular Science "Boom"?', 30.

childless married couples have been portrayed as being incomplete, unfulfilled, and not as happy as those couples with children . . . Articles such as this one help to present the complete picture and show people that they do have a choice. It is encouraging to see a magazine confront this issue squarely.'[77] Another letter says: 'Finally, some scientific support for the idea . . . that not everyone should have children and that, in fact, many people are happier without them . . . it is time that not having children was viewed as as "normal" an option as having them.'[78] One woman plainly celebrated Campbell's article: 'Hurrah! At last the myth surrounding "motherhood" is beginning to explode.'[79] Some of the letters were more personal. One childless woman felt empowered by the article to react to stigmatizing questions: 'I'm thinking of carrying the article with me to be presented at a moment's notice to any friend or relative who asks "Why don't you have any children?"' Other letter writers regarded the quality of life survey as a form of life counselling: 'In the near future I may have to make a decision which would leave me childless. Your research may help in that decision.' Yet another woman wrote: 'Your article provided a stimulus to reconsider why I want children. It's been helpful in my thinking.'[80] In these letters the normative dimension of quality of life knowledge is especially evident. People were less interested in how happy their compatriots were than in knowing how they themselves should live in order to be happy.

Angus Campbell evidently felt encouraged by the myriad of positive responses. In *Harper's Weekly* he published another popular article devoted to the issue of childless marriages. In this piece, entitled 'Childless or Child-Free', he argued: 'It appears very probable that "freedom from children" will become a more attractive value in American society . . . Our research does not give any reason to believe that the people who make this choice will consider the quality of their lives diminished in any way by the fact that they are not parents.'[81] The results of his quality of life survey

[77] Bentley Historical Library, Angus Campbell Papers, Box 8, Publications: The American Way of Mating, letter, 21 May 1975.

[78] Bentley Historical Library, Angus Campbell Papers, Box 8, Publications: The American Way of Mating, letter, 15 June 1975.

[79] Bentley Historical Library, Angus Campbell Papers, Box 8, Publications: The American Way of Mating, collected letters.   [80] Ibid.

[81] Bentley Historical Library, Angus Campbell Papers, Box 8, Publications: Childless or Child-Free (1975).

only partly supported this conclusion, particularly as it found that a huge majority of married couples actually had children. Moreover, couples without children were not asked if they were voluntarily childless, and in an era in which the word 'choice' gained dominance and spilled over into more and more discourses,[82] it seems unimaginable that childless couples who did not 'choose' not to have children could reach high levels of life satisfaction too. Thus, strictly speaking, the results of the Quality of American Life study offered no evidence that ways of living or value orientations were changing in this regard.

However, in interactions between social scientists, media reports, social movements, and lay people, quality of life increasingly came to be regarded as a purely subjective phenomenon shaped by individual personal choices rather than by social or physical circumstances. Tellingly, Campbell used the word 'child-free' in the title of his article—a word that did not exist before the 1970s. Unlike the word 'childless', which was associated with deprivation, 'child-free' gave agency to couples as it indicates a voluntary choice not to have children. In these discourses, quality of life knowledge became a means of normalizing ways of living that diverged from the social norm by reinterpreting them as freely chosen 'lifestyles'—another word that did not exist before the mid 1960s.

In the 1970s two new kinds of people emerged—or, in Ian Hacking's terminology, were 'made up':[83] the child-free husband and the child-free wife. In the process of this subject formation, childlessness increasingly came to be regarded as the result of rational decision-making and as a legitimate way to pursue happiness. The letters cited above indicate that studies on quality of life were used to foster this new form of subjectivity. The creation of the child-free subject was facilitated by semantic shifts that categorized people and their behaviour in new ways. But it was also made possible by newly accessible social knowledge that circulated between the social sciences, the media, social movements, and concerned people who were looking for strategies to fight stigmatization. In the 1970s the phenomenon of 'happy childlessness' was increasingly represented—in the double sense of presented and produced—by words, figures, facts, and nar-

---

[82] Daniel T. Rodgers, *Age of Fracture* (Cambridge, Mass., 2011), 10–11.

[83] Ian Hacking, 'Making up People', in Thomas C. Heller, Morton Sosna, and David E. Wellbery (eds.), *Reconstructing Individualism: Autonomy, Individuality, and the Self in Western Thought* (Stanford, 1986), 222–36.

ratives, and these representations embodied a shift in social norms and values at least in some parts of the population. Therefore, this is an example of how quality of life knowledge became a driver of changing values.

These observations, however, do not mean that the ensuing value changes coincided with the supposed fundamental transformations that Ronald Inglehart described as a 'silent revolution', as the changes were too limited for that in at least three respects. First, the appropriation of new social knowledge and its translation into new subjectivities were limited to those parts of the population in which the new words, facts, and meanings were circulating—thus to well-educated, overwhelmingly White, middle- and upper-class demographics. Second, the news of happy child-free couples did challenge norms of family and reproduction, but these effects were limited to heterosexual, married couples. The quality of life studies in the 1970s were remarkably oblivious to all forms of sexual relations outside the norm of heterosexuality. Moreover, the finding of happy childlessness referred only to *married* couples, as the social scientists emphasized. Thus, in respect to marriage, quality of life knowledge encouraged adjustment to norms, as the surveys seemed to confirm the conventional wisdom that married people were significantly more satisfied with life than singles or divorced persons. Third, the value orientations which were incorporated into the new subjects of happily child-free individuals could only partly be described as 'post-material'. To be sure, concerns for 'self-fulfilment' were at the core of child-free activism in the 1970s. But activists likewise mentioned 'financial stability' as one of the perks of the child-free lifestyle,[84] and thus embraced a 'material value', in Inglehart's terminology.

In her history of the family in the USA, Isabel Heinemann convincingly argues that there was no single 'value change' in the twentieth century; rather, there were incremental shifts in norms and attitudes, and these were heterogeneous, contested, and frequently accompanied by backlashes.[85] This is also true for the 1970s. The decade was an era of social movements, changing representations, and rapidly circulating social knowledge that fostered new subjectivities while challenging norms of family life and reproduc-

---

[84] Healey, 'Rejecting Reproduction', 142.

[85] Isabel Heinemann, *Wert der Familie: Ehescheidung, Frauenarbeit und Reproduktion in den USA des 20. Jahrhunderts* (Berlin, 2018), 441–3.

tion. Although values were changing in the 1970s, the direction and scope of these changes was in practice less clear than the assertion of a global shift from material values toward quality of life would suggest.

V. *Conclusion*

The history of the booming field of quality of life studies brings into focus the often neglected but important role of the social sciences in changing values during the 1970s. It reveals that social scientists were not just passive 'discoverers' of a new value orientation towards quality of life. Rather, many of them—including Ronald Inglehart— were involved in the social indicators movement, which explicitly aimed to promote quality of life as a new societal goal and value. In retrospect, social scientists obscured their own contribution to this new orientation by claiming that it was part of a fundamental but silent value change that 'occurred within individuals'. This view tends to neglect the crucial role of statistics, surveys, reports, papers, words, and figures as tools for promoting particular values and for defining or extending the realm of what was regarded as 'normal'. Thus, instead of speculating on what 'occurred within individuals', this essay makes the case for focusing on what happened outside them. In other words, historians of value transformations should deal with the material embodiments of values: the representations of the social world.

In the 1970s these representations underwent huge changes. Most obviously, there were semantic shifts. 'Child-free', 'lifestyle', and—of course—'quality of life' were all new terms that did not exist before the mid 1960s and whose usage strikingly increased in the 1970s. The mere use of these phrases could challenge social norms. Therefore, these new terms were not just indicators of new value orientations, but also crucial factors in their development. Moreover, new realms of social knowledge took shape around these terms. Changes in society that had not previously been represented in words, numbers, or facts became visible, and this visibility gave them normative power. Quality of life studies translated vague phenomena into nameable and quantifiable social issues that could be publicly discussed and politically assessed. Among these 'quantified facts', psychological elements of subjective well-being gained importance in the 1970s. Representations of attitudes, values, perceptions, and feelings became more persuasive and found their way into political programmes. These shifts towards subjective and psychological dimensions of the social were an important prerequisite for framing the ongoing transformations of the 1970s as a fundamental change in values.

Social knowledge about quality of life was not only represented in published social science studies, but also in popular scientific papers, in newspaper articles, and in letters written by private individuals. The above discussion has shown that this newly produced and broadly circulating quality of life knowledge was used, adopted, and transformed by various actors—from government officials and international organizations to mass media, NGOs, and social movements. These circulations had an impact on social relations. Quality of life knowledge was reshaped to promote new forms of subjectivity, to challenge traditional norms, and to extend the scope of socially accepted ways of living. Thus, changing value orientations in the 1970s were also enabled by epistemic shifts that altered the dominant representations of the social world. All these multifaceted changes were monitored, debated, and contested: they were neither 'silent' nor unidirectional.

4

Historicizing Love and Partnership: A Grass-Roots Perspective on Value Change in Marriage in East Germany

Lisa Dittrich

In recent years, we have become somewhat distanced from each other . . . an excess of work on my husband's side . . . We have not yet really known a family life with time for each other . . . Nevertheless, our life is not empty; it is not that we have nothing to say to each other, on the contrary. We are ideologically on the same side, complementing each other in a way that is seldom the case between spouses. I help him with his studies . . . My husband came and still comes to me with all his worries, enjoyments, and experiences of the day, we consult each other about everything, exchange opinions, and are happily united on the state of our political and economic development, on educational questions, etc. Only one thing has always been a poor relation for us: we have never been really happy with each other.[1]

In this letter dating from 1962, a 48-year-old housewife outlines what was considered a good marriage in East Germany at the time. Yet she was writing to a marriage counsellor because her husband had started an affair. She struggled to find explanations for why her marriage, although close to the ideal, was not working, and she saw the reasons in their infrequent sexual activity and a lack of emotions. A 'good marriage' was at odds with strong feelings such as joy or love. The question of how to solve this conflict between the stability of marriage and an individual's search for self-fulfilment in love occupied married couples, marriage counsellors and other family experts, politicians, and the courts from the end of the 1950s to the fall of the Berlin Wall.

Attitudes to love and emotion in intimate relationships were transformed during the long 1970s and became more important,[2] while

[1] Hauptstaatsarchiv (hereafter HStA) Dresden, 12741, Neubert Papers, 85, G.S. to Rudolf Neubert, 22 Dec. 1962. All translations are the author's own.
[2] See e.g. Anthony Giddens, *The Transformation of Intimacy: Sexuality, Love and Eroticism*

marriage was deinstitutionalized.[3] Sociologists and historians have explored this transformation in the USA and Western Europe, but less attention has been paid to whether a similar social change happened on the other side of the Iron Curtain. In 1955 the East German leadership introduced a new marriage code, defining marriage as a relationship based on love. This fundamental legal redefinition raises the question of whether an emotionalization of marriage and intimate relationships took place in East Germany as well as in the Western world. This essay explores the culture of marriage and coupledom as expressed in the ideals and perceptions of marital partners, as well as in political and legal debates. Issues relating to gender are only briefly touched upon, and examined in more detail where gender differences can be detected in the expression of the ideals and perceptions of marriage and love.

Taking this approach, the argument picks up recent strands from two fields of research: the proliferation of marriage for love and the study of value change, mostly in relation to German scholarship. Thus, the essay combines a long-term perspective with a focus on the 1970s, which makes it possible to question periodization. Research on the spread of marriage for love has long concentrated on the emergence of this ideal in the Victorian era.[4] The twentieth century is rarely studied, although it is a basic assumption in social science that in the twentieth century the phenomenon became normal across the classes in the Western world.[5] Although relationships and marriage in East Germany have been a focus of interest in the social sciences,[6] especially in the post-reunification period, historians have

---

in *Modern Societies* (Stanford, Calif., 1992); Andreas Reckwitz, *Das hybride Subjekt: Eine Theorie der Subjektkulturen von der bürgerlichen Moderne zur Postmoderne* (Weilerswist, 2006), 525–54; Sven Reichardt, 'Von "Beziehungskisten" und "offener Sexualität"', in id. and Detlef Siegfried (eds.), *Das Alternative Milieu: Antibürgerlicher Lebensstil und linke Politik in der Bundesrepublik Deutschland und Europa 1968–1983* (Göttingen, 2010); Karla Verlinden, *Sexualität und Beziehungen bei den '68ern': Erinnerungen ehemaliger Protagonisten und Protagonistinnen* (Bielefeld, 2015); Nina Verheyen, 'Der ausdiskutierte Orgasmus: Beziehungsgespräche als kommunikative Praxis in der Geschichte des Intimen seit den 1960er Jahren', in Peter-Paul Bänziger et al. (eds.), *Sexuelle Revolution? Zur Geschichte der Sexualität im deutschsprachigen Raum seit den 1960er-Jahren* (Bielefeld, 2015), 181–98.

[3] See François de Singly, *Le Soi, le couple et la famille* (Paris, 1996), 159–60; Hartmann Tyrell, 'Ehe und Familie: Institutionalisierung und Deinstitutionalisierung', in Kurt Lüscher, Franz Schultheis, and Michael Wehrspaun (eds.), *Die 'postmoderne' Familie: Familiale Strategien und Familienpolitik in einer Übergangszeit* (Konstanz, 1988), 145–56.

[4] See Andreas Gestrich, *Geschichte der Familie im 19. und 20. Jahrhundert* (Munich, 2013), 72–3. [5] See de Singly, *Le Soi, le couple et la famille*, 159–60.

[6] e.g. Jutta Gysi, 'Die Zukunft von Familie und Ehe: Familienpolitik und Familienfor-

been researching these topics only for the past fifteen years or so.[7] Such studies deal with the political and legal treatment of marriage in the context of the women's labour market and family policy, with sexuality, and with fundamental questions about the private sphere under state socialism. The emotional side of relationships, by contrast, has not been examined in depth.[8] But a recent study of literature and film has shown how different ideals of love were articulated and discussed in the closely monitored East German media from the 1950s to 1990.[9]

Existing social science research and historiography on value change in East Germany debate whether to confirm or deny the existence of value change in East Germany in the 1970s and 1980s.[10] Those who affirm that value change took place usually imply that East Germany lagged behind the Western world.[11] In contrast, historical case studies of the GDR claim that sexual liberalization and equality in gender relations came about particularly early in the

schung in der DDR', in Günter Burkart (ed.), *Sozialisation im Sozialismus: Lebensbedingungen in der DDR im Umbruch* (Weinheim, 1990), 33–41; Norbert F. Schneider, *Familie und private Lebensführung in West- und Ostdeutschland: Eine vergleichende Analyse des Familienlebens, 1970–1992* (Stuttgart, 1994).

[7] See Donna Harsch, *Revenge of the Domestic: Women, the Family, and Communism in the German Democratic Republic* (Princeton, 2007); Josie McLellan, *Love in the Time of Communism: Intimacy and Sexuality in the GDR* (Cambridge, 2011); Anja Schröter, *Ostdeutsche Ehen vor Gericht: Scheidungspraxis im Umbruch 1980–2000* (Berlin, 2018); Eva Schäffler, *Paarbeziehungen in Ostdeutschland: Auf dem Weg vom Real- zum Postsozialismus* (Wiesbaden, 2017); Christopher Neumaier, *Familie im 20. Jahrhundert: Konflikte um Ideale, Politiken und Praktiken* (Berlin, 2019); from the perspective of the private, see also Paul Betts, *Within Walls: Private Life in the German Democratic Republic* (Oxford, 2010); Andrew I. Port, 'Love, Lust, and Lies under Communism: Family Values and Adulterous Liaisons in Early East Germany', *Central European History*, 44/3 (2011), 478–505.

[8] Till Großmann's project on love in the self-help literature of Eastern Germany promises enlightenment here. However, the focus of the unfinished study is on the self in state socialism rather than on the question of marriage. First results in Till Großmann, 'Moral Economies of Love and Labor in the GDR: Family Values and Work Ethics in Advice Correspondence, circa 1960', in Ute Frevert (ed.), *Moral Economies* (Göttingen, 2019), 213–37.

[9] See John G. Urang, *Legal Tender: Love and Legitimacy in the East German Cultural Imagination* (Ithaca, NY, 2010).

[10] Supporting the existence of value change, see e.g. Thomas Gensicke, *Mentalitätsentwicklungen im Osten Deutschlands seit den 70er Jahren: Vorstellung und Erläuterung von Ergebnissen einiger empirischer Untersuchungen in der DDR und in den neuen Bundesländern von 1977 bis 1991* (Speyer, 1992); denying, see e.g. Heiner Meulemann, *Werte und Wertewandel: Zur Identität einer geteilten und wieder vereinten Nation* (Weinheim, 1996).

[11] e.g. Jan W. van Deth, 'Wertewandel im internationalen Vergleich: Ein deutscher Sonderweg?', *Aus Politik und Zeitgeschichte*, 29 (2001), 23–30; Andreas Rödder, 'Wertewandel im geteilten und vereinten Deutschland', *Historisches Jahrbuch*, 130 (2010), 421–33.

East.[12] We therefore need to ask whether the transformation of marriage and partnerships in East Germany took place mainly in the 1970s and 1980s, or whether it had started earlier. To answer this, my essay will trace developments in marriage culture using a chronological analysis from the 1950s to the beginning of the 1980s. The essay builds on the work of Niklas Luhmann and recent historical research on emotions,[13] which understand emotions and love as historically constructed and assume that different ideas of love exist and are modified over time.[14] Many social science studies, by contrast, present a teleological development towards love-based relationships, sexual freedom, and partnership.[15] The more recent historical research on value change also criticizes the straightforward narratives of liberalization or individualization, common in social science research,[16] as ahistorical. These studies differentiate values from norms and historicize them by examining political and public debates.[17]

Following on from this, my essay traces the many shifts in the ideals of marriage and love, along with disputes about the 'proper' management of marriage, by analysing exchanges between married couples and marriage counsellors (letters, self-help books), biographical interviews, the censored press, and political and legal

[12] See Harsch, *Revenge of the Domestic*, chs. 5–7; McLellan, *Love in the Time of Communism*, chs. 2–4; Dagmar Herzog, *Sex after Fascism: Memory and Morality in Twentieth-Century Germany* (Princeton, 2005), ch. 5.

[13] See Niklas Luhmann, *Liebe als Passion: Zur Codierung von Intimität* (Frankfurt a.M., 1994; 1st edn. 1986), available in English translation as *Love as Passion: The Codification of Intimacy* (Cambridge, 1986); for the history of emotions see e.g. Jan Plamper, *Geschichte und Gefühl: Grundlagen der Emotionsgeschichte* (Munich, 2012).

[14] For an approach of this sort see Andrea Leupold, 'Liebe und Partnerschaft: Formen der Codierung von Ehen', *Zeitschrift für Soziologie*, 12/4 (1983), 297–327; Elke Reinhardt-Becker, *Seelenbund oder Partnerschaft? Liebessemantiken in der Literatur der Romantik und der Neuen Sachlichkeit* (Frankfurt a.M., 2005); Reckwitz, *Das hybride Subjekt*; Sylka Scholz, Karl Lenz, and Sabine Dreßler (eds.), *In Liebe verbunden: Zweierbeziehungen und Elternschaft in populären Ratgebern von den 1950ern bis heute* (Bielefeld, 2013); in historical research, Ingrid Bauer and Christa Hämmerle (eds.), *Liebe schreiben: Paarkorrespondenzen im Kontext des 19. und 20. Jahrhunderts* (Göttingen, 2017).

[15] See e.g. Eva Illouz, *Why Love Hurts: A Sociological Explanation* (Cambridge, 2012); for democratization see Giddens, *The Transformation of Intimacy*.

[16] e.g. Ulrich Beck and Elisabeth Beck-Gernsheim, *Individualization: Institutionalized Individualism and its Social and Political Consequences* (London, 2002).

[17] See e.g. Bernhard Dietz, Christopher Neumaier, and Andreas Rödder (eds.), *Gab es den Wertewandel? Neue Forschungen zum gesellschaftlich-kulturellen Wandel seit den 1960er Jahren* (Munich, 2014); Isabel Heinemann (ed.), *Inventing the Modern American Family: Family Values and Social Change in 20th Century United States* (Frankfurt a.M., 2012); Neumaier, *Familie im 20. Jahrhundert*.

developments. My main sources are the correspondence of the marriage counsellor Rudolf Neubert (1898–1992), which includes about 3,000 letters from married individuals seeking advice between the 1950s and the early 1970s, and some 100 letters to Jutta Resch-Treuwerth (1941–2015), the agony aunt of the youth magazine *Junge Welt*, dating from around 1980. Thus, the essay can include different perspectives and actors and tell the in-depth story of the transformations in marriage culture in East Germany.

Research on historical value change often draws on the quantitative data of social science research for want of alternative sources with which to analyse changing practices, and thus imports all the methodological problems of quantitative survey research.[18] I follow a different path that focuses on the ideas and notions that guide social actions, without using the concept of value as an abstract construct. To be more precise, I shall look at how ideas inform practices of married life, as reflected in discussions between married couples and their marriage counsellors and other professionals. It is only this focus on the perspectives of married couples themselves that allows us to examine the social spread of marriage for love, and to fully grasp developments within marriage and intimate relationships.

Methodologically, the question arises whether this sort of qualitative, bottom-up approach focusing on the discussion of ideals is compatible with the study of a change in values in the sense of a general replacement of principles. To answer this, a specific aspect of the putative value change will be singled out—namely, the question of post-rational principles. I shall examine whether emotional behaviour and ideals replaced rational principles in marriage management over time. This essay will first explore ideals of socialist marriage in the 1950s and 1960s (section I) before turning to practices of marriage counselling during the same period (section II). Using letters to counsellors as a source, I shall focus on individual romantic

[18] For methodological criticism of the use of quantitative data from social science research in historical studies see Rüdiger Graf and Kim Christian Priemel, 'Zeitgeschichte in der Welt der Sozialwissenschaften: Legitimität und Originalität einer Disziplin', *Vierteljahrshefte für Zeitgeschichte*, 59/4 (2011), 479–508; Benjamin Ziemann, 'Sozialgeschichte und empirische Sozialforschung: Überlegungen zum Kontext und zum Ende einer Romanze', in Pascal Maeder, Barbara Lüthi, and Thomas Mergel (eds.), *Wozu noch Sozialgeschichte? Eine Disziplin im Umbruch: Festschrift für Josef Mooser zum 65. Geburtstag* (Göttingen, 2012), 131–49; defending the approach, Bernhard Dietz and Christopher Neumaier, 'Vom Nutzen der Sozialwissenschaften für die Zeitgeschichte: Werte und Wertewandel als Gegenstand historischer Forschung', *Vierteljahrshefte für Zeitgeschichte*, 60/2 (2012), 293–304.

longings, the changing demands made of marriage partners, and the loosening of the regulations governing marriage as time went on. With the advent of the 1970s, state policies and counselling practices changed, the concept of partnership assumed new meanings, and the ideals of mature and romantic love competed with each other (section III).

I. *The New Socialist Marriage: Stability and Mutuality*

The newly founded GDR fundamentally reorganized the legal framework for marriage in 1955 as part of the revolutionary transformation of state and society. The regulations based marriage on love, thus codifying the ideal of socialist marriage formulated by Friedrich Engels (1820–95). This was used in the Cold War competition to distinguish between socialist marriage and the 'bourgeois', economically based 'provider marriage', and between the gender-specific public, male realm and the private, female one. At that time, it was assumed that freeing the institution of marriage from its economic function would automatically result in happy marriages and bring about true love.[19] The marriage code defined marriage as a 'community established for life' based on 'mutual love and respect' whose aim was the 'joint development of the marriage partners and the raising of children'.[20]

Two aspects of the reorganization which were central to the attitude of the state towards love and marriage in the following decades must be singled out here. First, the law defined the purpose of marriage, unlike the German Civil Code of 1900. Marriage was to ensure that children were brought up and that the married couple developed in the interests of socialism. Thus, marriage had a societal purpose to fulfil. This went hand in hand with the state's claim that it educated families to achieve this ideal. Second, the law displayed a certain ambivalence in regard to making it easier to dissolve marriages and a desire for stable families.[21] In succession to the National Socialist legal provision, the GDR law adopted the principle of irreconcilable differences as a reason for divorce.

[19] Schäffler, *Paarbeziehungen in Ostdeutschland*, 194.

[20] Petra Fischer-Langosch, *Die Entstehungsgeschichte des Familiengesetzbuches der DDR von 1965* (Frankfurt a.M., 2007), 69.

[21] Ibid. 105–6; Ute Schneider, *Hausväteridylle oder sozialistische Utopie? Die Familie im Recht der DDR* (Cologne, 2004), 238–46.

The antisemitic, racial, and eugenic provisions of the National Socialist Marriage Act of 1938 had already been repealed by the Allied Control Council in its modified Marriage Act of 1946.[22] Implementing a new basis for divorce, the law of 1955 made it possible to dissolve marriages without need for 'absolute' grounds (such as adultery).[23] However, the law did place restrictions on those wanting to divorce. The definition of marriage emphasized its lifelong character, and absolute grounds no longer guaranteed divorce.[24] The law prescribed that there had to be 'serious' grounds decided on by the courts, which were to assess whether the marriage still had meaning, not only for the partners, but also for society.[25] The attempt to stabilize marriages despite a fundamental opening up was also reflected in court practice: in divorce proceedings in the 1950s, more pressure was exerted on couples to remain married than in the 1940s.[26]

The desire to guarantee marital stability was expressed even more clearly in the writings of marriage guidance counsellors and in statements by married couples seeking advice. In the late 1950s and 1960s, both expressed an ideal of a good marriage that went far beyond the provisions of the law—one in which marriage was defined as an emotional bond, a 'union of heart and mind'.[27] But the ideal was based mainly on the idea of marriage as two partners mutually complementing each other. Mutual 'support' implied a certain degree of equality, albeit one that was distinct from gender equality. The image of an ideal marriage was linked to the partners agreeing on 'ideological' questions,[28] mutual complementarity of character,[29] sharing joys and concerns, coping with problems together,[30] the joint building of a 'home' or of careers, and spending

[22] For the National Socialist law and its implementation see Dirk Blasius, *Ehescheidung in Deutschland im 19. und 20. Jahrhundert* (Frankfurt a.M., 1992), 188–223.

[23] Schneider, *Hausväteridylle oder sozialistische Utopie?*, 240; Fischer-Langosch, *Die Entstehungsgeschichte des Familiengesetzbuches*, 23–6.

[24] Port, 'Love, Lust, and Lies', 491.

[25] Schneider, *Hausväteridylle oder sozialistische Utopie?*, 243–4.

[26] Betts, *Within Walls*, 95–100.

[27] Rudolf Neubert, *Das neue Ehebuch: Die Ehe als Aufgabe der Gegenwart und Zukunft* (Rudolstadt, 1957), 272.

[28] HStA Dresden, 12741, Neubert Papers, 97, H.S. to Rudolf Neubert, 24 Apr. 1968; HStA Dresden, 12741, Neubert Papers, 167, M.C. to Rudolf Neubert, 28 Sept. 1971, and L.O. to Rudolf Neubert, 5 Jan. 1971.

[29] HStA Dresden, 12741, Neubert Papers, 85, I.T. to Rudolf Neubert, 20 Oct. 1963.

[30] HStA Dresden, 12741, Neubert Papers, 85, G.S. to Rudolf Neubert, 22 Dec. 1962; Neubert, *Das neue Ehebuch*, 272.

time together.[31] From the 1960s it also became particularly associated with participating in classic leisure activities such as dancing, sport, or attending cultural events.[32] The basic norms that marriage was built on were understanding,[33] harmony, consideration,[34] loyalty, and faithfulness.[35] The concept of mutuality consisted of guidelines for behaviour, some of which could be followed by taking rational action, such as selecting a complementary spouse. Beyond the traditional values listed above, love and other emotions (such as joy) were also required.

This concept of mutuality was not only central to the thinking of GDR marriage counsellors and married couples seeking advice: it also had a history in Germany. Marriage guidance from National Socialist times, such as the well-known book *Das Leben zu Zweien*[36] by Walther von Hollander (1892–1973)—probably the best-known marriage counsellor in print and audio media in the early Federal Republic—expressed an ideal of marriage in which the partners complemented each other. Of course, this was not the only concept of a good marriage under the Nazi dictatorship, where eugenic and racial elements dominated. Yet at the same time more romantic ideas were cultivated, for example in the worlds of film and popular music.[37] It is therefore important to emphasize here that the idea of mutuality was adopted again in East and West Germany, having been largely purged of racist ideas and eugenics. It was passed on at the micro level and at the level of the media and journalistic discourse.

[31] HStA Dresden, 12741, Neubert Papers, 97, H.S. to Rudolf Neubert, 24 Apr. 1968; HStA Dresden, 12741, Neubert Papers, 85, I.T. to Rudolf Neubert, 20 Oct. 1963.

[32] HStA Dresden, 12741, Neubert Papers, 97, H.S. to Rudolf Neubert, 24 Apr. 1968; HStA Dresden, 12741, Neubert Papers, 167, M.C. to Rudolf Neubert, 28 Sept. 1971, and L.O. to Rudolf Neubert, 5 Jan. 1971; HStA Dresden, 12741, Neubert Papers, 96, H.G. to Rudolf Neubert, 23 Jun. 1975; Neubert, *Das neue Ehebuch*, 272.

[33] HStA Dresden, 12741, Neubert Papers, 85, L.S. to Rudolf Neubert, 21 Apr. 1964, I.T. to Rudolf Neubert, 20 Oct. 1963.

[34] HStA Dresden, 12741, Neubert Papers, 23, S.F. to Rudolf Neubert, 9 Sept. 1957.

[35] HStA Dresden, 12741, Neubert Papers, 85, G.S. to Rudolf Neubert, 22 Dec. 1962. Similar ideals of marriage can be found in the following guides: Gerhard Weber and Danuta Weber, *Du und ich* (Berlin, 1957); Wolfhilde Dierl and Hans-Joachim Müller, *Liebe, Ehe — Scheidung?*, 2nd edn. (Leipzig, 1958).

[36] Walther von Hollander, *Das Leben zu Zweien: Ein Ehebuch. Betrachtungen und Geschichten* (Berlin, 1940).

[37] See e.g. Gabriele Czarnowski, *Das kontrollierte Paar: Ehe- und Sexualpolitik im Nationalsozialismus* (Weinheim, 1991); Lisa Pine, *Nazi Family Policy, 1933–1945* (Oxford, 1997); Torsten Reters, *Liebe, Ehe und Partnerwahl zur Zeit des Nationalsozialismus: Eine soziologische Semantikanalyse* (Dortmund, 1997).

II. *Rudolf Neubert's Marriage Counselling in the 1950s and 1960s*

The individual right to decide on the continuation of the marriage was the main reason why—in letters to the marriage counsellor Rudolf Neubert—married couples argued for a different model from companionate marriage and mutuality.[38] The social hygienist and physician Neubert was a well-known author of self-help books in the GDR, including probably the best-known marriage guide in East Germany, *Das neue Ehebuch* (1958). Since the Weimar Republic he had advocated a holistic approach to health care which was intended to result in a physically and mentally balanced lifestyle. He worked for the Museum of Hygiene in Dresden in the early 1930s but lost his position for political reasons in 1933, although he had become a member of the Nazi Party (NSDAP) in the same year. Like other marriage counsellors of the time,[39] he focused on sex education in his work. The Nazis' racist guidelines for marriage had been deleted from the laws of the GDR in a deliberate attempt at demarcation, and the socialist state abandoned eugenic provisions largely for the same reason.[40] Nonetheless, eugenic ideas remained present in a weak form, as self-help books by Neubert and others show.[41] Neubert himself had a career as a university professor and family expert in the GDR, having previously been appointed scientific director of the Hygiene Museum in 1946 before being dismissed the following year because of his Nazi past.[42]

---

[38] e.g. HStA Dresden, 12741, Neubert Papers, 97, I.B. to Rudolf Neubert, 20 Nov. 1968; HStA Dresden, 12741, Neubert Papers, 23, S.R. to Rudolf Neubert, 12 Dec. 1954; HStA Dresden, 12741, Neubert Papers, 23, J.J. to Rudolf Neubert, 28 Oct. 1958.

[39] See e.g. Hans-Joachim Hoffmann and Peter G. Klemm, *Ein offenes Wort: Ein Buch über die Liebe*, 2nd edn. (Berlin, 1957); Lykke Aresin, *Sprechstunde des Vertrauens: Fragen der Sexual-, Ehe- und Familienberatung* (Rudolstadt, 1968).

[40] For the family law see Schneider, *Hausväteridylle oder sozialistische Utopie?*, 210–14; for traces of eugenic thinking in the abortion law see Michael Schwartz, 'Abtreibung und Wertewandel im doppelten Deutschland: Individualisierung und Strafrechtsreformen in der DDR und in der Bundesrepublik in den sechziger und siebziger Jahren', in Thomas Raithel, Andreas Rödder, and Andreas Wirsching (eds.), *Auf dem Weg in eine neue Moderne? Die Bundesrepublik Deutschland in den siebziger und achtziger Jahren* (Munich, 2009), 113–30.

[41] See e.g. Rudolf Neubert, *Die Geschlechterfrage: Ein Buch für junge Menschen* (Rudolstadt, 1956), 93–4; Irene Uhlmann (ed.), *Kleine Enzyklopädie: Die Frau* (Leipzig, 1961), 63–4. For the non-eugenic tradition of social hygiene in the GDR see Udo Schagen, 'Sozialhygiene als Leitkonzept für Wissenschaft und Gesellschaft: Der Bruch mit dem Biologismus in der Medizin der SBZ', in Rüdiger vom Bruch, Uta Gerhardt, and Aleksandra Pawliczek (eds.), *Kontinuitäten und Diskontinuitäten in der Wissenschaftsgeschichte des 20. Jahrhunderts* (Stuttgart, 2006), 223–32.

[42] Großmann, 'Moral Economies', 221.

According to Neubert, he began to receive letters from people seeking advice after attending his sex education lectures.[43] He seems always to have answered these letters personally,[44] and in his second marriage guide—*Fragen und Antworten zum Neuen Ehebuch und zur Geschlechterfrage*—he published a selection of them anonymously and without having asked for permission.[45] The letters to Neubert did not deal exclusively with questions of sexuality and contraception; he was also consulted on other problems besetting intimate relationships. The state marriage counselling services that operated in the 1950s in East Germany, by contrast, concentrated largely on contraception and sex education, as well as on sexual problems such as impotence or frigidity; emotional problems in relationships came into focus only later.[46] In addition, many people were generally suspicious of going to state marriage counselling because this meant submitting to state intervention.[47] A letter to Neubert was a way of talking to a stranger about one's problems without having to turn to a state agency, thus circumventing the interference of official bodies. This space was relatively free of ideological preconceptions, as the only sporadic references to socialist ideals show.[48]

The ideal of mutuality was most typically rejected in the letters in which men and women talked about their extramarital affairs or those of their partners.[49] Infidelity was not a new problem in marriage; it was historically the main reason for divorce in Germany in the nineteenth and twentieth centuries. In divorce law based on the principle of fault, adultery was an absolute ground

---

[43] Rudolf Neubert, *Fragen und Antworten zum Neuen Ehebuch und zur Geschlechterfrage*, 2nd edn. (Rudolstadt, 1962), 6.

[44] See HStA Dresden, 12741, Neubert Papers, 23–6, 30, 59–100, 112, 215.

[45] Neubert, *Fragen und Antworten*.

[46] Harsch, *Revenge of the Domestic*, 296; for marriage guidance institutions in general see Schäffler, *Paarbeziehungen in Ostdeutschland*, 178–91; Martin Fischer, *Dienst an der Liebe: Die katholische Ehe-, Familien- und Lebensberatung in der DDR* (Würzburg, 2014); Erik Huneke, 'Sex, Sentiment, and Socialism: Relationship Counseling in the GDR in the Wake of 1965 Family Law Code', in Scott Spector, Helmut Puff, and Dagmar Herzog (eds.), *After* The History of Sexuality: *German Genealogies with and beyond Foucault* (New York, 2012), 231–47; for contemporary descriptions see Aresin, *Sprechstunde des Vertrauens*, 16; Peter Brauer, 'Entwicklung der Ehe- und Sexualberatung der Deutschen Demokratischen Republik aus historischer Sicht' (Ph.D. thesis, Akademie für Ärztliche Fortbildung, Berlin, 1980).

[47] See Schäffler, *Paarbeziehungen in Ostdeutschland*, 187.

[48] Großmann, 'Moral Economies', 227.

[49] e.g. HStA Dresden, 12741, Neubert Papers, 97, I.B. to Rudolf Neubert, 20 Nov. 1968; HStA Dresden, 12741, Neubert Papers, 23, J.J. to Rudolf Neubert, 28 Oct. 1958.

for divorce. Even when absolute grounds were abolished in East Germany, however, infidelity remained an important reason for divorce, alongside violence and alcoholism.[50] In their letters about extramarital affairs and wanting to end their marriages, men and women of different ages fell back on the ideal of marriage for love, which the state had already enshrined in the marriage law reform—but they modified it.[51] In contrast to the state's concept of marriage that aimed to reconcile love and marital stability, in the letters about infidelities the central point of reference was the romantic concept of love, including sexual fulfilment. Love was not necessarily the original reason for marriage. For the generation born in the 1910s and the 1920s, oral history interviews show that economic concerns were a powerful motivation for marrying, as well as the desire to solve everyday problems together.[52] Moral imperatives were important as the number of 'shotgun weddings' was still very high in the 1940s, 1950s, and 1960s,[53] and until the end of the 1970s the birth of a child was still a reason for marrying in the GDR.[54] Although married couples were given preference in the allocation of housing, in letters this was not typically given as a reason for tying the knot: couples writing to counsellors or the press rarely stated housing concerns as a reason for marriage. In sociological studies, however, interviewees emphasized the instrumental character of marriage in improving one's chances on the housing market in the GDR.[55]

[50] Regarding the statistics for East Germany, it should be noted that other categories were constantly introduced to prevent comparability and thus reserve for the state a monopoly on the interpretation of social reality. This ultimately makes it impossible to compare the various grounds for divorce, and a comparative assessment is therefore always only an approximation. See Blasius, *Ehescheidung in Deutschland*; Lothar Mertens, *Wider die sozialistische Familiennorm: Ehescheidung in der DDR 1950–1989* (Opladen, 1998), 56, 58–68; Harsch, *Revenge of the Domestic*, 295.

[51] HStA Dresden, 12741, Neubert Papers, 23, J.J. to Rudolf Neubert, 28 Oct. 1958, and S.R. to Rudolf Neubert, 12 Dec. 1954; HStA Dresden, 12741, Neubert Papers, 167, C.S. to Rudolf Neubert, undated [c.1971–2]; HStA Dresden, 12741, Neubert Papers, 97, A.S. to Rudolf Neubert, 10 May 1969.

[52] Archiv Deutsches Gedächtnis, Institut für Geschichte und Biographie der Fernuniversität Hagen, holding DDR 87, interview with R.W. conducted by Lutz Niethammer on 31 Aug. 1987, interview with H.H. conducted by Dorothee Wierling on 11 June 1987, interview with R.H. conducted by Alexander von Plato on 29 July 1987, and interview with L.S. conducted by Alexander von Plato on 27 Apr. 1987.

[53] See Johannes Weyer, 'Liebe Leserinnen', *Für Dich*, 38 (1963), 3.

[54] See e.g. Bundesarchiv (henceforth BArch), Resch-Treuwerth Papers, N 2709-16, Jutta Resch-Treuwerth to E.S.

[55] For the allocation policies see Elizabeth D. Heineman, *What Difference Does a*

But even in marriages which were entered into for pragmatic, more rational reasons, the concept of love still played a role. In 1954, for instance, a woman seeking advice wrote that she 'liked her husband but did not feel what is called love . . . But I talked myself into it before the marriage. I have already bitterly regretted that I did not question myself better, and for longer.'[56] In 1958 another woman, who had started an affair, complained:

> My husband is completely unemotional. Nothing can move him, neither Hiroshima nor a beautiful poem, neither my gall bladder surgery nor his boy's first cry (he was there when he was born). I was missing something. I was looking for love. I first sought it from him, but I could not and cannot bear his kisses. Not even the actual act of love . . . For seven years, I was absolutely faithful to my husband. I cannot talk to him about anything . . . When I read your book, I became so unhappy. What is it to be satisfied?[57]

While the Marriage Act did not further define love as the basis of marriage, the letters to Neubert elaborated an ideal of romantic love.[58] For the letter writers, love was defined by deep feelings[59] and sexual satisfaction,[60] and in some letters it was explicitly distinguished from 'a good comradely relationship without any tenderness'.[61] Love promised self-realization,[62] 'great' or 'complete' happiness,[63] and

Husband Make? Women and Marital Status in Nazi and Postwar Germany (Berkeley, 1999), 185; Eva Maria Maier, 'Die Frauenpolitik der SED unter besonderer Berücksichtigung der Ära Honecker: Motivation, Anspruch, Wirklichkeit' (Ph.D. thesis, University of Stuttgart, 1997), 161–4, 180–1, 208–10; for the surveys see Johannes Huinink, 'Familienentwicklung und Haushaltsgründung in der DDR: Vom traditionellen Muster zur instrumentellen Lebensplanung', in Bernhard Nauck, Norbert F. Schneider, and Angelika Tölke (eds.), *Familie und Lebensverlauf im gesellschaftlichen Umbruch* (Stuttgart, 1995), 39–55, at 51–2.

[56] HStA Dresden, 12741, Neubert Papers, 23, S.R. to Rudolf Neubert, 12 Dec. 1954.

[57] HStA Dresden, 12741, Neubert Papers, 23, J.J. to Rudolf Neubert, 28 Oct. 1958.

[58] For the ideal of romantic love see e.g. Karl Lenz and Sylka Scholz, 'Romantische Liebessemantik im Wandel?', in Anja Steinbach, Marina Hennig, and Oliver Arránz Becker (eds.), *Familie im Fokus der Wissenschaft* (Wiesbaden, 2014), 93–116.

[59] HStA Dresden, 12741, Neubert Papers, 167, H.B. to Rudolf Neubert, 25 Apr. 1971, and C.S. to Rudolf Neubert, no date [c. 1971–2].

[60] e.g. HStA Dresden, 12741, Neubert Papers, 97, A.S. to Rudolf Neubert, 10 May 1969, and H.S. to Rudolf Neubert, 24 Apr. 1968; HStA Dresden, 12741, Neubert Papers, 23, G.L. to Rudolf Neubert, 2 Apr. 1958, J.J. to Rudolf Neubert, 28 Oct. 1958, and S.R. to Rudolf Neubert, 12 Dec. 1954; HStA Dresden, 12741, Neubert Papers, 167, H.B. to Rudolf Neubert, 25 Apr. 1971, and C.S. to Rudolf Neubert, no date [c.1971–2]; HStA Dresden, 12741, Neubert Papers, 85, G.S. to Rudolf Neubert, 22 Dec. 1962.

[61] HStA Dresden, 12741, Neubert Papers, 23, G.L. to Rudolf Neubert, 2 Apr. 1958.

[62] HStA Dresden, 12741, Neubert Papers, 23, J.J. to Rudolf Neubert, 28 Oct. 1958.

[63] HStA Dresden, 12741, Neubert Papers, 167, H.B. to Rudolf Neubert, 25 Apr. 1971, and C.S. to Rudolf Neubert, no date [c.1971–2].

was associated with absolute exclusivity. The lover was supposed to be completely focused on the beloved, to be there for him or her, and to do everything in order to 'merge completely'[64] with the other.[65]

Moving forward in time to letters written between the late 1950s and the early 1970s, clear shifts can be seen in approaches to the topic of love. While marriage remained the preferred form of cohabitation and there was—as a rule—no fundamental criticism of marriage as a concept (even by those who experienced an absence of love in marriage), the demands made of a marriage partner began to change. Above all, the letters of the late 1950s and the early 1960s demonstrate that people struggled with the decision of whether to end their marriage. It is impossible to verify whether the longing for love or for the stability of marriage gained the upper hand, and how this was reflected in practice in individual cases, as the sources do not provide any information on this. Those seeking advice typically asked whether they could give in to their individual desires for emotional and physical satisfaction and thus fail in their responsibility towards their spouses and children, or towards the institution of marriage and society.[66] They expressed sympathy with their spouses: 'I am so sorry that I have to disappoint him [my husband] so much, but I cannot pretend to love.'[67]

The woman who complained about her emotionally cold husband responded to Neubert's advice to concentrate on herself instead of on the extramarital affair as follows: 'What you are asking me to do . . . is very, very difficult, because I love him [my boyfriend] so much that I could leave everything behind and go to him.'[68] Another woman asked whether 'one can endure such a coexistence [without love] in the long run without perishing from it'.[69] This almost rhetorical question illustrates an incipient change.

[64] HStA Dresden, 12741, Neubert Papers, 23, J.J. to Rudolf Neubert, 28 Oct. 1958.

[65] HStA Dresden, 12741, Neubert Papers, 22, E.M. and M.S. to Rudolf Neubert, 17 Sept. 1962; HStA Dresden, 12741, Neubert Papers, 97, R.T. to Rudolf Neubert, 5 Jan. 1969.

[66] HStA Dresden, 12741, Neubert Papers, 23, G.L. to Rudolf Neubert, 2 Apr. 1958, and J.J. to Rudolf Neubert, 28 Oct. 1958.

[67] HStA Dresden, 12741, Neubert Papers, 23, S.R. to Rudolf Neubert, 12 Dec. 1954.

[68] HStA Dresden, 12741, Neubert Papers, 23, J.J. to Rudolf Neubert, 28 Oct. 1958.

[69] HStA Dresden, 12741, Neubert Papers, 97, I.B. to Rudolf Neubert, 20 Nov. 1968.

The letter writers at the end of the 1960s who wrestled with the idea of making a break more typically asserted their right to pursue happiness:

I don't have a bad conscience about the whole thing [the extramarital affair] (although I also think a lot about whether what I'm doing is right, especially towards him [my husband]), but I still think that I'm a little bit right about what I'm doing. Why should I give up the other man who really brought some sunshine into my life again? The one I look forward to seeing, on account of whom I can be cheerful and enjoy many things again.[70]

However, they did not only discuss being right in the moral sense. Others went so far as to demand changes in the legal framework:

I cannot divorce like this. First, I would deprive a helpless mother of her last hope. She would never cope with the boy and the household alone. Secondly, this marriage will probably not be dissolved under the new Family Code (article 24) because it would mean unreasonable hardship for the spouse and the child. But it is also unreasonable hardship for the other spouse if the . . . healthy spouse first has to fall ill because of a lack of sexual balance. For such cases of hardship there is no additional provision in FGB [family code] article 24.[71]

The correspondence between Neubert and the letter writers makes it clear that two different ideals of marriage were in competition here.

The new sense of entitlement was not influenced by gender or age. The first two quotations are from women in their early twenties and early thirties respectively, the last one from a man born in 1911.[72] Studies of divorce and contemporary interpretations see a gender-specific transformation in the 1960s because more and more women were seeking divorce. Contemporaries and later historians attribute this to the increasing emancipation of women.[73] The letter writers' claims to be seeking fulfilment in love at the expense of an existing marriage do not support this interpretation—though the questioning of a marriage is one thing and its dissolution by divorce,

---

[70] HStA Dresden, 12741, Neubert Papers, 167, C.S. to Rudolf Neubert, no date [c.1971–2].

[71] HStA Dresden, 12741, Neubert Papers, 97, A.S. to Rudolf Neubert, 10 May 1969. The reference to Art. 24 demonstrates an in-depth knowledge of the new family law, which had introduced this restrictive passage into the divorce law.

[72] Apart from age and gender, it is not always possible to classify the letter writers precisely. Professions are usually referred to in the letters only in the case of higher education. See also Großmann, 'Moral Economies', 226.

[73] See Port, 'Love, Lust, and Lies', 496; Harsch, *Revenge of the Domestic*, 294; Mertens, *Wider die sozialistische Familiennorm*, 27–8.

where economic possibilities naturally play a much greater part, is another. In any case, how did politicians, marriage counsellors, and the editors of the state-monitored media respond to these demands by men and women?

III. *Changing Policies and Practices in the Late 1960s and 1970s*

The East German state's ideal remained the nuclear family with two to three children as the nucleus of socialist society, although in the 1960s and 1970s having illegitimate children began to lose its moral stigma.[74] Non-marital relationships remained undesirable.[75] From the late 1950s to the end of the GDR, East German leaders struggled with steadily rising divorce rates, which in the 1980s were among the highest in the world.[76] In response, the East German leadership began to promote marriage in the late 1960s and early 1970s by offering housing privileges, establishing marriage schools, matchmaking institutes, and marriage counselling centres, and introducing educational measures.[77]

Nevertheless, there is evidence of a tendency to weaken the focus on stable marriage as the goal of family policy, especially in the handling of divorce. The Family Act of 1965 softened the definition of marriage as the cornerstone of society. The meaning of marriage was no longer defined by its importance for society and for the couple, as in 1955. Rather, its social meaning was defined only in terms of its significance for the couple and their children.[78] Shifts can also be observed in the state's influence on people seeking divorce. This, however, became evident only at the beginning of the Erich Honecker era in 1971. In the aftermath of the Marriage Decree of 1955 a reconciliation procedure had been adopted, legally ensuring state intervention.[79] Divorce judges had the task of giving advice to

---

[74] See McLellan, *Love in the Time of Communism*, 56; Schäffler, *Paarbeziehungen in Ostdeutschland*, 130–6.

[75] For the first years of the GDR see Schneider, *Hausväteridylle oder sozialistische Utopie?*, 196–200; for the later years see Schäffler, *Paarbeziehungen in Ostdeutschland*, 127–48.

[76] See e.g. Anna Kaminsky, *Frauen in der DDR* (Berlin, 2016), 160–7; Harsch, *Revenge of the Domestic*, 216–18; Mertens, *Wider die sozialistische Familiennorm*, 13.

[77] See Schäffler, *Paarbeziehungen in Ostdeutschland*, 111–13, 120–7; for the marriage institutes see Kaminsky, *Frauen in der DDR*, 153; for the question of housing, Maier, 'Frauenpolitik der SED', 161–4, 180–1, 208–10.

[78] See Schneider, *Hausväteridylle oder sozialistische Utopie?*, 243.

[79] Betts, *Within Walls*, 97–8, 101–3; Schneider, *Hausväteridylle oder sozialistische Utopie?*, 244–5.

couples seeking divorce so that they could work on their marriage in order to save it.[80] At the beginning of the 1970s the purpose of this reconciliation procedure shifted from an exclusive focus on individual couples seeking a divorce to the general education of society as a whole.[81] And in the 1970s and 1980s even less pressure was exerted on those wanting to divorce to withdraw their plans.[82] Divorce was finally recognized by the political leadership as a social reality and a progressive achievement of socialism, rather than a problem of the social order that needed to be remedied.[83]

The practice of counselling for marriages in crisis was also adapted, although, as previously, the stability of marriage remained central. In marriage counselling the change was reflected in an increasing recognition of individual demands and a willingness to recommend divorce. In the 1950s, for example, Rudolf Neubert explained that love was important for marriage but was not its basis, and he declared that love was more than just sex.[84] Playing down romantic feelings, he represented a sober idea of love that was compatible with his ideal of mutuality: 'At the beginning of every good marriage is the love between two people. Love is not what you can read in Freud's book—an inherited animal instinct . . . Nor is love what van de Velde describes: a physiological reflex process. Love is a relationship with a person, reciprocity, affection, respect, and attention.'[85]

At the end of the 1950s other guides also warned of the dangers of passion.[86] Ten years later, Neubert still did not see lack of love as a reason for divorce. A woman longing for love had become pregnant by another man in order to have a reason for divorce, but her husband recognized the child, and in 1968 the marriage counsellor answered her desperate complaint about her 'hopeless' situation as follows:

---

[80] See Inga Markovits, *Gerechtigkeit in Lüritz: Eine ostdeutsche Rechtsgeschichte* (Munich, 2006), 98–106; Betts, *Within Walls*, 92–115.

[81] For the anti-divorce policies in general see Schäffler, *Paarbeziehungen in Ostdeutschland*, 148–213.

[82] See Betts, *Within Walls*, 108–15; Schröter, *Ostdeutsche Ehen vor Gericht*, 112–21.

[83] See Irene Uhlmann (ed.), *Kleine Enzyklopädie: Die Frau*, 2nd edn. (Leipzig, 1989), 227–8; Mertens, *Wider die sozialistische Familiennorm*, 23, 44; Betts, *Within Walls*, 108; Schäffler, *Paarbeziehungen in Ostdeutschland*, 191–2.

[84] HStA Dresden, 12741, Neubert Papers, 23, Rudolf Neubert to E.L., 4 July 1957, and to P.H., 11 May 1957. [85] Neubert, *Das neue Ehebuch*, 135.

[86] See Weber and Weber, *Du und ich*, 19; and Dierl and Müller, *Liebe, Ehe — Scheidung?*, 31.

What is this, the great love? What do you expect from it? . . . You probably need the encouragement of a woman with life experience or an older man with life experience who tells you what life is all about. You will then be much less worried about your own little happiness and will ask your husband to make you happy and be a good mother to your children. The rest will take care of itself.[87]

Nevertheless, in certain cases Neubert gave in to the individual's wishes. From the 1960s onwards, Neubert advised women to prepare for a life alone when they complained about fundamental character differences, or about husbands who were incorrigible 'tyrants' and controlled their wives, sometimes committing acts of violence.[88]

Moreover, at the level of individual counselling, Neubert considered sex before marriage necessary at the turn of the 1970s to prevent any difficulties in this area from becoming a problem in a future marriage.[89] His 1956 sex education guide for young people had argued clearly against premarital sex.[90] But now the social hygienist took part in the transformation that has been characterized as 'sexual evolution'. This liberalization had limits in the GDR, which tolerated sexuality only within certain norms. For example, homosexuality only gradually came to be acknowledged, and socially was largely not accepted. Heterosexual intercourse was meant to take place within a loving relationship.[91] At the same time, as already mentioned, sexuality was a field in which marriage counselling played a part from the very beginning of the socialist state, but its importance increased in the 1970s.[92] The 1970s was the 'golden age of sex manuals',[93] which had the goal of improving sex life under real socialism.[94]

---

[87] HStA Dresden, 12741, Neubert Papers, 97, Rudolf Neubert to I.B., no date [c.Nov. 1968].

[88] See the replies to the following letters attempting to reconcile the couples: HStA Dresden, 12741, Neubert Papers, 23, Rudolf Neubert to S.F., 11 Sept. 1957, and Rudolf Neubert to I.W., 29 Oct. 1958; HStA Dresden, 12741, Neubert Papers, 97, Rudolf Neubert to I.B, no date [c.1965–70]; HStA Dresden, 12741, Neubert Papers, 167, Rudolf Neubert to H.B., 2 May 1971; for a rare case in which divorce was advised see HStA Dresden, 12741, Neubert Papers, 85, Rudolf Neubert to I.T., 2 Dec. 1963.

[89] e.g. HStA Dresden, 12741, Neubert Papers, 167, Rudolf Neubert to M.C., 28 Sept. 1971.   [90] See Neubert, *Die Geschlechterfrage*, 140–58.

[91] See Dagmar Herzog, 'East Germany's Sexual Evolution', in Katherine Pence and Paul Betts (eds.), *Socialist Modern: East German Everyday Culture and Politics* (Ann Arbor, Mich., 2010), 71–95; McLellan, *Love in the Time of Communism*; Schäffler, *Paarbeziehungen in Ostdeutschland*, 84–110.

[92] See Aresin, *Sprechstunde des Vertrauens*.   [93] Betts, *Within Walls*, 103.

[94] See Schäffler, *Paarbeziehungen in Ostdeutschland*, 86–7.

A growing willingness to allow for individual sexual needs and the possible dissolution of marriages can also be seen in legal practices in the course of the 1960s. Divorce petitions by women were now granted because of the 'patriarchalism' of husbands who did not respect their wives, or who clung to traditional roles and claimed the power to make decisions. Different lifestyles and attitudes to life were considered grounds for divorce and sexual needs were also recognized; overall, the courts were more likely to agree to dissolve a marriage.[95]

The counsellors' and politicians' ideal of a good marriage assumed a new shape, which was intended to guarantee stability in the face of increasing demands for sexual and emotional fulfilment. Social science and historical value change studies have shown that the concept of the 'socialist lifestyle' promoted from the late 1960s offered increasing room for individual self-fulfilment.[96] Moreover, a new concept enhanced the possibilities for individual development within relationships: partnership. Eva Schäffler uses the term *Kameradschaft* (comradeship) for a new concept of the 1960s which had already been common during the Weimar Republic and was, in part, used synonymously in East Germany. However, comradeship in the context of marriage was increasingly replaced by the terms 'partner' and 'partnership', as a full-text search of the SED's official Party newspaper *Neues Deutschland* and the *Berliner Zeitung* shows. The latter was a daily newspaper in the GDR capital, and though subordinate to the SED Central Committee, it was often somewhat more critical than the official Party newspaper.[97] During the 1960s, partnership became the central term for relationships in East Germany,[98] although it did not appear in the 1965 Family Code. This code, mentioned above, included the marriage decree of 1955, which remained largely identical in wording, and in addition saw marriage as based on love and affection in a relationship between two equal but economically independent individuals. The elaboration of the second

[95] See Betts, *Within Walls*, 100–8.

[96] See Christopher Neumaier and Andreas Ludwig, 'Individualisierung der Lebenswelten: Konsum, Wohnkultur und Familienstrukturen', in Frank Bösch (ed.), *Geteilte Geschichte. Ost- und Westdeutschland 1970–2000* (Göttingen, 2015), 239–82, at 271–2; Gensicke, *Mentalitätsentwicklungen im Osten Deutschlands*, 61.

[97] See Schäffler, *Paarbeziehungen in Ostdeutschland*, 194.

[98] See Christa Wolf, 'Drum prüfe, wer sich ewig bindet', *Für Dich*, 37 (1963), 18–19; Johannes Weyer, 'Liebe Leserinnen', *Für Dich*, 38 (1963), 3; interview with Helga Hörz, *Berliner Zeitung*, 5 Apr. 1970, 11; the series 'Reicht Liebe zum Eheglück?', *Berliner Zeitung*, 13 Sept.–1 Nov. 1975.

point went further than the law of 1955 and strengthened the idea of gender equality.[99]

The main features of the partnership model can be traced back to the early twentieth-century attempts to reform marriage made by the women's movement and the movement for sexual reform. Here, too, female sexual reformers in their marriage counselling books and young socialists developed ideas of marriage based on love, companionship, and responsibility, in which both partners were to be given space for development.[100]

In the new model, partnership was a permanent task for the couple. According to the advice pages of East German women's magazines and daily newspapers, partnership was the framework within which individuals could evolve into 'socialist personalities',[101] and within which they would receive support for their individual development. The emphasis on mutual assistance in development was also found in the definition of marriage in the Family Act of 1965.[102] In an expert discussion on marriage, a university lecturer in ethics at the Humboldt University of Berlin, Helga Hörz (born 1935), explained: 'Marriage—this is often ignored—is a task for both partners involved. This results in the subordinate task of helping the other partner in their further development and feeling responsible for each other in such questions as well.'[103]

This idea of mutual support referred primarily to male 'help' in the household and female employment, and was thus located in the context of efforts to increase women's participation in the labour market. Labour market policy in the early GDR initially aimed to integrate women into paid employment in general. In the 1960s a major professional qualification campaign for women was launched,[104] in the context of which the partnership model

---

[99] e.g. Schneider, *Hausväteridylle oder sozialistische Utopie?*, 191–6; Fischer-Langosch, *Die Entstehungsgeschichte des Familiengesetzbuches*, 177–81; Neumaier, *Familie im 20. Jahrhundert*, 459–60.

[100] e.g. Kirsten Reinert, *Frauen und Sexualreform: 1897–1933* (Herbolzheim, 2000), 23–32; Karen Hagemann, *Frauenalltag und Männerpolitik: Alltagsleben und gesellschaftliches Handeln von Arbeiterfrauen in der Weimarer Republik* (Bonn, 1990), 325–49.

[101] For the notion of the 'socialist personality', which had been posited since 1958, see Ilko-Sascha Kowalczuk, *Die 101 wichtigsten Fragen: DDR* (Munich, 2009), 43 4.

[102] See *Familiengesetzbuch der Deutschen Demokratischen Republik*, Art. 2 and Art. 5.

[103] Interview with Helga Hörz, *Berliner Zeitung*, 5 Apr. 1970, 11.

[104] See Gunilla-Friederike Budde (ed.), *Frauen arbeiten: Weibliche Erwerbstätigkeit in Ost- und Westdeutschland nach 1945* (Göttingen, 1997); Christine von Oertzen and Almut Rietzschel, 'Comparing the Post-War Germanies: Breadwinner Ideology and Women's

of marriage was adopted. Despite its utilitarian orientation, it is important to emphasize that the concept of partnership created a space for individual development within the framework of socialist society, which codified equality, at least nominally. The partnership model was also used as a way of containing the explosive power of love, particularly in the 1970s and 1980s. This can be seen in numerous letters from readers about their problems and in the responses of journalists in newspapers and magazines.[105] The disputes that took place in the monitored newspapers and magazines had the character of *Aussprachen*.[106] Behind this concept was the idea of talks held within political, workplace, and residential collectives to prepare legal modifications, or to discuss problems in order to solve them collectively. The aim was to have an educational impact on society while maintaining a channel to the general public's mood. From the 1950s, letters to the editor in East Germany were formally treated as *Eingaben* (petitions), another form of communication with the same purpose.[107] As a result of state control of the media, those who wrote letters to the newspaper were closer to the socialist ideal than those who wrote personal letters to Neubert. The former used well-known coded language to prove that they were politically reliable. We cannot entirely rule out that the editors themselves wrote parts of the letters they printed, as in some cases different letters used identical wording.[108] However, there were also clear deviations within the editorial staff's final assessments, which were always printed at the end of these series running over several issues. We can therefore assume that the letters to the editor were not all

Employment in the Divided Nation, 1948–1970', in Angélique Janssens (ed.), *The Rise and Decline of the Male Breadwinner Family*? supplement 5 of *International Review of Social History*, 42 (1997), 175–96; Beate Clausnitzer, *Der Geburtenrückgang in der modernen Industriegesellschaft: Zum Spannungsverhältnis von Mutterschaft und Erwerbsarbeit am Beispiel der DDR* (Berlin, 2016).

[105] See Editors of *Für Dich*, 'Ein lehrreicher Streit', *Für Dich*, 9 (1963), 23; Eberhard Bormann, 'Was ist die große Liebe?', *Für Dich*, 4 (1963), 14–15; the series 'Reicht Liebe zum Eheglück?'; R.J., 'Briefe an Susanne', *Berliner Zeitung*, 28–29 May 1983, 11; Monika Harrar, 'Briefe an Susanne', *Berliner Zeitung*, 11–12 June 1983, 11.

[106] For *Aussprachen* see Schneider, *Hausväteridylle oder sozialistische Utopie?*, 271–2; Großmann, 'Moral Economies', 228.

[107] See Ellen Bos, *Leserbriefe in Tageszeitungen der DDR: Zur 'Massenverbundenheit' der Presse 1949–1989* (Opladen, 1993); for *Eingaben* see Felix Mühlberg, 'Eingaben als Instrument informeller Konfliktbewältigung', in Evemarie Badstübner (ed.), *Befremdlich anders: Leben in der DDR*, 2nd edn. (Berlin, 2000), 233–70.

[108] See Ursula Melcher, 'Briefe an Susanne', *Berliner Zeitung*, 10 Mar. 1963, 9, and Gisela Schmid, 'Briefe an Susanne', *Berliner Zeitung*, 17 Feb. 1963, 11.

invented,[109] and interpret them as expressing the officially accepted and partly independent voices of individuals. They allow us to trace, to some extent, changes in the perceptions held by married couples themselves, although they cannot be used as equivalents for the Neubert and Resch-Treuwerth letter collections to fill the temporal gaps between the sources in the 1970s and 1980s.

> True love matures, is beautiful, and proves its worth when it is shaped by the noble human relationships that are characteristic of our socialist order—by comradeship and helpfulness, by mutual respect and sacrifice, by mutual understanding and trust, by the meaning and purpose that both partners give to their lives, by the work they do on themselves to be wise and good companions to their partners.[110]

This was how the editors of *Für Dich* expressed the concept of partnership, along with a certain ideal of love. *Für Dich* was the largest GDR women's magazine, read especially by middle-aged women from a wide range of social backgrounds.[111] As in this quotation, the marriage counsellors and columnists referred to the concept of mature love, which contrasted with passionate, romantic love: 'The value and meaning of marriage lie not only in passionate love, but above all in experiencing and bearing together the weal and the woe.'[112] Jutta Resch-Treuwerth quoted this saying by the author Leonhard Frank (1882–1961) in her book of letters to the editor published in 1982. Resch-Treuwerth was the leading editor and columnist of *Junge Welt*, the official daily newspaper of the socialist youth movement Free German Youth and an institution in sex education in the late GDR.[113]

The idea of mature love put forward in this saying was based on 'good knowledge of each other', 'respect', 'trust', and 'helpfulness', as

---

[109] For an *Aussprache* of this sort, see the series 'Reicht Liebe zum Eheglück?'.

[110] Editors of *Für Dich*, 'Ein lehrreicher Streit'; see also Bormann, 'Was ist die große Liebe?', 14.

[111] For *Für Dich* see Dietrich Löffler, 'Publikumszeitschriften und ihre Leser: Zum Beispiel: *Wochenpost, Freie Welt, Für Dich, Sibylle*', in Simone Barck, Martina Langermann, and Siegfried Lokatis (eds.), *Zwischen 'Mosaik' und 'Einheit': Zeitschriften in der DDR* (Berlin, 1999), 48–60, at 53, 59.

[112] See Jutta Resch-Treuwerth, *Leben zu zweit: Briefe unter vier Augen* (Berlin, 1982), 109.

[113] Jutta Resch-Treuwerth was a journalist by training and worked for the column for over a decade. See ⟨http://www.jutta-resch-treuwerth.de/⟩ [accessed 27 July 2020], and Uta Kolano, *Kollektiv d'amour: Liebe, Sex und Partnerschaft in der DDR* (Berlin, 2012), 107–16.

well as sexual relationships.[114] Love meant more than a deep feeling of attachment and exclusive devotion to the other in a partnership. Some of the additional ingredients in the concept of love were already expressed in the ideal of mutuality. For Neubert and other counsellors, love was also associated with trust, respect, compassion, understanding, companionship, care, consideration, and a sense of duty.[115] The two ideals of marriage—mutuality and partnership—included love but tied it to other things, and developed notions of love that competed with the romantic ideal. The subordination of the ego to traditional values, such as duty and respect for the other, was central to these ideas of love.

'Working on marriage' also played a central part in the concept of partnership and mature love. As early as the 1950s and especially in the 1960s, Neubert and other authors of marriage guides had already drawn on the ideas of personal development and 'education in marriage'.[116] Constant 'adaptation' and the 'renunciation of personal needs' were seen as solutions to conflict.[117] Conversations between spouses about possible conflicts were considered important, but the advice was that initially one should 'always first consider whether a hard word is necessary, whether it would be better to leave it unsaid!'[118] In other words, emotions that threatened the stability of the relationship were to be repressed. Self-control, politeness, and consideration remained a recipe for solving conflicts in the 1970s and 1980s, and thus other elements central to the concept of mutuality were carried forward into the notion of mature love and partnership.[119]

At the same time, in the 1960s a different way of dealing with conflicts began to appear. Individual psychological counselling was increasingly pursued within institutional marriage counselling.[120]

[114] e.g. BArch, Resch-Treuwerth Papers, N 2709-16, Jutta Resch-Treuwerth to I.P.; Wolfgang Polte (ed.), *Unsere Ehe*, 3rd edn. (Leipzig, 1969), 28–31; in general, for the containment of love in the ideal of comradely marriage or partnership, see Schäffler, *Paarbeziehungen in Ostdeutschland*, 194.

[115] See Weber and Weber, *Du und ich*, 9–10; and Dierl and Müller, *Liebe, Ehe — Scheidung?*, 31.

[116] See Neubert, *Die Geschlechterfrage*, 27; Dierl and Müller, *Liebe, Ehe — Scheidung?*, 110; Aresin, *Sprechstunde des Vertrauens*, 93; for Neubert, see also Großmann, 'Moral Economies', 227.   [117] Aresin, *Sprechstunde des Vertrauens*, 93.

[118] Dierl and Müller, *Liebe, Ehe — Scheidung?*, 28.

[119] e.g. BArch, Resch-Treuwerth Papers, N 2709-17, Jutta Resch-Treuwerth to H.K., 14 Nov. 1979; Monika Wiedemeyer, 'Endstation Scheidung', *Für Dich*, 12 (1975), 46.

[120] See Brauer, *Entwicklung der Ehe- und Sexualberatung*, 97; Harsch, *Revenge of the Domestic*, 290–1.

Dialogue and *Aussprache* also began to feature in marriage guidance and the relevant pages of the press as a new form of marriage management. The new solution was a rationalization of emotions. The aim was to become aware of one's own feelings and those of one's partner in order to be able to develop an understanding for him or her, and thus to achieve a harmonious marriage.[121] This idea of two individuals working on themselves complemented the earlier idea of self-control and self-education in marriage.

This process was also intended to create more space in the relationship for the other person beyond the utilitarian aspect of women's gainful employment. Couples were supposed to recognize each other as individuals, as various letters to agony aunts in the 1970s show: 'There is a common Marxist world-view, a mutual good will to live well together; each [partner] also tries to tolerate the habits of the other, or to adapt more and more without giving up their own personality.'[122] In this sense, tolerance not only towards the peculiarities of the other person, but also towards extramarital affairs of the partner, was advised.[123]

The potential incompatibility between fulfilment in love and stability in marriage remained, despite the partnership model offering space for individual development and love,[124] an increasing openness to divorce, and the relaxation of interventionist policies. In 1970 *Für Dich* posed the question 'What is marriage without love?', and in 1975 the *Berliner Zeitung* asked its readers to discuss whether love was enough for a happy marriage.[125] The discussions on the topic of love

---

[121] e.g. Monika Wiedemeyer, 'Ehekrise', *Für Dich*, 37 (1975), 46; Karlen Vesper, 'Laserstrahlen in Operationssälen', *Neues Deutschland*, 1 Apr. 1987, 4; for the scientific background of this new form of socialist social management and its analysis in Neubert's counselling see Großmann, 'Moral Economies', 231–6.

[122] E. Fernahl, 'Briefe an Susanne', *Berliner Zeitung*, 25 Oct. 1975, 14; see also M. Feyerabend, 'Briefe an Susanne', *Berliner Zeitung*, 4 Oct. 1975, 14; and Inge D., 'Briefe an Susanne', *Berliner Zeitung*, 25–26 June 1983, 11.

[123] See Schäffler, *Paarbeziehungen in Ostdeutschland*, 195–8.

[124] Writing theoretically on this conflict, see Günter Burkart, 'Arbeit und Liebe: Über die Macht der Liebe und Arbeit an der Partnerschaft', in id. and Kornelia Hahn (eds.), *Grenzen und Grenzüberschreitungen der Liebe: Studien zur Soziologie intimer Beziehungen*, vol. ii (Opladen, 2000), 165–98; Cornelia Koppetsch, 'Die Pflicht zur Liebe und das Geschenk der Partnerschaft: Paradoxien in der Praxis von Paarbeziehungen', in Johannes Huinink, Klaus Peter Strohmeier, and Michael Wagner (eds.), *Solidarität in Partnerschaft und Familie: Zum Stand familiensoziologischer Theoriebildung* (Würzburg, 2001), 219–39.

[125] See 'Ganz unter uns gesagt: Was ist die Ehe ohne Liebe?', *Für Dich*, 20 (1970), 46; the series 'Reicht Liebe zum Eheglück?'.

demonstrate that it was still necessary to negotiate the meaning and role of love. Most of the replies printed by the editors in both series gave preference to 'mature' love and partnership,[126] or pointed out that love must include more than passion to result in a successful marriage. For example, one reader wrote: 'The partnership proves its worth only when you live together. Many people—not only the young—confuse sexual desire and being in love with love.'[127]

However, there were dissenting voices. Although the partnership model was already being developed in the 1960s, it did not leave any traces in the correspondence with Neubert, and struggles between marriage and feelings of love were still a topic in personal correspondence with counsellors at the end of the 1970s.[128] There were also implicit rejections of the concept of mature love in the press debates. One woman complained about her husband in the column 'Ganz unter uns gesagt' (Off the Record), as he did not engage with her in any way: 'I believe I can't live without love, which I don't understand only in terms of sexual love. I have been missing a tender word or a gentle embrace for three years.'[129] Danuta Weber, author of a guide to marriage, responded in a psychologizing and matter-of-fact manner, referring to mutual respect and advising the woman to work on her respect for her husband in order to bring about a different relationship in the long term. The partnership model represented an attempt to create a space for individual self-fulfilment, where love would also have a place. However, the arguments about love in the 1970s clearly show that tensions persisted. The search for romantic fulfilment continued to conflict with the desire for stable marriages.

IV. Conclusion

In summary, there was a change in the GDR's culture of marriage between the late 1950s and the 1980s. It manifested itself in negotiations between marital partners, marriage counsellors, the

---

[126] See R.J., 'Briefe an Susanne'; Harrar, 'Briefe an Susanne'.

[127] D. Reichart, 'Briefe an Susanne', *Berliner Zeitung*, 27 Sept. 1975, 11; see also the letters by F. Arendt, S. Bechert, and G.H. in the same edition.

[128] See e.g. BArch, Resch-Treuwerth Papers, N 2709-13, P.B. to Jutta Resch-Treuwerth, 4 Oct. 1979.

[129] R. St., 'Ganz unter uns gesagt: Ist mein Mann ein Egoist?', *Für Dich*, 18 (1975), 46; insisting on the importance of romantic love see also R. Wittig, 'Briefe an Susanne', *Berliner Zeitung*, 11 Oct. 1975, 13.

monitored public, and politics. Legally, the concept of marriage for love was codified in East Germany in 1955. At the same time, married couples and marriage counsellors put forward a different concept that was intended to ensure stability and contained rational components as well as emotional aspects. The ideal of mutuality was a relationship based on reciprocity and a certain degree of equality, characterized by two complementary personalities sharing everyday life. It also included an idea of love in which emotional bonds between lovers had to be accompanied by other ingredients, such as trust or a sense of duty.

By the end of the 1950s, this ideal was challenged by an individually articulated longing for love and sexual fulfilment which adopted the ideal of marriage for love, but radicalized it. In East German marriage culture, couples began to search for the romantic ideal of complete merging with, and self-fulfilment in, the other in terms of love and sexuality. While this search initially led to doubts about how to deal with people expressing these desires, in the late 1960s and early 1970s married individuals successfully asserted their right to give in to this longing. Marriage counsellors began to react differently to those seeking advice; they supported divorce in specific cases and regarded premarital sex as desirable. The policy of the state had also changed since the 1960s. Initially, the state had increased its efforts to curb the rising divorce rate, but by the early 1970s it relaxed this policy in response to demands from below. Individual, emotional reasons for divorce were increasingly recognized from the 1960s, and the legal pressure on those wishing to divorce decreased.

At the same time, a different model of marriage developed from the mid 1960s and remained dominant until the end of the GDR: partnership. In this model, marriage was conceived of as a contract between two equal, economically independent individuals who were united by love. This model explicitly offered room for self-fulfilment since it regarded the development of the individual as an essential part of the relationship. It was combined with a concept of love that was less intense than in the earlier concept of mutuality. In partnership, love was to be achieved through a process of permanently working on and for the individuals in the partnership, thereby rationalizing their emotions. However, this attempt was never completely successful because marriage partners still referred to love as an absolute feeling going beyond conjugal responsibility in order to explain the specific problems of marriages in crisis.

What does this case of transformation tell us about changes in marriage culture in East Germany and beyond, about the concept of value change, and about the history of the GDR? The negotiations over ideals show that marriage culture in East Germany had already begun to change in the 1950s, much like the culture of sexuality and gender relationships. As in the UK, the increased reference to love in marriage ideals started in the period after the Second World War. In the UK, an ideal of marriage based on self-realization and a transcendentally charged attachment to the other person increasingly displaced the ideal of mutual understanding and care, although pragmatic and material considerations still played a role at first.[130] Studies on the UK and the USA have also shown that the concept of working on a marriage became relevant in the context of marriage counselling during the course of the twentieth century, shifting from an emphasis on the idea of adaptation to a focus on psychological maturation or personal development.[131] These similarities call for comparative studies asking whether these changes in marriage culture were common to the Western world as a whole and occurred in the same time periods. Likewise, they put a question mark over the idea of a common East–West divide in the European history of marriage and family.[132] From a German perspective, it is astonishing that the transformation seems to have begun earlier in East Germany than in West Germany. A systematic comparison would be required to corroborate this assumption based on the existing literature on West Germany.

The East German development of marriage culture was not a

---

[130] For the concept of mutuality in contemporary Britain see Marcus Collins, *Modern Love: An Intimate History of Men and Women in Twentieth-Century Britain* (London, 2003); Simon Szreter and Kate Fisher, *Sex before the Sexual Revolution: Intimate Life in England 1918–1963* (Cambridge, 2010); for the increasing role of love in marriage see Claire Langhamer, *The English in Love: The Intimate Story of an Emotional Revolution* (Oxford, 2013).

[131] See Rebecca L. Davis, *More Perfect Unions: The American Search for Marital Bliss* (Cambridge, Mass., 2010); Teri Chettiar, 'Treating Marriage as "the Sick Entity": Gender, Emotional Life, and the Psychology of Marriage Improvement in Postwar Britain', *History of Psychology*, 18/3 (2015), 270–82; for love as work in general see Kristin Celello, *Making Marriage Work: A History of Marriage and Divorce in the Twentieth-Century United States* (Chapel Hill, NC, 2009).

[132] See e.g. the project KASS at the Max Planck Institute for Social Anthropology ⟨https://www.eth.mpg.de/3542341/kas⟩ [accessed 16 Nov. 2020].

linear process, as the concept of value change generally implies.[133] It is more appropriate to speak of long-term adjustments than of an 'era of change'. I have shown that different ideals of marriage coexisted and competed over time. Any modification in these ideals was the result of constant negotiations between marriage partners, politicians, and family experts. The ideals discussed were not hermetically sealed units, but consisted of various different building blocks that were exchanged, modified, and reused. For example, claims for romantic love from the 1950s drew on the legal code, while the notion of partnership took up the idea of working on marriage from the concept of mutuality and modified it. These simultaneous transformations show how necessary it is not only to examine the history of love and marriage from a political and legal perspective or from that of the experts, but to listen to the voices of the marriage partners themselves and to examine their ideals in order to get the full picture. Consistently taking a grass-roots perspective would make it possible to re-examine these initial findings on value transformations regarding marriage and love. Perhaps developments in West Germany and elsewhere in the 'West' would also look less linear and clear-cut if the grass roots were taken into account.

It would also make sense to pursue another issue that could not be sufficiently considered here. It appears that the search for love was not gender-specific. Nevertheless, it would be worth investigating what ideas of gender relations were considered and practised in the concepts of marriage and sexuality outlined above. In particular, the abandonment of the breadwinner model in the socialist state raises questions around developments in gender relations in marriage culture.

Only by consistently historicizing the language of the sources in the negotiated exchanges between macro and micro levels has it been possible to show that value changes took place by means of resumptions and shifts in meaning. Such shifts cannot be identified in any analysis that uses ahistorical catch-all terms such as 'individualization' or 'liberalization'. While the term 'post-rational value change' is somewhat more specific, my analysis has shown that it is not helpful to assume a post-rational era in marriage culture. Although love as the guiding principle of marriage was codified

---

[133] Cf. Schäffler, *Paarbeziehungen in Ostdeutschland*; Neumaier, *Familie im 20. Jahrhundert*; Mertens, *Wider die sozialistische Familiennorm*.

in law as a post-rational ideal and demanded by married couples, other concepts of love developed at the same time that rationalized emotions and merged with other, more traditional values, such as respect. The grass-roots approach shows that the concept of post-rational value change can function as a heuristic means for identifying specific elements, but not as a description of the entire social transformation. It therefore seems more instructive to give space to the full breadth of historical debates. Perhaps the consistent integration of a grass-roots perspective will allow us to develop a more complex understanding of how changes in values and ideals take place as a whole. From a theoretical point of view, I would like to suggest that the idea I have presented of building blocks as a tool for interpreting the moral transformations of societies should be further developed.

PART II

Experiments with the Post-Rational Self

5

Youth Cultures, New Religiosities in West Germany, and the Search for Meaning in the Long 1970s

ISABEL RICHTER

When the German journalist Sven Michaelsen interviewed the philosopher Peter Sloterdijk for the *Süddeutsche Zeitung* in 2014, Sloterdijk remembered Munich in the mid 1970s as 'saturated with encounter-culture, esoteric discos, meditation centres, and self-awareness groups, all with a Californian flavour of primal scream and all that'. He had heard rumours of the 'super-guru' Bhagwan Shree Rajneesh, who 'had everything down pat from the Upanishads to German idealism and Wittgenstein'. Sloterdijk stayed in Rajneesh's ashram in Pune in 1979 and received his mala, a string of beads used in meditation, from the guru himself: 'I had this guru give me the mala with his portrait.' He returned to Germany after just four months, but in his interview with Michaelsen he remarked that 'after Pune I was psychologically no longer available at my German address'.[1]

He characterized his cohort as obsessed with the truth, with adjusting their 'psychological screws', and with the belief that 'psychosis' was 'their best friend'.[2] In retrospect, Sloterdijk saw Pune as one of the crucial turning points of his life. The presence of a guru, sexuality as a tool for self-realization, and thinking and acting beyond the rational Western self definitely have positive connotations here. This is remarkable given the negative coverage of youth religions in West Germany from the late 1970s, when many German popular magazines published series on the mass murder-suicides by members of the Peoples Temple movement in Guyana

[1] Sven Michaelsen, '"Man denkt an mich, also bin ich": Der Philosoph Peter Sloterdijk spricht über seine Selbsterfahrungstrips bei Bhagwan in Poona, seine langjährige Fehde mit Jürgen Habermas und seinen Plan, einen erotischen Roman zu schreiben', *Süddeutsche Zeitung Magazin*, 45, Nov. 2014, 42–57, at 46. [2] Ibid.

in 1978. This development had been an issue of concern to West German Christian and theological circles since the early 1970s: the term 'new youth religions' (*Neue Jugendreligionen*) was used for the first time in a document put out by the Protestant Press Association in Munich in 1974. The Protestant theologian Friedrich-Wilhelm Haack also started his critical research in the 1970s. Until well into the 1980s, authors with a Christian theological background tended to describe the phenomenon as a threat to teenagers and young people, and one which would require serious deprogramming to overcome.[3]

In the historiography of the USA and many Western European countries, the 1970s have been seen quite differently: as a period of crisis;[4] as a crisis and transformation of the work-oriented society (*Arbeitsgesellschaft*);[5] as a decade of transition from modernity to postmodernity;[6] as a contradictory period defying clear definition;[7] as a great shift (*Umbruchsphase*) in Eastern Europe;[8] and as a decade of structural change 'after the boom'.[9] The 'post-boom paradigm' characterizes the recent historiography of the Federal Republic of Germany.[10] Based on the notion of a stable, postwar order

[3] Friedrich-Wilhelm Haack, *Neue Jugendreligionen* (Munich, 1974); id., *Jugendreligionen: Ursachen, Trends, Reaktionen* (Munich, 1977); Johannes R. Gascard, *Neue Jugendreligionen: Zwischen Sehnsucht und Sucht* (Freiburg i.Br., 1984); Daniel Kraus, ' "Jugendreligionen" zwischen Fluch und Segen', *Praxis der Kinderpsychologie und Kinderpsychiatrie*, 48/3 (1999), 192–201.

[4] Frank Bösch (ed.), *A History Shared and Divided: East and West Germany since the 1970s*, trans. by Jennifer Walcoff Neuheiser (New York, 2018), 14; Simon Reid-Henry, *Empire of Democracy: The Remaking of the West since the Cold War, 1971–2017* (New York, 2019), 58 ff.

[5] Lutz Raphael, 'Arbeitsbiografien und Strukturwandel "nach dem Boom": Lebensläufe und Berufserfahrungen britischer, französischer und westdeutscher Industriearbeiter und -arbeiterinnen von 1970 bis 2000', *Geschichte und Gesellschaft*, 43/1 (2017), 32–67.

[6] See Andreas Rödder referring to Jean-François Lyotard in his *Wertewandel und Postmoderne: Gesellschaft und Kultur der Bundesrepublik Deutschland 1965–1990* (Stuttgart, 2004).

[7] Konrad H. Jarausch, 'Krise oder Aufbruch? Historische Annäherungen an die 1970er-Jahre', *Zeithistorische Forschungen/Studies in Contemporary History*, 3/3 (2006), 334–41, at 339.

[8] Claudia Kraft, 'Paradoxien der Emanzipation: Regime, Opposition und Geschlechterordnungen im Staatssozialismus seit den späten 1960er-Jahren', *Zeithistorische Forschungen/Studies in Contemporary History*, 3/3 (2006), 381–400, at 383.

[9] Anselm Doering-Manteuffel and Lutz Raphael, *Nach dem Boom: Perspektiven auf die Zeitgeschichte seit 1970*, 2nd edn. (Göttingen, 2008). See also Anselm Doering-Manteuffel, Lutz Raphael, and Thomas Schlemmer (eds.), *Vorgeschichte der Gegenwart: Dimensionen des Strukturbruchs nach dem Boom* (Göttingen, 2016).

[10] See Doering-Manteuffel and Raphael, *Nach dem Boom*; Doering-Manteuffel,

in West Germany, the structural change of the 1970s has been interpreted mainly from a political and economic perspective. Postwar economic prosperity, an increase in paid holidays, and the availability of new transport technologies from the 1960s had allowed a growing number of people to travel. While the authors of the 'post-boom paradigm' identify religion (among other areas) as a pivotal sphere of structural change,[11] they do not discuss it in detail. Historians such as Arthur Marwick have spoken of the 1960s as a 'cultural revolution' in order to highlight the importance of cultural change. Others have suggested the notion of a 'silent revolution' and the birth of a post-materialist society.[12] However, the transformation of the religious landscape in the 1960s and 1970s has not received much attention in this context.

The growing interest in Eastern wisdom and Buddhist and Hindu traditions fuelled new spiritualities from the 1960s. Religiosity— a vision which blended various religious and spiritual traditions beyond church membership and closed communities of faith— experienced a multifaceted renaissance in the 1970s. The mindsets, agency, and experience of the new religiosities in West Germany in the 1970s were profoundly shaped by a transcultural exchange of knowledge and practices. This essay explores the impact of two Indian gurus who were particularly popular among young adults in the 1960s and 1970s: Maharishi Mahesh Yogi and Bhagwan Shree Rajneesh. I shall argue that the increasing interest in their teachings was not necessarily an expression of postmodern lifestyle choices or a spiritual marketplace for practitioners, but rather reflected new values and forms of religiosity. Many Western followers linked these spiritual practices with emancipatory practices based on 1970s ideals such as 'authenticity', 'spontaneity', 'creativity', and an 'integral life'.[13] These new values were 'conceptions of the desirable',[14] and,

Raphael, and Schlemmer (eds.), *Vorgeschichte der Gegenwart*; Ulrich Herbert, *Geschichte Deutschlands im 20. Jahrhundert* (Munich, 2014), ch. 17, published in English as Ulrich Herbert, *A History of Twentieth-Century Germany*, trans. by Ben Fowkes (Oxford, 2019).

[11] See Doering-Manteuffel and Raphael, *Nach dem Boom*, 12, and Herbert, *Geschichte Deutschlands*, 911.

[12] See Arthur Marwick, *The Sixties: Cultural Revolution in Britain, France, Italy, and the United States, c.1958–c.1974* (London, 1998); Ronald Inglehart, *The Silent Revolution: Changing Values and Political Styles among Western Publics* (Princeton, 1977). For the 1960s as 'cultural revolution' see also Axel Schildt and Detlef Siegfried (eds.), *Between Marx and Coca-Cola: Youth Cultures in Changing European Societies, 1960–1980* (New York, 2005).

[13] See Joachim C. Häberlen, *The Emotional Politics of the Alternative Left: West Germany, 1968–1984* (Cambridge, 2018), 5. These shared values of immediacy and an integral
[See p. 116 for n. 13 cont. and n. 14

for many practitioners, served the purpose of experiencing life beyond the rational Western self.

In the 1960s and 1970s the movements led by Maharishi Mahesh Yogi and Bhagwan Shree Rajneesh gave new youth religiosities popular forms, and were an expression of post-rational values in West Germany. In this essay I shall show, first, that Western encounters with Eastern philosophy, mysticism, and religious notions can be traced back to the late eighteenth and nineteenth centuries. Second, I shall describe the two Indian gurus in the postwar world and show how their teachings led to transnational flows of knowledge and practices as these were appropriated in West Germany. Third, I shall investigate the voices of contemporary critics, insiders, and dropouts who commented on these trends in autobiographical texts and memoirs published between the 1970s and the present day.

I. *Eastern Spirituality in Western Minds*

Western intellectuals who challenged the dominance of Western traditions of rationalism and the Enlightenment discovered Eastern religious ideas and practices long before the 1960s. In Germany, the notion of India as mystical, sublime, and timeless can be traced back to late eighteenth-century linguistics, to German Romanticism, and to discourses on the Orient in the nineteenth century.[15] Buddhism became fashionable among the educated upper classes in Germany in the late nineteenth century.[16] Eastern teachings, religions, and body–mind practices were widespread in both the international theosophical and the *Lebensreform* movements, where they were interpreted in specifically Western terms, and they seemed to promise a way out of a contemporary society driven by efficiency and increasingly ubiquitous technology.[17] In the German-speaking

life are also seen in the linkage between spiritual seekers and alternative milieux in West Germany. See Sven Reichardt, *Authentizität und Gemeinschaft: Linksalternatives Leben in den siebziger und frühen achtziger Jahren*, 2nd edn. (Berlin, 2014), 815.

[14] For an understanding of values see Clyde Kluckhohn, 'Values and Value-Orientations in the Theory of Action: An Exploration in Definition and Classification', in Talcott Parsons and Edward Shils (eds.), *Toward a General Theory of Action* (Cambridge, Mass., 1951), 388–433, at 395.

[15] See Elija Horn, *Indien als Erzieher: Orientalismus in der deutschen Reformpädagogik und Jugendbewegung 1918–1933* (Bad Heilbrunn, 2018), 65 ff.

[16] See Bernd Wedemeyer-Kolwe, *'Der neue Mensch': Körperkultur im Kaiserreich und in der Weimarer Republik* (Würzburg, 2004), 131.

[17] Jan Stottmeister, *Der George-Kreis und die Theosophie, mit einem Exkurs zum Swastika-*

countries around 1900, the burgeoning interest in Asia extended to Indian philosophy, Buddhism, and Hinduism. Contemporaries viewed this increasing interest as a response to a crisis of contemporary culture and a loss of spiritual potential among the Western churches. In the early twentieth century—which saw the beginnings of psychoanalysis—it was first and foremost Carl Gustav Jung who studied Indian philosophy and myths while developing his concept of the self.[18]

Spiritual teachers from Japan and India had found a growing audience in the Western world since the nineteenth century. The first World Parliament of Religions was held in 1893 in Chicago with the ambitious goal of establishing a dialogue between the religions. Among those who stepped onto the stage were the Abbot of Engakuji in Kyoto and his student, Daisetz Teitaro Suzuki (1870–1966). Suzuki was to become one of the most prominent voices of the Zen movement in the West. During the first half of the twentieth century he published numerous essays and books in English which introduced Zen ideals to Western audiences. Suzuki spent eleven years in the United States (1897 to 1908) as an assistant to Paul Carus (1852–1919), a German theologian and philosopher who had emigrated to America. During this period, Suzuki was influenced by contemporary intellectual currents, such as the ideas of the German Protestant theologian Friedrich Schleiermacher (1768–1834), who regarded intuition and feeling as the essence of religion. Suzuki also studied the writings of the American philosopher William James (1842–1910), who argued that non-dualist knowledge acquired via 'pure experience' could overcome the dualism inherent in empiricism.[19]

Another Asian spiritual teacher who also attended the first World Parliament of Religions in Chicago was Swami Vivekananda, a spiritual mediator of Hinduism. He was warmly received in both the

Zeichen bei Helena Blavatsky, Alfred Schuler und Stefan George (Göttingen, 2014), 47–8; Isabel Richter, 'Alternativer Tourismus in den 1960er und 1970er Jahren: Transkulturelle Flows und Resonanzen im 20. Jahrhundert', in Alexander Gallus, Axel Schildt, and Detlef Siegfried (eds.), Deutsche Zeitgeschichte — transnational (Göttingen, 2015), 155–78, at 162; Jared Poley, 'Rudolf Steiner and the Theosophy of Greed', in Joanne Miyang Cho, Eric Kurlander, and Douglas T. McGetchin (eds.), Transcultural Encounters between Germany and India: Kindred Spirits in the Nineteenth and Twentieth Centuries (London, 2014), 55–67.

[18] See Richter, 'Alternativer Tourismus', 161–2.

[19] See Selected Works of D. T. Suzuki, 4 vols. (Berkeley, 2015–), vol. ii: Pure Land, ed. James C. Dobbins (2015), p. xiv.

USA and Europe.[20] In the first third of the twentieth century, Kriya yoga, focusing on meditation and breath control, was additionally introduced to European and American audiences by Paramahansa Yogananda. His following grew steadily after he established the Self-Realization Fellowship in 1920 in Los Angeles. Yogananda's *Autobiography of a Yogi* (1946) became an international postwar bestseller, combining autobiographical reflections with an introduction to Indian philosophical traditions.

II. *Transcultural Flows: Travelling Indian Gurus in the Postwar World*

The increasing interest in Eastern wisdom in the 1970s was nurtured by Western spiritual seekers returning from overland trips to India. Well-known celebrities and travellers to India, such as Ram Dass in 1967 and the Beatles in 1968, introduced wider audiences to Indian spirituality. In addition, the establishment in West Germany of meditation centres connected to Indian gurus who travelled internationally had a significant impact. Maharishi Mahesh Yogi, for instance, who introduced transcendental meditation (TM) to the Western world, began lecture tours in the USA in 1959 and visited West Germany in 1960. The first German TM centre was founded in 1960 in Bonn, followed by a second in Bremen in 1967.[21]

We know little about Maharishi Mahesh Yogi's biography. He was born in 1917 in Madhya Pradesh, a state in central India, and met his guru, Swami Brahmananda Saraswati, a prominent regional leader in Advaitic (non-dualistic) Hinduism, in 1940. Both Mahesh's guru and his parents insisted that he complete a university education before he officially took up a disciple's life in 1941.[22] After his guru's death in 1953, Maharishi Mahesh Yogi embarked on a pilgrimage through India and began to give public lectures. He became a well-known speaker in India, introducing meditation not only to renunciates but to householders, the second (and largest) of

---

[20] See Dorothea Lüddeckens, *Das Weltparlament der Religionen von 1893: Strukturen interreligiöser Begegnung im 19. Jahrhundert* (Berlin, 2002), 186–7; Wedemeyer-Kolwe, 'Der neue Mensch', 141. For the reception in the USA see Philip Goldberg, *American Veda: From Emerson and the Beatles to Yoga and Meditation. How Indian Spirituality Changed the West* (New York, 2010), 70–1.

[21] See Religionswissenschaftlicher Medien- und Informationsdienst e.V. (henceforth REMID) Marburg, 'Kurzinformation Religion: Transzendentale Meditation (TM)' ⟨http://remid.de/info_tm⟩ [accessed 15 June 2020].

[22] Douglas E. Cowan and David G. Bromley, *Cults and New Religions: A Brief History* (Malden, Mass., 2008), 51–2.

the four traditional stages of male Hindu life.[23] His international travel took off in the late 1950s.

By the time the Beatles heard one of his talks in the UK in 1967, Maharishi Mahesh Yogi was already well known in the West. The Canadian Paul Saltzman, who photographed the Beatles in the Maharishi's ashram in Rishikesh, remembers his own introduction to TM. His teacher Raghvendra taught him to repeat a mantra:

> how to say the sound silently, within, and just easily follow it, listen to it until it faded to silence; and how to repeat this until I experienced a transcending of normal waking consciousness. I closed my eyes and tried it for a few minutes and Raghvendra asked me to describe what I was experiencing, to make sure I was using the technique properly.[24]

This account underlines the importance of a guru for the practice of meditation in the late 1960s, but also emphasizes meditation as a practice based on experience. Saltzman's reports and photographs of the Beatles in Rishikesh contributed significantly to the TM boom in many Western countries. By the 1970s, TM had 300,000 followers worldwide.[25]

During that decade, the first introductions to TM were published in English and German.[26] In 1975 West German psychiatrist Jürg Wunderli mentioned, in a comparison of Eastern and Western wisdom, that TM enjoyed great popularity, and he also publicized the positive effects associated with it: destressing, a healthier life, the solution to all problems, and, ultimately, nothing less than bliss.[27] But the strong resonance of TM in particular can probably also be traced back to aspects that Peter Russell praised in his introduction to TM. According to Russell, TM was suitable for everyone from physicians to policemen and housewives, requiring a commitment of only twenty minutes twice a day, and without the need for a long-term relationship with a guru.[28] But TM required an initiation. Only

[23] Ibid. 53.

[24] Paul Saltzman, *The Beatles in Rishikesh* (New York, 2000), 49.

[25] Goldberg, *American Veda*, 168.

[26] See e.g. Harold Bloomfield et al., *Transzendentale Meditation: Lebenskraft aus neuen Quellen* (Düsseldorf, 1976); Bernhard Müller-Elmau, *Kräfte aus der Stille: Die transzendentale Meditation* (Düsseldorf, 1977); Peter Russell, *The TM Technique: An Introduction to Transcendental Meditation and the Teachings of Maharishi Mahesh Yogi* (Boston, 1976).

[27] Jürg Wunderli, *Schritte nach innen: Östliche Meditation und westliche Mystik* (Freiburg i.Br., 1975), 92, 101.

[28] Russell, *The TM Technique*, 15.

certified teachers could teach TM after having completed a standard course of instruction, and fees for this varied from country to country. An advanced meditation practice would typically include the TM-Sidhi programme ('yogic flying') and an alternative healthcare programme called 'Maharishi Ayurveda'. Reliable statistical data on the number of practitioners in West Germany in the 1970s do not exist. Where numbers are given in the secondary literature, they refer to the number of official initiations in TM courses by 1980: 60,000 to 100,000 in West Germany.[29] We do not know, however, how TM was practised, or for how long. Concerning the numbers of followers in Germany, there are discrepancies between the data published by TM centres, which suggest that there were 200,000 practitioners in 2001, and data produced by critics of TM, who estimated that there were only 50,000 followers in the same year.[30]

Maharishi Mahesh Yogi claimed he had rediscovered a form of meditation which could be traced back to one of the classic works of Indian philosophy, the *Yoga Sutras of Patanjali*, compiled some time between 500 BCE and 400 CE.[31] TM also merged the teachings of Krishna, the Buddha, and Shankara, an eighth-century CE Hindu reformer and theologian. Yet TM was introduced in the West neither as neo-Hinduism nor as a religion, but rather as a 'technology of consciousness', supporting practitioners to realize their full mental potential.[32]

Unlike Maharishi Mahesh Yogi, Bhagwan Shree Rajneesh did not travel extensively in the 1970s. The Rajneesh movement is therefore a good example of transcultural flows of knowledge and practices. Rajneesh was born in 1931 as Chandra Mohan Jain in Madhya Pradesh. He studied philosophy and worked as an editor for a local newspaper before he started to teach philosophy at the Sanskrit College in Raipur and became a public speaker. He moved to Mumbai in 1970, where he gave lectures and began to receive Indian and international guests in his residence. After adopting the title 'Bhag-

[29] Reinhard Hummel, *Indische Mission und neue Frömmigkeit im Westen: Religiöse Bewegungen Indiens in westlichen Kulturen* (Mainz, 1980), 97. The origin of this number is not footnoted and remains unclear.

[30] REMID, 'Kurzinformation Religion'; for the varying data and estimates in West Germany see also James A. Beckford (ed.), *New Religious Movements and Rapid Social Change* (London, 1986), 250.

[31] For the ongoing debate among scholars over how to date the *Yoga Sutras* see David Gordon White, *The Yoga Sutra of Patanjali: A Biography* (Princeton, 2014), ch. 13.

[32] Cowan and Bromley, *Cults and New Religions*, 54.

wan Shree Rajneesh' in 1971, he moved to his first ashram in Pune in 1971 with a small group of disciples.[33]

Rajneesh's meditation technique, labelled 'dynamic meditation', was especially suited to a Western audience. It reached West Germany in the late 1970s. Rajneesh's devotees stood out, and not only because of their orange clothes. From Berlin to Wiesbaden they were popular with young people for their hip dance clubs, which provoked some journalists to speak of a veritable 'red flood'.[34] Rajneesh's meditation, developed especially for Western practitioners, quickly became popular in West Germany. His interpretation of dynamic Kundalini meditation foregrounded physical activity. In four stages lasting fifteen minutes each, shaking the body was followed by dancing, meditation, and stillness.[35] Rajneesh justified this method with reference to the basic constitution of humans, which he saw as deeply neurotic. He appreciated other techniques such as Zen meditation or TM and admitted their benefits up to a certain point. But in his version of 'dynamic' or 'chaotic' meditation, release, liberation, purification, and transformation were the key elements.[36]

Rajneesh's teachings have been described as a synthesis of Indian traditions and religiosity, Tantrism, Western esotericism, and practices common in humanistic psychology and the human potential movement. Humanistic psychology was a postwar development in reaction to the perceived limits of Freudian psychoanalysis or Burrhus Frederic Skinner's behaviourism. Its proponents, such as Carl Rogers and Abraham Maslow, rejected the view that behaviour was determined by one's childhood, and encouraged patients' capacity to grow, with the goal of self-fulfilment by removing obstacles and through change in the present. The Esalen Institute founded in 1962 in Big Sur, California, was a hub of the human potential movement in the 1960s. Fritz Perls, who coined the term 'gestalt therapy' and practised in Esalen in the 1960s, deliberately refrained from analysing his patients' past, which he regarded as an unnecessary rationalization and described as 'mind-fucking'.[37] Sensory awareness beyond mere mind-centred perceptions, altered states of consciousness,

[33] Hummel, *Indische Mission*, 221; Hugh B. Urban, *Zorba the Buddha: Sex, Spirituality, and Capitalism in the Global Osho Movement* (Oakland, Calif., 2015), 58.

[34] See 'Bhagwan: Glaube und Mammon', *Der Spiegel*, 5 Feb. 1984.

[35] Bhagwan Shree Rajneesh, *Meditation: The Art of Ecstasy*, ed. Ma Satya Bharti (New York, 1976), 233–4.   [36] Ibid. 26 ff.

[37] Frederick S. Perls, *Gestalt Therapy Verbatim*, compiled and ed. by John O. Stevens (Lafayette, Calif., 1969), 158.

acceptance of oneself and others, spontaneity, identification with humanity, democratic values, and creativity were highly valued ideals within self-exploration settings during the 1960s and 1970s.[38]

These principles of person-centred therapy were also adapted to create a group model. The goal of encounter groups in the 1960s was for members to perceive each other in 'authentic ways', to experience 'genuine' inner feelings, and to develop honest relationships. Carl Rogers, an early proponent of encounter groups in the USA, called for a group leader to act as a non-authoritarian facilitator, creating a non-threatening atmosphere for group members. In 1978 *Time Magazine* dubbed Rajneesh's ashram 'Esalen East' because he started to adapt his programme after being visited by 'graduates of the "human potential" movement' and Esalen 'experts' in the 1970s.[39] The exploration of altered states of consciousness, a devaluation of rationality, mind, and intellect, and an increased focus on personal growth and transformation linked humanistic psychology and counter-cultural psychedelic explorations to meditation and notions of an awakened consciousness in neo-Hinduism in the 1960s and 1970s. In Rajneesh's ashram in Pune, the daily schedule included dynamic meditation, talks by Rajneesh, and work assignments. The Indian ashram was also popular because of its encounter groups and the free sexuality it promoted.[40] Rajneesh's followers, the sannyasins, also opened centres in many major cities in West Germany. The ashram in Freiburg, for instance, started with fifty members. By 1982 it had eighty inhabitants and included a doctor's practice, a carpenter's workshop, and a bakery. It also produced food and sold its produce at the local farmers' market.[41] Other centres in West Germany ran restaurants and popular dance venues.

III. *Critical Voices*

Some critics embraced and welcomed these changes in the religious landscape during the 1970s. Others spotlighted the shortcomings,

---

[38] See Jeffrey J. Kripal, *Esalen: America and the Religion of No Religion* (Chicago, 2007), ch. 7.

[39] '"God Sir" at Esalen East', *Time Magazine*, 16 Jan. 1978, 59.

[40] See e.g. Michaelsen, 'Man denkt an mich, also bin ich', 46–7; Hugh Milne, *Bhagwan: The God that Failed* (London, 1986), 151–2, 159.

[41] Ralf Strittmatter, 'Als die Sannyasins nach Freiburg kam', *Badische Zeitung*, 11 Feb. 2018 〈[http://www.badische-zeitung.de/suedwest-1/als-die-sannyasins-nach-freiburg-kam-149241373.html〉 [accessed 30 July 2021].

and contributed to the ambivalent reception which these ways of searching for meaning received in the 1970s. The Beatles doubtless stimulated the boom in transcendental meditation. The group's stay in Maharishi Mahesh Yogi's ashram in Rishikesh in 1968 encouraged some of their fans to try TM. George Harrison praised the meditative high:

> We can have anything that money can buy. And all the fame we could dream of. And then what? It isn't love. It isn't health. It isn't peace inside . . . Meditation and the Maharishi have helped make the inner life rich for me. I get higher than I ever did with drugs.[42]

Whereas George Harrison was attracted by the way in which TM helped its practitioners to turn away from the material world and achieve a high without drugs, John Lennon valued the religious openness of TM teachings. According to Lennon, the practitioners' religious background was not an issue in the ashram: 'You can make it with meditation if you're a Christian, a Mohammedan or a Jew. You just add meditation to whatever religion you've got.'[43]

The British philosopher and former Anglican priest Alan Watts, who had experimented with LSD and later popularized Eastern wisdom for a mainly Western audience (including a German one) from the 1960s, also advocated meditation. He did not favour any specific Eastern tradition in his 1971 introduction to meditation, however, when he recommended going 'out of your mind at least once a day . . . because by going out of your mind, you come to your senses'. Alan Watts compared an overly rational existence to 'a very rigid bridge which because it has got no give, no craziness in it, is going to be blown down in the first hurricane.'[44] For Watts, meditation meant getting in touch with a reality beyond the world of symbols and representations. Similarly, as we saw, Peter Sloterdijk highlighted the crucial change in his attitude towards rationality after staying in Rajneesh's ashram in the 1970s. Sloterdijk recalled that his experiences in the ashram triggered a process which he characterized as the Eastern expansion of consciousness ('die Osterweiterung der

---

[42] Paul Saltzman, *The Beatles in Rishikesh* (New York 2000), 98.

[43] Keith Badman, *The Beatles off the Record* (London, 2000), quoted from Goldberg, *American Veda*, 152.

[44] Alan Watts, 'Meditation: Introduction to a Contemplative Ritual', NYC, 1971 ⟨https://drive.google.com/open?id=1aRHOq-lS5oX3nRGdTgQRpg_YfP7–otWj⟩ [accessed 15 Oct. 2019].

Vernunft'), making him feel an intense, profound exhilaration and relieving him of the depression of his generation.[45]

The negative coverage around youth religions started in the late 1970s, when most of the German popular magazines published series on the murder-suicides by more than 900 members of the Peoples Temple movement in its jungle commune in Guyana in 1978.[46] The Protestant theologian Friedrich-Wilhelm Haack, a critic since the early 1970s, pointed out that followers of the new youth religions were usually educated, intellectually open-minded, and socially motivated teenagers and young adults. He diagnosed the loss of a feeling of belonging and of security (*Geborgenheitsverlust*), angst about the future, and performance pressure as key motives for their receptiveness to new religious movements. Haack mentioned youth religions and dropping out in the same breath as alternative political movements, terrorism, drugs, counter-culture, and hippie communes.[47] According to Haack, these groups and movements were so attractive because they offered a strong sense of belonging, a sense of a future beyond capitalist careers, and the achievement of the followers' goals and aspirations. Haack saw the specific danger presented by youth religions as lying in the threat of personality changes. But he also pointed to the loss of a mainstream, middle-class life for young adults who had quit their jobs and apprenticeships, experienced the loss of relationships, abandoned private property, and sometimes descended into a life of crime.[48]

Until well into the 1980s, authors with a Christian theological background continued to describe the phenomenon as posing a threat to teenagers and young adults who might be lost for ever to what Johannes Gascard called the 'gluttony of the soul' ('Freßsucht der Seele'), which required serious 'deprogramming'.[49] Other voices emphasized the neo-liberal structures of many youth religions. While in the late 1970s and early 1980s magazines and newspapers such as *Der Spiegel* and *Bild* identified Rajneesh as a 'sex guru' and head of a 'sex monastery' in Pune, academic papers drew attention to his pronounced sense of profit. He was said to be a yogi who knew how to blend his spiritual offerings with late twentieth-century capitalism

---

[45] Michaelsen, 'Man denkt an mich, also bin ich', 46.

[46] Jeff Guinn, *The Road to Jonestown: Jim Jones and Peoples Temple* (New York, 2017).

[47] Haack, *Jugendreligionen*, 71, 75.   [48] Ibid. 42, 57.

[49] Haack, *Neue Jugendreligionen*; id., *Jugendreligionen*; Gascard, *Neue Jugendreligionen*; Kraus, '"Jugendreligionen" zwischen Fluch und Segen'.

and who, time and again, was able to adapt his range of practices as products to changing customer preferences.[50]

After a while, dropouts and meditation teachers who had left the scene added their voices to the chorus of criticism. Hugh Milne had lived in Rajneesh's entourage since 1973, worked as his bodyguard, and, having grown disillusioned, left the guru in 1982. He wrote in 1986 that Rajneesh's central goal from the late 1970s was economic success.[51] Former TM teacher Joe Kellett raised the issue of the TM movement taking advantage of people's psychological vulnerabilities. In 1980 some German former teachers of TM reflected critically on their meditation practices. Therese Schulte, for instance, mainly criticized the TM movement's market structure, but she also found totalitarian echoes in TM courses and noted the lack of freedom of speech.[52] Finally, autobiographies and self-narratives focused on sexism and sexual harassment:

'It was typical of the group leaders that they would pick out which woman they wanted, then lock the door after the rest of the group left and get it on with whomever they wanted to', says ex-Rajneesh disciple Roselyn Smith. 'Group leaders got lots of sex. In fact, the guys on the outside, who worked in other parts of the ashram, would call the group leaders the "pussy pool." They were the guys who had all the fun. There was tremendous sexism going on there, yet they tried to make you believe that because Rajneesh was picking women to run all those departments he really believes in liberated women.'[53]

It docs not come as a surprise that dropouts who published their experiences drew rather critical conclusions. There is some evidence that gender played an important role in communities of new religiosities, but the role of gender as a tool of self-realization in sexuality undoubtedly needs further research.

[50] See '"Die liebende Gabe, die mich durchdringt": Spiegel-Reporter Willhelm Bittorf über den Ashram in Poona und die Suche nach östlicher Weisheit', *Der Spiegel*, 8 Mar. 1981; Hugh B. Urban, 'Osho, from Sex Guru to Guru of the Rich: The Spiritual Logic of Late Capitalism', in Thomas A. Forsthoefel and Cynthia Ann Humes (eds.), *Gurus in America* (Albany, NY, 2005), 169–92.   [51] See Milne, *Bhagwan*, 246.

[52] See Therese Schulte, *Transzendentale Meditation und wohin sie führt: Abschiedsdisput einer TM-Lehrerin* (Stuttgart, 1980), 154, 237–8, 240–1; Joe Kellett, '"Falling down the TM Rabbit Hole": How Transcendental Meditation Really Works. A Critical Opinion' ⟨http://www.suggestibility.org⟩ [accessed 14 June 2020]; Ulrike Schrott, *Maharishi Good Bye* (Salzburg, 2010); Claire Hoffman, *Greetings from Utopia Park: Surviving a Transcendent Childhood* (New York, 2016); Joel Kramer and Diana Alstad, *The Guru Papers: Masks of Authoritarian Power* (Berkeley, 1993).

[53] Win McCormack, 'Bhagwan's Sexism: Rajneesh's Dirty Work was Usually Left to Women', *The New Republic*, 12 Apr. 2018 ⟨https://newrepublic.com/article/147871/bhagwans-sexism⟩ [accessed 30 July 2021].

IV. *Conclusion*

Historicizing the 1970s in West Germany means taking a closer look at religion and religiosities and their transnational dimensions. It is certainly possible to interpret the Rajneesh and TM movements as lucrative business models launched by Indian gurus and their followers in the 1970s. This essay has focused on these two movements as popular forms of new youth religiosities and expressions of post-rational values in West Germany. First and foremost, the practices and attitudes of their devotees were associated with post-rational ideals. Experiences going beyond the perceived rational self were crucial in the 1970s because exploring and transcending the self in meditation was linked with the hope of ending alienation and the Western notion of the detachment of body and mind. TM and the Rajneesh movement resonated particularly strongly with educated, young, and counter-cultural milieux. Ideals linked to meditation in the 1970s, such as 'destressing', an 'integral life', and 'authenticity', reflected the counter-cultural roots of Rajneesh's and Maharishi Mahesh Yogi's early followers. Activists in the West German alternative left of the 1970s, in particular, tried to transform themselves by means of emotional practices. Their political imagination was shaped by a specific understanding of rationality and its questionable status. From their point of view, the power of rationality was based on the ability to categorize and separate. As they saw it, this rationality was 'cold', 'technical', 'bureaucratic', divided people, and made 'authentic' personal connection with others impossible.[54] But as the many introductions to meditation published in the 1970s show, TM and the Rajneesh movement also gained popularity beyond the counter-cultures.

Maharishi Mahesh Yogi's TM and Rajneesh's teachings blended different religious traditions and, in the case of Rajneesh, added Western therapeutic approaches to a philosophy of self-realization. Both movements were expressions of a trend that started in the late 1960s and established a specific form of religiosity: a vision which blended various religious and spiritual traditions beyond church membership and closed communities of faith, and a religious bricolage that allowed practitioners to choose spiritual practices and communities without a prescribed set of religious traditions. Many

---

[54] See Häberlen, *Emotional Politics*, 78.

scholars associate the expression 'spiritual but not religious' with do-it-yourself and pick-and-mix religion, a spiritual marketplace, believing without belonging, religion as long as it is personally useful, and the 'self-technologies' that started the wellness industry.[55] Others point to the spread of post-Christian spirituality and a 'spiritual turn', or a 'religion of no religion'. Be it Esalen as the epicentre of body–mind explorations since the 1960s, the spread of post-Christianity since the 1980s in Western European countries and the USA, or the sacralization of the self,[56] there is no question that a considerable erosion of church-based religion took place 'after the boom'.[57] This is not intended to construct a direct link between West Germans leaving the Christian churches and the rise of new religious movements during the 1970s. However, the promise of individual happiness and liberation resonated with many young people who were tired of obeying the moral laws of

[55] See Wade Clark Roof, *Spiritual Marketplace: Baby Boomers and the Remaking of American Religion* (Princeton, 1999); David Lyon, *Jesus in Disneyland: Religion in Postmodern Times* (Cambridge, 2000); Adam Possamai, 'Alternative Spiritualities and the Cultural Logic of Late Capitalism', *Culture and Religion*, 4/1 (2003), 31–45; Maik Tändler, *Das therapeutische Jahrzehnt: Der Psychoboom in den siebziger Jahren* (Göttingen, 2016), 360. For an overview of the recent literature on the phrase 'spiritual but not religious' see also Tuhina Ganguly, 'Connecting their Selves: The Discourse of Karma, Calling, and Surrendering among Western Spiritual Practitioners in India', *Journal of the American Academy of Religion*, 86/4 (2018), 1014–45, at 1015 ff.

[56] See Kripal, *Esalen*; for a statistical analysis from the 1980s, including Germany and the USA, see Dick Houtman and Stef Aupers, 'The Spiritual Turn and the Decline of Tradition: The Spread of Post-Christian Spirituality in 14 Western Countries, 1981–2000', *Journal for the Scientific Study of Religion*, 46/3 (2007), 305–20, at 310; Pascal Eitler, '"Selbstheilung": Zur Somatisierung und Sakralisierung von Selbstverhältnissen im New Age (Westdeutschland 1970–1990)', in Sabine Maassen, Jens Elberfeld, Pascal Eitler, et al. (eds.), *Das beratene Selbst: Zur Genealogie der Therapeutisierung in den 'langen' Siebzigern* (Bielefeld, 2011), 161–81.

[57] See Thomas Großbölting, *Losing Heaven: Religion in Germany since 1945*, trans. from the German by Alex Skinner (New York, 2017), 106 ff. See also Martin Greschat, 'Protestantismus und Evangelische Kirche', in Axel Schildt, Detlef Siegfried, and Karl Christian Lammers (eds.), *Dynamische Zeiten: Die 6oer Jahre in den beiden deutschen Gesellschaften* (Hamburg, 2000), 544–81, at 546 ff.; Karl Gabriel, 'Zwischen Aufbruch und Absturz', ibid. 528–43, at 537; Benjamin Ziemann, 'Religion and the Search for Meaning, 1945–1990', in Helmut Walser Smith (ed.), *The Oxford Handbook of Modern German History* (Oxford, 2011), 693–714, at 694, 706. Some authors foreground not the erosion process, but a profound transformation of the Catholic Church in the FRG which came with the increasing application of social science knowledge; see Benjamin Ziemann, *Encounters with Modernity: The Catholic Church in West Germany, 1945–1975*, trans. from the German by Andrew Evans (New York, 2014). On new departures in teaching in disciplines such as political theology and liberation theology, and the rise of evangelical fundamentalism within the Catholic and Protestant churches, see also Ziemann, 'Religion', 700.

the Judaeo-Christian tradition, which had lost its credibility for many young people in West Germany after the Second World War and Vietnam. TM and the Rajneesh movement were not among the anti-authoritarian movements of the 1970s. Instead of looking to Western religious authorities, people sought new and different spiritual authorities, such as gurus. The new religiosities could be group-oriented like the Rajneesh movement, but they related primarily to the body–mind, to action, and, above all, to the experiences of the practitioners. Their followers questioned not authority as such, but the authority of detached rationality.

I am not dismissing the many who continued to frequent traditional Christian churches and synagogues at this time. Even vague estimates of 60,000 to 100,000 TM initiations in 1980 indicate that TM practitioners were still a minority compared with those who attended Christian services. But to what extent did minorities and practitioners at the margins of contemporary religiosities provide insights into value and attitude shifts in the 1970s? Several aspects come into play: ideals linked to the new religiosities were based on experiential spirituality instead of looking for moral authority in God and Scripture. The Rajneesh movement in particular offered body-centred practices which promised popular new key features such as spontaneity, creativity, authenticity, and an integral life. Challenging rationality and the intellectual mind as technical, cold, and detached, new youth religions promoted a melange of different Eastern spiritual traditions and therapeutic settings, promising healing for the rigid and stressed Western body–mind. These trends are unimaginable without the transcultural flows of knowledge and experience of the 1960s and 1970s, and they gained momentum on the margins not only of West German society, but also in India and the US counter-culture. Furthermore, new youth religions also drew attention to the angst of the majority. From the late 1970s, social science researchers and mainstream media increasingly perceived new youth religions such as TM and the Rajneesh movement as a threat to the nuclear family, prosperity, and mental health. And although they were minority pursuits, they were considered to be serious temptations for young people in general.

It is interesting to note that both movements have undergone a transformation since the 1980s. Neither has established itself as a mainstream religious group, but both still exist as communities offering healing and an integral life. Although some core members still 'explicitly interpret their engagement with the group religiously', TM centres offer meditation courses and Ayurvedic treatments which are not generally perceived as spiritual practices today.[58] Rajneesh left India in 1981, founded Rajneeshpuram, a religious intentional community in Wasco County, Oregon, and renamed himself Bhagwan Shree Rajneesh in the 1980s. Allegations of criminal activities in the commune and immigration fraud forced him to leave the USA in 1985. He returned to India as Osho and died in Pune in 1990. While few people identify as Osho-followers in the early twenty-first century, dynamic meditation is still a highly popular practice offered in yoga studios, workshops, and by many hospitals treating psychosomatic disorders.[59] The 'gluttony of the soul' which so alarmed the contemporaries of the 1970s has left only feeble echoes in today's world.

[58] Mikael Rothstein, *Belief Transformations: Some Aspects of the Relation between Science and Religion in Transcendental Meditation (TM) and the International Society for Krishna Consciousness (ISKCON)* (Aarhus, 1996), 34; Dorothea Lüddeckens and Rafael Walthert, 'Das Ende der Gemeinschaft? Neue religiöse Bewegungen im Wandel', in eid. (eds.), *Fluide Religion: Neue religiöse Bewegungen im Wandel. Theoretische und empirische Systematisierungen* (Bielefeld, 2010), 19–54, at 33.

[59] Lüddeckens and Walthert, 'Das Ende der Gemeinschaft?, 31.

6

Goodbye Reforms, Hello *Kaif*: The Shift from Intellectual Dissent to a Nonconformism of Feeling(s) in the Later Soviet Union

Juliane Fürst

In 1933, shortly after Hitler had taken power in Germany, a group of Leningrad students sat down to formulate their political thoughts. Under the name Youth Organization of Internationalists, Communists, and Socialists they wrote down six central criticisms of the Stalinist system, including one in which they mused about the relative evils of fascism and Stalinism.[1] The students were arrested for this 'crime' in 1938, at the height of the purges, and are not likely to have survived. They disappeared into the bowels of Stalinist terror. We know about them only because one of their successors in the political underground dug out their documents from the St Petersburg Party archives for his study of dissent against the Soviet regime. Veniamin Iofe, then head of the St Petersburg section of the human rights organization Memorial, had also been a member of an underground youth collective that criticized Soviet reality and politics, albeit thirty years later, in the early 1960s. His group, operating under the name Kolokol (Russian for 'bell' and a reference to Alexander Herzen's nineteenth-century newspaper of the same name), was part of a broader wave of what Iofe was to define as 'neo-Leninist dissent'. Like their prewar peers, Iofe and his fellow dissenters were convinced of the primacy of words as identifiers and creators of culture. Yet this was no longer the ideologically

I would like to thank several colleagues who responded to a call for comments on the idea of an 'emotional change', pointed me towards rereadings, and encouraged or disagreed with my working assumption: Jan Behrends, David Brandenberger, Jonathan Brunstedt, Johanna Conterio Geisler, Anna Fishzon, Mischa Gabowitsch, Catriona Kelly, Lisa Kirschenbaum, Anatoly Pinsky, Serguei Oushakine, Alexander Titov, Josephine von Zitzewitz, and Zbigniew Wojnowski.

[1] Veniamin Iofe, *Novye etiudy ob optimizme* (St Petersburg, 1998), 46.

charged world of the 1930s. A closer look at the environment in which the young zealots of Kolokol were operating reveals that youth opposition had diversified. In their first incarnation as a Komsomol patrol group in the late 1950s, the future members of Kolokol had hunted down so-called *stiliagi*—a kind of Soviet Teddy Boys. The very existence of this subculture was an indication that 'wordy' reform programmes were on their way out and style was on its way in. *Stiliagi* were youngsters who defined themselves through a love of music and fashion. Iofe and his friends had initially despised them for their superficiality, but over time had to concede that freedom was not served by persecuting them, or anyone else—a fact which ultimately turned the members of Kolokol from extra-loyal citizens of the Soviet state into fierce critics.[2]

By the time Iofe wrote his study of Soviet opposition, the Soviet Union was no more. To a certain extent it looked as if people like him, who had called for 'our and your freedom', had won.[3] He published his work at the tail end of the 1990s—a decade rich in revelations from the archives, including evidence of several dozen underground opposition groups. Iofe concluded that he and his friends had come up with essentially the same ideas and demands as countless other 'other-thinkers' (from the Russian *inokomyslaiushchie*) had done before them. More often than not, Soviet political dissidence drew on the same language and thought processes as official rhetoric. Unkindly labelled 'terrifying mimicry' of the Soviet system by one scholar, these texts were nonetheless written at high personal risk, since even small deviations from the political norm continued to be punished harshly even in post-Stalin times.[4] But it was already clear that the downfall of the USSR was not the outcome of this intellectual struggle between Soviet leaders and their ideological critics. Rather, one could argue that the last decades of the Soviet

---

[2] Valerii Ronkin, *Na smenu dekabriam prikhodiat ianvari* (Moscow, 2003); Iofe, *Novye etiudy*, 97–106.

[3] Slogan adopted by the Soviet-era human rights movement spearheaded by, among others, Andrei Sakharov, Ludmila Alexeeva, and Yuri Orlov. See Joshua Rubenstein, *Soviet Dissidents: Their Struggle for Human Rights* (London, 1981); Barbara Martin, *Dissident Histories in the Soviet Union: From De-Stalinization to Perestroika* (London, 2019).

[4] Serguei Oushakine, 'The Terrifying Mimicry of Samizdat', *Public Culture*, 13/2 (2001), 191–214; Liudmila Alexeeva, *Istoriia inakomysliia v SSSR* (Moscow, 2001); Erik Kulavig, *Dissent in the Years of Khrushchev: Ten Stories about Disobedient Russians* (Basingstoke, 2002); Benjamin Nathans, 'Talking Fish: On Soviet Dissident Memoirs', *Journal of Modern History*, 87/3 (2015), 579–614; Juliane Fürst, 'Prisoners of the Soviet Self? Political Youth Opposition in Late Stalinism', *Europe–Asia Studies*, 54/3 (2002), 353–75.

Union were permeated by emotional disagreements—not in the sense that emotions ran very high, although they did in the very last years, but more in the sense that people had started to express their views through emotions. Identity was increasingly defined by how they related emotionally—rather than ideologically—to the system in which they lived. Or indeed how they did *not* relate emotionally to the system. One of the defining pictures of the last few Soviet years is the overcrowded Luzhniki Stadium in Moscow in 1988, where over 100,000 young people listened to Viktor Tsoi and his band Kino sing 'we want change' (literally 'we wait for change'—*my zhdem peremen*). This change was not presented in the form of an ideological programme or a political flyer. It was not an intellectual argument that rumbled through the stadium. It was a 'feel'—a feel that united a large number of people in a community of coolness, otherness, and a vague sense of defiance.

Clearly, something significant had changed when Tsoi's lines became the anthem of perestroika. Possibly, this change consisted precisely in the fact that so many people felt that nothing had changed and nothing was ever going to change—expressed later by one of the most eloquent representatives of the last Soviet generation, Alexei Yurchak, as *Everything was Forever, Until It Was No More*. Historical analysis has pointed to change even in the years that became known as *zastoi*, or stagnation.[5] Yet there is ample evidence that Soviet people *felt* the inertia, the repetition, the predictability of Soviet life. They felt both secure and bored by Brezhnev's 'little deal' with them.[6] They judged the system of which they were part by how it made them *feel* rather than by the finer points of political debate. And it was this feeling that made people go out and demand change when perestroika and glasnost allowed them to do so. The Soviet people abandoned the Soviet project because of a sense of ennui, desperation, anger, and disillusionment, as well as one of adventure, hope, and enthusiasm for something new or different. Whatever it was, it was more often than not expressed via a terminology of sense, feelings, and affect. Change, freedom, equality, justice, and conscience were all terms that were loaded with emotions. Gorbachev had started an intellectual argument about reform (an

---

[5] Alexei Yurchak, *Everything was Forever, Until it was No More: The Last Soviet Generation* (Princeton, 2006); Dina Fainberg and Artemy M. Kalinovsky (eds.), *Reconsidering Stagnation in the Brezhnev Era: Ideology and Exchange* (Lanham, Md., 2016).

[6] James R. Millar, 'The Little Deal: Brezhnev's Contribution to Acquisitive Socialism', *Slavic Review*, 44/4 (1985), 694–706.

approach he had learnt during his own socialization at the time of Khrushchev's Thaw) and was met by an emotional tsunami that swept him and the Soviet Union away.

This essay will argue that this emotional tsunami gathered force as a paradigm change at some point in the long 1970s. It will claim that the use of vocabulary of 'feelings' to express dissidence and nonconformism was the consequence of a shift in emotional regimes throughout Soviet society, including in the field of official propaganda and rhetoric. The entire Soviet discursive field moved towards a more subjective, more sensual, and more affective rhetoric emphasizing well-being and 'mindfulness' from about the mid 1960s onwards. This does not mean that there were no emotional ties between the Soviet system and citizenry before this period. On the contrary, Stalinism relied heavily on the affective powers of the leader and his cult.[7] Nonetheless, there was a qualitative difference. The sheer extent to which escapist and (at first sight) non-political practices were embraced by the Soviet population, and especially the younger generation, as a mechanism for negating the Soviet system was a hallmark of late socialism. Popular disappointment with the mostly empty promises of the Thaw era facilitated a shift in emphasis away from a dissenting discourse framed in (usually socialist) political vocabulary to one that privileged expressions, practices, and images belonging to the realm of 'feel'. Renewed repression of political 'other-thinkers' under Brezhnev also channelled—by sheer necessity and for reasons of prudence and self-preservation—dissent away from the political arena. This might not have been a conscious decision, but it was simply less dangerous to break the norm by feeling excited about the Beatles than by writing an alternative Party programme, even though both these things went straight to the heart of the Soviet system. In youth slang, the positive vibes of a feeling outside the official canon became known as *kaif*—a term derived from Arabic which is best translated as pleasure, but whose multilayered meanings are hard to capture in a single word. *Kaif* signalled both cultural opposition and evasion; pleasure and purpose; mysticism and consumption; ecstatic 'highs' and tranquil 'downs'. And the rapid rise to popularity of the term *kaif*—it was abso-

---

[7] On the use and importance of emotions see e.g. Jan Plamper, *The Stalin Cult: A Study in the Alchemy of Power* (New Haven, 2012); Malte Rolf, *Das sowjetische Massenfest* (Hamburg, 2006); and Sheila Fitzpatrick, 'Happiness and *Toska*: An Essay in the History of Emotions in Pre-War Soviet Russia', *Australian Journal of Politics & History*, 50/3 (2004), 357–71.

lutely ubiquitous in the 1980s, having been almost unknown in the 1960s—is already an indication of the extent to which Soviet youth identity, and hence implicitly Soviet youth protest, had changed in the meantime.[8]

While there was an inherently Soviet logic to the paradigm shift from reforms to *kaif*, it was also spurred on by a wave of global events and phenomena that altered the way in which protests were enacted and expressed in this period. The counter-culture and protest movements of the 1960s and 1970s were only partially underpinned by political and intellectual ideology. A significant part of them relied on emotional tropes such as hope (most prominent in the rhetoric of the civil rights movement), love, harmony, and peace (as propagated by the hippie culture), as well as anger and hate, which propelled the more radical and terrorist offshoots of the 1960s protest movement. The primacy of feeling even 'emotionalized' the political causes and texts which had high currency in those years, such as Mao's *Little Red Book*, opposition to the Vietnam War, or the civil rights movement.[9] Again, this is not to say that programmatic statements such as the one written by the Leningrad students in 1933 entirely disappeared from the scene in the long 1970s. The New Left had many detailed written programmes in its arsenal, both globally and in the Soviet Union.[10] But somehow, even here, the politics of feeling could not be ignored as part of the discourse—not least because forms of protest had diversified significantly and lifestyle choices had become part and parcel of political opposition.[11] Sitting, singing, chanting, tripping, and even just listening to music or living communally were now part of the canon of dissent. Protest became as much about what one felt as about what one thought (fully realizing that the two cannot be read separately, but mutually conditioned each other).

[8] Aleksandr Fain and V. Lur'e, *Vse v kaif!* (n.p., 1991); Nancy Traver, *Kife: The Lives and Dreams of Soviet Youth* (New York, 1989).

[9] For discussions on the nexus between political protest and emotions see (among many) Alexander C. Cook (ed.), *Mao's Little Red Book: A Global History* (Cambridge, 2014); Joachim C. Häberlen, Mark Keck-Szajbel, and Kate Mahoney (eds.), *The Politics of Authenticity: Countercultures and Radical Movements across the Iron Curtain, 1968–1989* (New York, 2019); Robert Gildea, James Mark, and Anette Warring (eds.), *Europe's 1968: Voices of Revolt* (Oxford, 2013); and James M. Jasper, *The Emotions of Protest* (Chicago, 2018).

[10] Van Gosse, *Rethinking the New Left: An Interpretative History* (New York, 2005).

[11] For the West, see (among others) Joachim C. Häberlen, *The Emotional Politics of the Alternative Left: West Germany, 1968–1984* (Cambridge, 2018); Jasper, *The Emotions of Protest*; and Anna von der Goltz, *The Other '68ers: Student Protest and Christian Democracy in West Germany* (Oxford, 2021)

Expressing dissent was now done by mobilizing the senses—the emotional ones as much as the physical, the intellectual, and the instinctive. I deliberately use the nebulous term 'feel' to describe this new sensuality, because it is more comprehensive than 'emotion' and closer to the kinds of words that 1970s youths would have used themselves.

When attempting to make such a large and sweeping argument, some caveats are appropriate. First of all, shifting paradigms are a messy affair and never absolute. Shifts are not the equivalent of breaks and are rarely linear. There are numerous counter-examples to my claim that protest and dissidence acquired more emotionally connotated instruments of expression. The most obvious example has already been cited in the first paragraphs of this essay: Gorbachev's reform programme was a throwback to the very earnest statements of the so-called *shestidesiatniki* (literally 'sixties generation', referring to people who had been committed to the ideas and culture of the Thaw as young adults). His ideas were picked up not only by state and Party representatives, but also by ordinary people across the Soviet Union, demonstrating that the hope for political and cultural reforms had not been entirely replaced by the quest for *kaif*. Second, the specific details of perestroika reform never figured as prominently among young people as the 'feel' of liberation and change that they embodied, since their impact was often experienced on an affective level in this societal stratum. Third, looking at dissent goes hand in hand with a certain focus on the intelligentsia, since it was always the urban, educated classes who set the tone in the Soviet Union with respect to nonconformist discourse. And one final caveat: all of this is written with the Soviet heartlands in mind. It goes without saying that every region, every periphery, and every ethnic or religious minority had its own specific discursive fields, which at times ran parallel to the trends outlined above, and at times eclipsed them.

I. *From Reforms to Rock*

Veniamin Iofe's underground organization Kolokol was a last outpost of what was once a very powerful trend. Its members' transformation from earnest, faithful Soviet citizens who wanted to change their country for the better by patrolling the streets in the name of public order into earnest, dissenting Soviet citizens who wanted to change their country for the better by publishing political pamphlets was, as Iofe himself observed, the classic path taken from the 1930s to the 1960s. The members were also classic in their composition—educated young people, often the children of intelligentsia, with a disproportionate percentage of Jewish members. They fitted neatly into Yuri Slezkine's outline of the Jewish relationship with the Soviet project, following a trajectory from shared aspirations for education and change and ending in divisive disappointment and discrimination. Their mode of dissent was one they had learnt from the system they wanted to reform: logical argumentation on the basis of Marxist, class-based thinking, revolving around the terms 'equality' and 'freedom'. It would be untrue to claim that similar groups from similar backgrounds did not also come into existence later on. Indeed, in the mid 1970s another politically aware student group was active in Leningrad's youth scene—one whose members also had a past as activists in the official Soviet system and were made up of the Jewish intelligentsia. Andrei Reznikov, Arkadii Tsurkov, Aleksandr Skobov, and their female companions and helpers Irina Flige and Irina Lopotukhina were politically located somewhere between anarchism, social democracy, Maoism, and syndicalism. They published the underground journal *Perspektiva*, for which they were soon arrested. But there was an important context to their existence. *Perspektiva* was typed and produced on the ground floor of the hippie commune Yellow Submarine, with active input from the members living upstairs. Although the commune eventually faltered in 1978 under the tension between those who were more politically inclined and those who favoured a more escapist, counter-cultural lifestyle, the line between the two camps cannot be drawn clearly. For instance, the second issue of *Perspektiva* carried a special feature covering an event that was decidedly 'apolitical', but which raised the young anarchists' hopes that there was still some revolutionary potential in Soviet youth.[12]

In fact the event in question never actually took place. It has become known as 'the concert that never happened'—a little-known curiosity that was successfully buried by the Soviet press. It all started with an announcement in *Leningradskaia pravda* about a concert to take place on 4 July 1978 that would feature, apart from

---

[12] Juliane Fürst, 'We All Live in a Yellow Submarine: Dropping Out in a Leningrad Commune', in ead. and Josie McLellan (eds.), *Dropping out of Socialism: The Creation of Alternative Spheres in the Soviet Bloc* (Lanham, Md., 2017), 179–206.

several Soviet Estrada stars such as Alla Pugacheva and Veselye Rebiata, the crème de la crème of Western rock music, including Santana, the Beach Boys, and Joan Baez. No wonder that news of this event spread like wildfire among young people who had never heard a Western band play in their country. Originally the concert was part of a plan to shoot a film about the internationalism of Soviet youth, which, however, was never sanctioned for production. By the time the project was shelved, the newspaper advertisement had been forgotten. But the young people who had read the announcement and written to their friends about it still remembered the exciting news. They gathered on time at Palace Square, and when it became apparent that they were waiting in vain, they got angry. The crowd staged an ad hoc demonstration with chants ranging from 'Santana' to 'Down with psychiatric hospitals', which was finally put down by police armed with water cannons.[13] The buoyant mood that lasted among Leningrad youth for some time afterwards was expressed in a letter from Aleksandr Karev to a friend in which he wrote about his state of mind after the riots:

WE ARE MANY Believe me. I did not think that something like this was possible. Our moral state (it could not be better), and a conviction that now one has to do something, that one should not wait for something, are heating up the atmosphere and grip a great and invisible mass of people! Drop your scepticism. Believe me. Already our almanacs are being published. Exhibitions with our artists, our concerts, and our theatre are organized. People are uniting—that is now the most important thing. Did we ever dream of such luck? This is a myth, which IMPACTS ON REALITY, and prepares people for the fights against the existing conditions. I believe and am prepared to give everything for this.[14]

The interesting thing was that Karev was the kind of youth who would have been a classic *shestidesiatnik* ten years earlier. He was a student from an intelligentsia family, interested in Leo Tolstoy and his ideals (which had the whiff of dissent by itself), and eager to change the world. The same was true of Skobov and Reznikov, the publishers of the story about the concert that never happened, who had doubts about their hippie housemates due to the hippies' political apathy and inertia. They suspected that these long-haired young rock fans

[13] Aleksandr Skobov, '*Perspektiva*: Zhurnal novykh levykh', in Viacheslav Dolinin and Boris Ivanov, *Samizdat: Po materialam v konferentsii '30 let nezavisimoi pechati, 1950–80 gody* (St Petersburg, 1993), 105–14.

[14] The Wende Museum, Los Angeles, Fond Karev, Letter Karev, 16 Apr. 1979.

lacked intellectual gravitas. And yet they could not dispute that it was these same young people who had been behind the disturbances on Palace Square in July 1978. Intrigued by the hippies and their network, Andrei Reznikov and his girlfriend Irina Flige even made a point of visiting a hippie gathering in a wood in the Baltics, only to have the frightened hippies flee from them because they did not look the hippie part. This was all a far cry from the programmatic statements of earlier young dissidents and nonconformists. At the same time, Skobov, Reznikov, and Tsurkov's *Perspektiva* was also full of rather dry ideological texts. The thing that was new to the mix was rock music. It was Santana, the Beach Boys, and Joan Baez—and to a certain extent the queen of Soviet Estrada, Alla Pugacheva—who had exercised the young rioters on Palace Square. It was English-language pop songs that got their blood boiling—songs which most young Soviets could not even understand. Yet what seems at first sight to be a complete reversal in youth interests reveals itself, on closer inspection, to be a gradual, logical development with its own Soviet, socialist trajectory.

The official canon of Marxism–Leninism is not poetic, but art and literature were important vehicles for Soviet ideology from the very beginning. The Soviet project was enthusiastically supported by many of the most avant-garde voices in literature, including that of Vladimir Mayakovsky, whose conceptualist poetry expressed the young revolutionary generation's desire to break old, bourgeois norms. His poems, full of allusions, open endings, and iconoclastic metres, enthused Soviet youth in the 1920s and 1930s, even if his name faded under Stalin. It was only in 1958, with the unveiling of a monument to him on the square bearing his name in Moscow, that Mayakovsky came to the attention of Soviet youth again. In the 1950s poetry was an accepted pastime, identifier, and mobilizer for young people. An officially sponsored campaign of poetry writing was in full swing, fuelling a number of official, semi-official, and underground youth poetry circles. The boundaries between them could be fluid, as the literary circle of the Leningrad Mining Institute learnt when its officially produced almanac was burnt in 1957 for containing a reference to the Soviet invasion of Hungary.[15] Meanwhile, in Moscow, readings under the Mayakovsky monument escaped the control of the Komsomol, who had initiated them, and attracted a

---

[15] Emily Lygo, *Leningrad Poetry 1953–1975: The Thaw Generation* (Oxford, 2010), 47–8; Vladimir Britanishskii, *Vykhod v postranstvo* (Moscow, 2008), 7–12.

number of self-styled and nonconformist young poets, along with an even larger audience excited by this public nonconformity. One of the participants, the later famous dissident Vladimir Bukovsky, declared even at the time that the content of the poems was secondary. What mattered was the spirit of defiance they produced within their audience. Some poems became battle hymns for recalcitrant Moscow youth. Yuri Galanskov's 'Manifesto of Man' leaves no doubt about the primacy of feeling:

> I'll go out on the square
> and into the city's ear
> I'll hammer a cry of despair . . .
> This is me,
> calling to truth and revolt,
> willing no more to serve,
> I break your black tethers,
> woven of lies . . .
> And I'm falling and soaring,
> half-delirious,
> half-asleep . . .
> And I feel
> man
> blooming in me.[16]

   In the late 1950s and the early 1960s, out of this general veneration of poetry, the so-called 'bards'—Soviet singer-songwriters— were born. Melodies were mostly secondary in the songs of Bulat Okudzhava and Aleksandr Galich (and even more so in the work of their successor Vladimir Vysotsky), which were based primarily on the power of the word, but they were crucial vehicles for creating emotional communities. They provided the Soviet 1960s with a specific soundtrack. It was a soundtrack that emphasized words, but these words became part of the rhythm, and the rhythm part of the style, of the period. And into this environment the Beatles dropped like a bomb in the mid 1960s, introducing the English language to the vocabulary of dissent. The interesting thing about English is that in the Soviet context it was a sort of non-language—or to adapt a term coined by Svetlana Boym, a half-language.[17] Few

[16] Vladimir Bukovsky, *To Build a Castle: My Life as a Dissenter*, trans. Michael Scammell (New York, 1978), 119–20

[17] Svetlana Boym, *Common Places: Mythologies of Everyday Life in Russia* (Cambridge, Mass., 1994).

Soviet young people were proficient in English, but most understood a little. English texts thus offered signposts to meaning, but left much room for personal interpretation and undefined yet highly emotional responses to what was left ununderstood, misunderstood, or half-understood. As such, fragments of English songs became clues to a whole litany of associations which did not have to be uttered in full to be understood by the community of those who had imbibed the songs and their lyrics. In other words: the half-articulated nature of English songs provided a sensual soundscape—an ephemeral impression that lasted only as long as the sound lasted, but which left a powerful memory of the mood it had created. And since rock music was viewed with extreme suspicion by the authorities, these sensual soundscapes became landscapes of nonconformism and dissent.[18]

Several historians of the Soviet creative intelligentsia have identified the 1960s as the decade that contained both the apogee of intellectual reformism and a decided turn towards emotional discourses that appealed to the senses and inner states of the people. Vladislav Zubok describes how post-1965 dissenting voices took on even the most central terrain of Bolshevik ideology: 'The interpretation of Soviet history and Marxism–Leninism itself, once the monopoly of the regime, had suddenly become explosive material in the hands of the writers, historians, and philosophers.'[19] One of the most famous and most contested cases was that of the historian Aleksandr Nekrich, who in April 1965 published a revisionist history of the first few months of the Great Fatherland War in which he sharply criticized Stalin's decisions in June 1941, yet did not overstep the lines drawn in Khrushchev's secret speech of 1956. Despite initial approval by the censors, the book soon fell foul of the authorities and was subjected to criticism. To the authorities' surprise, Nekrich's colleagues rallied around his interpretation and him personally in a Party assembly designed to denounced him. They insisted on 'the truth' in history, hence making both an intellectual as well as an emotional judgement. (Interestingly, one of those supporters was the father of the famous Russian American historian Yuri Slezkine.)[20]

---

[18] Artemy Troitsky, *Back in the USSR: The True Story of Rock in Russia* (London, 1987); Polly McMichael, 'Prehistories and Afterlives: The Packaging and Re-Packaging of Soviet Rock', *Popular Music and Society*, 32/3 (2009), 331–50.

[19] Vladislav Zubok, *Zhivago's Children: The Last Russian Intelligentsia* (Cambridge, Mass., 2009), 269.

[20] Jonathan Brunstedt, *The Soviet Myth of World War II: Patriotic Memory and the Russian Question in the USSR* (Cambridge, 2021), 177–8.

The very same project of 'reforming' history was pursued by Emil Kardin, who wrote an exposé of Soviet historical imprecisions called 'Legends and Facts', which appeared in the famous literary journal *Novyi Mir*, edited by the writer Aleksandr Tvardovskii, in 1966. The article debunked some of the most cherished myths of Soviet revolutionary and military history: the battleship *Aurora*, which supposedly fired the first shots in the storming of the Winter Palace; the battles of Pskov and Narva in 1918; and the heroic last stand of the so-called Panfilovites, who were said to have saved Moscow from the German army in 1941.[21] (The controversy over the Panfilovite story and its lack of veracity has more recently also resulted in the long-serving head of the Russian archive services losing his job.)[22]

More and more historian dissenters, such as the brothers Zhores and Roy Medvedev, fought the Party on other parts of its own terrain in both samizdat and official publications. Alexander Esenin-Volpin challenged the authorities on the issue of Soviet legality, insisting on upholding the Soviet constitution, while a number of economists, such as Vasilii Nemchinov, questioned the wisdom of price-fixing and other socialist practices. In his study *Zhivago's Children*, Zubok also describes these years as the high point of the Akademgorodok district in Novosibirsk, where scientists built up a quasi-civil society under the ideological aegis of the socialist state.[23] Yet eventually Brezhnev cracked down on Nekrich in 1967, and symbolically on the entire reformist intelligentsia in 1968 by sending tanks into Prague. The notion that reforms were marching in a linear trajectory towards socialism with a human face was decisively debunked. Zubok's chapter on the years 1968–85 is entitled 'The Long Decline'. This is to be understood as the decline not of the intelligentsia or of dissent as such (which if anything became more mainstream), but of a particular type of reformist ideal which characterized the heroes of *Zhivago's Children*. Zubok chose the title of his book very carefully. Pasternak's novel *Doctor Zhivago* is a heart-breaking story of love between doomed people, but it is also (and possibly foremost)

---

[21] Denis Kozlov, *The Readers of* Novyi Mir: *Coming to Terms with the Stalinist Past* (Cambridge, Mass., 2013), 263–94.

[22] Tom Balmforth, 'Russian Archive Chief Out after Debunking Soviet WW II Legend', *Radio Free Europe/Radio Liberty*, 17 Mar. 2016 ⟨https://www.rferl.org/a/mironenko-state-archive-chief-removed-from-post-panfilov-legend/27619460.html⟩ [accessed 17 June 2021].

[23] Zubok, *Zhivago's Children*, 276–90. See also Paul Josephson, *New Atlantis Revisited: Akademgorodok, the Siberian City of Science* (Princeton, 1997).

a revisionist narrative of revolutionary history—in other words, a proposal for reform.[24]

The same people who followed the Nekrich controversy with interest, read *Novyi Mir* with gusto, and sympathized with the dissidents calling for more freedom of speech, were simultaneously engaged in another project that at first glance looks akin to the reformist cause, but on closer observation turns out to be quite different: the adulation and idealization of all (or many) things Western, ranging from popular culture to high-brow intellectual products. Eleonory Gilburd has written an insightful account of the Soviet relationship with high-brow Western culture, which she characterizes as a love affair with something that seemed full of promise precisely because of its remoteness and its mediated nature—aspects which allowed people to project all the hopes and feelings that they were wary of directing at the Soviet project lest they be disappointed (again).

It has already become apparent that there was no strict division between system and dissenters in terms of reformist ambitions. *Novyi Mir* was an official journal. The historian Nekrich worked at the Academy of Sciences, and the critical economists were employed by government universities. Yet the collaboration between system and people was even more pronounced when it came to fostering this love affair with Western mass culture. Gilburd argues that the translation of works by Erich Maria Remarque and J. D. Salinger unleashed an emotional response among their Soviet readers. In the case of Remarque, she argues, the translation allowed his novel *Three Comrades* to be read with an emphasis on friendship and love rather than on its pessimism. This chimed well with a contemporary obsession on the part of official youth propaganda outlets, especially the new journal *Iunost'*, with 'love' as a spiritual and emotional concept.[25] A few years later, Salinger's *Catcher in the Rye* also left a linguistic–emotional imprint. Salinger's liberal use of youth slang opened up in its Russian translation a sense of 'feeling young and free' simply by using certain words that were specific enough to a particular generation and mindset to create a spiritual

---

[24] Boris Pasternak, *Doctor Zhivago*, trans. Max Hayward and Manya Harari (London, 1958); Peter Finn and Petra Couvée, *The Zhivago Affair: The Kremlin, the CIA, and the Battle over a Forbidden Book* (London, 2015).

[25] Kristin Roth-Ey, *Moscow Prime Time: How the Soviet Union Built the Media Empire that Lost the Cultural Cold War* (Ithaca, NY, 2011).

community.[26] Vasilii Aksenov continued this trend with novels set in the Soviet youth scene, in which he used a slangy prose style learnt during his years as a *stiliaga*. His *Ticket to the Stars* was read as a Soviet version of Salinger, giving the author an aura of Americanness even before his emigration.[27] Gilburd points out that this interpretation overlooked the socialist realist qualities of Aksenov's novel.[28] But that would have hardly bothered young readers. The trajectory of the narrative was not the point. The point was that a linguistic code such as slang was employed less for its meaning than for its symbolic function as an entrance card to an emotional community—the community of the young and progressive. This brings us back to the notion of English as a half-language. Language in the Soviet 1960s was not only a means of transporting content. Rather, it was manipulated to produce a rhyme, a sound, a feeling, or an image—whether as poetry, as slang, or as words hailing from the fabled America or its language. In the early 1970s no self-respecting Soviet rock band sang in Russian. The vibrant DIY rock scene relied on good to excellent imitations of classic American and British songs, with performers often singing lyrics they did not understand but whose code melded them and their audience into a community of feeling. By virtue of being linked to America and the world on the other side of the Iron Curtain, that feeling was defiant without ever having to articulate details, plans, or visions of the future. The moment lasted only a few years. From 1973–4 onwards, bands such as Time Machine and Aquarium started to experiment with rock songs in Russian, reconnecting with the tradition of the bards but with a proper soundtrack. The fact that rock in itself transmitted a certain whiff of dissent was by then well established. The hippie-poet Guru, alias Arkadii Slavorosov, penned a long ode to the character, quality, and function of rock within the 'tribe' of nonconformist youth. It contains the lines:

ROCK—existence—this is a spiritual ritual, a kind of irrational knowledge contrasting with pragmatic fulfilment of common sense. ROCK does not tolerate evaluation. It is neither good nor bad. Often precisely what may seem

---

[26] Eleonory Gilburd, *To See Paris and Die: The Soviet Lives of Western Culture* (Cambridge, Mass., 2018), 103–57.

[27] Bradley Gorski, 'Manufacturing Dissent: *Stiliagi*, Vasilii Aksenov, and the Dilemma of Self-Interpretation', *Russian Literature*, 96–8 (2018), 77–104.

[28] Gilburd, *To See Paris and Die*, 147–9.

illiterate and tasteless to an intelligent, informed connoisseur causes the most powerful resonance.[29]

It was a straight line from here to Viktor Tsoi and his cry for change.

II. *From Reforms to Symbols*

With the sound of language turning into cypher, words themselves became necessarily less important. It is no coincidence that samizdat came to prominence with the 1960s generation of 'reformers'. They wanted to put their alternative vision for a better state into words in the hope that these words would one day become a reality. In the course of this endeavour, samizdat became much more than the political discourse of the 1960s, as it came to include hard-to-get foreign novels as well as yoga manuals and many other things. But the vision of a better world, or criticism of the existing one, remained its engine.[30] And, of course, words remained at the centre of samizdat activity, regardless of whether the content was directly or only indirectly political (all of samizdat was political since it sidestepped the state's publishing monopoly). Yet although the youth of the 1970s read samizdat extensively, they supplemented the written word with a variety of other non-verbal markers that became symbols of dissent. In line with the rise of rock as a collective emotive (something that evokes emotions), dissent against the Soviet system and reality came to be expressed through appearance, spaces, graffiti, and handicrafts, and in other material, spatial, or symbolic ways.

This was nothing new. Indeed, one can observe such trends within the Bolshevik tradition itself—for instance in the early revolutionary period, when revolutionary fervour found expression not only in ideology, but in personal clothing, forms of living such as communes, and a certain way of speaking, walking, and acting that was seen as breaking bourgeois norms. Later, in the postwar years, the *stiliagi* ushered in the era of subcultures for the Soviet Union, protesting against 'normality' by sporting dandy-like clothing. I argue that the 1970s saw an explosion of outward markers of dissent that stood

---

[29] [Anon.], 'Arkadii Slavorosov ("Guru") i Serhei Zhutov: Kanon', *Papa Lesha* ⟨https://papa-lesha.ru/lib/guru/canon⟩ [accessed 14 May 2021].

[30] Josephine von Zitzewitz, *The Culture of Samizdat: Literature and Underground Networks in the Late Soviet Union* (London, 2020); Ann Komaromi, 'Samizdat and Soviet Dissident Publics', *Slavic Review*, 71/1 (2012), 70–90.

in stark contrast to the emphasis on inward states in earlier years. It is no coincidence that 'inner freedom' was a trope much in use by the Soviet dissenters of the 1960s.[31] The outer façade gave little away in those years. Bohemians and quasi-beatniks followed the existentialist fashion of black turtlenecks and checked shirts, but remained respectfully within the framework of the Soviet dress code, even when dancing the twist or rocking to the sounds of the new beat music in their dormitories.

This changed dramatically with the arrival of the next youth subculture—the first to call itself explicitly global. Artemy Troitsky, a contemporary rock critic from a privileged communist family, claimed that 'the hippie thing changed youth virtually overnight'.[32] And indeed, Soviet hippies not only expressed themselves to a large extent non-verbally, but were also highly visible—at least enough to get the police and authorities agitated about their appearance on the street. Hippies distinguished themselves through their hair and clothing, through the flowers they used as ornaments and identifiers of their character, through their gender-bending attire of loose-fitting shirts, trousers, and skirts, and through their desire to showcase their style to the world—as a provocation, but more importantly, because they believed that their style encapsulated the essence of their beliefs.[33] Style was the lingua franca in both East and West. Many contemporary observers testified that hippie beliefs distinguished themselves by their vagueness, their unspoken associations, and their strong emotional coding, which was not easily captured in words.[34] For hippies to communicate, it was thus necessary to be visible in public. They needed an audience to explain who they were, just as the generation of 1960s reformers needed a readership. It is no coincidence that hippies assembled at the most central places in Moscow: Mayakovsky Square, where ten years earlier young people had read unsanctioned poetry; the Psichodrom, the courtyard in front of the old Moscow State University building directly opposite the Kremlin; cafés, benches, and

[31] Zubok, *Zhivago's Children*; Philip Boobbyer, *Conscience, Dissent and Reform in Soviet Russia* (Abingdon, 2005).

[32] Artemy Troitsky, *Back in the USSR: The True Story of Rock in Russia* (London, 1987).

[33] Juliane Fürst, *Flowers through Concrete: Explorations in Soviet Hippieland* (Oxford, 2021).

[34] Hunter S. Thompson, 'The Hippies', *Distrito47*, 3 Feb. 2014 ⟨https://distrito47.word-press.com/2014/02/03/the-hippies-by-hunter-s-thompson/⟩ [accessed 14 May 2021]; W. J. Rorabaugh, *American Hippies* (New York, 2015); Timothy Miller, *The Hippies and American Values*, 2nd edn. (Knoxville, 2011).

monuments on Gorky Street, Moscow's most prestigious boulevard; and other prominent locations. These places also happened to be representations of Soviet power—the university, the Kremlin, the government buildings and flagship stores on Gorky Street. This made them attractive to the hippies, who challenged the meaning of these spaces through their presence. Without Soviet power, there was no thrill—and no thrill, no hippies.

This symbiosis of creating and chasing thrills—*kaif*—extended not only to places, but also to things. The most important item in the canon of the *kaif*-infused materiality of alternative youth in the Soviet bloc has to be the American blue jeans. This item of clothing, whose value rested in a small label with the words 'Wrangler' or 'Levi's', and whose authenticity was tested by rubbing matches on the fabric (the matches had to turn blue), was almost all symbol. Soviet young people knew this very well, because quite a number of them made money by producing fakes. They bought denim-like fabric in Soviet shops, dyed it at home, distressed the finished products, and sold them on the street to youngsters who occupied lower positions in the knowledge community. The sellers of fakes wore authentic jeans, not their own products. Yet the difference was only in the material—in their minds, everyone ended up with an authentic piece of the West. As Alexei Yurchak has pointed out, the West itself was an imaginary whose existence rested on the feeling its presence generated among those who partook in the celebration of its mystical energy.[35] Jeans did not have to be illegal in order to become symbols of dissent; rather, the fact that they were declared items of dissent created the feeling that sustained their continued success. In other words, the regime itself, with its uncool consumer items and its arrogant disdain for those who loved jeans, created the conditions in which wearing jeans could become an act of dissent. However mild this dissent was, wearing jeans was a clear statement that Western things mattered. Ferenc Hammer has written a wonderful interpretation of the place of jeans in János Kádár's Hungary:

The key thing was that jeans enabled the wearer to transcend boundaries between conventional fields of action. Jeans received from a politically privileged relative became a source of aesthetic pleasure. A pair of Levi's acquired from a dangerous and remote black market could become the source

[35] Yurchak, *Everything was Forever*.

of the owner's sex appeal. Sitting like a free-floating hippie in a denim suit in an armchair in a village disco could operate as a source of privilege. In these stories, privilege is transformed into aesthetic pleasure, aesthetics into sensual appeal, sex appeal into authority, freedom into exclusivity, lack of freedom into opportunity and so on. But all of these magical transformations were possible only because of the political restrictions on the acquisition of jeans imposed by the Kádár regime.[36]

The 'symbolification' of the discourse of dissent was accompanied by the rise of nonconformist artists as the most visible face of bohemian resistance. If the 1960s were the years of political, reformist dissidence, characterized by a short but ground-breaking demonstration for the observance of the constitution on Pushkin Square in December 1965, the visible support for the writers Iulii Daniel and Andrei Siniavskii during their trial in 1966, and the foundation of the *Chronicle of Current Events* in 1968, then the 1970s clearly belonged to the circle of recalcitrant artists around Oscar Rabin, who began staging illegal open-air exhibitions. The most infamous of these, the September 1974 exhibition in Beliaev, a suburb of Moscow, also provided one of the most symbolic images of the struggle between regime and nonconformists when the unsanctioned exhibition was closed down and bulldozers flattened the artworks. The outcry in the Western media, which by now had become a powerful instrument for shrewd artists, was such that two weeks later another open-air exhibition was allowed, this time in Izmailovo Park. In 1975 it was followed by two exhibitions at the VDNKh (the grounds of the Exhibition of the National Economy), the second of which was marred by scandal as the Moscow authorities confiscated several works just before the opening and the artists refused to open the exhibition until the items were returned. Interestingly, two of the pieces in question were among the most symbolic in their dissent. One was a large straw nest by the Donskoi group, in which at times people 'nested'. The other was an enormous hippie flag created by the group Volosy ('Hair'). Both celebrated alternative communities—one with reference to family and biological ties, the other by taking a red Soviet flag and using patches to turn it into a codification of hippie beliefs: love and peace, yin and yang, a guitar, a piece of denim, and—most controversially—a crossed-out image of a border post

[36] Ferenc Hammer, 'Sartorial Manœuvres in the Dusk: Blue Jeans in Socialist Hungary', in Frank Trentmann and Kate Soper (eds.), *Citizenship and Consumption* (Basingstoke, 2008), 51–68, at 60–1.

with the words 'country without borders' stitched next to it. The latter exercised the authorities much more than the huge poppy right in the middle of the flag, which symbolized the hippies' love for its intoxicating properties.

This exhibition indeed signalled the end of the nonconformist artists' acceptance in the official sphere; yet their paintings and artworks continued to attract huge crowds in semi-official and unofficial settings. The 1970s were the decade of the image and the artist rather than of the reformer and the dissident. Painters and conceptual artists were at the forefront of civil disobedience and recalcitrance. They were the most visible expression of 'otherness' in the eyes of the public—precisely because they were allowed to act in a semi-official sphere. Yet they themselves also felt that this was their era, despite—or precisely because of—'stagnation'. And they were keenly aware of the ways in which official cultural policy endowed them with an aura of bravery, adventure, and relevance. Georgii Kizeval'ter wrote in the introduction to his volume of artists' memoirs on the 1970s:

Nobody attempts here to diminish the importance of the hopes of the Thaw in the 1960s or the maniacal–suggestive performance culture of the 1980s or to single out for admiration the years when stagnation reached its apogee. And yet, if you put these decades next to each other, you see their faces are not dissimilar, like children of different fathers.[37]

His friend Aleksandr Kosolapov recalls the 1970s as a time when 'we swam free'. Leonid Sokov claims that the 1970s were a 'turning point in the Russian fine arts'. Artistic dissent, although political because of its precarious legality outside the accepted Soviet canon and institutions, was in essence aesthetic in nature and as such addressed itself more to people's senses than to their intellectual thoughts.[38] As Joseph Bakshtein has expressed it, nonconformist art was an answer to both Soviet practice and the value underpinning it, including its aesthetics:

The creation of this nonconformist tradition was impelled by the fact that an outsider in the Soviet empire stood alone against a tremendous state machine, a great Leviathan that threatened to engulf him. To preserve one's identity in this situation, one had to create a separate value system, including a system of aesthetic values.[39]

[37] Georgii Kizeval'ter (ed.), *Eti strannye semidesiatye, ili poteria nevinnosti: Esse, interv'iu, vospominaniia* (Moscow, 2010), 5–6. [38] Ibid. 141, 254.

[39] Joseph Bakshtein, 'A View from Moscow', in Alla Rosenfeld and Norton T. Dodge (eds.), *Nonconformist Art: The Soviet Experience 1956–1986* (London, 1995), 331–40, at 332.

As in the case of poetry, the boom of aesthetics as a form of dissent did not come from nowhere. There is much evidence to suggest that Soviet propaganda also underwent a change in its rhetoric and presentation. The Soviet state, Soviet society, and Soviet life were now often depicted as objects of beauty capable of creating emotional and affective communities by the power of their high-minded ideals. This was part and parcel of Khrushchev's shift away from measuring Soviet success purely in terms of political power to an approach that privileged people's material and spiritual well-being.[40] It is no coincidence that two of Khrushchev's famous ad hoc debates happened in places connected to material and aesthetic pleasure: a kitchen and a modern art exhibition. Both his discussion with Nixon in the showroom kitchen of the 1959 American National Exhibition in Moscow and his clash with nonconformist artist Ernst Neizvestnyi at the Manege exhibition in 1962 demonstrated that Khrushchev saw the Soviet project not solely as an economic project or a player on the international scene, but as a competition for people's hearts and minds. The Soviet Union was to be the better state, measured by the crucial index of human happiness. This metric encompassed both a certain standard of living (and here one had to catch up with the USA, as Khrushchev asserted that the USSR would do within a few decades in his argument with Nixon) and a moral and aesthetic superiority (over which Khrushchev battled with Neizvestnyi in his attack on modern art, which Khrushchev judged to be not only ugly but also immoral). Soviet culture took the cue and responded throughout the 1960s with a repertoire of cultural production that emphasized aesthetics and morality. Thaw-era Soviet cinema burst onto the international scene—not only because late Stalinism had produced so few films overall, but also because it had its very own aesthetics, which, while often tackling difficult social questions, undoubtedly transmitted a specifically Soviet beauty. Thaw-era films dealing with the painful memory of war (such as *Ivan's Childhood* or *The Cranes are Flying*) were shot at beautiful angles, providing almost unseemly pictures of horror and death. There was beauty even in the suffering of Soviet people.

Serguei Oushakine has pointed out that the 1960s discourse on materiality had a similar dual motivation. On the one hand, materialism was condemned as something bourgeois, Western, and anti-

---

[40] Susan E. Reid, 'The Khrushchev Kitchen: Domesticating the Scientific–Technological Revolution', *Journal of Contemporary History*, 40/2 (2005), 289–316.

collective; on the other, more and more publications celebrated the beauty of things, along with their value as products of crafts-manship and as objects of aesthetic pleasure. Oushakine calls it the 'simultaneous fight for and against things in the 1960s and 70s'.[41] Both aspects ultimately aimed to generate an emotional response: anti-materialism stirred a sense of moral righteousness, while appre-ciation evoked the satisfaction of aesthetic pleasure. Yulia Karpova comes to a similar conclusion when she observes that in the 1960s Soviet design no longer justified the production of things through their 'indispensability . . . to people's daily lives, but [through] the rich potential of the material to express complex ideas'. For instance, 'the ceramic artist could now be like a sculptor or, even better, a painter'.[42]

III. *From Reforms to 'How I Feel'*

The interplay between official rhetoric and tropes and those used by people who wanted to position themselves against or outside Soviet norms becomes even more apparent when we look at another facet of the 'politics of feeling': the rise of 'how I feel'. Emphasis on personal emotions was not new to the Soviet 1960s and 1970s, but, I argue, it gained more prominence throughout Soviet society than in previous decades. It permeated not only cinematic production, but also public discourse in newspapers and journals, which privileged topics and stories that explored the inner emotional states of Soviet citizens. Even the atheist project changed in the long 1970s with the recognition that people clung to spirituality regardless of gains made in technology and especially in space exploration, which was used as evidence against the existence of God. Alongside a renewed propaganda effort to instil an awareness of scientific knowledge and thinking, there was also an attempt to use religious symbols (churches, religious paintings and artefacts, and so on) as vectors for the promotion of 'aesthetic and patriotic emotions'. Behind this considerable rethinking of the meaning of atheism was widespread concern over the spiritual emptiness of Soviet youth in particular—a void that had been less urgent when radical policies had taken care

[41] Serguei Oushakine, *Servantiki zastoia: O krasote i pol'ze sovetskogo veshchizma, Tret'iakovskaia galereia, Nenavsegda. K vystavke Nenavsegda 1968–1985* (Moscow, 2020), 24.

[42] Yulia Karpova, *Comradely Objects: Design and Material Culture in Soviet Russia, 1960s–80s* (Manchester, 2020), 160.

of the emotional needs of young people. Now 'building communism' (and the beauty this supposedly entailed) had to suffice as a source of motivation and inspiration for the young.[43] Polly Jones identifies a similar need to fill a spiritual hole in her analysis of the Fiery Revolutionaries series of books, which retold the stories of many important actors in the Russian Revolution. As is already apparent in the name of this highly popular series, the emotional world of both its protagonists and its readers was positioned unusually prominently, with the clear aim of evoking an emotional response. In order to achieve this goal, the conservative state publishing house Politizdat even commissioned authors from the fringes of the officially sanctioned community of writers and allowed the inclusion of intimate personal details from the lives of the heroes under discussion. As it transpired, the titles produced by the most 'difficult' and least conformist writers became the most popular among readers.[44]

In many respects, the most concerted effort to appeal to people's affect was the new veneration of the Great Fatherland War, whose memory Brezhnev was determined to use in order to stabilize and legitimize the Soviet project overall. While the emotional campaign for a unifying patriotic memory was mostly a success, in general the rise of emotionality worked against the state. This was not only true for those who were critical of some aspects—or even at times the totality—of the Soviet system. 'How I feel does not match Soviet reality' increasingly became the basis of a general sense of alienation, distancing, and estrangement. While the term 'individualization' captures some aspects of this development, it is misleading, because the new primacy of feeling was not necessarily anti-collective. Rather, it created new collectives, based on shared emotions, affect, and sensual perceptions.

During the Thaw, the discourse on the seminal Soviet trauma of the Great Fatherland War had shifted from a rhetoric of victory with Stalin at the centre to a delicate probing of the wounds, injuries, and consequences of war and its links to that other great trauma: the years of the Stalinist terror, which saw hundreds of thousands of Party and army members arrested and, in many cases, executed.[45]

[43] Victoria Smolkin, *A Sacred Space is Never Empty: A History of Soviet Atheism* (Princeton, 2018), 205–9.

[44] Polly Jones, *Revolution Rekindled: The Writers and Readers of Late Soviet Biography* (Oxford, 2019).   [45] Brunstedt, *Soviet Myth*.

Marko Dumančić has shown how films of the long 1960s in particular questioned the myths of both male and female participants in
the war, shattering the certainty of patriotic heroism by portraying
Soviet people as weak, fallible, and conflicted. Here was a war represented not as a battle of arms and ideologies, but as a field of personal
conflicts and dilemmas of conscience.[46] This came to a halt with
Brezhnev's instrumentalization of war commemorations to enforce
national and ideological unity from the mid 1960s onwards. Heavily promoted by the national faction in the leadership, especially
KGB head Aleksandr Shelepin and Komsomol boss Sergei Pavlov,
these commemorations sported a strongly Russocentric slant and,
given their public and propagandistic nature, allowed little room
for ambiguity, alternative memories, or moral doubts.[47] Brezhnev's
ever more extensive annual celebrations continued to encourage an
emotional and spiritual engagement with the war and soon with
Victory Day itself—a practice that Putin has resumed and perfected,
despite the dwindling numbers of surviving veterans. There is much
debate about the roots and motivations behind the rise of 9 May
as a participatory mega-event, but all commentators agree that
the commemorations gathered more and more emotional energy
throughout the period of stagnation, with some even suggesting that
Victory Day was designed to serve as a distraction.[48]

Overall, Brezhnev's project to create community through shared
commemoration and veneration of the war effort paid dividends.
While alienating to those who did not identify with the official
line (including large swathes of the Soviet Union's population
in the newly annexed Western territories), Soviet patriotism and
Russian patriotism were and remain genuinely popular sentiments.
The beatification of the Second World War unleashed unintended
consequences on a different level. The state's invitation to engage
with Sovietness on a spiritual, aesthetic, and emotional level was a
result of a certain alienation and indifference among young people,
but it generated exactly these sentiments among those who did not
want to be Soviet. This desire for non-Sovietness had already found

[46] Marko Dumančić, *Men out of Focus: The Soviet Masculinity Crisis in the Long Sixties*
(Toronto, 2021).
[47] N. Mitrokhin, *Russkaia partiia: Dvizhenie russkikh natsionalistov v SSSR, 1953–1985
gody* (Moscow, 2003).
[48] Nina Tumarkin, *The Living & the Dead: The Rise and Fall of the Cult of World War II
in Russia* (New York, 1994); Brunstedt, *Soviet Myth*; Mischa Gabowitsch, *Pamiatnik i
prazdnik: Etnografiia Dnia Pobedy* (St Petersburg, 2020).

a growing community in the 1960s among people who resented the interference of the state in their life choices and hence had set about building alternative universes for themselves in their kitchens, their dachas, or simply in their private lives. As the sociologists Aleksandr Genis and Petr Vail' have concluded, unofficial culture in many ways reversed official culture in the 1960s.[49] When official culture asked for affection, the easiest way to resist was to withhold the requested emotion—or worse, bestow it on someone else, such as the often-invoked West or, more specifically, the hated USA. With its emphasis on building a spiritual and emotional relationship, the Soviet system provided a route to dissent that sidestepped politics. That fitted well with a society that had grown tired of politics after six decades of socialist mobilization and, more recently, one long decade of reformist hopes and false starts.

The late Soviet 'how I feel' could take many forms, and few of them were explicitly political. In its most widespread form, it was tightly bound up with 'what I have', as the allure of jeans as an item that was both rare and forbidden has already demonstrated. It also neatly corresponded to the aforementioned efforts by Soviet designers to evoke complex and affective reactions from users. Jeans were only one small part of an empire of things and practices that constituted the personal world of the average 1970s Soviet citizen— a world whose fabric was woven ever tighter and that acted more and more as a divider and shield against the official world, with which it nonetheless often overlapped. While Vladimir Shlapentokh has propagated the idea of growing privatization as early as the 1980s, his strict dichotomy between private and public is these days widely renounced.[50] Yet the idea of late Soviet citizens creating a universe infused with meaningful practices which they engaged in independently from or in spite of the state has gained credence in a more symbiotic form. Alexey Golubev has written about repairing objects both as a response to material reality and as an act of self-empowerment and self-realization undertaken precisely because there was no state to step into the void of broken things.[51] Golubev has developed this idea of an affective nexus between state and

---

[49] Aleksandr Genis and Petr Vail', 60e: Mir sovetskogo cheloveka (Moscow, 1988).

[50] Vladimir Shlapentokh, Public and Private Life of the Soviet People: Changing Values in Post-Stalin Russia (New York, 1989).

[51] Alexey Golubev and Olga Smolyak, 'Making Selves through Making Things: Soviet Do-It-Yourself Culture and Practices of Late Soviet Subjectivation', Cahiers du monde russe, 54/3–4 (2013), 517–41.

citizen with reference to a variety of items, including stairwells, streetscapes, and basement gyms—all of which were spaces located within the Soviet universe that were used to further individual self-realization.[52] Pointing to another paradox, Anna Ivanova has explored foreign-currency shops, which excluded the normal Soviet consumer but created a vibrant private trade network for all manner of things that were not necessities, but luxury items valued as an emotive.[53] Even Soviet hippie culture oriented itself by Soviet reality, using its features to build a world in which hippies could pretend to live a non-Soviet life. Soviet hippies thus remained residents of the Soviet Union while living emotionally in a different world.[54] All the studies I have mentioned share a (sometimes unarticulated) emphasis on feeling as an important driver of relationships with the regime. Implicitly, they categorize this feeling as a new platform of dissent in that they explore forms of feeling that were not connected to the hegemonic emotional regime, even if they still relied on that emotional regime in order to define themselves.

One arena in which late Soviet popular feeling played out most notably was that of spirituality and religion. After sixty years of atheist propaganda, the Soviet authorities were dismayed to find in the 1970s that religion was far from dead; on the contrary, it seemed to be undergoing a renaissance on a variety of levels. The urban intelligentsia flocked to a number of monasteries and priests who not only spread the Gospel, but were often known to be hostile towards the Soviet system. Father Dmitrii Dudko, who served in Moscow at the Preobrazhenskii Monastery and Cemetery in the 1960s and early 1970s, and after 1973 in remote villages in the Moscow region, was one of the best-known representatives of this new type of Orthodox priest. His sermons, which took the form of question-and-answer sessions, attracted members of the Moscow bohemian scene who in the past had flocked to semi-legal literary and political gatherings. Now their quest for knowledge was augmented by their quest for spirituality. Dudko was only the tip of an iceberg. Konstantin Skrobotov (Father Nikolai) at the Elokhovskii Monastery in the Kaluga region became a magnet for alternative youth as he spoke to them in their slang, while

---

[52] Alexey Golubev, *The Things of Life: Materiality in Late Soviet Russia* (Ithaca, NY, 2020).

[53] Anna Ivanova, *Magaziny 'Berezka': Paradoksy potrebleniia v pozdnem SSSR* (Moscow, 2017).   [54] Fürst, *Flowers through Concrete*.

in the village of Otradnoe Father Vladimir Shibaev attracted a more conservative crowd, whom he introduced to the idea of new martyrs, including former Tsar Nicholas II. In an interview in 2012 he spoke of 'the spiritual awakening of youth not only in Moscow but across the whole country' that characterized those years.[55] The 1970s also saw the foundation of Aleksandr Ogorodnikov's Christian Seminary and Sandris Ria's ecumenical community, both of which saw hundreds if not thousands of young people passing through. And finally, the Western craze for Eastern religion also engulfed the Soviet Union, with a wide variety of esoteric and spiritual beliefs and practices making the rounds. The list of fascinations is diverse: yoga, vegetarianism, kabbalah, Hare Krishna, Nicholas Roerich, Nikolai Gumilev, Daniel Kharms, Tolstoy and Tolstoyism, and much more besides.[56]

Certainly, 'to be on the search' was an important feature of youthful identity in the Soviet 1970s, and this state of mind—this feeling—seems to have been more important than what could actually be found. Many youngsters were interested in some, or many, or indeed all of the intellectual preoccupations named above. Curiosity was valued most among so-called 'progressive' youth—a self-definition that encompassed an ever-growing constituency among Soviet young people and whose meaning included a certain ironic distancing and alienation from the official Soviet project. It was the sense of adventure, the feeling of trespassing, and the excitement of what might be round the corner that drove the search—not the prospect of finding something, which by definition would bring the search to an end. Hence, the late Soviet years saw strange bedfellows among dissenters, united by little else than the feeling of dissent. The graffiti of the 1980s saw swastikas and peace signs appear side by side, just as Siberian punk bands could be both extremely provocative and extremely patriotic.[57] *Kaif* transcended many borders, but it was a firm enemy of non-*kaif*. And non-*kaif* was everything that was boring, official, or regulated. It is interesting to note that perestroika not only revived the reformist manifestos

[55] Aleksandr Petrov, 'Takaia strashnaia deistvitel'nost'', *Pravda*, 13 Aug. 2012 ⟨https://www.pravda.ru/faith/1124708-trust/⟩ [accessed 27 Oct. 2021].

[56] Birgit Menzel, Michael Hagemeister, and Bernice Glatzer Rosenthal (eds.), *The New Age of Russia: Occult and Esoteric Dimensions* (Munich, 2012); Fürst, *Flowers through Concrete*.

[57] Yngvar B. Steinholt, 'Siberian Punk shall Emerge Here: Egor Letov and Grazhdanskaia Oborona', *Popular Music*, 31/3 (2012), 401–15.

of the 1960s. Its official culture also came scrambling to get a piece of that elusive feeling of *kaif* that propelled the so-called *neformaly* youth communities—the hippies, punks, football fans, weightlifters, break-dancers, neo-*stiliagi*, and so on. These communities were now studied, courted in the press, and invited to talk shows. But that is another story.

The value change from intellectual dissent to a politics of change, which I have outlined here, was not unique to the Soviet 1970s. While certain factors were specific to the Soviet Union and the socialist bloc—the disillusionment about the dashed hopes for reforms in the 1960s translating into a less direct confrontation with socialist reality in the 1970s—the rise of emotionality as an expression and mode of nonconformism also rode the wave of the global zeitgeist. The diffusion of language into cyphers of feeling was at the heart of the beatnik project, while the increased reliance on symbols and exterior markers was to no small extent propelled by the hippie movement going global. Protests all over the world in this period looked for authenticity, whose meaning was identified more by a feeling than by any empirical definition of what it meant to be 'authentic'.[58] Decolonization in the Global South triggered a more political debate. The protests of the late 1960s echoed through Western Europe in the following decade in the form of radical left-wing discourses, which included political violence and terrorism. Ecological causes started to gather momentum, culminating in the rise of green movements in the following decade. And yet here too, feeling was an omnipresent motor. Odd Arne Westad concludes his musings about 1968 with the thought that the global significance of this year was 'not primarily about revolution, or class struggle, or even feminism. It was about autonomy, very often personal and individual rather than collective.'[59] The global 1970s were the decade in which these new ideas, self-identifications, and resulting feelings were developed, put into practice, and refined. They changed how people related to the system they lived in—and especially how they dissented from it. The reverberations of this change are still with us, in both the East and the West.

---

[58] Joachim C. Häberlen, Mark Keck-Szajbel, and Kate Mahoney (eds.) *The Politics of Authenticity: Countercultures and Radical Movements across the Iron Curtain, 1968–1989* (New York, 2020).

[59] Odd Arne Westad, 'Was There a Global 1968?', in Chen Jian, Martin Klimke, Masha Kirasirova, et al. (eds.), *The Routledge Handbook of the Global Sixties: Between Protest and Nation-Building* (Abingdon, 2018), pp. xx–xxiii, at p. xxii.

7

Ecstatic Bodies as Actors of Change: Drugs and Sexuality in West Germany's Alternative Milieu during the Late 1960s and Early 1970s

KRISTOFF KERL

In 1969 Joseph Berke visited Kommune 1 in Berlin. Berke was a New Yorker who lived in London during the 1960s and 1970s and was involved in counter-cultural activities during this time, and he also collaborated with the famous psychiatrist Ronald D. Laing. During his stay in Kommune 1, Berke constantly smoked cannabis with the communards, some of whom engaged in overt sexual activity. He also discussed ways of achieving changes in society with them—mainly with Rainer Langhans and Dieter Kunzelmann. According to Berke's report, Langhans explained that Kommune 1 had fundamentally reshaped its theoretical and practical approach to revolutionizing society. Denouncing the 'traditional activities of the Left' as useless and the left-wing movements of the previous years as 'carbon copies of the bourgeois system', he claimed that it was a *sine qua non* for fundamental societal change that people should 'undergo a radical transformation in areas where it really matters, in themselves and their relationships with others'.[1] Langhans's modified conception of radical societal changes went along with a fundamentally new attitude towards the use of drugs. While the communards had previously seen cannabis, LSD, and other substances as simply 'bourgeois tricks' to keep young people distracted from starting a political revolution, by the time of Berke's visit they had come to regard cannabis and LSD as important means for achieving a fundamental reconfiguration of the self and,

I thank the Alexander von Humboldt Foundation for generously supporting the research for this essay. I would also like to thank the editors of this volume, as well as Florian Schleking and Detlef Siegfried, for commenting on earlier drafts.

[1] Joseph H. Berke, 'Kommune 1 Visited', in id. (ed.), *Counter Culture* (London, 1969), 138–42, at 140.

by extension, of society.[2] Some doubts about the political effects of psychedelic substances remained, however, and Berke tried to dispel them by referring to the experiences of counter-cultural actors in the United States: 'I tried to point out that their experience was related to a cyclic movement of political action (old left variety), turning on and dropping-out, and repoliticization at another level, as has been experienced by many people in the States and elsewhere (Rubin, Yippies, etc.).'[3]

As Berke's visit to Berlin indicates, the politicized use of psychedelic substances, fuelled by transnational contacts, spread in counter-cultural scenes in West Germany from the late 1960s. Historians have shown that the often ritualized use of psychedelics played an important role in the politics of the self, in the shaping of an alternative identity, and in processes of community formation.[4] Counter-cultural politics of (psychedelic) ecstasy aimed to transform society. The notion that the ecstatic body was a factor in the struggle for social and cultural change was based on how counter-culturalists placed the body and the mind in relation to each other. For them, the two were inextricably entangled, constituting a body–mind complex. As we shall see in the first part of my essay, this conception had repercussions for counter-cultural notions of the political. The alternative Left rejected Western capitalist modes of sociation and the underlying form of rationality as 'repressing' the body, but did not reject all forms of rationality per se.[5] Against this backdrop, states of (psychedelic) ecstasy were understood as a force that contributed to the 'liberation' of the body, and—because of the interconnectedness

---

[2] Ibid. 141–2.   [3] Ibid. 142.

[4] Will Morris, 'Spiel Appeal: Play, Drug Use and the Culture of 1968 in West Germany', *Journal of Contemporary History*, 49/4 (2014), 770–93; Sven Reichardt, *Authentizität und Gemeinschaft: Linksalternatives Leben in den siebziger und frühen achtziger Jahren* (Berlin, 2014), 831–55; Isabel Richter, 'Die Osterweiterung des Bewusstseins: Techniken der Selbstentgrenzung in den langen 1960er-Jahren', *Mittelweg 36*, 25/4–5 (2016), 107–26; Florian Schleking, 'Drogen, Selbst, Gefühl: Psychedelischer Drogenkonsum in der Bundesrepublik Deutschland um 1970', in Pascal Eitler and Jens Elberfeld (eds.), *Zeitgeschichte des Selbst: Therapeutisierung — Politisierung — Emotionalisierung* (Bielefeld, 2015), 293–326; Detlef Siegfried, *Sound der Revolte: Studien zur Kulturrevolution um 1968* (Weinheim, 2008), 66–8; Robert P. Stephens, *Germans on Drugs: The Complications of Modernization in Hamburg* (Ann Arbor, 2007); Klaus Weinhauer, 'Der Westberliner "Underground": Kneipen, Drogen und Musik', in rotaprint 25 (ed.), *agit 883: Bewegung, Revolte, Underground in Westberlin, 1969–1972* (Berlin, 2006), 73–83.

[5] Detlef Siegfried, 'Rausch und Rationalität: Ästhetiken der Gegenkultur um 1968', in Wolfram Kinzig, Jochen Sautermeister, and Nathalie Thies (eds.), *Rausch: Ekstase zwischen Bacchanal und Cognitive Enhancement* (Baden-Baden, 2020), 103–15, at 114.

of body and mind—as a means of creating an 'authentic' subject and, by extension, a new society. In the second part of the essay I shed light on the intersections between the use of substances such as psychedelics or cannabis and sexual politics, which were also of great significance in the alternative politics of 'liberating' the subject. In this context I scrutinize how contemporaries used cannabis and psychedelics to have new and more satisfying sexual experiences. In the alternative discourse, knowledge of the erotic and sexual effects of LSD and cannabis (substances such as mescaline and psilocybin were of only minor importance in West Germany) played a significant role. The consumption of these substances was conceived of as a driving force of the 'sexual revolution'—a construction which served as an important motive for using them.

Furthermore, I argue that ideas about these substances' sexual and erotic effects had repercussions on the sexual activities and experiences of at least some users. Following scholars such as Norman E. Zinberg and Angus Bancroft, I understand a drug's effect to be a combination of the substance itself, the setting (the socio-material context in which the substance is consumed), and the set—in the words of Bancroft, 'the mental frame which the user brings to their drug use'.[6] In relation to psychedelic sex, this means that knowledge of and expectations about the drug's sexual effects influenced sexual outcomes. Thus, ideas of what sex would be like under the impact of psychedelics or cannabis created new sexual experiences. The variety of erotic and sexual effects attributed to these substances meant that users' experiences differed significantly. However, the drugs' sexual effects not only resulted from knowledge of the substances, but were also influenced by the users' habitus— that is, their internalized sexual morals, attitude towards sexuality, and ways of handling sexual desires.

Before I come to the first part of the essay, I would like to point to a topic in the history of counter-cultural substance use that has received little scholarly attention to date: the role of gender. Since using drugs and having sex are gendered bodily practices, the category of 'gender' affected how people in alternative milieux used substances, and how they experienced the ecstatic states resulting

[6] Angus Bancroft, *Drugs, Intoxication and Society* (Cambridge, 2009), 67; Jonathan Herring, Ciaran Regan, Darin Weinberg, et al., 'Starting the Conversation', in eid. (eds.), *Intoxication and Society: Problematic Pleasures of Drugs and Alcohol* (Basingstoke, 2013), 1–30, at 11; Norman E. Zinberg, *Drug, Set, and Setting: The Basis for Controlled Intoxicant Use* (New Haven, 1984).

from their consumption.[7] Historians such as Robert P. Stephens have already pointed to the gendering of psychedelic discourse around 1970—for example, its reinforcement of male sexual fantasies.[8] Stephens's observation is certainly correct, and it is not the aim of this essay to airbrush sexism out of the alternative politics of ecstasy. Yet it is also necessary to recognize that at least in the years around 1970, some people used psychedelics to undermine the heteronormative and sexist gender order. I shall point to some facets of gendered discourses and practices of counter-cultural drug use, but further research is required.

I. *Ecstatic Bodies in West Germany's Alternative Left around 1970*

As was the case with earlier subcultural groups such as the so-called *Gammler*, body practices played an important role in the alternative milieu which began to emerge during the late 1960s and constituted a significant cultural and social force in West Germany until the early 1980s.[9] Although counter-cultural actors differed significantly in their world-views, they were united in the notion that societal problems in the West grew out of the hegemonic cultural conditions. By modifying these conditions, they aimed to make a better life possible within the existing Western, capitalist framework. In a longer perspective, they strove for societal transformation and the creation of a society characterized by values such as solidarity, sustainability, naturalness, self-fulfilment, and holism.[10]

In counter-cultural politics the body and body practices assumed great importance. Body practices were ways of creating and strengthening a sense of counter-cultural belonging.[11] Furthermore, members of the alternative milieu saw the body as an important aspect

---

[7] Fiona Measham, '"Doing Gender"—"Doing Drugs": Conceptualizing the Gendering of Drugs Cultures', *Contemporary Drug Problems*, 29/2 (2002), 335–73. For the connection between gender and cultures of affect see Andreas Reckwitz, 'Umkämpfte Maskulinität: Zur historischen Kultursoziologie männlicher Subjektformen und ihrer Affektivitäten vom Zeitalter der Empfindsamkeit bis zur Postmoderne', in Manuel Borutta and Nina Verheyen (eds.), *Die Präsenz der Gefühle: Männlichkeit und Emotion in der Moderne* (Bielefeld, 2010), 57–79.   [8] Stephens, *Germans on Drugs*, 238.

[9] Sven Reichardt and Detlef Siegfried, 'Das Alternative Milieu: Konturen einer Lebensform', in eid. (eds.), *Das Alternative Milieu: Antibürgerlicher Lebensstil und linke Politik in der Bundesrepublik Deutschland und Europa 1968–1983* (Göttingen, 2010), 9–24, at 15; Reichardt, *Authentizität und Gemeinschaft*, 14. For the body practices of the *Gammler* see Joachim C. Häberlen, *The Emotional Politics of the Alternative Left: West Germany, 1968–1984* (Cambridge, 2018), 68; Stephens, *Germans on Drugs*, 64–8.

[10] Reichardt and Siegfried, 'Das Alternative Milieu', 9.

[11] Häberlen, *Emotional Politics*; Bodo Mrozek, 'Walle, walle, nimm die schlechten

of their striving for a fundamental reconfiguration of the self and the creation of a so-called 'authentic' subject, which they regarded as essential for societal change. They assumed that societal conditions would materialize in the body and vice versa. They described Western societies as dominated by a Western capitalist rationality, resulting in a 'repressed' body which they believed caused individual and societal problems.[12] Against this backdrop, body practices and body experiences were important forces in the process of creating new types of subjectivity and new modes of sociation, and thus provided a fertile ground for body politics.[13]

Effervescent and ecstatic states played a significant role in the project of 'liberating' the body from the shackles of Western capitalism.[14] Counter-culturalists searched for ecstatic experiences in many places—at home and abroad—and in many ways, using different objects and techniques. They regarded the state of ecstasy as a way of overcoming psychological, physical, and emotional problems caused by conditions in Western societies. In 1984 Raymond Martin, a colourful protagonist of West Germany's counter-cultural milieu, wrote in retrospect about the AAO-Kommune:[15] 'For each form of neurosis caused by an upbringing in the nuclear family, the AA-Kommune finds a form of ecstasy to reveal and cure it.'[16]

Lumpenhüllen: Body Politics der Langhaarigkeit in Lebensreform um 1900 und alternativem Milieu um 1980', in Detlef Siegfried and David Templin (eds.), *Lebensreform um 1900 und Alternativmilieu um 1980: Kontinuitäten und Brüche in Milieus der gesellschaftlichen Selbstreflexion im frühen und späten 20. Jahrhundert* (Göttingen, 2019), 271–91; Andreas Reckwitz, *Das hybride Subjekt: Eine Theorie der Subjektkulturen von der bürgerlichen Moderne zur Postmoderne* (Weilerswist, 2006), 474–82; Reichardt, *Authentizität und Gemeinschaft*, 629–35; Siegfried, *Sound der Revolte*, 62–4.

[12] Häberlen, *Emotional Politics*, 76–91.

[13] Pascal Eitler, 'Die "sexuelle Revolution": Körperpolitik um 1968', in Martin Klimke and Joachim Scharloth (eds.), *1968: Handbuch zur Kultur und Mediengeschichte der Studentenbewegung* (Stuttgart, 2007), 235–46; Häberlen, *Emotional Politics*, 3; Dagmar Herzog, *Sex after Fascism: Memory and Morality in Twentieth-Century Germany* (Princeton, 2005), 153–83; Massimo Perinelli, 'Lust, Gewalt, Befreiung: Sexualitätsdiskurse', in rotaprint 25 (ed.), *agit 883*, 85–99; Siegfried, *Sound der Revolte*, 63–4; Reichardt, *Authentizität und Gemeinschaft*, 629–30. For the politicization of emotions in the alternative Left see Joachim C. Häberlen and Jake P. Smith, 'Struggling for Feelings: The Politics of Emotions in the Radical New Left in West Germany, c.1968–84', *Contemporary European History*, 23/4 (2014), 615–37.

[14] Reckwitz, *Das hybride Subjekt*, 461.

[15] For the AAO-Kommune (also known as AA-Kommune) see, among others, Reichardt, *Authentizität und Gemeinschaft*, 686–98.

[16] Raymond Martin, 'Die AA-Kommune: Vom Bürgerschrecken zur Institution', *Liebe*, 1 (Oct. 1984), 16–21, at 19.

Martin's comment points not only to the importance of ecstatic and euphoric states in alternative politics of the self, but also to the many kinds of ecstasy that were used to shape the 'authentic' subject.

Some described giving birth at home as a 'natural' practice and experience that could produce an ecstatic state—an idea that was also common in the counter-culture of the United States.[17] Others used collective experiments with pain as a way of inducing ecstasy and trance.[18] At least in some cases, counter-culturists used modern technologies to achieve an ecstatic bodily state. In an article published in the magazine *Germania*, one author recommended the use of a machine called an Alphaphon that stimulated the user's brain. It was believed to induce contemplative and euphoric states similar to those resulting from 'controlled drug experiences and meditative techniques'.[19]

The main ways of achieving ecstatic states in the years around 1970, however, were listening and dancing to music, using substances, and having sex. These three activities were often closely connected in achieving ecstatic states.[20] In the following, I focus first on the use of psychedelic substances and cannabis, and then on overlaps between the 'psychedelic revolution' and the 'sexual revolution'.

II. *Politics of Psychedelic Ecstasy around 1970*

Fuelled both by media reports about the use of LSD in the United States and by transnational contacts and travel, the use of substances became an important body practice from the late 1960s.[21] The British counter-cultural magazine *International Times* reported

---

[17] Allen Cohen and Stephen Walzer, *Childbirth is Ecstasy* (1971; repr. Petaluma, 2011); Elke Dufner, [no title], *Päng*, 10 (1974), 3.

[18] Wolf Mein and Lisa Wegen, *Die Pop-Kommune: Dokumentation über Theorie und Praxis einer neuen Form des Zusammenlebens. Ein Report* (Munich, 1971), 87–9.

[19] [Anon.], 'Alpha-Wellen', *Germania*, 3 (Spring 1972), 35–6. Although the author asserted that the Alphaphon was able to create states comparable to those resulting from meditation and controlled drug use, he also stated that the 'high' induced by the machine was different from the ecstasy (*Rausch*) resulting from the use of alcohol and consciousness-expanding drugs.   [20] Reckwitz, *Das hybride Subjekt*, 477.

[21] Reichardt, *Authentitzität und Gemeinschaft*, 834–5; Stephens, *Germans on Drugs*, 56–68; Jakob Tanner, 'Amerikanische Drogen — europäische Halluzinationen', in Angelika Linke and Jakob Tanner (eds.), *Attraktion und Abwehr: Die Amerikanisierung der Alltagskultur in Europa* (Cologne, 2006), 267–88, at 283; Bernd Georg Thamm and Walter Schmetz, *Drogenkonsumenten im Untergrund* (Berlin, 1973), 31; Richard van Ess, *Der Underground war amerikanisch: Vorbilder für die deutsche Undergroundpresse* (Tübingen, 2018), 518–28.

enthusiastically on this development, with reference to the ongoing 'dope revolution' in Berlin: 'In the last six months everybody has turned on; all the Communards are stoned out of their heads, leaving only the straight, unimaginative ideologues to make the speeches.'[22]

The rapid increase in substance use—described in the media as a 'drug wave'—was a topic of intense and heated public debate, stimulated scientific research, and encouraged the passing of the Federal Drug Law (*Betäubungsmittelgesetz*) in West Germany in 1971.[23] Counter-cultural drug use, however, was attacked not only by the societal 'mainstream' and the extreme right, but also by important factions and actors on the Left.[24] In addition to the K-Gruppen, which regarded drugs as a means of exploitation and repression by the ruling class, other left-wing actors, such as Klaus Rainer Röhl, the editor of *konkret*, were also opposed to the politics of substance use.[25]

The alternative Left took a different view of drug-induced states of ecstasy. Despite the fact that parts of the alternative milieu overlapped with the heroin scene that developed in West Germany around 1970—or perhaps because of this—counter-cultural discourses drew a sharp line between 'hard drugs' such as heroin, opium, barbiturates, and amphetamines on the one hand, and cannabis and psychedelic substances such as LSD, mescaline, and psilocybin on the other. With few exceptions—for instance, the West Berlin group Der Zentralrat der umherschweifenden Haschrebellen (The Central Council of the Wandering Hash Rebels) advocated the use of opium and heroin in some of its earlier leaflets—the majority of the alternative Left was opposed to the use of 'hard drugs'.[26]

---

[22] Felix Scorpio, 'Berlin: The Politics of Acid', *International Times*, 11 Apr. 1969, 3.

[23] Detlef Briesen, *Drogenkonsum und Drogenpolitik in Deutschland und den USA: Ein historischer Vergleich* (Frankfurt a.M., 2005), 284–7; Klaus Weinhauer, 'The End of Certainties: Drug Consumption and Youth Delinquency in West Germany', in Axel Schildt and Detlef Siegfried (eds.), *Between Marx and Coca-Cola: Youth Cultures in Changing European Societies, 1960–1980* (New York, 2007), 376–97, at 381.

[24] Some actors on the extreme right framed the spread of drug use in Germany in an antisemitic way and constructed Jews as the driving force behind the so-called drug wave: Wolfgang Massmann, 'Rauschgift zersetzt Deutschland', *Deutsche National-Zeitung*, 31 July 1970, 7.

[25] *konkret*, 26 Feb. 1970, front page; also in Stephens, *Germans on Drugs*, 207; Reichardt, *Authentizität und Gemeinschaft*, 848–9; Peter Viebahn, 'Politgammler, Haschrebellen und eine verlorene Tochter', *twen*, 11/12 (Dec. 1969), 55–63, at 61.

[26] Reichardt, *Authentizität und Gemeinschaft*, 856–8; Weinhauer, 'Der Westberliner "Underground"', 79–80.

According to them, these drugs created a 'kind of Hitlerian fascist mentality' and a 'grey, dull personality', and enslaved their users instead of liberating them by making them addicted and causing an unpolitical retreat and isolation from society.[27] Counter-culturalists considered that these effects meant that 'hard drugs' barred the way to the 'liberation' of the body and the creation of the new subject.

In contrast to 'hard drugs', psychedelics and cannabis were seen as important means of transforming and improving the self. In the words of historian Florian Schleking: 'The drug-body became the object and agent of techniques of the self for changing one's own consciousness, one's own perceptions, and one's own emotions.'[28] Counter-culturalists argued that using these substances to this end required a particular knowledge of the body, a carefully chosen setting, and specific guidelines prescribing the 'correct' emotional and mental preparations.[29] Members of the alternative milieu believed that if drugs were used in the right way, the resulting ecstatic states could serve the creation of the alternative subject and the alternative society in different ways. First, seeing cannabis-induced highs as a way of enhancing their ability to communicate and to improve the relationship between themselves and their environment, counter-culturalists used psychedelics and cannabis to shape a counter-cultural identity and to create and strengthen a communal sense of belonging.[30] Second, some advocates of militant politics praised cannabis for inciting clashes with the police and for shaping a militant subject.[31] Third, the notion that psychedelic highs allowed users to expand their consciousness and gain new insights about

---

[27] Allen Ginsberg, 'Speed', *Love*, 3, n.d. [1970], p. [19]; Rudi Wormser, *Drogen, Erfahrung und Erkenntnis: Selbstzeugnisse, Dokumente, Analysen* (Neuwied, 1973), 78.

[28] Schleking, 'Drogen, Selbst, Gefühl', 296.

[29] Kristoff Kerl and Florian Schleking, 'Rausch, Körper, Geschichte: Überlegungen und Perspektiven', *Body Politics*, 6/10 (2018), 13–60, at 29–37; Schleking, 'Drogen, Selbst, Gefühl'; id., 'Psychedelic Fears: Drug Use as an Emotional Practice in West Germany around 1970', *Storicamente*, 11/24 (2015), 1–23 ⟨https://doi.org/10.12977/stor607⟩.

[30] [Anon.], 'Cornelia: Eine Blume von Bambule ist gestorben', *Hundert Blumen*, 8 (Summer 1973), 5; Morris, 'Spiel Appeal', 776–7; Reichardt, *Authentizität und Gemeinschaft*, 840–1; Schleking, 'Drogen, Selbst, Gefühl', 295, 313, 323; Ronald Steckel, *Bewusstseinserweiternde Drogen: Eine Aufforderung zur Diskussion* (Berlin, 1970), 93; Tanner, 'Amerikanische Drogen', 277; Klaus Weinhauer, 'Drug Consumption in London and Western Berlin during the 1960s and 1970s: Local and Transnational Perspectives', *Social History of Alcohol and Drugs*, 20/2 (2006), 187–224, at 196.

[31] Ralf Reinders and Ronald Fritzsch, *Die Bewegung 2. Juni: Gespräche über Haschrebellen, Lorenz-Entführung, Knast* (Berlin, 2003), 21–7; Bodo Saggel, *Der Antijurist oder die Kriminalität der schwarzen Roben & Bruchstücke aus meinem Leben* (Berlin, 1998), 94.

themselves was widespread in the alternative milieu—an idea that was influenced by the main protagonists of the 'psychedelic revolution' in the United States, such as Richard Alpert, Ralph Metzner, and especially Timothy Leary, whose book *Politics of Ecstasy* was published in Germany in 1970, and who was widely read in West Germany's counter-culture.[32] The anonymous author of an article entitled 'Haschisch', which was published in the magazine *Love*, presented psychedelics and cannabis as being able to create a state of ecstasy which allows users to escape a reality of 'bourgeois forced fictions consisting of nineteenth-century platitudinous rationalism and the exhausted everyday life of achievement and consumption'.[33]

The direction taken by the 'liberation' of the self could vary significantly in the alternative milieu, and the different currents often overlapped. For some, the main driving force was the idea that the use of psychedelics allowed them to have spiritual and mystic experiences seen as suppressed by Western, capitalist rationalism.[34] Others associated the mind-expanding powers of psychedelics and cannabis mainly with radical societal changes.[35] In 1972 the magazine *Germania* published an article about the new alternative culture, which it described as 'a drug culture'. Claiming that LSD allows the user to become more 'authentic' and more of a human being, the article linked the experience of LSD to the creation of a libertarian, communist subjectivity: 'The social form of the new culture is, of course, communism. Our communism is electricity plus a smile, technology plus your energy . . . Our communism is anarchy because everybody is his own prime minister, representative, highest judge . . . Let us populate the world with human beings!'[36] Describing 'our communism' as the result of the interplay between electricity/technology and the 'liberation' of the body (smile, energy) in 'a drug culture',

---

[32] Reichardt, *Authentizität und Gemeinschaft*, 850–2; Schleking, 'Drogen, Selbst, Gefühl', 311–17; Jakob Tanner, '"Doors of Perception" versus "Mind Control": Experimente mit Drogen zwischen kaltem Krieg und 1968', in Birgit Griesecke, Marcus Krause, Nicolas Pethes, et al. (eds.), *Kulturgeschichte des Menschenversuchs im 20. Jahrhundert* (Frankfurt a.M., 2009), 340–72, at 365–6.

[33] [Anon.], 'Haschisch', *Love*, 2, n.d. [1969], pp. [4–6, 15], at [4]: 'bürgerliche Zwangsfiktion, aus plattem Rationalismus des neunzehnten Jahrhunderts, aus dem vernutzten Alltag von Leistung und Konsum'.

[34] Richter, 'Osterweiterung des Bewusstseins', 110–14; Schleking, 'Drogen, Selbst, Gefühle', 304–6.

[35] Stephens, *Germans on Drugs*, 78–80; Morris, 'Spiel Appeal', 785–7.

[36] Gila, Annette, Antje, et al., 'Was wir so dachten!', *Germania*, 3 (Spring 1972), 26–7, at 27.

the article detected a close relationship between the 'rational' and the impact of ecstatic experiences. 'Reason' and the psychedelic 'liberation' of the body were not thought of as antagonistic forces, but as complementary ones that together laid the foundations for a libertarian, communist subjectivity and society.

In addition to the ways mentioned above in which counter-culturalists used substances in reconfiguring the self, drugs also played a significant role in the alternative politics of sexuality. In the following, I examine how ecstatic experiences were conceived of as a tool in the ongoing 'sexual revolution'. As we shall see, the 'psychedelic revolution' and the 'sexual revolution' were closely entangled and fuelled each other on the alternative Left.

III. *Drugs and Sexuality around 1970*

The so-called 'sex wave' hit West Germany in the mid 1960s. New methods of birth control, the increasing representation of mostly female naked bodies in the media, the rising numbers of erotic and pornographic products, and the pluralization of sexual morals undermined the conservative sexual culture of West Germany's post-fascist society.[37] The alternative milieu had an ambivalent relationship with liberal, consumer-oriented, capitalist changes in the field of sexuality. On the one hand, the ubiquitous depictions of naked bodies and sex, new methods of birth control, and the increased discussion of sex—both scientific and non-scientific— paved the way for an alternative politics of sexuality. On the other, counter-culturalists denounced the consumer-oriented, capitalist attitude towards sexuality which resulted in its commodification. For them, sexuality played an important part in the struggle for a new subject and society.[38] Drawing on theoreticians such as Wilhelm Reich and Herbert Marcuse, they made the 'liberation' of an allegedly repressed sexuality an integral part of their broader body politics.[39] From counter-cultural perspectives, the 'liberation'

---

[37] Eitler, 'Die "sexuelle Revolution"'; Herzog, *Sex after Fascism*, 141.

[38] Timothy Scott Brown, *West Germany and the Global Sixties: The Antiauthoritarian Revolt, 1962–1978* (Cambridge, 2013), 304–20; Reichardt, *Authentizität und Gemeinschaft*, 651.

[39] For the wide reception of Wilhelm Reich and Herbert Marcuse in the late 1960s see (among others) Eitler, 'Die "sexuelle Revolution"', 237–40; Jens Elberfeld, 'Freudomarxismus und 68er Aufklärung', in Sven Lewandowski and Thorsten Benkel (eds.), *Schlüsselwerke der Sexualtheorie* (Wiesbaden, forthcoming); Herzog, *Sex after Fascism*, 158–60.

of sexuality demanded new attitudes towards sex as well as new sexual practices. Against this backdrop, historians have argued that the counter-cultural 'sexual revolution' did not 'liberate' sexuality, but implemented a new sexual regime.[40]

After the drug culture became a visible and hotly debated phenomenon in the late 1960s and early 1970s, ongoing changes in the field of sexuality became in many ways closely related to drug use. In the United States, psychedelic substances had already been used in therapeutic settings to treat sexual 'problems' in the early 1960s. In the mid 1960s, Constance A. Newland's book *My Self and I* was published in Germany.[41] It reported the LSD-based psychoanalytic therapy undertaken by the author and how she overcame her problems in achieving orgasm. From the late 1960s, the alleged sexual effects of psychedelic substances and cannabis became a topic of public interest in West Germany.[42] In addition to (popular) scientific articles and books, newspapers, the yellow press, and magazines reported on the alleged effects of drugs on sexual morals and sexual experience, often in a sensationalized and sexualized way.[43]

Many contemporaries—especially conservatives—presented the use of drugs as a force driving the changes in the sexual morals and practices of young people in general, and of young women

[40] Franz X. Eder, 'The Long History of the "Sexual Revolution" in West Germany', in Gert Hekma and Alain Giami (eds.), *Sexual Revolutions* (Basingstoke, 2014), 99–120, at 99–100; Eitler, 'Die "sexuelle Revolution"', 236–7.

[41] Constance A. Newland, *Abenteuer im Unbewußten: Das Experiment einer Frau mit der Droge LSD* (Munich, 1964), 46; first published as *My Self and I* (New York, 1962).

[42] For the 'sexual revolution' in West Germany see, among others, Peter-Paul Bänziger, Magdalena Beljan, Franz X. Eder, et al. (eds.), *Sexuelle Revolution? Zur Geschichte der Sexualität im deutschsprachigen Raum seit den 1960er Jahren* (Bielefeld, 2015); Eitler, 'Die "sexuelle Revolution"', 235–46; Herzog, *Sex after Fascism*.

[43] Günter Amendt, *Haschisch und Sexualität: Eine empirische Untersuchung über die Sexualität Jugendlicher in der Drogensubkultur* (Stuttgart, 1974); Rolv Heuer, Herman Prigann, Thomas Witecka, et al., *Helft Euch Selbst! Der Release-Report gegen die Sucht* (Hamburg, 1971), 11; Peter Kirchgässer, *Haschisch und Marihuana: Beobachtungen in zwanzig Fällen* (Munich, 1969), 14, 16; Nicolaus Neumann, 'Drogen: Berichterstattung der bundesdeutschen Presse', in Gemeinnütziger Verein zur Bekämpfung des Drogen- und Rauschmittelmißbrauchs — konkret e.v. (ed.), *Sucht ist Flucht: Drogen und Rauschmittelmissbrauch in der Bundesrepublik. Analysen, Berichte, Forderungen* (Hamburg, 1972), 212–32, at 217–18, 232; Theo Löbsack, *Die unheimlichen Möglichkeiten, oder: Die manipulierte Seele*, 4th edn. (Düsseldorf, 1969), 194, 201–2; Karl-Ludwig Täschner, *Das Cannabis-Problem: Die Kontroverse um Haschisch und Marihuana aus medizinisch-soziologischer Sicht* (Wiesbaden, 1979), 112–19; Rudolf G. Wormser, *Drogenkonsum und soziales Verhalten bei Schülern: Eine empirische Untersuchung der Zusammenhänge von Drogengebrauch, Leistung, Persönlichkeit und Sexualität* (Munich, 1973), 190–206.

in particular. They deplored that young women, while under the influence of drugs, could become victims of 'immoral' men or even engage deliberately in premarital sex.[44] By describing drugs as a threat to the sexual order, critics hoped to restore conservative sexual morals and contain the 'drug wave' at the same time, but the outcome was different. Against the backdrop of the ongoing 'sexual revolution', the debates and reports on the sexual effects of drugs fuelled interest in these substances by making them attractive to young people looking for new sexual experiences.[45]

Counter-culturalists shared the idea that drugs had a significant impact on sexual experience, but they constructed, framed, and evaluated these alleged effects differently. They drew a sharp distinction between the sexual impact of psychedelics and cannabis on the one hand, and drugs such as opioids on the other. Both were connected to the aspiration of 'liberating' sexuality, but in fundamentally different or even antagonistic ways. Whereas counter-culturalists, as we shall see, understood and used psychedelics and cannabis as tools that enabled them to have new sexual experiences, they constructed a strong opposition between heroin/drug addiction and 'liberated' sex. They saw the use of heroin as preventing the changes in sexuality that they aspired to.[46] They presented opioid use as 'repressing' sexual desires and, in the case of addiction, as causing its users to engage not in 'liberating' sex, but in sex acts that they considered to be exploitative, such as sex work.[47]

In addition to believing that substances such as heroin caused or perpetuated the 'repression' of sexuality, counter-culturalists also considered the 'repressive' attitude towards sex in Western societies to be one of the causes of drug habits—a view which was

---

[44] Günther Bauer, *Rauschgift: Ein Handbuch über die Rauschgiftsucht, den Rauschgifthandel, die Bekämpfungsmaßnahmen und die Hilfen für Gefährdete* (Lübeck, 1972), 85; Hermann Dobbelstein, *Porno und Hasch: Aus der Sprechstunde eines Arztes* (Freiburg i.Br., 1971), 27–30; Stephens, *Germans on Drugs*, 232–43; Wormser, *Drogenkonsum*, 190.

[45] Hu, 'Rajneeshstädte', *Materialdienst*, 45/2 (July 1982), 205–6, at 206, Wormser, *Drogenkonsum*, 200.

[46] William S. Burroughs, 'Opium, Morphium', *Love*, 2, n.d. [1969], pp. [2–3, 16–18], at [18]; Hamburger Institut für Sozialforschung (HIS), Flugblatt-und Broschüren-sammlung, SBe 431 Subkultur-Bewegungen G3 Kommune 1, folder 'Zentralrat der Haschrebellen. Es ist Zeit zu zerstören', 'Teach In'; Klaus Weinhauer, 'Heroinszenen in der Bundesrepublik Deutschland und in Großbritannien der siebziger Jahre: Konsumpraktiken zwischen staatlichen, medialen und zivilgesellschaftlichen Einflüssen', in Reichardt and Siegfried (eds.), *Das Alternative Milieu*, 244–64, at 260.

[47] [Anon.], 'Wahre Comiks [*sic*]', *Hundert Blumen*, 4 (Nov. 1972), 16; Stephens, *Germans on Drugs*, 219–21, 247; Wormser, *Drogen*, 43.

shared by left-wing researchers such as Günter Amendt.[48] In the summer of 1971, the magazine *Fizz* published a letter to the editor dealing with substance use. Differentiating between the deliberate, mind-expanding use of psychedelics and cannabis, and the use of drugs as a means of escaping reality, the letter writer (who called herself 'female comrade') described the excessive and permanent use of drugs as a 'substitute satisfaction, especially for a lack of sexual satisfaction and recognition'.[49] The idea that 'repressed' sexuality was an important factor in the development of a type of personality prone to drug addiction was also expressed in alternative addiction therapy.[50] In a questionnaire which the drug counselling organization Release used to obtain detailed information about its service users, 12 out of 126 questions related to topics such as sexual experiences as a child, parents' attitudes towards sexuality, and problems in achieving orgasm.[51]

IV. 'Liberating' Sexuality via Psychedelic Substances

In contrast to the negative relationship they saw between sexuality and 'hard drugs', counter-culturalists regarded psychedelics and cannabis as tools which allowed their users to have new sexual experiences—a notion that fuelled the use of psychedelic substances during the late 1960s and early 1970s.[52]

If used in the right set and setting, counter-culturalists claimed, these substances would serve the 'sexual revolution'.[53] According to the psychedelic discourse, the body under the influence of drugs paved the way for the creation of a sexually 'liberated' subject by reshaping the user's consciousness, sensuality, and desires. First, assuming that socialization in Western societies created a

[48] Amendt, *Haschisch und Sexualität*, 108.

[49] [Anon.], 'Leserbrief', *Fizz*, 6 (Summer 1971), 5, repr. in Udo Koch and Klaus Decker (eds.), *Fizz Reprint 1–10* (Berlin, 1989).

[50] HIS, *Release*, REL 221, folder 1, Drogenberatungsstelle München, 'Psychologisches Behandlungsprogramm für Opiat und Amphetamin Abhängige', 5.

[51] HIS, *Release*, REL 111, folder 3, Interessenverband pädagogischer Forschungsprojekte e.V., 'Wie's bei dir lief'.

[52] Steckel, *Bewusstseinserweiternde Drogen*, 53.

[53] [Anon.], 'Playboy Interview: Timothy Leary. A Candid Conversation with the Controversial ex-Harvard Professor, Prime Partisan and Prophet of LSD', *Playboy*, Sept. 1966 〈https://ia800706.us.archive.org/34/items/playboylearyinte00playrich/playboylearyinte00playrich.pdf〉 [accessed 28 Nov. 2020]; Reichardt, *Authentizität und Gemeinschaft*, 651; Steckel, *Bewusstseinserweiternde Drogen*, 52.

sexually repressed body unaware of its 'natural' sexual feelings and desires, they saw psychedelics and cannabis as enabling users to re-explore their body and recognize its 'natural' demands. Rolf-Ulrich Kaiser, a central figure on the alternative music scene in West Germany, supported his statement that these substances could expose their users' sexual needs by referring to Tuli Kupferberg, lead singer of the famous band The Fugs.[54] Second, alternative leftists claimed that psychedelics and cannabis could be used to have new sexual experiences and discover new sexual and erotic feelings. Members of the famous High-Fish-Kommune even described sex under the influence of LSD as bearing no comparison with sex without LSD.[55]

In the following, I trace ideas about the power of cannabis and psychedelics to change sexual experience. What potential did counter-culturalists see in these substances? In general, discourses on the 'liberation' of sexuality fundamentally shaped counter-cultural expectations of the substances' effects on sex. As we shall see, these expectations not only fuelled the use of these substances, but also influenced the sexual and erotic experiences achieved under their influence.

V. Drugs at the Wet Dream Film Festival

In the striving for the 'liberation' of sex via psychedelics and cannabis, the possibility of (temporarily) removing feelings of sexual shame and 'bourgeois inhibitions' was of great importance and made these substances an attractive tool for people searching for new sexual experiences.[56] Their alleged disinhibiting effects meant that counter-culturalists used cannabis and acid to initiate sexual encounters and to create an atmosphere which allowed them to transgress dominant sexual morals. Whether at home, at parties

---

[54] Rolf-Ulrich Kaiser, *Fuck the Fugs: Das Buch der Fugs* (Cologne, 1969), p. [26]. For more information on Rolf-Ulrich Kaiser see, among others, Detlef Siegfried, *Time is on my Side: Konsum und Politik in der westdeutschen Jugendkultur der 60er Jahre* (Göttingen, 2017), 601–23; Alexander Simmeth, *Krautrock transnational: Die Neuerfindung der Popmusik in der BRD 1968–1978* (Bielefeld, 2016), 90–101.

[55] Mein and Wegen, *Die Pop-Kommune*, 96.

[56] Jan Herha, 'Erfahrungen mit Haschisch: Ergebnisse einer Befragung von 234 Konsumenten von Cannabis und anderen Drogen in Berlin (West) 1969/70' (Ph.D thesis, Freie Universität Berlin, 1973), 103; Steckel, *Bewusstseinserweiternde Drogen*, 52; Wormser, *Drogenkonsum*, 206.

and events such as festivals, or travelling abroad, using drugs and having sex were often closely entangled.[57]

The close connection between drugs and sex is shown by the Wet Dream Film Festival (WDFF). This was organized by members of the counter-cultural sex magazine *Suck*'s editorial team in Amsterdam in 1970 and 1971, including Jim Haynes, Germaine Greer, William Levy, and Willem de Ridder.[58] The international audience included supporters of 'sexual liberation' such as Betty Dodson, Jefferson Poland, and Richard Neville, writers such as Fernando Arrabal and Jean Genet, and pornographer Al Goldstein. The festival aimed to serve the cause of 'liberating' sex, and attendees were required to join an organization called Sexuality Egalitarian and Libertarian Fraternity (SELF) in advance of the festival.[59]

Whereas the first WDFF screened only erotic and pornographic films, the second and larger festival also had an extensive accompanying programme which included (sex) parties and a boat tour lasting several hours. Several hundred people with different social and cultural backgrounds from many countries attended both festivals, which made them an important transnational contact zone. One attendee described the second festival as a 'gathering of groovy people from all over Europe who came to groove, get high, laugh and watch pornographic movies'.[60] Jim Haynes also emphasized the sense of belonging and the international connections created by the festival:

We are a tribe: The Sex Freaks of Europe. We believe that our bodies are holy. Our bodies are made to touch. We want to reach out and experience others. We have come to Amsterdam because in this corner of Europe it is possible for us to express ourselves openly. . . . Many people [who] met during the first Wet Dream, between the two, [or] during the second, are still meeting each other. This was one of the main purposes of the Festival: to bring SUCK readers and SUCK contributors together so that they might 'cum' to know

---

[57] [Anon.], 'A Week in the Fondle Park', *Suck*, 6, n.d., 10; Mein and Wegen, *Die Pop-Kommune*, 49–50, 69, 82.

[58] Elena Gorfinkel, 'Wet Dreams: Erotic Film Festivals of the Early 1970s and the Utopian Sexual Public Sphere', *Framework: The Journal of Cinema and Media*, 47/2 (2006), 59–86, at 63.

[59] International Institute of Social History, Amsterdam (IISH), Bill Levy: Suck and Wet Dream Film Festivals Collection, folder 70, [Anon.], 'S.E.L.F. Statement'.

[60] Les Frank, 'You Have Seen my Cock: Now Read my Story', in William Levy (ed.), *Wet Dreams: Films and Adventures* (Amsterdam, 1973), 32–5, at 33.

one another. And out of this coming together, we might evolve a new spirit, a new confidence thru our communal strength.[61]

Around sixty people from West Germany participated in the WDFF, with some of them attending in both 1970 and 1971. This made West Germans the fourth largest national group, exceeded only by participants from the Netherlands (around 227), the UK (around 109), and France (around 104).[62] Among the German participants were important figures from West Germany's counter-culture, such as Bernd Brummbär and Felix de Mendelssohn. Reports on the festival, published in magazines such as *Pardon* and *Twen*, introduced the event to West Germans who did not attend the festival in Amsterdam.[63]

The presence of police officers at the first festival in 1970 meant that the festival organizers discouraged the smoking of cannabis during the film screenings.[64] Whether attendees heeded this advice is unknown. However, we do know that the use of drugs was widespread during the second WDFF, and that it was closely related to new sexual experiences. Participants reported that 'hash cake and group sex were very popular' at a party in the Lido club, which was part of the programme accompanying the festival in 1971.[65] Regarding the boat tour, Bernd Brummbär remembers: 'We smoked a few joints, Doris and Fatima were tripping, we were dancing, kissing, touching, feeling full of love—warm bodies. Then we fucked, we fucked, we fucked, we fucked, and we fucked. It blew my mind, I had the most incredible fuck of my life.'[66]

At least some of the organizers and participants saw some drugs as important means of having 'liberated' sexual experiences. This is shown in the book *Wet Dreams*, which was edited by William Levy and

[61] Jim Haynes, 'Jim's Journals 2', in Levy (ed.), *Wet Dreams*, 36–8, at 38.

[62] [Anon.], 'Cast of Characters: S.E.L.F. Members from Both Festivals', in Levy (ed.), *Wet Dreams*, 259–61. The list of people who attended one or both Wet Dream Film Festival(s) is incomplete and excludes some of the attendees mentioned in the essays in the *Wet Dreams* book. Thus, the number of participants was higher than mentioned above.

[63] IISH, Bill Levy: Suck and Wet Dream Film Festivals Collection, folder 24, telegram from Verlag Bärmeier und Nikel, 23 Nov. 1970; folder 69, [Anon.], 'List of all S.E.L.F. members'.

[64] IISH, Bill Levy: Suck and Wet Dream Film Festivals Collection, folder 70, Wet Dream Film Festival programme.

[65] Lady Angel, 'Brummbär Treats my Cunt as a Really Precious Thing', in Levy (ed.), *Wet Dreams*, 3–5, at 3; Joan Buck, 'Some of my Best Friends Made Love There', ibid. 24–6, at 25.

[66] Brummbär, 'I Met Lady Angel at the Wet Dream Film Festival', in Levy (ed.), *Wet Dreams*, 6–8, at 7.

published in 1973. It contains reports by numerous participants in the festival. A short article in the book introduces the 'official festival dealer', accompanied by a photograph of him, naked, captioned: 'This is the man, holding the grass, he used to make the cake which helped create the Festival's sexually charged atmosphere.'[67] The close link between sex and drugs, established here by describing cannabis as contributing to 'the Festival's sexually charged atmosphere', is also conveyed in a cartoon printed in the *Wet Dreams* book. It shows a seller walking through the crowded cinema auditorium, advertising her products: 'Porn novels, dirty pictures, aphrodisiac chocolates, vibrators, masks, boots, whips, handcuffs, hashish, marijuana, LSD, leather, corsets, cocaine.'[68] The inclusion of substances such as cannabis, LSD, and cocaine in the list of sex toys and other objects used to arouse desire and intensify sexual pleasure underlines that at the WDFF these drugs were seen and used as sexual stimulants.

The festival not only provides insights into the role of drugs in the politics of 'sexual liberation', but also sheds some light on the significance of gender in the counter-cultural politics of ecstasy around 1970. In general, the ratio of men to women at the WDFF was roughly two to one, suggesting that the idea of such a sex film festival was more attractive to men than to women.[69] One reason for the gender imbalance was the dominance of the male gaze in most sex films, which was criticized by some women who attended the event.[70] In her article 'Cunt Positive Women Getting it Together', the famous feminist Betty Dodson, who was a member of the festival jury, complained that 'most porno films are made by men and are still very double standard'. However, this diagnosis did not lead her to criticize sex films per se as sexist, but rather created the wish to 'produce sex films that will be sensuous and effective turn ons, and teach-ins with the women having real orgasms'.[71]

The reduction of women to sex objects also coincided with work on the 'liberation' of female sexuality in reports by other women who

[67] [Anon.], 'Official Festival Dealer', in Levy (ed.), *Wet Dreams*, 44–5, at 44.

[68] Siné, 'Siné in Amsterdam', in Levy (ed.), *Wet Dreams*, 96–100, at 97.

[69] [Anon.], 'Cast of Characters'. I identified the gender of the participants by their names—a problematic method: first, it only allows participants to be grouped into the binary categories 'man' and 'woman'; second, in some cases the first name is not fully given in the listing.

[70] Joan Buck and Lady Angel, 'I am Constantly Trying to Change', in Levy (ed.), *Wet Dreams*, 28–9, at 28.

[71] Betty Dodson, 'Cunt Positive Women Getting it Together', in Levy (ed.), *Wet Dreams*, 48–55, at 51.

visited the WDFF.[72] Despite complaints about sexism, many women enthusiastically told stories of desire-driven, orgastic sex and new sexual experiences during the festival—whether sex with a stranger, group sex, or with a partner of the same sex (which also applied to men). A female participant from Germany praised the freedom and agency she experienced at a sex party held during the festival: 'The only interest I had by this time was to fuck Brümbar [*sic*] as long and as much as I could (I don't often have the opportunity). And this was possible, one could really do what one wanted to, without feeling bad: fuck, dance, hear music, drink, eat, talk, and smoke dope.'[73]

As already mentioned, the use of substances was ubiquitous at the festival and women (as well as men) often engaged in sex under their influence. Unfortunately, most of the women's reports do not elaborate on how these substances contributed to the shaping of their sexual experiences. A report by one woman, however, indicates that at least for some, taking drugs was closely linked to 'liberating' sexual experiences. After she smoked cannabis with a friend and got 'really high', she had sex with him in a way that she conceived as increasing her female agency: 'I fuck him on top. All the way, sucking him first, then riding home. First time, solo for the whole trip. A little chilly on the back but good to be with a guy who isn't at all uptight about me being on top. Opening more and more doors. Doesn't seem political, didn't feel more powerful but felt more possibilities.'[74]

The reports written by attendees on their experiences at the Wet Dream Film Festival show that the use of substances such as psychedelics and cannabis—and in some cases also cocaine—made new sexual experiences more intense. However, the reports provide little information about how these substances influenced and changed the sensual feelings and experiences of the users. I shed light on this issue in the following section.

VI. *The Intensification of Orgasms and the Eroticization of the Whole Body*

Counter-culturalists argued that drug use intensified sensual perception, which made these substances highly useful for those seeking

---

[72] Any Rousseau, 'The Mad Boat of Amsterdam', in Levy (ed.), *Wet Dreams*, 104–7, at 104–5.

[73] Barbara Breiteneicher, 'Too Much for Me', in Levy (ed.), *Wet Dreams*, 23.

[74] Lynne Tillman, 'Everyone Has a Story', in Levy (ed.), *Wet Dreams*, 138–41, at 141.

a more satisfying and pleasurable sexuality.[75] In this sense, Rudi Wormser claimed: 'People who are already sensual experience tenderness, skin contact, and sexuality so much more intensely that they use hashish only for that purpose.'[76]

The intensification of bodily sensations and the reduction of inhibitions, counter-culturalists believed, allowed the user to have new erotic and sexual experiences. Notions about the drug-induced reshaping of sexuality were strongly influenced by contemporary knowledge, which circulated in discourses on the 'sexual revolution'. Drawing on Wilhelm Reich, many members of the alternative Left saw having long and intense orgasms as an important demand of the 'sexual revolution'.[77] The use of psychedelics and cannabis was seen as a way of achieving that goal. According to Ronald Steckel, LSD, mescaline, and psilocybin have the capacity 'to intensify the sexual experience to the point of ecstasy'.[78] In 1966 'the prophet of LSD' Timothy Leary stated in an interview with the magazine *Playboy* that 'a woman will inevitably have several hundred orgasms' if she has sex in a 'carefully prepared, loving LSD session'.[79] Against the backdrop of the alleged sexual power of LSD, some contemporaries explicitly connected the drug with Wilhelm Reich's politics of orgasm. In an article entitled 'Sex, Religion & LSD', published in the Berlin magazine *Love*, Allan D. Coult develops a psychedelic version of Wilhelm Reich's theory of orgasm. He depicts LSD as a tool that enables its users to realize the goals of Reich's somatic psychotherapy. As an indicator of the therapy's success, he describes the patient's capacity to experience a 'perfect orgasm'. According to the author, LSD could pave the way to such an orgasm.[80]

The discursive construction of psychedelics and cannabis as tools to improve the ability to orgasm not only influenced users' expectations about the bodily effects of the substances, but also shaped their sexual experiences.[81] In a study conducted in Munich

---

[75] Mein and Wegen, *Die Pop-Kommune*, 82; Schleking, 'Drogen, Selbst, Gefühl', 320; Steckel, *Bewusstseinserweiternde Drogen*, 52.   [76] Wormser, *Drogen*, 97–8.

[77] Franz X. Eder, 'Die lange Geschichte der "Sexuellen Revolution" in Westdeutschland (1950er bis 1980er Jahre)', in Bänziger, Beljan, Eder, et al. (eds.), *Sexuelle Revolution?*, 25–59, at 48; Eitler, 'Die "sexuelle Revolution"'; Reichardt, *Authentizität und Gemeinschaft*, 654; Nina Verheyen, 'Der ausdiskutierte Orgasmus: Beziehungsgespräche als kommunikative Praxis in der Geschichte des Intimen seit den 1960er Jahren', in Bänziger, Beljan, Eder, et al. (eds.), *Sexuelle Revolution?*, 181–98.

[78] Steckel, *Bewusstseinserweiternde Drogen*, 24.   [79] [Anon.], 'Playboy Interview'.

[80] Allan D. Coult, 'Sex, Religion & LSD', *Love*, 4, n.d. [1970], pp. [5–9], at [8].

[81] Herha, 'Erfahrungen mit Haschisch', 103.

from December 1968 to August 1969, Peter Kirchgässer interviewed fourteen men and six women aged between 18 and 30.[82] Asked why they used cannabis and what their experiences had been, some interviewees stated that they had had intensified orgasms under the influence of the drug.[83]

However, Kirchgässer's interviews also show that the sexual experiences of users differed. While four adolescents in the sample had experienced more intense orgasms, the other participants did not share this experience. Some of them stated that cannabis did not have any sexual or erotic effects on them.[84] Others reported a cannabis-induced reduction in their sexual potency and desire for coitus.[85] Instead of wanting more orgastic genital sex, they felt an intense longing for caresses and tenderness under the influence of cannabis. This experience points to the second main sexual effect attributed to cannabis and LSD.

In the context of the 'sexual revolution' there was a powerful idea that the whole body, and not only the genital area, should be a source of erotic pleasure. An important advocate of this idea was Herbert Marcuse, who described the primacy of genital sexuality and the resulting de-eroticization of the rest of the body as the result of the capitalist performance principle.[86] The demand to eroticize the whole body was also part of counter-cultural discourses on psychedelic sex. In an article by Timothy Leary and Ralph Metzner, published in translation in *Love*, the authors describe caressing as a source of orgasmic delight: 'A simple caress can be of the orgasmic intensity usually experienced only in genital effusion.' Furthermore, they linked this 'psychedelic sexual experience' to the pan-eroticism described in 'Eastern texts such as the Kama Sutra',[87] a description which points to the orientalization of drug use and sexuality in parts of the Western counter-culture.[88] In his interview with *Playboy*,

---

[82] Kirchgässer, *Haschisch und Marihuana*, 12.　　　[83] Ibid. 14, 18, 34, 36.
[84] Ibid. 24, 30.　　　　　　　　　　　　　　　　　　　　[85] Ibid. 22.
[86] Häberlen, *Emotional Politics*, 54–5, 186; Joachim C. Häberlen, 'Feeling like a Child: Dreams and Practices of Sexuality in the West German Alternative Left during the Long 1970s', *Journal of the History of Sexuality*, 25/2 (May 2016), 219–45, at 223; Herbert Marcuse, 'Die Re-Erotisierung des ganzen Körpers und die Befreiung von der Arbeit', in Barbara Eder and Felix Wemheuer (eds.), *Die Linke und der Sex: Klassische Texte zum wichtigsten Thema* (Vienna, 2011), 115–18; Reichardt, *Authentizität und Gemeinschaft*, 654.
[87] Ralph Metzner and Timothy Leary, 'Über das Planen psychedelischer Erfahrungen', in *Love*, 2, n.d. [1969], pp. [7–14], at [13].
[88] Eitler, 'Die "sexuelle Revolution"', 243–4; Elija Horn, 'Sexuelle Befreiung aus Indien: Jugendkulturelle Verknüpfung von "östlicher Spiritualität" und Sexualität

Timothy Leary also saw LSD as having the capacity to turn the whole body into an erogenous zone. He reported on a moment when his wife tenderly touched the palm of his hand while he was tripping on LSD. According to Leary, 'a hundred thousand end cells exploded in my hand in soft orgasm. Ecstatic energies pulsated up my arms and rocketed into my brain, where another hundred thousand cells softly exploded in pure, delicate pleasure.'[89]

Again, as with orgasms, this idea affected the physical experiences of some contemporary users of cannabis and psychedelics. In an article published in the German news magazine *Der Spiegel*, a young woman from Berlin described sex under the influence of hash as follows: 'Under the influence of hash I slept with my boyfriend more beautifully than before. The skin all over my body was more sensitive than usual, even in places where I usually don't respond, such as under the shoulder blades.'[90] Others also framed their physical experiences in a similar way. They reported on 'skin eroticism' (*Hauterotik*), a 'genitalization of the body' (*Genitalisierung des Körpers*), 'orgastic skin ecstasy' (*orgastischer Hautempfindungsrausch*) and an 'orgasm-like sensation' (*orgasmusähnliches Gefühl*) when petted tenderly while under the influence of cannabis.[91] The notion that psychedelics and cannabis enabled users to have ('better') genital orgasms and allowed them to experience the whole body as a source of erotic and sexual pleasure played a major role in counter-cultural discourses on and practices of psychedelic sexual 'liberation'.

In addition, some counter-culturalists linked psychedelic drugs to the transformation of sexuality in other ways. Sometimes the effects of cannabis were described as enabling men to be more responsive to the erotic or sexual desires of their female partners and to engage more harmoniously in sex acts.[92] In a study on drug use among school students, Rudolf Wormser quotes experience reports from Barbara Lewis's book *The Sexual Power of Marijuana*, which he introduces as shedding light on the sexual effects of hashish. According to a male respondent, marijuana allowed him

um 1918 und um 1980', in Siegfried and Templin (eds.), *Lebensreform um 1900 und Alternativmilieu um 1980*, 195–212; Richter, 'Osterweiterung des Bewusstseins', 110–14; Schleking, 'Drogen, Selbst, Gefühl', 314–15.

    [89] [Anon.], 'Playboy Interview'.

    [90] [Anon.], 'Hasch: Tibet ist überall', *Der Spiegel*, 10 Nov. 1969, 76–102, at 96.

    [91] Herha, 'Erfahrungen mit Haschisch', 115; Kirchgässer, *Haschisch und Marihuana*, 20, 40.

    [92] Kirchgässer, *Haschisch und Marihuana*, 22, 33.

to feel how his partner experienced the sex act: 'I notice from the beginning how long it takes the girl to orgasm, how far away she is from it, and I am at exactly the same point, coming closer to orgasm at the same speed. When I feel her orgasm, the contraction of the vagina, I feel exactly like her, I can resonate, put myself completely in her position, I am her.'[93] The idea that using cannabis resulted in more sensitive and empathetic male sexual performance also framed the experience of another young man. In his view, taking cannabis resulted in 'a large increase of feelings with deep sensations of tenderness but without aggressive sexuality. This surprised him as 'he had always been sexually aggressive'.[94]

Some counter-culturalists also came to regard the use of psychedelics and cannabis as weakening the heteronormative order. Some of the main protagonists of the 'psychedelic revolution' initially described the therapeutic use of LSD as a 'cure' for homosexuality. In the article 'LSD and Sexuality', which was published in the *Psychedelic Review*, Richard Alpert reported on his 'successful' treatment of a homosexual man in LSD therapy.[95] In addition, in his interview with *Playboy*, Leary described LSD as stabilizing the heteronormative order. Seeing homosexuality as 'sexual perversion[s]' resulting from 'freaky, dislocating childhood experiences', he regarded LSD as 'a specific cure for homosexuality'.[96] However, Leary changed his views on this issue under the impact of 'gay liberation' in the late 1960s. He then saw acid as freeing its user from 'artificial social expectations' and allowing him to 'see himself as he really is'.[97]

Against the backdrop of views on homosexuality becoming more plural around 1970 and, as Benno Gammerl argues, of borders between heterosexual and homosexual orientations becoming more fluid, some alternative voices went further than Leary.[98] They described cannabis and psychedelics as forces that actively undermined heteronormativity by queering the sexual desires of their users. The anthology *Acid*, which was edited by Rolf Dieter Brinkmann and Ralf-Rainer Rygulla and went through fifteen editions

---

[93] Wormser, *Drogenkosum*, 206.   [94] Kirchgässer, *Haschisch und Marihuana*, 34.
[95] Richard Alpert, 'LSD and Sexuality', *Psychedelic Review*, 10 (1969), 21–4, at 23.
[96] [Anon.], 'Playboy Interview'.
[97] Michael-Francis Itkin, 'Psychedelics and Gay Liberation: The Battle of Algiers', *Gay Sunshine*, 6 (1971), 18–19, at 19.
[98] Benno Gammerl, 'Ist frei sein normal? Männliche Homosexualitäten seit den 1960er Jahren zwischen Emanzipation und Normalisierung', in Bänziger et al. (eds.), *Sexuelle Revolution?*, 223–44, at 230–1.

in West Germany between 1969 and 1981, contains an article by US counter-culturalist Parker Tyler in which he enthusiastically attributed to LSD the effect of queering the sexual desires of users and causing states of 'hetero-homosexual promiscuity'.[99] The effect of enabling its users to have same-sex experiences was also ascribed to cannabis. A student from Berlin was full of praise that the use of cannabis allowed 'bourgeois inhibitions' to be 'overcome, also towards men'.[100]

The fact that people used LSD both to 'overcome' homosexuality and to undermine heteronormativity suggests that the sexual effects of psychedelics and cannabis were not inherent properties of these substances, but depended on the user's attitudes and expectations. The close link between the set and the substance's sexual effects might also have had repercussions for the efficacy of psychedelics and cannabis as tools for 'liberating' sexuality in general. According to Günter Amendt in his *Haschisch und Sexualität* (1974), which scrutinizes sexuality in the drug subcultures of Hamburg, Munich, Frankfurt, and West Berlin,[101] the close connection between the drug's sexual effects and the users' internalized and embodied attitudes towards sex placed limits on the politics of psychedelic sexuality. The interviewees in Amendt's study described the alleged sexual power of LSD and cannabis as an important reason for their use of these substances. However, drug use did not fundamentally change the sex lives of the large majority of Amendt's interviewees. Rather, the influence of drugs on their users' sex lives was in line with their previous sexual development. People who were sexually uninhibited experienced an increase in sexual pleasure via drugs, and people with a 'problematic' sexuality experienced an increase in their sexual aversion.[102] Furthermore, only a small number of interviewees who had had completely new sexual experiences under the influence of drugs said that they were able to repeat these experiences without the help of drugs.[103]

---

[99] Parker Tyler, 'Männer, Frauen und die übrigen Geschlechter oder: Wie es euch gefällt, so könnt ihr es haben', in Rolf Dieter Brinkmann and Ralf-Rainer Rygulla (eds.), *Acid: Neue amerikanische Szene* (Berlin, 1981), 250–65, at 260–1.

[100] Herha, 'Erfahrungen mit Haschisch', 103.

[101] Amendt, *Haschisch und Sexualität*, 26.

[102] Ibid. 107.

[103] Ibid. 109.

VII. *Conclusion*

The politics of psychedelic ecstasy underline the huge significance of the body in West Germany's counter-cultural milieu, where the body and the mind were not separated from each other and juxtaposed in opposition, but closely entangled and interlaced. This made the body an important actor not only in the project of shaping an 'authentic' subject, but also in the production and reproduction of societal conditions. According to members of the alternative milieu, the 'suppression' of the body in Western capitalist societies caused mental and emotional problems in Western subjects and, by extension, societal ills and problems. In turn, the 'liberated' body was constructed as a force for societal transformation. Thus, it was a requirement on the alternative Left to work on and reshape the body–mind.

A way to 'liberate' the body from the shackles of Western capitalism and its underlying mode of rationality was by experiencing ecstatic states. To this end, counter-culturalists made use of a variety of body practices. Psychedelic substances and cannabis played an important role in ecstatic work on the self during the late 1960s and early 1970s. Their use was thought of not merely as a pleasurable practice, but as a means of transforming the subject and society. Against the backdrop of the close entanglement of mind and body, the psychedelic 'liberation' of the body aimed to open up new levels of consciousness via new bodily experiences. The ecstatic body became an actor in societal change. Despite its aim of overcoming Western capitalist rationality, however, it would be misleading to characterize the alternative Left as a whole as an anti-rational force. At least among sections of the alternative Left, overcoming Western modes of rationality and sociation did not mean the overcoming of 'reason' per se. Rather, they aspired to a form of society arising from an interplay between rational thinking, psychedelic knowledge acquisition, and (psychedelic) feeling.

The use of psychedelics and cannabis to 'liberate' the body was fuelled by the close links that the alternative discourse constructed between these substances and the ongoing 'sexual revolution'. Seeing 'hard drugs' (such as heroin) and drug addiction as antagonists of the sexual 'liberation', counter-culturalists made the psychedelic body an actor in 'liberating' sex. They used substances to overcome 'bourgeois inhibitions' and transgress sexual morals, as we have seen in the case of the Wet Dream Film Festival. The psychedelic body also enabled a new kind of sexual feeling. Being in a state of ecstasy allowed (some) drug users to have sexual experiences which conformed to the demands of the contemporary sexual revolution: Wilhelm Reich's politics of orgasm and Herbert Marcuse's eroticization of the whole body. Users reported intensified and multiple orgasms and were amazed at the states of 'orgastic skin ecstasy' they achieved.

Some also tried to use cannabis and acid to overcome heteronormativity and sexism, the latter of which was widespread in the counter-cultural politics of sexuality. At least in the years around 1970, some women, as we have seen in the case of the WDFF, used these substances to act out their desires, enjoy sexual pleasures, and behave actively and dominantly in sexual intercourse with men, while others saw these substances as a means of queering sexual desire and thus of undermining heteronormativity.

During the first half of the 1970s, the use of LSD lost ground significantly. Cannabis, by contrast, continued to be used frequently on the alternative Left in the second half of the decade. Its use still played an important part in shaping a counter-cultural identity and strengthened the sense of belonging on the alternative Left. The 'sexual revolution', criticized by the feminist movement for its often sexist character, also rapidly lost its appeal, and thus the use of psychedelics and cannabis to 'liberate' sexuality declined in significance in the following years.

PART III

Consumerism and Politics

8

'Full board with a pang of conscience': Value Changes and Tourist Travel to the Western Dictatorships in Europe

PATRICIA HERTEL

In the spring of 1969 the editor of *Lenkrad*, the magazine of the automobile association Auto Club Europa, sparked a readers' debate over tourism boycotts of Spain, Greece, and Portugal.[1] During a May rally of the West German Trade Union Confederation (Deutscher Gewerkschaftsbund, or DGB), the founding body of the Auto Club, young Greek women had sold ballpoint pens bearing the slogan 'No tourist money for the dictatorship in Greece' in both Greek and German. The *Lenkrad* editor asked his readers: would a tourist boycott help overcome the authoritarian regime in Greece, as well as in countries such as Spain and Portugal, as the message on the pens suggested? Or would it only harm the population and therefore miss its target? The answers from readers were diverse. One person highlighted Germany's own dictatorial experience: 'It is primarily the German government's task to oppose the Greek dictatorship in the name of our people—to the extent that we have learnt from our past. As the government is apparently not doing this, a tourist embargo would simultaneously be a demonstration against this undemocratic stance.' Other readers doubted the efficacy of a tourist boycott, fearing that it would do far more damage to the 'little people' already suffering from political oppression. The most optimistic respondent hoped that mass tourism to countries with authoritarian regimes had the potential to 'change the material, ideational, and intellectual structures of a country'. Furthermore,

This essay is based on Patricia Hertel, *Europe's Favourite Dictatorships: Southern Authoritarianism, Tourism, and the 'Free West', 1945–1975*, forthcoming with De Gruyter. The research was funded in part by the Swiss National Science Foundation, projects 158422 and 171484.

[1] Claus Page, 'Touristen-Embargo', *Lenkrad*, May/June 1969, 4.

he referred to 'free mobility' as a distinctive feature of the geopolitical discourse of 'the West': 'What sort of democratic position limits
one's freedom of movement because others should also have it?'[2]

This debate is one example of a discussion on tourism to Spain,
Portugal, and Greece—countries with authoritarian governments
that were considered to be ambivalent members of the geopolitical
'West' in the 1960s and 1970s. This essay deals with debates in the
UK, West Germany, and Sweden as examples of discourses that
also took place in other Western European countries. Journalists in
both the mainstream press and more specialist publications, readers,
members of trade unions and parties on the Left, and grass-roots
activists discussed whether going on holiday to these countries was
compatible with democratic principles, anti-authoritarianism, and
free movement. These exchanges shed light on a core interest of
this volume: the redefinition of politics in the 1960s and 1970s,
through which lifestyle and consumerism became instruments for
individuals to express their personal values. This essay explores
how different historical actors and social groups—travel agents,
politicians, activists, journalists, and individual travellers—ascribed
different values to tourism according to their respective interests,
economic needs, and personal beliefs. It covers the period from the
tourism boom of the 1960s, when Portugal, Greece, and especially
Spain established themselves as popular destinations for an increasing spectrum of middle- and working-class tourists, to the political
transitions to democracy in these countries during the 1970s. The
transnational perspective of this essay foregrounds the so-called
'North–South' divide within non-Communist Europe, an entity
that was in political, economic, and social terms far more heterogeneous than the geopolitical discourse of 'the West' would suggest.[3]
I argue that discussions of whether to go on holiday to a country
with an authoritarian regime forged the new notion of 'politically
conscious tourism', which was related to the idea of 'politically conscious consumerism'. This reveals a process of value change: from a
pragmatic understanding of consumerism to one that foregrounded

---

[2] 'Letters to the editor', *Lenkrad*, July/Aug. 1969, 6–7.

[3] Patricia Hertel, Martin Baumeister, and Roberto Sala (eds.), *Die Verhandlung des
Westens: Wissenseliten und die Heterogenität Westeuropas nach 1945*, special issue of *Comparativ*,
25/3 (2015). For concepts of the European 'South' and its relation with the 'West' see
also Martin Baumeister and Roberto Sala (eds.), *Southern Europe? Italy, Spain, Portugal,
and Greece from the 1950s until the Present Day* (Frankfurt a.M., 2015); Philipp Müller and
Clara Maier (eds.), *Konstrukt Südeuropa*, special issue of *Mittelweg 36*, 27/5 (2018).

self-assertion and individual conviction—in this case, in the field of politics. While this understanding was still a minority view in the 1960s and 1970s, it became more mainstream in subsequent decades in questions of economy, society, and environment.

This emerging new understanding of tourism has to be seen in the context of three general features that historical scholarship has highlighted as pivotal characteristics of the 1960s and 1970s. First, there were new forms and expressions of a politicization of everyday life in the 1960s—something that was emblematically expressed in the slogan 'the personal is political', first used in the feminist movement.[4] Scholars have rightly argued that the politicization of everyday life should not be taken as a given; in order to assess its meanings and impact, it is important to ask what different groups and individuals considered to be 'personal' and 'political', and what reasons they had to do so.[5] As well as in education, domestic labour, parenthood, sexuality, music, fashion, or hairstyles, this politicization can also be analysed in the diverse values projected onto tourism in general, and onto the authoritarian regimes within the geopolitical 'West' in particular.

The second driver of value discussions in tourism was the growing concern for human rights, which historians have identified as an important factor in the making of European identity in the post-war decades. The earliest activities of Amnesty International were directed at Western Europe and its colonies, and European activists considered Greece to be a 'second Vietnam'.[6] While activists—especially but not exclusively on the Left—openly attacked human

---

[4] The slogan was first used as the title of an essay by the US feminist Carol Hanisch in 1969, though the title was chosen by the editors. See Carol Hanisch, 'The Personal is Political: The Women's Liberation Movement Classic with a New Explanatory Introduction' ⟨http://www.carolhanisch.org/CHwritings/PIP.html⟩ [accessed 15 June 2019].

[5] Detlef Siegfried, 'Demokratie und Alltag: Neuere Literatur zur Politisierung des Privaten in der Bundesrepublik Deutschland', *Archiv für Sozialgeschichte*, 46 (2006), 737–50, at 750.

[6] Tom Buchanan, 'Human Rights, the Memory of War and the Making of a "European" Identity, 1945–1975', in Martin Conway and Kiran Klaus Patel (eds.), *Europeanization in the Twentieth Century: Historical Approaches* (Basingstoke, 2010), 157–71, at 165–6; Tom Buchanan, '"The Truth Will Set You Free": The Making of Amnesty International', *Journal of Contemporary History*, 37/4 (2002), 575–97; Kim Christiaens, 'Europa als "Dritte Welt": Europäische Perspektiven auf globalen Aktivismus während des Kalten Krieges', in Frank Bösch, Caroline Moine, and Stefanie Senger (eds.), *Internationale Solidarität: Globales Engagement in der Bundesrepublik und der DDR* (Göttingen, 2018), 235–62, at 243–51; Kim Christiaens, '"Communists are No Beasts": European Solidarity Campaigns on Behalf of Democracy and Human Rights in Greece and

rights violations in Spain, Greece, and Portugal and its colonies, European governments manifested such concerns more discreetly. The pragmatic working relations in economic, military, and foreign policy that conservative governments had cultivated with Portugal and Spain in the 1950s continued under the increasing number of social democratic governments in the 1960s and 1970s, as many studies on international relations have shown.[7]

The third factor that influenced value debates was the unprecedented prosperity which translated into considerable consumer clout and new consumer preferences. The tourist boom of the 1960s was set in motion by the introduction of paid holiday entitlement in a growing number of countries, cheaper transport, higher aircraft passenger capacities, and a broader range of destinations. In particular, charter flights and package holidays converted tourism from a privilege reserved for wealthy elites into an affordable new habit for the lower middle and working classes.[8] In 1960 a third of West Germans took a holiday, and a third of these holidaymakers went abroad. By the late 1970s, both of these categories had doubled to 60 per cent. In 1968, West German tourism abroad surpassed domestic tourism for the first time. In the UK, the number of holidaymakers travelling abroad rose from 1.5 million in 1955 to 4 million in 1972.[9] This increase in tourism came with new con-

---

East–West Détente in the 1960s and Early 1970s', *Contemporary European History*, 26/4 (2017), 621–46, at 630–5.

[7] Birgit Aschmann, *'Treue Freunde . . .'? Westdeutschland und Spanien 1945 bis 1963* (Stuttgart, 1999); Carlos Sanz Díaz, 'España y la República Federal de Alemania (1949–1966): política, economía y emigración entre la Guerra Fría y la distención' (Ph.D. thesis, Universidad Complutense de Madrid, 2005) ⟨http://biblioteca.ucm.es/tesis/ghi/ucm-t28931.pdf⟩ [accessed 3 Dec. 2020]; Antonio Muñoz Sánchez, *El amigo alemán: el SPD y el PSOE de la dictadura a la democracia* (Barcelona, 2012); Pedro Aires Oliveira, *Os despojos da aliança: a Grã-Bretanha e a questão colonial portuguesa 1945–1975* (Lisbon, 2007); Thomas Schroers, 'Die Außenpolitik der Bundesrepublik Deutschland: Die Entwicklung der Beziehungen der Bundesrepublik Deutschland zur Portugiesischen Republik 1949–1976' (Ph.D. thesis, Universität der Bundeswehr Hamburg, 1998); Rui Lopes, *West Germany and the Portuguese Dictatorship 1968–1974: Between Cold War and Colonialism* (New York, 2014); Stefan A. Müller, David Schriffl, and Adamantios T. Skordos, *Heimliche Freunde: Die Beziehungen Österreichs zu den Diktaturen Südeuropas nach 1945: Spanien, Portugal, Griechenland* (Vienna, 2016).

[8] On package tours see Christopher M. Kopper, 'The Breakthrough of the Package Tour in Germany after 1945', *Journal of Tourism History*, 1/1 (2009), 67–92. On charter flights see Peter J. Lyth, '"Gimme a Ticket on an Aeroplane": The Jet Engine and the Revolution in Leisure Air Travel, 1960–1975', in Laurent Tissot (ed.), *Construction d' une industrie touristique aux 19ᵉ et 20ᵉ siècles: perspectives internationales* (Neuchâtel, 2003), 111–22.

[9] Axel Schildt, 'Across the Border: West German Youth Travel to Western Europe',

sumer preferences for sunny beaches and a stable climate. Among the destinations that catered perfectly to the new trend were those with a long tradition in foreign tourism, such as Italy,[10] but they also included destinations whose tourist clientele in the nineteenth and early twentieth centuries had to a large extent been domestic, such as the Iberian Peninsula. In the 1960s Greece, Portugal, and especially Spain established themselves as tourist destinations for a broad clientele.[11] In 1973—the peak year for tourism before the oil

in Axel Schildt and Detlef Siegfried (eds.), *Between Marx and Coca-Cola: Youth Cultures in Changing European Societies, 1960–1980* (New York, 2006), 149–60, at 150; Sina Fabian, *Boom in der Krise: Konsum, Tourismus, Autofahren in Westdeutschland und Großbritannien 1970–1990* (Göttingen, 2016), 130; Bill Cormack, *A History of Holidays 1812–1990* (London, 1998), 70. All tourist numbers can only be taken as approximations given the variety of methods and data used in different statistics.

[10] Till Manning, *Die Italiengeneration: Stilbildung durch Massentourismus in den 1950er und 1960er Jahren* (Göttingen, 2011).

[11] For overviews of Spanish tourism after 1945, as well as for promotion abroad, see e.g. Sasha D. Pack, *Tourism and Dictatorship: Europe's Peaceful Invasion of Franco's Spain* (New York, 2006); Ana Moreno Garrido, *Historia del turismo en España en el siglo XX* (Madrid, 2007); Justin Crumbaugh, *Destination Dictatorship: The Spectacle of Spain's Tourist Boom and the Reinvention of Difference* (Albany, 2009); Alicia Fuentes Vega, *Bienvenido, Mr. Turismo! Cultura visual del boom en España* (Madrid, 2017); Moritz Glaser, *Wandel durch Tourismus: Spanien als 'Strand Europas', 1950–1983* (Konstanz, 2018); Jorge Villaverde and Yvonne Galant (eds.), *¿El turismo es un gran invento? Usos políticos, identitarios y culturales del turismo en España* (Valencia, 2021); Ana Moreno Garrido and Jorge Villaverde, 'De un sol a otro: turismo e imagen exterior española (1914–1984)', *Ayer*, 114 (2019), 95–121; Carolin Viktorin, 'All Publicity is Good Publicity? Advertising, Public Relations, and the Branding of Spain in the United Kingdom, 1945–69', in Carolin Viktorin, Jessica C. E. Gienow-Hecht, Annika Estner, et al. (eds.), *Nation Branding in Modern History* (New York, Oxford, 2018), 124–48; Patricia Hertel, 'Ein anderes Stück Europa? Der Mittelmeertourismus in Expertendiskursen der Nachkriegszeit, 1950–1980', *Comparativ*, 25/3 (2015), 75–93; ead., '1960: el turismo llega a España', in Xosé M. Núñez Seixas (ed.), *Historia mundial de España* (Barcelona, 2018), 837–44. There is far less research on tourism to Portugal. See e.g. Paulo Pina, *Portugal: o turismo no século XX* (Lisbon, 1988); Flávio Lopes and Teresa Gamboa, *90 anos de turismo em Portugal: conhecer o passado, investir no futuro* (Lisbon, 2001); Jorge Mangorrinha (ed.), *História de uma viagem: 100 anos de turismo em Portugal (1911–2011)*, 2 vols. (Ponta Delgada, 2012); Eva Milheiro, 'Turismo', in António Reis, Maria Inácia Rezola, and Paula Borges Santos (eds.), *Dicionário de história de Portugal: o 25 de Abril*, 8 vols. (Porto, 2016), viii. 200–6; Raphael Costa, 'The "Great Façade of Nationality": Some Considerations on Portuguese Tourism and the Multiple Meanings of Estado Novo Portugal in Travel Literature', *Journal of Tourism History*, 5/1 (2013), 50–72. On tourism in Greece during the dictatorship see Michalis Nikolakakis, 'The Colonels on the Beach: Tourism Policy during the Greek Military Dictatorship (1967–1974)', *Journal of Modern Greek Studies*, 35/2 (2017), 425–50; id., 'Representations and Social Practices of Alternative Tourists in Post-War Greece to the End of the Greek Military Junta', *Journal of Tourism History*, 7/1–2 (2015), 5–17; id., 'Tourism, Body and Seaside Recreational Practices in Postwar Greek Society Until 1974', in Kostis Kornetis, Eirini Kotsovili, and Nikolaos Papadogiannis (eds.), *Consumption and Gender in Southern Europe since the Long 1960s* (London, 2016), 103–17.

crisis—these three countries together received more than 40 million foreign visitor arrivals, of which Spain alone attracted the lion's share with 34.5 million.[12]

The first part of this essay deals with the way in which tourism experts, such as economists, tourism researchers, travel agents, and travel journalists, used a certain set of values in order to promote tourism in the 1960s and 1970s. The second part explores the ways in which political opponents of the Spanish, Portuguese, and Greek dictatorships in the UK, Sweden, and West Germany advocated a tourist boycott of the three authoritarian regimes, as well as the reactions to these appeals in the travel industry and in public discussions. The third part analyses the impact of the political transitions in Greece, Spain, and Portugal on tourism and tourist promotion in the 1970s.

I. 'Development' and 'Peace': Values in Promoting Tourism in the 1960s

Tourism was part of the 1960s growth euphoria. Increasing travel stirred the expectations of politicians, economists, and tourism researchers, who considered the sector a suitable instrument for economic development. Where basic infrastructure existed, experts argued, investments in tourism were cheaper and easier than industrial investments on account of the high involvement of the service sector.[13] The concept of 'development through tourism' was fostered by academic and non-academic tourism experts and put into practice through bilateral and international agreements on technical assistance, development aid, and beneficial legislation.

Much like other governments of less industrialized countries across the world, the authoritarian regimes in Spain, Greece, and Portugal embraced tourism as an important source of foreign currency. Internally, however, leading politicians and economists disagreed on the place that tourism should occupy in the national economy and society. In Spain, Franco never had much interest in tourism, but he accepted the efforts of his tourism officials,

---

[12] OECD, *Tourism Policy and International Tourism in OECD Member Countries 1974: Evolution of Tourism in OECD Member Countries in 1973 and the Early Months of 1974* (Paris, 1974), 104, 121, and 129.

[13] Klaus Frentrup, *Die ökonomische Bedeutung des internationalen Tourismus für die Entwicklungsländer* (Hamburg, 1969), 14–20; Hans Keller, 'Schweizerische Entwicklungshilfe im Fremdenverkehr', in Schweizerischer Fremdenverkehrsverband, *Fremdenverkehr, Integration und Entwicklungshilfe* (Bern, 1962), 29–36, at 29–30.

such as Manuel Fraga Iribarne, Minister for Information and Tourism from 1963 to 1969, to modernize the sector and enhance Spain's image abroad as a holiday destination. Fraga and his staff faced resistance in turn, as members of the regime's elites questioned the power of tourism as a strategic sector in the long run and saw the rapidly increasing revenues as nothing more than a supplementary source of currency.[14] In Greece, Athens, Rhodes, and Corfu were already established tourist destinations when the Colonels seized power in 1967. The regime expanded tourism to other zones, such as Thessaloniki and Crete. This created social frictions between the regime and local stakeholders, who criticized the lack of environmental protections and disagreed over hotel architecture and what sort of clientele to attract.[15] In Portugal, tourism had hitherto been concentrated on a few select spots, especially the Lisbon area, and addressed a rather affluent clientele. In the early 1960s the Estado Novo initiated the tourist development of the Algarve, the country's southern Atlantic coast, as the most promising region to attract foreign tourism on a larger scale. However, Portuguese tourism experts debated the question of how and to what degree the government should invest in tourism[16]— a sector that Prime Minister António de Oliveira Salazar tolerated but never really valued.

Despite such internal resistance and ambivalence within the regimes' elites, Spain, Portugal, and Greece, as so-called 'European developing countries',[17] benefited from the paradigm of 'development through tourism'. In 1962 the West German government granted Portugal 50 million DM for the construction of airports in Faro (Algarve) and Funchal (Madeira). These new airports connected remote regions more closely to the international market, and encouraged foreign travel agencies to promote these destinations.[18] The FRG in turn used this form of development aid to secure diplomatic support for its foreign policy, and especially for the Berlin

[14] Pack, *Tourism and Dictatorship*, 105–35.

[15] Nikolakakis, 'The Colonels on the Beach', 438–41.

[16] Sérgio Palma Brito, *Direcção-Geral do Turismo: contributos para a sua história* (Lisbon, 2011), 80.

[17] Matthias Schmelzer, 'Entwickelter Norden, unterentwickelter Süden? Wissenseliten, Entwicklungshilfe und die Konstruktion des Westens in der OEEC und OECD', *Comparativ*, 25/3 (2015), 18–35, at 26–8.

[18] John Carter, *Chandler's Travels: A Tour of the Life of Harry Chandler* (London, 1985), 125.

question.[19] Furthermore, legal regulations granting tax benefits for investments in 'developing countries' were used to secure markets for West German exports and investments abroad. Such regulations boosted the construction of tourist resorts in the Canary Islands, for example, but were also questioned and criticized.[20]

While tourism experts stressed the material importance of tourism, they also ascribed highly immaterial features to these new market opportunities. The United Nations Conference on International Travel and Tourism stressed the 'social, educational, and cultural impact of tourism', as well as its 'significant contribution to the promotion of international good will and understanding and to the preservation of peace between the peoples'.[21] The UN International Tourist Year in 1967 used the slogan 'Tourism—Passport for Peace', referring to the idea of 'peace through tourism', which has its roots in the interwar period.[22] The ideas of 'development through tourism' and 'peace through tourism' reinforced each other. This was visible in exchanges between tourism experts, as well as on a diplomatic level—for example, when the West German Minister of Transport Hans-Georg Seebohm described Faro airport during its inauguration as a 'visible proof of the friendship between our countries and a recognition of our collaboration for the preservation of peace'.[23] This was in sharp contrast to other development projects, such as the Cahora Bassa dam project in Mozambique, where donors, including West Germany and France, were accused of supporting the Portuguese colonial war.[24]

Tourism experts in academia, on national tourism boards, and

[19] Bundesarchiv Koblenz (BArch), B213, vol. 6643, letter from the West German Embassy Lisbon to the Federal Foreign Office, 30 Jan. 1970.

[20] Javier Márquez Quevedo, 'Turistas y cambio social durante el tardo-franquismo: campesinos, obreros y extranjeros en los inicios del turismo de masas en las Islas Canarias (1962–1975)', *Diacronie: Studi di storia contemporanea*, 36/4 (2018), 1–27, at 10–13.

[21] *United Nations Conference on International Travel and Tourism, Rome, 21 August–5 September 1963: Recommendations on International Travel and Tourism* (New York, 1963), 17.

[22] Sune Bechmann Pedersen, 'Peace through Tourism: A Brief History of a Popular Catchphrase', in Mats Andrén (ed.), *Cultural Borders and European Integration* (Göteborg, 2017), 29–37; id., 'A Passport to Peace? Modern Tourism and Internationalist Idealism', *European Review*, 28/3 (2020), 389–402.

[23] BArch, B 231, vol. 289, letter from the Deutsche Zentrale für Fremdenverkehr in Lisbon to the headquarters in Frankfurt, including the report 'Einweihung des Flugplatzes Faro in Anwesenheit des Bundesverkehrsministers Dr. Ing. Seebohm', 13 July 1965.

[24] Christiane Abele, *Kein kleines Land: Die Kolonialfrage in Portugal 1961–1974* (Göttingen, 2017), 218–35; Lopes, *West Germany and the Portuguese Dictatorship*, 108–24; Schroers, 'Die Außenpolitik der Bundesrepublik Deutschland', 100–8.

in international organizations saw their efforts to enhance the sector as a 'technical' affair of providing the necessary conditions and removing travel obstacles. On the level of promotion, experts, entrepreneurs, and politicians stressed the 'private' character of tourism, presenting it as a personal matter for each individual. In the late 1960s and early 1970s, opponents of the authoritarian regimes challenged these notions.

II. *'Human Rights' and 'Anti-Authoritarianism': Values in Contesting Tourism in the Late 1960s and Early 1970s*

The counter-image of tourism as a technical matter and a 'personal' affair was the interpretation of tourism as a political statement.[25] The background for this view was a redefinition of politics as something not limited to the actions of parties or elected politicians, but that permeated people's everyday life decisions and behaviour, including consumerism.[26] In that context, foreign opponents of the authoritarian regimes who condemned human rights violations, censorship, oppression, and the Portuguese colonial war attacked tourism to Spain, Portugal, and Greece. Anti-authoritarian opposition in countries such as Sweden, the UK, and West Germany came from members of parties, unions, and churches, or just from individuals following their personal convictions, whether they were militant communists or social democrats. Some activists merely pointed to the human rights situation in popular holiday destinations as a gesture of political education, while others called for tourist boycotts in order to show disapproval and to weaken the regimes. Such campaigns were mostly short-lived and not well orchestrated, but they became a common form of protest against the regimes in Spain, Greece, and Portugal, and inspired reflections as to whether tourism could or should be a political statement.

An early incident that sparked such a protest was the execution of political prisoner Julián Grimau García in Spain in 1963, an event that triggered domestic and international discussions over

[25] Patricia Hertel, '¿Privado o público? La dimensión política del turismo a España en los años 60 y 70', in Villaverde and Galant (eds.), *¿El turismo es un gran invento?*, 219–47.

[26] Benjamin Möckel, 'The Material Culture of Human Rights: Consumer Products, Boycotts and the Transformation of Human Rights Activism in the 1970s and 1980s', *International Journal for History, Culture and Modernity*, 6/1 (2018), 76–104.

whether Spain could be considered a *Rechtsstaat* (a state in which
the government and administration act in accordance with the
law, guarantee the rights of citizens, and are overseen by independent courts).[27] In many European countries there were demonstrations in front of Spanish embassies. In 1967 the coup of the
Colonels in Greece—a NATO member and historically the cradle
of democracy—shocked the Western European public. While European governments tried to strike a balance between expressing
moderate criticism of the junta and maintaining economic and military relations with it, activists protested in various ways against the
new regime.[28] For example, two British Labour MPs launched the
campaign 'Danger, Dictatorship! Stay away from Greece in 1968!',
distributing pamphlets and protesting outside the Greek tourist
office in London.[29] Similar activities took place in other European
countries. In leaflets, newspaper articles, and illustrations, activists
drew on a vast reservoir of tourist semantics and iconography in
their protest against the three regimes, using contrasts of sun and
shadow, fun and repression, and beach and prison in their appeals
to tourists' conscience. The Swedish weekly *Vecko-Journalen* warned
readers to 'beware of paradise' in Portugal, and juxtaposed a photograph of a girl bathing in the sea with one of a group of policemen
surrounding a man lying on a pavement, probably a dissident under
arrest: 'While you are enjoying the sun and the beautiful green
sea on the beaches of Estoril, students in the prison of Caxias are

[27] Lucia Herrmann, 'Juristisches Wissen aus der Zelle: Spanische kommunistische
Gefangene und der Deutungskonflikt über den franquistischen "Rechtsstaat" in
den 1960er-Jahren', *Werkstatt Geschichte*, 80 (2018), 57–74; Nicolás Sesma Landrín,
'Franquismo, ¿estado de derecho? Notas sobre la renovación del lenguaje político de
la dictadura durante los años 60', *Pasado y Memoria: Revista de Historia Contemporánea*, 5
(2006), 45–58.

[28] Carolina Labarta Rodríguez-Maribona, 'Países "políticamente delicados" e intere-
ses nacionales: la política exterior de los gobiernos laboristas de Harold Wilson hacia
las dictaduras del flanco sur de la Europa occidental (1964–1974)', in Ángeles
Barrio Alonso, Jorge de Hoyos Puente, and Rebeca Saavedra Arias (eds.), *Nuevos
horizontes del pasado: culturas políticas, identidades y formas de representación* (Santander,
2011), accompanying CD-ROM; Alexandros Nafpliotis, *Britain and the Greek Colonels:
Accommodating the Junta in the Cold War* (London, 2013); Helen Conispoliatis, 'Facing
the Colonels: How the British Government Dealt with the Military Coup in
Greece in 1967', *History*, 92/4 (2007), 515–35; Müller, Schriffl and Skordos, *Heimliche Freunde*, 235–325. See also the conference 'Greek–German Relations during the
Military Dictatorship in Greece (1967–1974)' held at the Friedrich Ebert Foundation
Bonn in October 2020 ⟨https://www.fes.de/themenportal-geschichte-kultur-medien-netz/
geschichte/veranstaltungen/greek-german-relations⟩ [accessed 3 Dec. 2020].

[29] 'Regent Street Patrol in Armoured Car', *Sunday Telegraph*, 25 Feb. 1968.

being tortured up the hill above the sea.'[30] Along the main roads leading to British airports at the beginning of the Easter holidays in 1970, Amnesty International placed posters that showed a sunny beach alongside dark, anonymous faces, reminding holidaymakers to 'Have a good time, but remember: Amnesty for Spain's political prisoners.'[31] Throughout Europe, institutions related to Spanish tourism were occasionally the target of anonymous overnight attacks with Molotov cocktails, including the Iberia office in Rome and two travel agencies in Copenhagen promoting holiday destinations in Spain in 1963, as well as the Spanish tourist offices in Stockholm and Zurich in 1970 and 1972 respectively.[32]

However, individuals, journalists, and politicians did not agree on whether tourist boycotts were an appropriate form of protest. Several European centre-left newspapers had significant reservations about such boycotts, despite their general criticism of the dictatorship. In the British *Guardian*, one journalist asked: 'Is it really the best to make one's tiny gesture of disapproval of a regime by taking one's sterling elsewhere? If the collapse of the tourist trade brought the collapse of the Greek economy, should we be able to rejoice . . . for who knows what anguish would come of it?'[33] Eka von Merveldt, a well-known travel journalist for the West German weekly *Die Zeit*, questioned tourism as a suitable form of political expression and commented: 'People on holiday are on another planet . . . The political conscience is on holiday too.'[34] In a similar vein, another West German journalist argued that not only the authoritarian regimes in Greece, Spain, and Portugal, but also the political and social conditions in Yugoslavia, Italy, or Turkey, could offer holidaymakers 'full board with a pang of conscience'.[35] Even politicians who clearly opposed the authoritarian regimes abstained

[30] Inga Grunden, 'Varning för paradiset!', *Vecko-Journalen*, 23 Apr. 1965.

[31] 'Anti-Spain Poster Campaign', *The Guardian*, 6 Apr. 1970; Henry Stanhope, 'Spain is in Amnesty's Black Book', *The Times*, 7 Apr. 1970; 'Protest over Holidays in Spain', *Daily Express*, 6 Apr. 1970.

[32] AGA, (03)49.003 17073, letter from the Spanish Tourist Office Rome to the Subsecretario de Información y Turismo, Servicio Exterior, 5 Mar. 1963; AGA, (03)49.005 25867, agency report OID/UPI, Copenhagen, 30 Apr. 1963; AGA, 26/7646, Spanish translation of an article in *Svenska Dagbladet*, 20 July 1970; Moisés Prieto, *Zwischen Apologie und Ablehnung: Schweizer Spanien-Wahrnehmung vom späten Franco-Regime bis zur Demokratisierung (1969–1982)* (Cologne, 2015), 72.

[33] Mary Stott, 'Holiday Immorality', *The Guardian*, 9 Jan. 1969.

[34] Ead., 'Ausnahmemenschen', *Die Zeit*, 14 Feb. 1969.

[35] Matthias Scheben, 'Vollpension mit Gewissensbissen', *Schwäbisches Tagblatt*, 4 July 1970.

from appeals for boycotts. Swedish Prime Minister Olof Palme collected money on Stockholm's streets for the democratic opposition,
but expressed doubts about the usefulness of a tourist boycott.[36]
Willy Brandt's private visit to Fuerteventura in 1972–3, which was
very much in the public eye in West Germany, indirectly countered
calls for a boycott from the Left. The Nobel Prizewinner served
as an implicit model for the politically conscious and economically
well-off middle classes who had a great affinity for travel, sending
a signal that it was possible to reconcile tourism to Spain with an
attitude of 'change through rapprochement'.[37]

   Travel agents in turn continued to stress the 'private' character of
tourism. Representatives of Swedish travel agencies in the Spanish
resort town of Torremolinos stated: 'The Swedes who come here
should not interfere in politics. They should stay at the beach and
have a good time.'[38] While such an attitude was relatively easy
for commercial tour operators to espouse, it was far more difficult
for travel agencies operating on behalf of groups ideologically
removed from or opposed to the regimes. This was especially
true for European trade unions, which vehemently opposed the
regimes in Spain, Portugal, and Greece. This anti-dictatorial stance
stood in opposition to another unionist concern: that of facilitating
members' travel and recreation, which they felt should not be
privileges of the affluent classes. In order to achieve this, affordable
destinations such as Spain, where the government controlled prices
in order to remain competitive on the international market, were
crucial. Unions that engaged in travel activities thus had to find
a way to reconcile commercial interests, social commitment, and
political values. In the selection of holidays offered by the Transport
and General Workers' Union—the biggest British union of these
years, with more than 1.5 million members—Spain, Portugal, and
Greece received only minor billing. This was probably due to the
policy of Jack Jones, the union's General Secretary from 1968 and
a former volunteer in the Spanish Civil War. After the execution
of five regime opponents in Spain in September 1975, Jones called
for a tourist boycott.[39] In West Germany, the board of the travel

---

[36] Carina Gråbacke, *När folket tog semester: Studier av Reso, 1937–1977* (Lund, 2008), 215.

[37] Hertel, '¿Privado o público?', 233–8.

[38] 'Franco har lyckats fint met Spanien', *Aftonbladet*, 3 Apr. 1967.

[39] Ian Aitken, 'Jones Fighting on Beaches', and 'Keep Franco in the Cold', *The Guardian*, 30 Sept. 1975.

agency Gemeinwirtschaftliches Unternehmen für Touristik (GUT), which was owned by West German unions, was well aware of the dilemma involved in offering trips to Greece and Spain and had to deal regularly with critical questions from union members. When a DGB board member asked GUT to evaluate the consequences of excluding Spain from its travel programme after the executions in 1975, the managing director had a clear answer: 'If the company were to pronounce a boycott of Spain, this would . . . mean financial ruin.'[40] By contrast, the travel agency Reso, owned by Swedish unions, ceded to public pressure as a result of the executions and offered to cancel customers' bookings free of charge. So many people took advantage of the opportunity that Reso had to stop offering trips from Sweden to Spain between October and December 1975 because they were no longer profitable.[41] However, Reso's Spanish tours did not cease completely as they continued from Norway and Denmark. A photograph of Hans Ericson, board member of the Swedish Trade Union Confederation (Landsorganisationen i Sverige), at a unionist holiday resort in Gran Canaria circulated in the Swedish press, offering visual confirmation that the boycott had definitively failed.[42]

The examples of GUT and Reso explain why, on a quantitative level, appeals for tourist boycotts ended in failure. The very nature of the tourism industry—its economic entanglements, mutual interests, and dependencies across national boundaries—made it impossible to draw clear lines whereby the destinations would be harmed more than the tourists' home countries. There were certainly people who heeded the calls for boycotts, but numbers of tourists never fell in a visible and enduring way as a result of such campaigns. However, the activists' most important aim was not to inflict enough financial damage on the dictatorships to bring about their demise. Rather, they sought to spark critical debate at home about human rights violations within the geopolitical 'West'. Furthermore, activists used appeals for boycotts to articulate personal convictions in an era that placed extraordinary emphasis on individual self-expression as the new central value. They did not condemn tourism as such, and

[40] Archiv des DGB im Archiv der sozialen Demokratie Bonn, 5/DGCR000125, letter from GUT to the DGB board, 30 Sept. 1975.

[41] Gråbacke, *När folket tog semester*, 216.

[42] Ibid. 218–19; 'Hans Ericson firade nyår i SAF:s spanska semesterby', *Aftonbladet*, 2 Jan. 1976; Thore Davidson, 'Här njuter Hans Ericson av Spaniens semestersol', *Aftonbladet*, 6 Jan. 1976.

only occasionally criticized capitalism or pointed to cases of social exploitation—topics that would feature much more prominently from the late 1970s and 1980s. Economic prosperity, paired with a new understanding of political expression, gave calls for boycotts a prominent place in political activism based on the idea of a politically conscious citizen and consumer, which was linked to the emerging idea of 'ethical consumerism'.[43]

III. *'Conscience' and 'Quality': Values in Renewing Tourism in the Mid and Late 1970s*

The mid 1970s brought a political and an economic caesura for tourism to Spain, Portugal, and Greece as all three authoritarian regimes ended within a short span of time. In Portugal, the revolution of 25 April 1974 forced the government into exile; in Greece, the Turkish invasion of Cyprus in summer 1974 struck a deathblow to the regime of the Colonels; and in Spain, Franco's death on 20 November 1975 ushered in a political opening set in motion by liberal politicians and the new head of state, King Juan Carlos. In all three countries, these events triggered complex and not entirely smooth processes of transition to democracy. Economically, the oil crisis in 1973 ended three decades of postwar growth. Unlike other sectors of the economy, the economic crisis did not cause a structural break in the tourism industry, which was less badly affected and quicker to recover than other sectors.[44] However, there was a noticeable impact in the short term. Increasing transport costs, depreciating currencies, rising unemployment, and waning consumer confidence all contributed to a significant drop in tourism

---

[43] For other calls for boycotts see Möckel, 'The Material Culture of Human Rights'; Sebastian Tripp, *Fromm und politisch: Christliche Anti-Apartheid-Gruppen und die Transformation des westdeutschen Protestantismus 1970–1990* (Göttingen, 2015), 107–86; Tehila Sasson, 'Milking the Third World? Humanitarianism, Capitalism, and the Moral Economy of the Nestlé Boycott', *American Historical Review*, 121/4 (2016), 1196–224. On ethical consumerism see Benjamin Möckel, 'Ethischer Konsum und zivilgesellschaftliches Engagement: Moralisierungsstrategien des privaten Konsums seit den 1960er-Jahren', in Nicole Kramer and Christine G. Krüger (eds.), *Freiwilligenarbeit und gemeinnützige Organisationen im Wandel: Neue Perspektiven auf das 19. und 20. Jahrhundert* (Berlin, 2019), 303–32.

[44] Fabian, *Boom in der Krise*, 263; Moritz Glaser, 'Urlaub als Umweltbelastung: Kritik am Paradigma "Wohlstand durch Tourismus" in Spanien während der 1970er-Jahre', *Zeithistorische Forschungen/Studies in Contemporary History*, 14/3 (2017), 420–41; Anselm Doering-Manteuffel and Lutz Raphael, *Nach dem Boom: Perspektiven auf die Zeitgeschichte seit 1970*, 3rd edn. (Göttingen, 2012), 125.

TOURIST TRAVEL TO EUROPEAN DICTATORSHIPS 201

in 1974 compared with the previous year—the first such fall in the postwar decades.[45] The collapse of some tour operators, along with growing criticism of the negative aspects of mass tourism, exposed the limits of the growth paradigm of the 1960s. These political and economic factors helped develop further the idea of a politically conscious tourist that had emerged in anti-authoritarian activism, albeit under different circumstances and with different features.

Regime changes and the oil crisis temporarily shattered the stability, as well as the low prices, that had been attractive to tourists. In Greece, the Cyprus crisis and the accompanying political upheaval took place in the midst of the summer holiday season of 1974. Some airports were temporarily closed and European governments issued travel warnings. Despite a drop of 31 per cent, however, tourism never came to a standstill.[46] One year later, tourism to Greece had recovered and even surpassed its pre-crisis level, reaching a new record of 3.1 million tourist arrivals.[47] Far more adversely affected was Portugal—a destination comparable to Greece in both size and tourist numbers. The general increase in transport costs, a cholera outbreak in the summer of 1974, and especially the political situation were disastrous for tourism. Between the revolution on 25 April 1974 and the first constitutional elections on 25 April 1976, the country had six provisional governments, experienced several new coup attempts, saw a wave of strikes, and was racked by social and political unrest. As a result, tourist numbers dropped significantly. The record of over 4 million visitors in 1973 fell by three quarters to 920,000 just two years later.[48] This decline could not be compensated by the specific 'political tourists' attracted by the revolutionary situation, such as Spanish opponents of the Franco regime travelling to Lisbon in order to participate in political demonstrations or just to enjoy liberties not possible in Spain,[49] or foreign European activists on a sort of

[45] OECD, *Tourism Policy and International Tourism in OECD Member Countries 1975: Evolution of Tourism in OECD Member Countries in 1974 and the Early Months of 1975* (Paris, 1975), 13, 17.

[46] Ibid. 107.

[47] OECD, *Tourism Policy and International Tourism in OECD Member Countries 1976: Evolution of Tourism in OECD Member Countries in 1975 and the Early Months of 1976* (Paris, 1976), 105.

[48] OECD, *Tourism Policy and International Tourism in OECD Member Countries 1974*, 121; id., *Tourism Policy and International Tourism in OECD Member Countries 1976*, 129.

[49] Rita Luís, 'El viaje como recusa cultural del franquismo: Españoles en Portugal en 1974–1975', *Acta Hispanica Supplementum*, 1 (2018), 31–50.

'leftist pilgrimage'.[50] The successive governments used vacant hotel rooms as accommodation for the so-called *retornados*—settlers of the former colonies who came to Portugal as a consequence of decolonization and political unrest—and this too was a deterrent for foreign tourists.[51] In Spain, the political transition did not trigger a similar disaster,[52] to the great relief of the tourism industry. Still, as the oil crisis affected the cheaper travel segment more than the high end of the market, foreign tourist numbers declined by about 12 per cent from 34.5 million arrivals in 1973 to 30 million in 1974. After a relatively stable period, they finally reached a new record with 40 million arrivals in 1978.[53] Even if Spain came through the crisis comparatively lightly, the economic and political changes showed promoters that tourism was no longer the business of unlimited growth and endless possibilities that it had appeared to be before 1973.

While the European tourism industry was dealing with political change and rising prices, it also had to react to growing criticism of the negative sides of mass tourism, especially in Spain. As early as the late 1960s, Spanish tourism officials had faced a dilemma between encouraging growth and preserving the environment—not so much for its own sake as to keep tourists satisfied. Activist groups in Mallorca and the Costa Brava campaigned for better environmental protections, which was also an indirect way of voicing criticism of the regime.[54] The Marxist Spanish sociologist Mario Gaviria accused foreign tour operators of 'neocolonialism'. He did not criticize tourism as such—on the contrary—but advocated for more Spanish control over the industry.[55] Furthermore, there was growing resentment of mismanagement, fraud, poor quality, and

---

[50] Nuno Pereira, 'Le mouvement suisse de 68 et le Portugal: de la dictature à la révolution (1962–1975)', in Janick Marina Schaufelbuehl (ed.), *1968–1978: Ein bewegtes Jahrzehnt in der Schweiz/Une décennie mouvementée en Suisse* (Zurich, 2009), 147–60.

[51] On accommodation for the *retornados* see Christoph Kalter, *Postcolonial People: The Return from Africa and the Remaking of Portugal* (Cambridge, 2022), 100–77.

[52] On Spanish tourism during the oil crisis see Marta Luque Aranda and Carmelo Pellejero Martínez, 'Crisis del petróleo, transición à la democracia y frenazo de la expansión turística en España, 1973–1985', *Cuadernos de Historia Contemporánea*, 37 (2015), 115–44.

[53] OECD, *Tourism Policy and International Tourism in OECD Member Countries 1974*, 129; id., *Tourism Policy and International Tourism in OECD Member Countries 1975*, 137; id., *Tourism Policy and International Tourism in OECD Member Countries 1978: Evolution of Tourism in OECD Member Countries in 1978 and the Early Months of 1979* (Paris 1979), 133.

[54] Glaser, *Wandel durch Tourismus*, 181–267; id., 'Urlaub als Umweltbelastung'.

[55] Mario Gaviria, *España a go-go: Turismo charter y neocolonialismo del espacio* (Madrid,

false promises among the European public. The increasing availability of standardized package holidays contrasted with travellers' desires to express their individuality.[56]

In this situation of manifold changes and growing criticism, tourism promoters began to court more discerning tourists. As a result, even politics—a topic that the tourism industry had preferred to ignore while the authoritarian regimes were in power—started to appear discreetly in tourist publicity materials. In April 1975 the president of the Greek tourist board stated: 'The previous regime . . . pursued a strategy of enormous expansion. We are now striving to improve the quality.'[57] In similar vein, the director of the Portuguese tourist office in West Germany addressed prospective holidaymakers with the words: 'Before, we were only interested in people who brought money to Portugal . . . We still are, but today we are also interested in those who have little money, but who are interested in what happens in Portugal. We also want tourists who carry their wealth in their heads rather than in their wallets.'[58] In the late 1970s the Spanish tourism ministry ran an advertisement in the Swiss press with the caption: 'While lying in the sand, have you never vowed to learn more about the land? Now's your chance, for Spain longs to be loved rather than just visited . . . In the long run, Spain will benefit more from these warm, fuzzy feelings than from cold, hard cash.'[59] While the authoritarian regimes had wanted tourists to have a good time and leave money in the country, but not to interact in any meaningful way with the locals, the new governments encouraged and welcomed such contacts and encouraged a deeper interest in the destination country. Occasionally, even foreign politicians supported such arguments, especially in the case of Portugal. During a publicity event, the Federal Republic's Chancellor Helmut Schmidt recommended the country as a holiday destination to West Germans.[60] Likewise,

---

1974); id., *El turismo de playa en España: chequeo a 16 ciudades nuevas del ocio* (Madrid, 1975); id., *El escándalo de la 'Court Line': bancarrota del turismo español* (Madrid, 1975).

[56] Sina Fabian, 'Massentourismus und Individualität: Pauschalurlaube westdeutscher Reisender in Spanien während der 1970er- und 1980er-Jahre', *Zeithistorische Forschungen/Studies in Contemporary History*, 13/1 (2016), 61–85.

[57] 'Bessere Qualität statt Wachstum', *Frankfurter Allgemeine Zeitung*, 24 Apr. 1975.

[58] 'Vor allem Information', *Frankfurter Rundschau*, 12 July 1975.

[59] Advertisement for the *rutas romanticas*, *Neue Zürcher Zeitung*, 26 Jan. 1978.

[60] Nuno Rocha, 'Esperam-se mais de 250 000 turistas alemães em 1977', *Publituris*, 1 Oct. 1976.

Swedish Prime Minister Olof Palme encouraged his fellow citizens to spend their holidays in Portugal 'as an expression of friendship with the Portuguese people and of solidarity with their ambition to consolidate and further democracy'.[61] This symbolic support was a friendly gesture made by two Social Democrats towards the Socialist government under Mario Soares, which both Schmidt and Palme also supported in other contexts.

Despite these new elements, this was not a complete makeover of the tourism strategy. Package beach holidays continued to be the main selling point, and the mainstream discourses of tourism promotion continued to avoid mentioning politics. Rather, tourism was used by politicians and economists to provide an element of continuity in a situation of political and economic change. Promoters facing an economic crisis at the same time as political transitions used a mixture of older and newer tourist values in order to sell a new and improved version of the popular destinations. The political changes offered an additional argument with which to sell holidays to a clientele striving to distinguish themselves from 'the masses' through their reflective approach to travel. The idea of a reflective tourist who focused on quality and was aware of the socio-political situation at their chosen destination gradually became a resource for promoting tourism—a trend that increased in subsequent decades.

IV. *Conclusion*

Tourism to Spain, Portugal, and Greece from the 1960s to the 1970s gives insights into discussions of values and value change processes. First, it sheds light on a new understanding of politics and politicization; second, it helps us assess the impact of individual behaviour on social structures; and third, it provides insight into the relationship between tourism and democratization.

First, from the 1960s onwards, opponents of the authoritarian regimes created new practices and discourses around tourism as an expression of personal values and political sympathies, in which they questioned the notion of tourism as a 'private' activity and promoted the idea that it was a political statement. By attacking tourism, foreign opponents of these regimes successfully raised public aware-

---

[61] 'O discurso de Olof Palme', *Publituris*, 15 Mar. 1976.

ness and stimulated debate in the mainstream media. However, this strategy did not affect the numbers of visitors to Spain, Portugal, and Greece in the 1960s. Far more successful was the strategy of the tourist industry—led by international experts, travel agents, and journalists—that presented tourism as a 'technical', 'personal', and 'non-political' activity. Tourism proved to be immune to political attacks on a quantitative level; however, the discussions encouraged a more reflective approach to choosing one's holiday destination.

Second, the strong appeal of going abroad on holiday provides a good example of how individual behaviour could influence social structures. In the 1960s and 1970s, growing individual wealth converted mass consumerism into a powerful expression of social preferences. The success of tourism is one of many examples showing the extent to which consumerism for private pleasure became a core asset for an increasing number of Europeans. This was true for British, West German, and Swedish tourists travelling south, as well as for Greek, Spanish, and Portuguese people who embraced new consumer values in contact with foreign tourists.[62] The appeal of tourism was affected by the oil crisis only to a limited extent, as Europeans continued to spend their money on travel. The growth in tourism that had started in the 1960s continued, and made it one of the world's leading industries over the following decades.

Third, the relationship between tourism and the democratization of the three Western dictatorial regimes in Europe is a complex one.[63] The triumph of the bikini on the beaches was interpreted as a symbol of new social freedoms embraced by the local population as a result of foreign influence, but also seen as a veil that disguised the less pleasant aspects of the regimes. In fact, the political impact of tourism was far more subtle and indirect: as governments and tourism entrepreneurs in democracies and dictatorships alike saw tourism as a win–win situation, their mutual interest in encouraging tourism created spaces of collaboration and co-operation in the diplomatic and economic spheres. While the authoritarian regimes were in power, these collaborations helped to integrate Spain, Portugal, and Greece at least selectively into the geopolitical 'West'. During the transitions to democracy, these existing tourist links contributed favourably to further political collaboration in bilateral

[62] Kornetis, Kotsovili, and Papadogiannis (eds.), *Consumption and Gender*.

[63] For an overview on that discussion see Glaser, *Wandel durch Tourismus*, 350–6.

relations, as well as in the process of integration into the European Community.

Tourism transcended the economic caesura of the oil crisis, the 'North–South' divide within Western Europe, and the political separation between 'democracies' and 'dictatorships' within the geopolitical 'West'. As travel emerged as a highly valued practice in European consumer societies, the boycott appeals of Western European activists offer an early example of how tourism was connected to political consciousness. After the transitions to democracy, an anti-authoritarian or democratic outlook ceased to be an argument against tourism to these countries, but ecological and social arguments began to pull more weight when choosing a destination. Debates over tourism during the period of authoritarian regimes gave rise to the idea of a politically and ethically 'conscious tourist', which still exists today.

9

Towards Expressive Humanitarianism: The Formative Experience of Biafra

Norbert Götz

Chronologies of humanitarian aid tend to focus on foreign crises that elicit mitigating responses, thus emphasizing the geopolitical dimension of emergency relief. Two important monographs of the 2010s, Michael Barnett's *Empire of Humanity* and Silvia Salvatici's *History of Humanitarianism*, represent this perspective. They both suggest that the years following the Second World War and the period after the Cold War represent the most significant turning points of twentieth-century humanitarianism.[1] However, the 'long 1970s' may be regarded as another geopolitical watershed, with new postcolonial conflicts emerging from the ruins of the old imperial order that had collapsed in the decades after the Second World War. Recent overviews of humanitarian history point to a decisive rupture in the late 1960s and early 1970s.[2] Many historians agree, especially with regard to the 1967–70 Biafran War (also known as the Nigerian Civil War). While much current research on humanitarianism emphasizes upheavals in connection with decolonization, the analysis suggested here—stressing economics, media, culture,

In addition to Christina von Hodenberg and participants in the conference 'An Era of Value Change: The Seventies in Europe', German Historical Institute London, 14–16 March 2019, I would like to express my gratitude to Georgina Brewis, Susan Lindholm, Carl Marklund, and Steffen Werther for their welcome insights and valuable contributions to this essay, which is funded in the framework of the project 'Civil Society without Boundaries: Nordic Humanitarianism Facing the Biafra Crisis' (Swedish Research Council grant 2021-01219).

[1] Michael Barnett, *Empire of Humanity: A History of Humanitarianism* (Ithaca, NY, 2011); Silvia Salvatici, *A History of Humanitarianism, 1755–1989: In the Name of Others* (Manchester, 2019), 7, first pub. as *Nel nome degli altri: storia dell'umanitarismo internazionale* (Bologna, 2015).

[2] Johannes Paulmann, 'Conjunctures in the History of International Humanitarian Aid during the Twentieth Century', *Humanity*, 4/2 (2013), 215–38; Kevin O'Sullivan, Matthew Hilton, and Juliano Fiori, 'Humanitarianisms in Context', *European Review of History/Revue Européenne d'Histoire*, 23/1–2 (2016), 1–15.

and civil society rather than geopolitics—will address both social movements and so-called NGOs.[3] It changes the principal question regarding humanitarian effort from the geopolitical 'what?' to a moral-economic 'how?', shifting the focus of discussion from crisis management directives imposed by the outside world to value-based choices made by aid agencies on the ground.

Thus, the present essay seeks to demonstrate that rather than being a function of external demand (which it typically falls short of), humanitarian supply is determined by its own inherent mechanisms of mobilization, production, and distribution. In this view, humanitarianism is primarily a matter of logistical capability and organizational responsiveness on the part of donor and aid agencies. While influenced by geopolitical factors, aid providers follow their own logic of discursive and technological development. This new perspective more broadly correlates humanitarian efforts with domestic politics and voluntary action. It focuses in particular on entangled developments around 1970 in the media and the voluntary sector, with regard to authentic witnessing and post-rational forms of engagement. In contrast to conventional geopolitical thought, which tends to depoliticize humanitarian organizations and see them either as neutral conveyors of necessities or as pawns engaged in Great Power games, this approach seeks to provide an analytical tool for the critical scrutiny of humanitarian agencies themselves.

The present essay engages with the 'long 1970s' as a period especially well suited to illustrate the significance of socio-cultural developments for understanding aid. At the same time, it seeks to dismantle the 'international relations prerogative' in humanitarian studies. This is part of a larger project that reconceptualizes humanitarian history from a moral economy perspective and suggests a new chronology correlated with socio-economic regimes, cultural developments, and value change. In this view, the era of elitist nineteenth-century laissez-faire liberalism was one of ad hoc humanitarianism that was largely dependent on personal relations and contingencies. By contrast, the years shaped by Taylorism and mass society (approximately 1900 to 1968) were characterized by organized humanitarianism, with a strong emphasis on economies of scale and effective altruism. Finally, the blend of individualized

---

[3] For a critique of the term 'non-governmental organization' see Norbert Götz, 'Reframing NGOs: The Identity of an International Relations Non-Starter', *European Journal of International Relations*, 14/2 (2008), 231–58.

post-material lifestyles and neo-liberal public management that has emerged over the past half century is best understood as expressive humanitarianism.[4]

I. *The Long 1970s and Expressive Humanitarianism*

According to Lilie Chouliaraki, whose research comparing humanitarian appeals of the 1970s and 1980s with those of recent years deals with the mediation of human suffering, the entire period since 1970 has been an 'age of global spectacle'. This era, she suggests, is typified by the market-compliant deployment of aid, the erosion of the grand narrative of solidarity, and the technologically driven rise of a narcissistic, self-expressive spectatorship. Chouliaraki sees these developments as creating an epistemic shift towards a subjective, emotional humanitarianism that is correlated with superficial morality and an emergent 'neoliberal lifestyle of "feel good" altruism'.[5] Similarly, anthropologist Mark Duffield, although he acknowledges the differences between the 1970s and the present, suggests that the decline of modern humanitarianism and the 'anthropocentric turn' brought about by its postmodern variant can be traced back to the Biafran War.[6] In addition, sociologist Monika Krause argues that, in parallel with this development, powerful results-based management tools were introduced that shifted rationales in the humanitarian sector from overarching societal to project-specific goals.[7] The concept of expressive humanitarianism encapsulates all these trends. They are also summarized in the formulation of 'sentimental alienation' by philosopher and public intellectual Alain Finkielkraut, which

---

[4] Norbert Götz, Georgina Brewis, and Steffen Werther, *Humanitarianism in the Modern World: The Moral Economy of Famine Relief* (Cambridge, 2020); eid., 'Humanitäre Hilfe: Eine Braudel'sche Perspektive', in Nicole Kramer and Christine Krüger (eds.), *Freiwilligenarbeit und gemeinnützige Organisationen im Wandel: Neue Perspektiven auf das 19. und 20. Jahrhundert* (Berlin, 2019), 89–119. See also Norbert Götz, '"Moral Economy": Its Conceptual History and Analytical Prospects', *Journal of Global Ethics*, 11/2 (2015), 147–62. Whereas our previous work illustrates the period of expressive humanitarianism with relief efforts during the famine in Ethiopia in the mid 1980s, the present essay examines the Biafran crisis of 1967–70, when the shift occurred from organized to expressive humanitarianism.

[5] Lilie Chouliaraki, *The Ironic Spectator: Solidarity in the Age of Post-Humanitarianism* (Cambridge, 2013), 52, 4 (quotations), 1–21.

[6] Mark Duffield, 'From Protection to Disaster Resilience', in Roger Mac Ginty and Jenny H. Peterson (eds.), *The Routledge Companion to Humanitarian Action* (London, 2015), 26–37, at 29 (quotation), 27.

[7] Monika Krause, *The Good Project: Humanitarian Relief NGOs and the Fragmentation of Reason* (Chicago, 2014), 87.

has shaped humanitarian efforts towards the end of the twentieth century.[8]

The concept of expressive humanitarianism refers to a choreography of aid that has been dramatized and mediatized, and to spectacular forms of aid intervention. It covers a cluster of paradoxical developments that analysts of society trace to a turning point in political culture and economy that took place around 1970.[9] Major factors are the post-material and post-rational value system that increasingly took hold in the middle classes in late capitalist societies, and the political economy accompanying the third industrial revolution. The wider cluster includes the growing importance of charisma and self-expressive lifestyles, the increasing fusion of philanthropy and advocacy, the notion of human rights, the utilization of mass media, spectacles of various kinds—such as populism, commercial branding, privatization, and 'projectification'—and the aggressive conduct of humanitarian intervention.

Of the many formative influences on present-day humanitarianism that can be traced back to the long 1970s, the Biafran crisis has been seen as a historical precursor of the ethnic conflicts that followed the Cold War.[10] Biafra is a landmark in at least four respects. First, as the earliest televised famine, it heralded an increasingly media-driven presentation of emergencies and relief efforts. Second, it saw a proliferation of voluntary relief organizations that sought to provide aid by directly linking broad donor groups with recipient populations while working out pragmatic standards of provision. Third, Biafra ushered in a growing concern for witnessing and reporting on distress and human rights violations. Fourth, it became the harbinger of an emphasis on spectacle, celebrity, and a broad involvement in humanitarian campaigns, which suited the new donor groups' progressive consumer lifestyle. Following a brief

---

[8] Alain Finkielkraut, *In the Name of Humanity: Reflections on the Twentieth Century* (New York, 2000), 93.

[9] Luc Boltanski and Eve Chiapello, *The New Spirit of Capitalism*, trans. Gregory Elliott (London, 2005), first pub. as *Le Nouvel Esprit du capitalisme* (Paris, 1999); Anselm Doering-Manteuffel and Lutz Raphael, *Nach dem Boom: Perspektiven auf die Zeitgeschichte seit 1970*, 2nd supplemented edn. (Göttingen, 2010; 1st edn. 2008); Thomas Borstelmann, *The 1970s: A New Global History from Civil Rights to Economic Inequality* (Princeton, 2012). The significance of the long 1970s as a turning point is also suggested by such astute observers as Ulrich Beck, Daniel Bell, Manuel Castells, Anthony Giddens, Agnes Heller, Ronald Inglehart, Naomi Klein, Christopher Lasch, Alain Lipietz, Jean-François Lyotard, and Samuel Moyn, among others.

[10] Jonathan Benthall, *Disasters, Relief and the Media* (London, 1993), 94.

overview of the Biafran conflict, these four constitutive elements of expressive humanitarianism will be discussed in the context of the relief effort that ensued.

II. *The Case of Biafra*

In May 1967, following a year of political turmoil and atrocities against the Christian Igbo people, the governor of the oil-rich Eastern Region of Nigeria, Lieutenant Colonel 'Emeka' Odumegwu Ojukwu, declared the territory independent and announced that its new name was the Republic of Biafra.[11] In geopolitical terms, this secession, which precipitated the Biafran War, remained a domestic postcolonial power struggle in West Africa. It did not morph into a Cold War or North–South conflict. Almost all African governments, Western authorities, and the Soviet bloc sided with the established state of Nigeria, and intergovernmental organizations kept aloof from what they considered an internal affair. Limited military capacity on both sides initially prevented an armed confrontation. From the beginning, however, Nigeria, backed by its neighbouring states and supported by the UK and the international system, imposed a blockade that effectively cut off the secessionist province's supplies. After brief successes in the summer of 1967, the Biafran military retreated despite continuous French arms deliveries. This was followed by a period of stalemate and then renewed federal advances in the spring of the following year. It soon became clear that Biafra had no chance of winning the war and could at best hope for a negotiated settlement. However, the few talks that took place between the parties were a failure.[12]

Six months after the war started, the food shortage in Biafra had become a famine, causing foreign missionaries and clergy in the secessionist territory to express alarm at the humanitarian situation. From Christian news outlets the reports made their way into the mainstream media, a development bolstered by Biafran propaganda activities and expatriate networks that reframed the issue of civil war as a matter of human rights and the survival of their people. Beginning in June 1968, when news and images of starving Biafran

[11] Chukwuemeka Odumegwu Ojukwu, 'The Declaration', in *Biafra: Selected Speeches and Random Thoughts of C. Odumegwu Ojukwu*, 2 vols. (New York, 1969), i. 193–6.

[12] John J. Stremlau, *The International Politics of the Nigerian Civil War, 1967–1970* (Princeton, 1977).

children appeared on the front pages of international newspapers and in TV reports, the cause of the breakaway province quickly won the hearts and minds of Western audiences. An agitated public demanded that aid agencies take humanitarian action. Governments were pressured to provide financial aid despite the complex political situation.[13] Biafra assumed the role of a 'Vietnam for Christians', according to a contemporary comment, demonstrating that it was not only leftist groups who aspired to 'an ideal world'.[14] In retrospect, however, it is widely agreed that the authorities in Biafra used the suffering of their people for political ends, applying a 'rhetoric of victimisation' to mobilize support from abroad while making the nations and organizations offering relief complicit in their war effort.[15]

There are various ways in which providing support to Biafra might have served a humanitarian objective, but instead it ultimately reinforced 'the course of heroic but suicidal sacrifice on which Biafra was set' by its leadership.[16] A commentator noted that while logistically Biafran relief was a 'historic feat'—one 'unrivalled anywhere for bravery'—it appears at the same time to have been 'an act of unfortunate and profound folly'.[17] Without aid, including income generated by purchases humanitarian agencies made in Biafra, the civil war would probably have ended in late summer 1968, one and a half years before Biafra's ultimate surrender on 15 January 1970. This was—and still is—difficult for churches and aid organizations to admit. They made considerable efforts in the

---

[13] Lasse Heerten, *The Biafran War and Postcolonial Humanitarianism: Spectacles of Suffering* (Cambridge, 2017), 89, 93, 96, 103–4. See also Arua Oko Omaka, *The Biafran Humanitarian Crisis, 1967–1970: International Human Rights and Joint Church Aid* (Madison, 2016), 62–4.

[14] Cited in Florian Hannig, 'The Biafra Crisis and the Establishment of Humanitarian Aid in West Germany as a New Philanthropic Field', in Gregory R. Witkowski and Arnd Bauerkämper (eds.), *German Philanthropy in Transatlantic Perspective: Perceptions, Exchanges and Transfers since the Early Twentieth Century* (Cham, 2016), 205–25, at 209. On the broad political background of the Biafran aid movement see also Florian Hannig, 'Mitleid mit Biafranern in Westdeutschland: Eine Historisierung von Empathie', *Werkstatt Geschichte*, 68 (2015), 65–77.

[15] Marie-Luce Desgrandchamps, 'Biafra: At the Heart of Postcolonial Humanitarian Ambiguities', *Humanitarian Alternatives*, 9 (2018), 8–19, at 11 (quotation); Alex de Waal, *Famine Crimes: Politics and the Disaster Relief Industry in Africa* (Oxford, 1997), 72–7.

[16] John de St Jorre, *The Nigerian Civil War* (London, 1972), 18. For the potential benefits of aid see Marie-Luce Desgrandchamps, *L'Humanitaire en guerre civile: la crise du Biafra (1967–1970)* (Rennes, 2018), 325.

[17] Ian Smillie, *The Alms Bazaar: Altruism under Fire. Non-Profit Profit Organizations and International Development* (London, 1995), 104.

aftermath of the war to deny the manipulation and perverse effects of their aid, which estimates say might have cost the lives of 180,000 or more people.[18] Journalist Tord Wallström, Biafra's most vocal advocate in Sweden at the time of the conflict, exemplifies the shift in perceptions in the longer run. Acknowledging that he had been naive, he later expressed his regrets for the time he had spent on the cause and for having made others work in vain.[19] Although Biafra moulded 'an entire generation of NGO relief workers', leading to the founding of new agencies and the transformation of old ones, the issues it raised makes it a sensitive subject for the aid industry.[20] In hindsight, Biafra represents a misconceived post-rational effort that vividly contrasts with the humanitarian aspiration to 'do no harm'; at the same time, it marks the inauguration of expressive humanitarianism.

III. Media

A recent study asserts that according to most contemporaries, 'the media created "Biafra"'.[21] An Irish missionary at the time even sought to convince a sceptical Ojukwu that the war would be 'won on the T.V. screen not in the battlefield'.[22] Awareness of the mounting humanitarian crisis in Biafra quickly spread after extensive coverage appeared on the first three pages of the British newspaper *The Sun* on 12 June 1968. It featured 'marvellous [*sic*] pictures of kids in great distress' and other 'very moving stuff', according to journalist Michael Leapman, who had brought the story to the attention of the British public.[23] On the same evening, UK-based television production company ITN broadcast a news report showing similar disturbing images. Although previous humanitarian emergencies had occasionally resulted in media coverage that seized the attention of the world,[24] this was the first time newspaper images and TV footage played such a dramatic role.

---

[18] Ibid.

[19] Tord Wallström, *Vi på jorden: möten med människor och miljöer* (Höganäs, 1993), 211, 217.   [20] de Waal, *Famine Crimes*, 73.

[21] Heerten, *Biafran War*, 146.

[22] Ken Waters, 'Influencing the Message: The Role of Catholic Missionaries in Media Coverage of the Nigerian Civil War', *Catholic Historical Review*, 90/4 (2004), 697–718, at 714.

[23] Cited in Paul Harrison and Robin H. Palmer, *News out of Africa: Biafra to Band Aid* (London, 1986), 29.

[24] Götz, Brewis, and Werther, *Humanitarianism in the Modern World*, 137.

The Biafran crisis came at a time when TV dominated the media landscape, and tabloids and Sunday news magazines mirrored and amplified TV coverage.

After the British publicity, Western media began to pay increasing attention to Biafra. The story moved from the inside columns of newspapers to the front page, then to editorials and illustrated feature stories. As with coverage of the Vietnam War, technological developments facilitated live, front-line photojournalism, with the result that conflicts around the globe invaded millions of homes in print and on TV, stirring emotions, inciting protests, and mobilizing solidarity. Famine images like those from Biafra had never reached a mass audience before and became prototypes of their genre. Their impact is unmistakable: a photograph from Biafra is the first of three famine pictures among *Time* magazine's selected hundred most influential photographs of all time, and as of April 2021, Wikipedia entries on 'Kwashiorkor', 'Starvation', and 'Famine' all had Biafran children as a signature image.[25]

Biafra was a transformative media event in Western societies. The scenes of malnourished, dying children became a shocking symbol of human vulnerability.[26] The way in which mediatization changed a horrific tragedy into 'charity infotainment' that drew in new donor groups is illustrated by the BBC children's show *Blue Peter*, which held its first overseas emergency appeal in 1968 for those afflicted by the Nigerian Civil War. Children were asked to send parcels of wool and cotton, which were subsequently sold to raise money, and their response was enough to buy three hospital lorries, six cars for emergency doctors, six rehabilitation vans, and medical supplies. The decision to show images of malnourished children to very young viewers at teatime prompted protest from some parents, but it was defended by the BBC and received praise from others. One mother wrote:

That was the first time my son had faced the grim realities of the world. True he is only 4½ . . . but how can we help them (our children) to be responsible people if they are not aware? Philip was not afraid, but was inspired to help.

[25] See *100 Photographs: The Most Influential Images of All Time* (New York, 2015); also ⟨https://en.wikipedia.org/wiki/Kwashiorkor⟩, ⟨https://en.wikipedia.org/wiki/Starvation⟩, and ⟨https://en.wikipedia.org/wiki/Famine⟩ [all accessed 19 Apr. 2021].

[26] Heerten, *Biafran War*, 107, 118–29, 141, 335. On the role of timely transmitted (moving) images see also Michael Gould, *The Struggle for Modern Nigeria: The Biafran War 1967–1970* (London, 2012), pp. xii–xiii.

He has been canvassing our childless neighbours and explaining the matter most clearly and now happily feels he has saved the African children.[27]

Prior to their declaration of independence, the Biafran authorities had hired an international lobbying agency to help them gain favour with foreign elites. By early 1968, the regime had adjusted its strategy and created a Directorate of Propaganda that engaged a number of public relations companies to address broader Western audiences. The most widely known of these agencies, Markpress, was funded by the French intelligence services. Their main message was that the Biafrans were 'a people under siege', threatened with genocide. This was amplified by expatriates, an emerging solidarity movement, and the media. Alluding to a legend that the Igbo people were descended from one of the lost tribes of Israel, Biafran propaganda suggested that their experience paralleled that of the European Jews murdered by the Nazis. As the Holocaust had not yet taken on the resonance that it carries today, this campaign made a pioneering contribution to its rise as the emblematic crime against humanity, while at the same time issuing a desperate warning about what might be the fate of the people in Biafra. As the images of starvation were reminiscent of photographs that had emerged from liberated Nazi concentration camps, this message began to resonate among a wider public in the West. A French opinion poll taken in September 1968 showed that sympathy for Biafrans exceeded that for both the Czechoslovak and Vietnamese peoples.[28] Nigerian officials regarded Germans as particularly susceptible to Biafran propaganda because of their country's history as the perpetrator of the Holocaust.[29]

However, despite slogans such as '"A" as in Auschwitz, "B" as in Biafra' and some visual similarities, the parallels were far-fetched.[30] The objective of Biafran propaganda was not ultimately to convince

[27] BBC Written Archives, T47/93/1, Biddy Baxter, 'Blue Peter Appeals: Rags to Riches', 6, 1976. See also Biddy Baxter, *Dear Blue Peter: The Best of 50 Years of Letters to Britain's Favourite Children's Television Programme* (London, 2008), 238. I owe this example to Georgina Brewis.

[28] Heerten, *Biafran War*, 63, 89–93, 129, 177, 179; on French funding see Rony Brauman, 'Dangerous Liaisons: Bearing Witness and Political Propaganda', 1 Oct. 2006 ⟨https://www.msf-crash.org/en/publications/humanitarian-actors-and-practice/dangerous-liaisons-bearing-witness-and-political⟩ [accessed 19 Apr. 2021].

[29] Stremlau, *International Politics of the Nigerian Civil War*, 342.

[30] Lasse Heerten, '"A" as in Auschwitz, "B" as in Biafra: The Nigerian Civil War, Visual Narratives of Genocide, and the Fragmented Universalization of the Holocaust', in Heide Fehrenbach and Davide Rodogno (eds.), *Humanitarian Photography: A History* (Cambridge, 2015), 249–74.

the outside world that a genocide was in the making, but rather to convey the belief that the Biafran people were fearful of being slaughtered en masse and, in their own view, were fighting a war of survival. The picture of an intractable conflict presented here was intended to bring about a political settlement with international support to replace the ongoing military showdown. In order for the strategy to work, it was crucial to show the world that the Biafrans were prepared to continue their struggle at all costs. According to post-conflict interviews with Biafran propaganda officers, 'maintaining domestic support for the rebellion . . . [was] more important and difficult than the mobilization of international public opinion'.[31]

Humanitarian aid workers and agencies did their best to promote media coverage. The ITN television reports that had led to a breakthrough in media attention were driven by an Irish Holy Ghost Father and his colleagues in Biafra, who eagerly served as press informants. In addition, the priest's congregation back in Ireland mounted and sustained a public relations campaign in Europe and North America.[32] The International Committee of the Red Cross (ICRC) significantly stepped up its briefings and press conferences during the Biafran War. Its commissioner-general for the Nigeria–Biafra operation was featured on the British television show *The Man of the Month*. The ICRC also produced two films, one on Biafra and one on Nigeria, and issued an unprecedented number of photographs because 'quite often the publication of a single photo has greater impact than a lengthy text'.[33]

The success of the Biafran solidarity campaign in West Germany has been attributed to 'the media's bias in favour of Biafra'— something also said of other countries.[34] In the UK, Michael Leapman won the Campaigning Journalist of the Year award for his reporting from Biafra.[35] Tord Wallström, who had been with Leapman on the flight out of Biafra, was awarded Sweden's Grand Prize for Journalism for addressing the Biafran famine earlier than

[31] Stremlau, *International Politics of the Nigerian Civil War*, 112 (quotation), 111.

[32] Waters, 'Influencing the Message'.

[33] Marie-Luce Desgrandchamps, '"Organising the Unpredictable": The Nigeria–Biafra War and its Impact on the ICRC', *International Review of the Red Cross*, 94/888 (2012), 1409–32, at 1428–9, quotation from Archives du Comité International de la Croix-Rouge (ACICR), Directorate briefing note, 9 Apr. 1969, 1431.

[34] Hannig, 'Biafra Crisis', 206. For the USA, see John A. Sambe, 'Network Coverage of the Civil War in Nigeria', *Journal of Broadcasting*, 24/1 (1980), 61–7.

[35] Harrison and Palmer, *News out of Africa*, 37.

others, having been on the scene, and for publicizing the issue in his reports.[36] This was a unique honour for someone working for a small provincial newspaper.

Many professional journalists 'turned ambassadors' for Biafra, openly taking a stance by making statements such as 'there is no point writing anything if you stay neutral'.[37] Others assured their Western readers that while the conflict might be difficult to understand from abroad, all that was needed was a humanitarian response— a response that was correlated with political sympathy. Moreover, the trope of genocide blurred the boundaries of humanitarian aid, the legitimacy of providing arms, and the urgency of humanitarian intervention. Asked by journalists what Biafra needed most—food or arms?—self-proclaimed president Ojukwu responded with a moral calculation: 'I must give priority to weapons. If we do not get food, many will die; if we do not get weapons, everybody is going to die.'[38] The failure of the media to challenge this logic and expose the entanglement of philanthropy with waging war illustrates how expressive humanitarianism was enabled by emotional, rather than reflective, journalism.

IV. *Voluntary Organizations*

Although it had declared itself a republic, Biafra had little success in advancing its cause with foreign governments. However, the country's missionary contacts safeguarded its connections with Christian churches worldwide, and this allowed the Biafran government to shift its communications focus from official diplomacy to transnational advocacy.[39] Buttressed by growing media attention, this strategy proved effective, and in the summer of 1968 Biafra became a 'ward' of Western civil societies, totally dependent on the support of voluntary organizations. However, the fact that aid was provided on terms dictated by the recipient was a novel development.[40] The Biafran crisis is widely regarded as the first humanitarian effort in which voluntary organizations involved in

[36] Lars-Erik Holmertz, *Historien om Stora Journalistpriset från starten 1966 till millennie-skiftet* (Stockholm, 2000), 71.

[37] Françoise Ugochukwu, *Torn Apart: The Nigerian Civil War and its Impact* (London, 2010), 36; Jean Buhler, *Tuez-les tous! Guerre de sécession au Biafra* (Paris, 1968), 222.

[38] Anders Beijbom, Britt Rengheden, and Rolle Ståhlström, *Rapport från Biafra: en tragedi i närbild* (Stockholm, 1968), 106 (quotation), 7.

[39] Heerten, *Biafran War*, 85.

[40] Stremlau, *International Politics of the Nigerian Civil War*, 238.

'dynamics of co-operation and rivalry' were the most significant agents.[41] Aid was largely delivered in ways that violated Nigeria's sovereignty. This was justified by stating that 'morality overrides law', or even by reference to a 'divine law',[42] and can be viewed as an early application of what later became the 'responsibility to protect'. The Biafran experience has been credited with playing a transformative role in the NGO moment of the long 1970s, as it was the starting point for a post-rational cult of action that declared that emergency relief took precedence over political analysis, and it saw the emergence of people-to-people engagement as well as the growth of an aid industry.[43]

Much of the early intelligence from Biafra came from a close-knit network of Irish missionaries in the area. They were particularly sensitive to the historical grievances of imperial domination, and they were alert to harbingers of famine. In addition, they regarded the Irish people as 'kin to the Biafrans'.[44] Missionaries were generally involved in the distribution of relief, but there were also activists among them who unabashedly showed their political solidarity and provided logistical military support. Irish protagonists had sent a humanitarian mercy flight to Biafra around Christmas 1967, and by March 1968 had founded a new relief organization called Africa Concern (later renamed Concern Worldwide, today Ireland's largest aid organization). The extended media coverage from June 1968 onwards, in which images were 'more eloquent than words', gave their campaign momentum.[45] Africa Concern was more militant than other organizations, and sold cargo space on their aircraft to arms suppliers.[46]

---

[41] Desgrandchamps, *L'Humanitaire en guerre civile*, 324 (quotation); de Waal, *Famine Crimes*, 73.

[42] Jürgen Lieser, *50 Jahre Ende des Biafra-Krieges: Ein Lehrstück für die Dilemmata der humanitären Hilfe in Gewaltkonflikten* (Freiburg i.Br., 2020), 21; Omaka, *Biafran Humanitarian Crisis*, 113.

[43] Kevin O'Sullivan, 'Humanitarian Encounters: Biafra, NGOs and Imaginings of the Third World in Britain and Ireland, 1967–70', *Journal of Genocide Research*, 16/2–3 (2014), 299–315; Bertrand Taithe, 'Reinventing (French) Universalism: Religion, Humanitarianism and the "French Doctors"', *Modern and Contemporary France*, 12/2 (2004), 147–58, at 148; Marie-Luce Desgrandchamps, Lasse Heerten, Arua Oko Omaka, et al., 'Biafra, Humanitarian Intervention and History', *Journal of Humanitarian Affairs*, 2/2 (2020), 66–78.

[44] Kevin O'Sullivan, *Ireland, Africa and the End of Empire: Small State Identity in the Cold War, 1955–75* (Manchester, 2012), 114 (citing bishop Joseph Whelan), 86, 108.

[45] Ibid. 115 (quotation), 90, 113–16.

[46] Omaka, *Biafran Humanitarian Crisis*, 98; Lieser, *50 Jahre Ende des Biafra-Krieges*, 33.

The Biafran War was a challenge for established humanitarian organizations such as the ICRC that were used to dealing discreetly with sovereign nation states. Their approach was not easily adaptable to the more vocal, fluid conditions of the times.[47] Nevertheless, in November 1967 the ICRC became an early supplier of medical goods in the civil war, and one of its former delegates has suggested that 'the modern ICRC was born in Africa, in the smoking ruins of Biafra', where it was 'brought to the baptismal font of a new humanitarian era'.[48] While the Biafran crisis highlighted ICRC deficiencies in management, fieldwork, and interactions with third parties (including the media), it was the crucible that transformed it into the organization it is today.[49]

Some have argued that neutrality in the Biafran War was impossible for humanitarian organizations.[50] Nevertheless, the ICRC upheld its traditional neutrality, and sought not to alienate the recognized Nigerian government on which it depended for access to the conflict area. The majority of the ICRC's relief, therefore, went to areas controlled by federal forces, and the federal military government in turn tolerated the fact that some of the relief was delivered to the insurgent province. However, the continuing flood of disturbing images from Biafra and personal experience on the ground made some Red Cross fieldworkers uncomfortable with the ICRC's tacit approach. Volunteers from the independent French Red Cross formed the Comité de Lutte contre le Génocide au Biafra, which became the nucleus of a defecting organization now known worldwide as Médecins sans Frontières (MSF, Doctors without Borders).[51] To them, 'Biafra became a second Solferino', and when MSF was formally founded in 1971, it answered the call for 'a new Dunant'.[52]

---

[47] Norbert Götz and Irène Herrmann, 'Universalism in Emergency Aid before and after 1970: Ambivalences and Contradictions', in Pasi Ihalainen and Antero Holmila (eds.), *Nationalism and Internationalism Intertwined: A European History of Concepts beyond the Nation State* (New York, forthcoming), 247–69.

[48] Jean-Marc Bornet, *Entre les lignes ennemies: délégué du CICR (1972–2003)* (Geneva, 2011), 87 (here cited from Desgrandchamps, 'Organising the Unpredictable', 1410).

[49] Desgrandchamps, 'Organising the Unpredictable', 1411.

[50] Jacinta C. Nwaka, 'When Neutrality Loses its Value: Caritas Airlift to Biafra, 1968–1970', *Journal of the Historical Society of Nigeria*, 22 (2013), 63–81.

[51] Marie-Luce Desgrandchamps, 'Revenir sur le mythe fondateur de Médecins sans frontières: les relations entre les médecins français et le CIRC pendant la guerre du Biafra (1967–1970)', *Relations Internationales*, 146 (Apr.–June 2011), 95–108.

[52] Finkielkraut, *In the Name of Humanity*, 84; Eleanor Davey, *Idealism beyond Borders:*

The student group Third World First's dissociation from Oxfam marked a similar break with tradition and the emergence of an openly politicized approach to aid.[53] It was around 1970 that humanitarianism became 'a field of competing positions' in earnest.[54] This foreshadowed the proliferation of humanitarian organizations in the following decades, each with its own background, profile, and agenda.[55]

ICRC aid to Biafra in November 1967 originated in a donation from the Holy See that was passed down through the Catholic relief organization Caritas Internationalis. During the winter and spring of 1968, Caritas used the services of an arms dealer to fly aid to Biafra. At the same time, it issued its first international appeal, calling public attention to the high child mortality and the estimated 3 million refugees in the Biafran territory. Early supporters of these relief efforts were organizations such as Oxfam and War on Want. German Caritas became actively involved in June 1968, but its regional branch in the diocese of Münster had already begun an aid programme in November 1967.[56] The Roman Catholic Church of Germany established a working group on human rights in order to provide their Biafran effort with a non-denominational veneer.[57]

Norwegian, Dutch, and Danish church relief committees also began collecting money for Biafra towards the end of 1967.[58] Among Protestants, a significant mobilizer of global support for the breakaway province was Akanu Ibiam, one of the presidents of the World Council of Churches, although this organization, too, sought a balanced approach in order not to alienate the federal Nigerian side and other members of the Council who lacked sympathy for the

---

The French Revolutionary Left and the Rise of Humanitarianism, 1954–1988 (Cambridge, 2015), 35–6. See also Götz and Herrmann, 'Universalism in Emergency Aid'.

[53] Georgina Brewis, *A Social History of Student Volunteering: Britain and Beyond, 1880–1980* (New York, 2014), 184–5.   [54] Krause, *Good Project*, 103.

[55] Kevin O'Sullivan, 'A "Global Nervous System"': The Rise and Rise of European Humanitarian NGOs, 1945–1985', in Marc Frey, Sönke Kunkel, and Corinna R. Unger (eds.), *International Organizations and Development, 1945–1990* (Basingstoke, 2014), 196–219.

[56] Lieser, *50 Jahre Ende des Biafra-Krieges*, 13–14. For Oxfam's agency in the Biafra crisis, which also included the use of ICRC channels, see Tehila Sasson, 'In the Name of Humanity: Britain and the Rise of Global Humanitarianism' (Ph.D. thesis, University of California, Berkeley, 2015), 28–37.

[57] Hannig, 'Biafra Crisis', 208.

[58] Hugh G. Lloyd, Mona L. Mollerup, and Carl A. Bratved, *The Nordchurchaid Airlift to Biafra, 1968–1970: An Operations Report* (Copenhagen, 1972), 5.

secessionist cause.[59] By the end of August 1968, as the ICRC found itself unable to negotiate systematic access to Biafra, the Nordic Lutheran churches created Nordchurchaid as a collective transport mechanism for the last air miles to Biafra, while the German churches co-ordinated the flow of relief from Europe to Africa.[60]

Following ecumenical appeals in spring 1968, a close transnational collaboration between various churches emerged by the autumn of that year, resulting in the founding of Joint Church Aid (JCA). This was a logistical umbrella organization for co-ordinating and pooling aid resources, including from Nordchurchaid and the German churches. It initially included twenty-five organizations from seventeen countries, later growing to thirty-three organizations from twenty-one countries. Sectarian distinctions were maintained in this ground-breaking 'humanitarian international': Catholic and Protestant relief landed in Biafra on alternating nights and was distributed through separate channels. Although pilots mused that JCA stood for 'Jesus Christ Airline', the aid consortium included the American Jewish Committee (its first non-Jewish engagement). JCA was dissolved after the Nigerian Civil War, but it became a model of interdenominational co-operation whose lasting impact can be seen in the increased significance of humanitarian organizations on the global stage following the long 1970s.[61]

Biafra is credited with having shaped both the present-day knowledge regime of humanitarianism and an enduring epistemic community. The large-scale collaboration stimulated transnational communication and learning processes in relation to the management of a huge project operating under difficult circumstances, and it brought about necessary changes in fieldwork practices. For example, in Biafra, aid agencies developed a pragmatic system of nutrition based on anthropometric measurements and fortified foods of the kind still in use today—something historian Tom Scott-Smith identifies with 'low modernism'.[62]

[59] Omaka, *Biafran Humanitarian Crisis*, 73–7; Hannig, 'Biafra Crisis', 208.

[60] Lloyd, Mollerup, and Bratved, *Nordchurchaid Airlift*, 3, 101.

[61] Lieser, *50 Jahre Ende des Biafra-Krieges*, 16–17, 25; Heerten, *Biafran War*, 175–6; Omaka, *Biafran Humanitarian Crisis*, 5, 97–8. The term 'humanitarian international' is adopted from Alex de Waal, *Mass Starvation: The History and Future of Famine* (Cambridge, 2018), 118.

[62] Tom Scott-Smith, *On an Empty Stomach: Two Hundred Years of Hunger Relief* (Ithaca, NY, 2020), 138. See also Joël Glasman, *Humanitarianism and the Quantification of Human Needs: Minimal Humanity* (London, 2020), 94.

In addition to secular and church-driven humanitarian organizations, a solidarity movement that lobbied the public and solicited
donations played a considerable role in the emergence of expressive humanitarianism. West Germany alone had more than ninety
Biafra committees at the time. After their *raison d'être* vanished,
the Hamburg-based Aktion Biafra-Hilfe (Action Biafra Aid) transformed itself into the Gesellschaft für bedrohte Völker (Society
for Threatened Peoples), a human rights organization that has
maintained a high profile in Germany over recent decades.[63] A symbiosis between voluntary organizations and the media sometimes
emerged, as journalists took leading roles in the Biafran solidarity
movement. Examples were Ruth Bowert in Germany and Tord
Wallström in Sweden.[64] During the Biafran crisis, voluntary agencies also learnt a great deal about the importance of using the
media effectively, and this became a major concern for the decade's
fledgling humanitarian organizations.[65]

V. *Bearing Witness*

Although not a primary concern, the engagement of public relations
firms by authorities in disaster areas was a new aspect of expressive humanitarianism. In an interview reflecting on the conflict,
Uche Chukwumerije, former head of the Biafran Directorate of
Propaganda, claimed that the role of Markpress, the Geneva-based
advertising agency that disseminated statements by the rebels, had
been widely exaggerated. According to him, first-hand accounts
by foreigners living in or visiting Biafra were far more significant,
including those of journalists, religious leaders, and parliamenta-
rians who were flown into Biafra and shown around.[66] Political
analysts agree that Markpress's most effective action was to bring
media representatives to Biafra.[67] According to a later account,
Biafran authorities made even more efficient use of their visitors'

---

[63] Hannig, 'The Biafra Crisis', 210–11.

[64] Ibid. 213; Wallström, *Vi på jorden*, 208.

[65] Aengus Finucane, 'The Changing Roles of Voluntary Organizations', in Kevin
Cahill (ed.), *A Framework for Survival: Health, Human Rights, and Humanitarian Assistance
in Conflicts and Disasters*, rev. edn. (New York, 1999), 245–56, at 248–9.

[66] Stremlau, *International Politics of the Nigerian Civil War*, 117.

[67] Waters, 'Influencing the Message', 703. For a more positive evaluation of
Markpress's impact see Omaka, *Biafran Humanitarian Crisis*, 69.

time by creating 'a "park" of starving people, where hundreds dying of hunger were gathered to await the cameras'.[68]

Sympathy was also aroused by press releases that likened the Biafran (or Igbo) people to their Western counterparts, to whom appeals for humanitarian aid were being addressed, in terms of persistence, discipline, as well as Christian faith and defiance in the face of hardship. An example of this sort of rhetoric is the summing up of the Biafran character by Irish public intellectual Conor Cruise O'Brien as 'a real thing' that consisted of 'egalitarian manners, thirst for education, commercial enterprise, self-reliance, and technical ingenuity'. Moreover, when speaking with Ojukwu, O'Brien believed he heard 'that his tone, when he said the word "civilian," altogether lacked that professional note of contempt which so many African officers have acquired from their instructors'.[69]

However, aside from their praise of the Biafran people, media and humanitarian organizations were mainly concerned to denounce the genocide that many believed was threatening the Igbos. Notably, in these accounts, Africans largely remained 'voiceless victims' who rarely figured by name as spokespeople or sources, but were often depicted as passive sufferers. Journalists tended to report the words of Western missionaries and aid workers, frequently including the emotional reactions of the observers themselves.[70] Thus, it was predominantly 'White saviour' testimony of the distress and horror of annihilation that circulated abroad. The 'second age of humanitarianism', as medical anthropologist Didier Fassin puts it, 'corresponds to the emergence of the witness—not the witness who has experienced the tragedy, but the one who has brought aid to its victims'.[71] Thus, although the circles of aid have expanded, it appears that the voices of aid recipients have tended to grow quieter in the course of humanitarian history.[72] Nevertheless, Biafran students and expatriates were involved in the mobilization of support.[73]

[68] Brauman, 'Dangerous Liaisons'.

[69] Conor Cruise O'Brien, 'Biafra Revisited', *New York Review of Books*, 22 May 1969.

[70] Desgrandchamps, *L'Humanitaire en guerre civile*, 327; Heerten, *Biafran War*, 142, 154, 334; Brauman, 'Dangerous Liaisons'; Waters, 'Influencing the Message', 709. For an account with African voices see Tord Wallström, *Biafra* (Stockholm, 1968).

[71] Didier Fassin, *Humanitarian Reason: A Moral History of the Present* (Berkeley, 2012), 206; first pub. as *La Raison humanitaire: une histoire morale du temps présent* (Paris, 2010).

[72] Götz, Brewis, and Werther, *Humanitarianism in the Modern World*, 303.

[73] Hannig, 'Biafra Crisis', 210–11. See also Archives of the Swedish Biafra Committee, The National Archives, Sweden.

Sometimes the attitudes of reporters on the ground clashed with the views of their home organizations. For example, the dispatches of BBC correspondent Frederick Forsyth were perceived as harming the interests of the UK and he was summoned back to London. He then returned to Biafra as a freelancer in order to continue his work.[74] Another obstacle to fully publicizing the crisis was the traditional discretion and neutrality of humanitarian actors, with the Red Cross movement a prime example. Its employees were required to work and stay silent, although there were occasions during the autumn of 1968 when the ICRC privately protested against Nigerian transgressions, such as the bombing of hospitals or the killing of ICRC volunteers. Yet when members of the French Red Cross entered Biafra to conduct an independent relief effort, their public descriptions of the horrors of war and calls for a political settlement were noted with approval by the ICRC.[75]

In contrast to the discreet attitude displayed by the Red Cross, French doctors renounced silence and inaugurated a new style of humanitarianism that used an effective rhetoric of testimony and advocacy. Later, once they had founded MSF, they called this approach *témoignage* (speaking out) and made it a distinctive feature of their organization. Both the message and the means were new to the aid sector. The same doctors organized protest marches and media events in France in order to raise awareness of Nigerian atrocities against civilians. Bernard Kouchner, MSF's charismatic spokesperson, later dubbed this activist humanitarian media strategy *loi du tapage* (the law of hype).[76] One critic mocked the 'florid expressions of humanitarian intent' that followed, and another called it a form of humanitarian theatre or carnival.[77] However, the deeper irony is that while Biafra expanded the scope of humanitarian action, the crisis that precipitated this change was fabricated by determined secessionists who exploited humanitarian aid. The question is whether this 'is just a historical curiosity, or

---

[74] Harrison and Palmer, *News out of Africa*, 15–16. See also Frederick Forsyth, *The Biafra Story: The Making of an African Legend* (Harmondsworth, 1969).

[75] Marie-Luce Desgrandchamps, 'Dealing with "Genocide": The ICRC and the UN during the Nigeria–Biafra war, 1967–70', *Journal of Genocide Research* 16/2–3 (2014), 281–97, at 291. The most prominent article was by Max Recamier and Bernard Kouchner, 'Deux médecins français témoignent', *Le Monde*, 27 Nov. 1968.

[76] Davey, *Idealism beyond Borders*, 3.

[77] Benthall, *Disasters, Relief and the Media*, 132 (quotation); Alex de Waal, 'The Humanitarian Carnival: A Celebrity Vogue', *World Affairs*, 171/2 (2008), 43–55, at 54.

whether it is an emblem of moral overreach, or even hubris, to which humanitarian agencies have succumbed again and again',[78] at least in the age of expressive humanitarianism.

VI. *Spectacle and Charisma*

As Bernard Kouchner later put it, 'a morality of extreme urgency was born' in Biafra.[79] The media, voluntary organizations, and individual witnesses all conveyed 'spectacles of suffering', showing images such as those of emaciated children with bloated stomachs, while analogies were drawn with other genocides.[80] The fact that Biafra's territory gradually shrank during the war caused a greater concentration of the population and made the distress even more graphic. As the area controlled by the secessionists was cut off from the sea and from the border with Cameroon, it became an overcrowded enclave strewn with refugee camps and encircled by hostile forces. The resulting claustrophobic atmosphere and the mounting logistical challenges for aid providers contributed to the sense of alarm.[81]

Under these circumstances, the delivery of humanitarian aid required an airlift that was the largest civilian endeavour of its kind, surpassed only by the US government's Berlin airlift of 1948–9. In all, approximately 7,500 flights delivered more than 90,000 tons of relief goods. Three-quarters of the supplies were provided by JCA, approximately one-fifth by the ICRC, and the rest by Africa Concern and the French Red Cross. The principal staging points were two islands in the Gulf of Guinea: São Tomé for church aid and Fernando Po (now Bioko) for the ICRC. Most of the relief flights landed at Uli airstrip in the besieged territory—a bush road that had been widened and soon became the second busiest African airport after Johannesburg. Increasing the spectacular nature of the airlift, it operated only at night, initially to slip through federal air defences, but later because Biafran leaders were using the humanitarian air traffic as a shield for the importation of arms.[82]

[78] David Rieff, *A Bed for the Night: Humanitarianism in Crisis* (New York, 2002), 85.

[79] Bernard Kouchner, *Charité-Business* (Paris, 1986), 11.

[80] Heerten, *Biafran War*.

[81] Lloyd, Mollerup, and Bratved, *Nordchurchaid Airlift*, 1–2.

[82] Michael I. Draper, *Shadows: Airlift and Airwar in Biafra and Nigeria 1967–1970* (Aldershot, 1999), 4; Stremlau, *International Politics of the Nigerian Civil War*, 244–5, 284.

Uli parish priest and Africa Concern co-founder Aengus Finucane observed that with the start of the relief operation, 'parish duties gave way to airport duties'.[83] A US church official's comment illustrates the impression the operation made:

To stand in Uli in the middle of a dark night . . . or to stand in the Sao Tomé airport and watch the planes take off in relays for Biafra, is a wondrous experience indeed! One wonders at the might of the Christian Church and the determination that we are our brother's keeper, and to see so visibly and hear so audibly what has been wrought.[84]

By August 1968 aid agencies had acquired their own means of transportation, but they were unable to get through Nigerian air defences. The stalemate was broken by Swedish blockade runner Count Carl Gustaf von Rosen, who flew humanitarian relief into the war zone at tree-top level for German Caritas, accompanied by two Swedish journalists. On the trip home from Uli, the dashing count took a *New York Times* reporter on board who accompanied him all the way to Rosen's home in Sweden. Like some of the aid organizers among the priests working in Biafra, Rosen immediately became a celebrity and, for a time, was the chief of operations for Nordchurchaid, which he had helped to found. After Rosen's breakthrough flight, journalists flocked to São Tomé, vying with aid workers for accommodation, applying for visas, and, according to the final report of Nordchurchaid, waiting '"like vultures" for anything exciting to happen'. The report further laments that Rosen's daily press conferences morphed into political and military deliberations that 'were the source of much unfortunate publicity for Nordchurchaid', to the point that people made 'accusations of weapon smuggling on the relief airlift which were absolutely unfounded'.[85] In fact, the freelance journalist who broke the story of military humanitarianism had tried to give the story a positive spin, suggesting that 'the church, perhaps for the first time in history, has here a chance to "bless" weapons with a good conscience'.[86]

[83] Finucane, 'Changing Roles', 245.

[84] James MacCracken, Executive Director of Church World Service (CWS), 'Disaster Report and Response No. 88-X' 2 April 1969, cited in Stremlau, *International Politics of the Nigerian Civil War*, 244.

[85] Lloyd, Mollerup, and Bratved, *Nordchurchaid Airlift*, 14 (quotations), 10; Carl Gustaf von Rosen, *Biafra: som jag ser det* (Stockholm, 1969), 17–19; Lloyd Garrison, 'Swede, Defying Blockade, Flies New Route to Biafra', *New York Times*, 14 Aug. 1968; 'A Legendary Swedish Aviator: Carl-Gustav von Rosen', *New York Times*, 21 Aug. 1968.

[86] 'Biafrauppgift: vapen smugglas med hjälpflyget', *Svenska Dagbladet*, 23 Sept. 1968.

Nevertheless, Rosen was forced to resign his post from Nord-churchaid, and his own account cites a lack of evidence and the general code of conduct rather than explicitly denying the allegations of arms smuggling.[87] In the following year, the working group of the Swedish Biafra Committee became aware of 'special actions' Rosen was preparing and decided 'not to put the content of [its] discussion on record'.[88] The affair concerned a private 'humanitarian intervention' with five light trainer aircraft nicknamed 'Biafran Babies' that were equipped with small-calibre rockets. During a period of leave from their ordinary jobs, Rosen and two Swedish colleagues built up a Biafran Air Force, trained local pilots, and flew raids with them against Nigerian airfields, damaging or destroying ten advanced fighter jets and transport planes. They also severely disrupted a Nigerian power plant.[89]

Despite Rosen's clandestine actions, the media were carefully briefed on the attack. At the time of the bombing, Rosen's book, *Biafra: som jag ser det* (Biafra: As I See It), written with the help of Tord Wallström, was in production. Although issued in several Nordic languages and in French (under the title *Le Ghetto biafrais tel que je l'ai vu*), its anti-British tone probably thwarted publication of the already translated English version. In the book, Rosen narrates his breaking of the blockade, urges greater respect for human rights, and suggests that the Biafran War had turned the meaning of the word 'humanitarian' upside down. It no longer signified a duty, according to Rosen, but had become a right that needed to be defended.[90] Rosen was a unique figure with his 'truly spectacular' engagement, but he also 'typified much of the passionate conviction of Biafra's supporters abroad'.[91] The general silence over Rosen's exploits over the following decades shows how hard the wider world has found it to come to terms with the Biafran legacy.[92]

[87] Rosen, *Biafra*, 29–30.

[88] The National Archives, Sweden, Archive of the Swedish Biafra Committee, vol. 1, Minutes, 7 Feb. 1969.

[89] Gunnar Haglund, *Gerillapilot i Biafra* (Stockholm, 1988); Lieser, *50 Jahre Ende des Biafra-Krieges*, 33.

[90] Rosen, *Biafra*, 57, 60. The manuscript of the English translation of Rosen's book is held by Archives and Special Collections, SOAS Library, University of London, GB 102 MS 321463/68.

[91] St Jorre, *Nigerian Civil War*, 338–9.

[92] See, however, Haglund, *Gerillapilot*; Draper, *Shadows*; Tony Byrne, *Airlift to Biafra: Breaching the Blockade* (Dublin, 1997); Heli von Rosen, *Carl Gustaf von Rosen: An Airborne Knight-Errant* (Stockholm, 2016).

Rosen's militancy benefited the Biafran cause tactically in the short term, supporting the breakaway region's efforts to transform its image from that of a helpless recipient of international charity into that of a nation to be taken seriously. However, this intervention came at a time when the ugly sides of its war meant that Biafra had lost some goodwill in the West. The humiliating air strike against the federal air fleet gave hardliners in the Nigerian government the upper hand. Around the time Rosen returned to Sweden, Nigerian federal forces shot down a Swedish Red Cross plane, claiming they had mistaken it for an enemy arms supply flight. Moreover, the federal government expelled the general commissioner of the ICRC. No global outcry followed these actions. Rather, the ICRC stopped its airlift and instead intensified its co-operation with the Nigerian Red Cross. Although the JCA scaled up its efforts over the following months in order to fill the void, Biafra's supplies were rapidly exhausted towards the end of 1969, and at the beginning of January 1970 the rebellion collapsed.[93]

Figures such as Rosen and Irish Holy Ghost Fathers such as Caritas airlift manager Anthony Byrne (also known at the time as 'the Green Pimpernel') proved popular—or perhaps notorious—and it was the archetypical images of 'priest and pilot' that came to symbolize the drama of delivering humanitarian aid to Biafra. The lower profile of the Red Cross relegated the figure of the doctor to the background, and Kouchner was still in the early stages of his career as a public figure. Attempts to tie celebrities or moral authorities to the cause of Biafra were sometimes successful, as was the case with Simone de Beauvoir, Jean-Paul Sartre, Günter Grass, and Helmut Gollwitzer. Martin Luther King's planned peacemaking mission to Nigeria and Biafra was precluded by his assassination shortly before he was to depart.[94] During the conflict, Ojukwu was perceived as a charismatic intellectual who inspired confidence in the cause of Biafra. In the 1960s he became the fourth African to appear on the cover of *Time* magazine.[95] With his history degree from Oxford and the habitus of a thoughtful father of the nation, Ojukwu's low-key appeal made him appear as not so much a soldier, but a trustworthy Third World

---

[93] Stremlau, *International Politics of the Nigerian Civil War*, 327–8, 334–8; August R. Lindt, *Generale hungern nie: Geschichte einer Hilfsaktion in Afrika* (Munich, 1983), 229, 242–7.

[94] Heerten, *Biafran War*, 94.

[95] Stremlau, *International Politics of the Nigerian Civil War*, 125, 213 n. 112; Hannig, 'Biafra Crisis', 213; Harrison and Palmer, *News out of Africa*, 15.

politician whose demeanour made him seem much older than he actually was.

At the time of the Biafran War, the world had not yet seen the mega-events and record-breaking charity singles that were to become a signature feature of expressive humanitarianism, including George Harrison's Concert for Bangladesh, the single 'Do They Know It's Christmas?', and the Live Aid events for Ethiopia. However, drawing on charity traditions, there were concerts for Biafra in different places in a variety of musical genres. Most notable was the Operation Airlift Biafra Benefit series held at Steve Paul's The Scene in New York in August and September 1968, during which the venue was temporarily renamed 'Biafra' and dozens of artists—among them Joan Baez and Jimi Hendrix, Blood, Sweat & Tears, and a *Hair* ensemble—demonstrated their compassion for 'kids who are dying prematurely from an overdose of politics and grownups'.[96] Some of the concert audiences were addressed by a missionary who made the dubious claim that he could tell 'from personal observation at least 3000 (Biafrans) are dying daily from malnutrition and that is a very, very conservative figure'.[97] A year later, John Lennon publicized the Biafran cause when, in a letter to Queen Elizabeth II, he returned his membership of the Most Excellent Order of the British Empire 'in protest against Britain's involvement in the Nigeria-Biafra thing, against our support of America in Vietnam, and against [his single] "Cold Turkey" slipping down the charts'.[98]

VII. *Conclusion*

An episode that occurred in July 1969 is emblematic of how the conventional approach to aid was being challenged by emerging expressive humanitarianism at the time. At a hearing on Biafra held by the US Senate Committee on the Judiciary, Edward M. Kinney of Catholic Relief Services maintained that 'the important thing is to stop the verbiage' and to get '"the other fellow" to take the lead'.[99] 'The other fellow' was a reference to official aid and a

---

[96] 'Operation Airlift Biafra Benefit', *The East Village Other*, 6 Sept. 1968. See also 'Performance at The Scene Raising Funds for Biafra', *New York Times*, 28 Aug. 1968; 'Music Business Comes to the Aid of Biafra', *Cash Box*, 7 Sept. 1968.

[97] '£3000 to Aid Biafrans', *Aberdeen Evening Express*, 26 Aug. 1968.

[98] 'John Lennon Sends Back his MBE', *The Times*, 26 Nov. 1969.

[99] *Relief Problems in Nigeria–Biafra: Hearings before the Subcommittee to Investigate Problems Connected with Refugees and Escapes* (Washington DC, 1969), 48–9.

manifestation of the governmentality in the tradition of organized humanitarianism that had dominated humanitarian efforts in the USA and elsewhere since the days of Herbert Hoover. In the same hearing, Hyman Bookbinder, a representative of the American Jewish Committee, disputed this statement. While conceding that rhetoric would not feed children, and at the same time praising his Christian colleagues for their excellent work, he pointed out that global public opinion had recently prevented the government of Iraq from hanging Jewish, Muslim, and Christian citizens in a public square. With regard to Biafra, he sombrely added, 'There are some situations that require a great sense of conscience bearing, a crying out—and this is that time.'[100]

This value-laden, emotional approach, while not tied to any particular voluntary background, resonated widely among representatives of different groups. In fact, the Christian relief efforts during the Biafran War were a major driver of early expressive humanitarianism. At the same time, organized and expressive modes of humanitarianism were not mutually exclusive. The rise of expressive humanitarianism did not imply a disorganization or downscaling of relief work. Rather, it exploited and reshaped existing practices of humanitarian solicitation, allocation, and accounting in a new era marked by the mutually reinforcing involvement of the media and civil society in emotionally charged and broadly publicized causes abroad.[101]

The Biafran crisis exemplifies what nowadays is called a 'complex emergency'.[102] We have seen that four factors gained special prominence in emerging expressive humanitarianism: the media, voluntary organizations, bearing witness, and spectacle. However, these are not independent variables, as they feed into one another. Moreover, this conjuncture facilitated an emphasis on action, raised the issue of 'human rights', and led to the drive for 'humanitarian intervention'—whether as tacit consent or the active utilization of force. Along with the airlift's technical dependency on military logistics and personnel, Biafra was 'the opening salvo for a new military humanitarian apparatus'.[103] It also became increasingly evident after Biafra that for many organizations 'association with

---

[100] Ibid. 50–1.
[101] Götz, Brewis, and Werther, *Humanitarianism in the Modern World*, 303.
[102] Omaka, *Biafran Humanitarian Crisis*, 111.
[103] Sasson, 'Name of Humanity', 45.

high-profile disasters was good for business'.[104] The prominent role played by aid agencies in emergency relief had a greater impact in attracting public attention than long-term development projects. All these ambiguous and intertwined factors confirm that the long 1970s saw the post-rational transformation of modern society.

Thus, 'Biafra changed everything', and it became a watershed in the history of humanitarianism.[105] As Finkielkraut points out, for the current humanitarian sector 'everything began in 1968, far away from the barricades and the graffiti, in a region known only to specialists of Africa'. In his view, the new philanthropy that emerged at the beginning of the long 1970s abandoned political morality, offering instead 'a form of narcissistic first aid, distributed from home, at no personal risk'.[106] While this polemic addresses most of those who gave money for the children and welfare of Biafra, the accusation fails to acknowledge the many pilots, airlift staff, and aid workers who lost their lives in the effort to feed millions of starving people.

Beginning with Biafra, voluntary organizations gained a reputation for efficiency, in part based on their ability to work with communities on the ground. The major relief efforts of the 1970s, such as Bangladesh in 1970–1, the Sahel area in 1973, and the Thai–Cambodian border region after the defeat of the Khmer Rouge in 1979, further contributed to the consolidation of the humanitarian sector. Celebrities and musicians became increasingly engaged in humanitarian activities, paving the way for Irish pop star Bob Geldof's global success with Band Aid and Live Aid during the 1980s. The Nigerian Civil War was a formative experience for Geldof, as it was for many others who populated the scene of expressive humanitarianism at the end of the twentieth and the beginning of the twenty-first century. Blackrock College in Dublin, the secondary school that Geldof attended, is operated by the Holy Ghost Congregation and was one of the major mobilizers of support for Biafra worldwide. The plight of the Biafrans is said to have had a major impact on Geldof's social consciousness.[107] However, human-made disasters remain a problematic field in which the values of

[104] Barnett, *Empire of Humanity*, 132.
[105] O'Sullivan, *Ireland, Africa and the End of Empire*, 92.
[106] Finkielkraut, *In the Name of Humanity*, 83, 94.
[107] Waters, 'Influencing the Message', 711.

voluntary organizations, the media, witness bearers, and celebrity performers—sometimes unawares—can collide with the players of power games.

PART IV

Rethinking Gendered Bodies

10

Feminism, the Sexual Revolution, and the Embodied Political Subject in France

Maud Anne Bracke

I. *Introduction*

In this essay I look at new experiences of sexual and reproductive autonomy, and the discourses they generated, from the perspective of women in France during the long 1970s. I consider experiences of bodily autonomy to be crucial to wider cultural change during this period, and analyse the new, gendered understandings of bodily autonomy by focusing on debates and activism around abortion. Such an analysis suggests that the feminist movement and its allies were key in placing autonomy in reproduction at the centre of a wider discourse of social change. Post-1968 feminism offered a new and original understanding of the embodied political subject—an understanding that foregrounded sexual and reproductive agency, and was embedded in the sexual revolution. This original notion of the embodied political subject carries long-term historical significance in relation to the European political and philosophical traditions of the Enlightenment and rationalism. While it was based on critiques both of the Cartesian dualist separation of body from mind and of the traditions of disembodied rationalism, it also built on and expanded feminist Enlightenment concepts of gendered political subjectivity.

Section II of the essay explores key aspects of the sexual revolution from the perspective of heterosexual women. The new sexual permissiveness, combined with the dissemination of the contraceptive pill, created novel opportunities but also difficulties in navigating sexual and reproductive practices, leading many women to be ambivalent vis-à-vis the sexual revolution, and prompting feminists to articulate sharp critiques. Navigating the issue of procreation (and its avoidance) amid the new contraceptive technology and the transformation of sexual cultures was thus a crucial dimension of the sexual revolution for heterosexual women. At the same time, the liberal climate instilled in women a fresh desire for sexual liberation, and offered them ways to express it. I argue that women's conflicted attitudes towards the sexual revolution—a heightened thirst for liberation as well as unease with the male-centred character of the new permissiveness—shaped the new principles of bodily autonomy and reproductive agency advanced by feminists in the 1970s.

Section III situates these new articulations of reproductive agency within the wider politics of the body practised by 1970s feminism. This was a new political language rooted primarily in abortion activism. In the long 1970s it was the issue of abortion, along with the question of sexual violence, that led feminist activists to arrive at a new understanding of the autonomy of the sexual subject and to distil a new notion of the embodied political subject who claims fundamental rights vis-à-vis the state and the law. I analyse these concepts by taking seriously the theoretical implications of activism, which is viewed not only as a mirror reflecting emerging ideas and the reconfiguration of values, but also as a site where theory and knowledge are produced. Bridging social history and the history of ideas, I understand 1970s feminist activism as articulating a notion of the sexed political subject that was historically new in its reframing of agency, individual rights, and the relationship between the individual, the state, and the law, but that also built on earlier feminist engagements with Enlightenment notions of the rational political subject. In the European context, the political subject had been conceptualized as embodied since at least the English Habeas Corpus Act (1679). Yet Enlightenment rationalism not only by and large neglected the citizen's body, but also understood it to be universally uniform—that is to say, it was explicitly or implicitly framed as male. I suggest here that 1970s feminism critiqued as well as carried forward the Enlightenment project of the rational political subject. Central to the 1970s feminist politics of the body was a critique of Cartesian dualism, which envisaged a gendered citizen driven by rationality and individual will, as well as by desires and emotions emanating from the body. As will be discussed in the final section, the 1970s feminist politics of the body can be situated in a feminist tradition of embodied rationalism, initiated in different ways by Mary Wollstonecraft and Olympe de Gouges. This proposed a new type of rational subject based on the integration, rather than the separation, of body and mind.

II. *Women's Sexual Revolution: Desire and Reproduction*

The sexual revolution of the 1960s and 1970s was experienced fundamentally differently by men and women, and depending on one's sexual practices and identities, and how one was socially situated along the lines of class and constructions of race and ability. Mapping the diversity of experiences of the sexual revolution is a necessary and compelling historiographic agenda, and one which has only been initiated in part.[1] While in the popular imagination a linear narrative exists of post-1945 sexuality tending towards ever growing individual liberation, historical analysis presents a more complex and less teleological picture of postwar sexual change. It distinguishes between the discourses of sexual liberation and the professed thirst for it, which were ubiquitous in the long 1960s, and the far messier reality of diverse experiences in the population at large. As Anne-Claire Rebreyend argues for France, the notion of sexual liberation needs to be approached with caution: the postwar period witnessed the introduction of new sexual norms—often internalized rather than explicitly policed by laws or institutions—but not the evaporation of sexual normativity altogether.[2] At the same time, some scholarship on the sexual revolution continues explicitly or implicitly to take male sexual experiences—heterosexual or homosexual—as the standard, with accompanying celebratory accounts of increasingly easy access to sex for young men during this period. Some research understands the 'sexual moment in politics'

[1] Among the extensive historiography on the sexual revolution in Europe, there are a few analyses which offer distinct perspectives by looking at social class, race, nationality status, gender, or disability. See Annette F. Timm and Joshua A. Sanborn, *Gender, Sex and the Shaping of Modern Europe: A History from the French Revolution to the Present Day* (Oxford, 2007); Dagmar Herzog, *Unlearning Eugenics: Sexuality, Reproduction, and Disability in Post-Nazi Europe* (Madison, 2018); Todd Shepard, '"Something Notably Erotic": Politics, "Arab Men", and Sexual Revolution in Post-Decolonization France, 1962–1974', *Journal of Modern History*, 84/1 (2012) 80–115; Franz X. Eder, 'National and Racial Images of the Sexual "Other" in the German-Speaking Countries (1950s–1970s)', *Sexuality and Culture*, 21/2 (2017), 362–81. Scholarship on social class and the sexual revolution in Western Europe is limited, but see Michael R. Haines, 'Occupation and Social Class during Fertility Decline: Historical Perspectives', in John R. Gillis, Louise A. Tilly, and David Levine (eds.), *The European Experience of Declining Fertility, 1850–1970: The Quiet Revolution* (Cambridge, Mass., 1992), 193–226.

[2] Anne-Claire Rebreyend, *Intimités amoureuses: France, 1920–1975* (Toulouse, 2008), 24.

to be associated primarily with male homosexual awakening and activism, and analyses it largely as separated from feminism or women's experiences.[3] Within this picture, key questions as to how women experienced the changing sexual norms remain unanswered. Moreover, historians' accounts of the sexual revolution are far better informed about changing public discourses of sex than about intimate experiences and practices. This is accentuated as far as woman are concerned,[4] and, surprisingly, is more strongly the case for the 1970s than for the 1950s or 1960s.[5]

The 'politicization of sex' has become a key concept in analyses of the sexual revolution of the 1960s and 1970s in the Western world, with regard to both homosexuality and heterosexuality.[6] For women engaging in sex with men, the politicization of sex was centred, I argue, on two axes: pleasure and (the avoidance of) procreation. Women reclaiming sex as pleasurable was a key tenet of feminist discourse. This was reflected in the linking of sexual pleasure and experimentation with women's liberation in the key feminist texts circulating in the Western world in the 1970s, including Kate Millett's *Sexual Politics*, the Boston Women's Health Book Collective's *Our Bodies, Ourselves*, and the Italian group Rivolta femminile's *We Spit on Hegel*, all published in 1970. French

[3] One example among others: Massimo Prearo, 'The 1970s Moment in Sexual Politics', in Julian Jackson, Anna-Louise Milne, and James S. Williams (eds.), *May 68: Rethinking France's Last Revolution* (Basingstoke, 2011), 137–47.

[4] On women's experience of the sexual revolution in France see Rebreyend, *Intimités amoureuses*, and Sarah Fishman, *From Vichy to the Sexual Revolution: Gender and Family Life in Postwar France* (Oxford, 2017).

[5] As argued in Dagmar Herzog, 'Sexuality in the Postwar West', *Journal of Modern History*, 78/1 (2006), 144–71. On women and sex in France before the sexual revolution see Anne-Marie Sohn, *Du premier baiser à l'alcôve: la sexualité des Français au quotidien (1850–1950)* (Paris, 1996).

[6] The notion of the politicization of sex has been articulated in varying ways. See Fiammetta Balestracci, *La sessualità degli Italiani: politiche, consumi e culture dal 1945 ad oggi* (Rome, 2020); Dagmar Herzog, *Sexuality in Europe: A Twentieth-Century History* (Cambridge, 2011); Julian Jackson, *Living in Arcadia: Homosexuality, Politics, and Morality in France from the Liberation to Aids* (Chicago, 2009); Michael Sibalis, 'The Spirit of May 68 and the Origins of the Gay Liberation Movement in France', in Lessie Jo Frazier and Deborah Cohen (eds.), *Gender and Sexuality in 1968: Transformative Politics in the Cultural Imagination* (New York, 2009), 235–53; Ludivine Bantigny, 'Quelle "révolution" sexuelle? Les politisations du sexe dans les années post-68', *L'Homme et la Société*, 189–90 (2013), 15–34. On the different and sometimes conflicting strategies of politicizing sex by feminist and gay liberation movements in France throughout the twentieth century see Sébastien Chauvin, 'Les aventures d'une "alliance objective": quelques moments de la relation entre mouvements homosexuels et mouvements féministes au xxᵉ siècle', *L'Homme et la Société*, 158 (2005), 111–30.

feminists took inspiration from all of these,[7] alongside key French-language texts such as Luce Irigaray's *Speculum de l'autre femme* (1974). However, this occurred within a wider cultural context in which many taboos persisted with regard to women, sexual pleasure, and sexual freedom, although growing numbers of mostly young women overcame inhibitions in narrating sexual pleasure in the public sphere. In France, as recent scholarship has highlighted, women's self-expression continued to be limited by the traditions of gendered decency or *pudeur*, also after 1968.[8] Moreover, in reaction to the opening up of new lifestyle choices for girls, including in dress and leisure opportunities and as expressed in films and books such as *Bonjour tristesse* (1954) by Françoise Sagan, a new discourse of the 'easy girl' emerged—a figure associated with miniskirts, premarital sex, and use of contraception, and in urgent need of societal policing.[9]

Feminist sexual politics in France and the Western world at large were marked by political battles on several fronts: not only against religion, conservatives among one's family and community, the law, and the double sexual standard, but in some respects also against the new permissiveness and the far greater visibility of sexual images in the public sphere compared with the 1950s. The latter most often meant a proliferation of naked women's bodies, and was problematized by feminists after 1968 as accentuated objectification. Feminists sharply critiqued the supposedly progressive post-1968 milieu of left-wing organizations and cultural critics, which was male-dominated, celebrated male virility, and adopted permissive sexual practices as a hallmark of radical lifestyles.[10] Such permissive sexual practices and cultures, as feminists pointed out, were based on a male subject driven by a sexual desire which was to remain uncontrolled by what they saw as bourgeois or outdated moral

---

[7] On the French adaptation of *Our Bodies, Ourselves* see Nesrine Bessaïh and Anna Bogic, '"Nous les femmes" de 1970 à 2017 à travers les traductions et adaptations de *Our Bodies, Ourselves* en français', *TTR: Traduction, Terminologie, Rédaction*, 29/2 (2016), 43–71.

[8] This is suggested by research conducted at the time and published in a much-debated study by Pierre Simon, leading figure of the French family planning association MFPF: Pierre Simon, *Rapport sur le comportement sexuel des Français* (Paris, 1972). See also Michelle Perrot (intro.), *Filles de mai: 68 dans la mémoire des femmes* (Paris, 2004).

[9] Rebreyend, *Intimités amoureuses*, 45.

[10] It should be noted, however, that in many instances radical left groups also critiqued the sexual revolution on the basis of an anti-capitalist analysis. This is argued for the case of France by Bantigny, 'Quelle "révolution" sexuelle?'.

codes. Young heterosexual men claimed free sexual expression and activity as a right, centred on the unbounded agency of the male individual.[11] Thus, the new permissiveness led many young women to feel they were left between a rock and a hard place: a sexual regime marked by taboo and guilt now seemed to be replaced, at least in some circles, by pressures to engage in 'free sex'. In this context, abortion, contraception, and the ability to regulate one's fertility formed the crux of the experiences and concerns of heterosexual women.

Feminists also denounced the 'phallocratic' sexual revolution for its heteronormativity, leading to the emergence of a lesbian movement, with the first organization, Gouines rouges, created in 1971. A feminist critique of the new, male-centred permissiveness also emerged in the context of the debates on legal reform concerning sexual violence in 1978. Yet despite these critiques, 1970s feminists did understand sexual liberalization as fundamentally benefiting women. In France, hundreds of letters sent to renowned philosopher and writer Simone de Beauvoir by feminist sympathizers between the 1950s and early 1970s revealed a discourse on the new sexual permissiveness that was by and large positive. Writing in 1972, one woman described how she had experienced the 'release of a new sexual energy that had long been repressed'.[12] In *Demain la société sexualisée*, Simone Iff, feminist activist engaged in the battles for legal contraception and abortion and president of the Mouvement français pour le planning familial (MFPF) between 1973 and 1980, argued for the dissemination of sexual knowledge across society and the breaking of taboos and traditional morality with regard to women and pleasure.[13] It was their ambivalent attitude towards the rapid sexual changes—embracing the principles of sexual liberation while rejecting some aspects of the male-centred sexual revolution—that allowed feminists to tease out the principle of bodily autonomy in reproduction.

Women's desire for sexual liberation reverberated beyond the

---

[11] Julian Bourg, '"Your Sexual Revolution is Not Ours": French Feminist "Moralism" and the Limits of Desire', in Frazier and Cohen (eds.), *Gender and Sexuality in 1968*, 85–113.

[12] Anne-Claire Rebreyend, 'May 68 and the Changes in Private Life: A "Sexual Liberation"?', in Jackson, Milne, and Williams (eds.), *May 68*, 148–60. See also Judith G. Coffin, *Sex, Love, and Letters: Writing Simone de Beauvoir* (Ithaca, NY, 2020).

[13] Marcel Besse, Simone Iff, and Werner Iff, *Demain la société sexualisée: le combat du Mouvement français pour le planning familial* (Paris, 1975).

circles of feminist activists. A unique collection of source material in France reflects the extent to which women's thirst for sexual liberation was a wider cultural phenomenon, changing for ever ordinary women's life choices and sense of self. Between 1967 and 1981 Menie Grégoire, a journalist and writer involved in family planning and women's work campaigning, ran a very popular radio show entitled *Allô Menie* on RTL, the commercial radio station broadcasting from Luxembourg. Thousands of French women of different ages and social backgrounds sent her letters in which they reflected on their life experiences. These, it emerged, were in many cases dominated by marital malaise, dissatisfaction with cultural norms and double standards, and the desire to experiment sexually and in terms of life choices. As analysed by Rebreyend, the letters featured open discussions of marriage breakdown, sex, pleasure, and emotions. The overriding themes were women's desire for autonomy in their sexual choices, a thirst for greater knowledge of their bodies and desires, and the wish for liberation from traditional morality and from their (moral, financial, legal) dependency on men.[14] These letters, along with the themes and discourses featured in widely read women's magazines such as *Elle* and *Marie-Claire*, reflected a widespread disillusionment among women regarding marriage. While often not rejecting marriage, the letters and the women's presence in the press revealed a desire for marriage to be centred on love, equal partnership, and sex as pleasure, as well as an acknowledgement that the reality of marriage was far removed from these ideals.[15]

Amid the crumbling of taboos and opening up of sexual possibilities, female sexual liberation crucially hinged on the ability to regulate one's fertility. Scholarship on France and England has demonstrated that within heterosexual couples, from the 1930s women began increasingly to take responsibility for reproductive decisions—whether to have children, how many, and when. More broadly, many historians agree that the feminization of reproductive agency across the Western world started well before the legalization and dissemination of the pill during the 1960s and 1970s.[16] As

---

[14] Rebreyend, 'May 68 and the Changes in Private Life'.

[15] Ead., *Intimités amoureuses*, 193–8.

[16] Alison MacKinnon, 'Were Women Present at the Demographic Transition? Questions from a Feminist Historian to Historical Demographers', *Gender & History*, 7/2 (1995), 222–40. However, the role men continued to play in intimate reproductive

Anne-Marie Sohn has demonstrated for France, the time from the 1930s to the 1950s was a pivotal phase during which reproductive agency within married couples gradually came to lie with women rather than men.[17] The fact that to an increasing extent women were openly claiming the right to space their children, to have them later, or not to have any at all, was also expressed in many letters sent to Menie Grégoire.[18] This feminization of reproductive agency in the intimate sphere was reflected more and more openly during the 1960s and 1970s in a public and political affirmation of female reproductive rights. In societal discourse, medical practice, and laws regulating contraception and abortion, human procreation came to be associated with women, their health, their life choices, their sexual practices, and their rights. This feminization of reproductive agency was particularly evident in France. For instance, in the French popular women's press the notion of contraception as a woman's choice was firmly established from around 1960.[19]

From the early 1960s, the legalization of contraception was widely debated, as the contraceptive pill started to circulate illegally. The main organization campaigning for legal contraception— the French family planning movement created in 1956 under the name Maternité heureuse and refounded as MFPF in 1959—was led by influential, highly educated women such as Evelyne Sullerot and Marie-Andrée Lagroua Weill-Hallé. MFPF's campaigns for birth control centred on women's rights and their choices. MFPF's explicit feminization of reproductive agency marked a significant break with traditional cultures of femininity, even if it was framed by a celebration of motherhood and did not challenge the pronatalism that characterized postwar French culture and politics.[20] The notion emerging in the 1950s and 1960s of women as 'family planners' formed part of a wider societal vision of women as efficient homemakers and therefore drivers of postwar recovery and

decisions is highlighted in Kate Fisher, '"She was quite satisfied with the arrangements I made": Gender and Birth Control in Britain 1920–1950', *Past and Present*, 169/1 (2000), 161–93.

[17] Anne-Marie Sohn, *Chrysalides: femmes dans la vie privée (XIXe–XXe siècles)*, 2 vols. (Paris, 1996).   [18] Rebreyend, 'May 68 and the Changes in Private Life'.

[19] Bibia Pavard, 'Contraception et avortement dans Marie-Claire (1955–1975): de la méthode des températures à la méthode Karman', *Le Temps des Médias*, 12 (2009), 100–13.

[20] Ead., 'The Right to Know: The Politics of Information about Contraception in France (1950s–80s)', *Medical History*, 63/2 (2019), 173–88.

modernization.[21] The responsibilization of women with regard to family planning became even more explicit during the discussions on legal reform concerning contraception, leading up to the 'Law relative to birth regulation' or Neuwirth Law of 1967. This abolished the law of 1920, which had banned the sale of non-natural birth control and the dissemination of 'anti-conception propaganda'. The Neuwirth Law legalized the pill and other forms of contraception and prescriptions were limited in number per woman and not free of charge. During the parliamentary and media discussions preceding the passing of the Neuwirth Law, supporters and opponents of legal contraception, while engaging in tense arguments, converged in one respect: the centring of the issue of contraception on women—their social roles, sexual lives, morality, and rights.[22] However, it was only in the context of abortion law reform and the emergence, around 1970, of a feminist movement unprecedented in its radicalism and visibility that the feminization of reproductive agency became a more encompassing discourse on women's reproductive rights.

III. *The Feminist Politics of the Body and Legal Change*

Feminists during the 1970s were not the first to politicize the question of reproduction, but they did so in new ways. Throughout modernity and arguably for longer, human procreation has been a crucial site of political negotiation and interference with individual lives and bodies, motivating a wide range of actors, and creating cultural norms, legal rights and restrictions, and medical processes. As Susan Gal and Gail Kligman argue, the public discussion of reproduction 'makes politics' in at least four ways: in establishing a relationship between states and individuals; in projecting a vision of cultural belonging; in creating coded arguments about morality and sex; and

---

[21] See e.g. Centre des Archives du Féminisme (henceforth CAF), Bibliothèque universitaire d'Angers, Collection Suzanne Képès, 19AF, 109, MFPF, 'Qu'est-ce que c'est le planning familial?', Paris, 1968. On women as drivers of postwar recovery and modernization see Rebecca J. Pulju, *Women and Mass Consumer Society in Postwar France* (Cambridge, 2011); Christine Bard, *Les Femmes dans la société française au 20ᵉ siècle* (Paris, 2001).

[22] Paul Ladrière and François-André Isambert, *Contraception et avortement: dix ans de débat dans la presse, 1965–1974* (Paris, 1979); Janine Mossuz-Lavau, *Les Lois de l'amour: les politiques de la sexualité en France de 1950 à nos jours* (Paris, 2002), 253–5. As Pavard argues in 'The Right to Know', in the 1980s state discourse framed knowledge of contraception not only as a woman's right, but as her duty.

in situating women as a specific type of citizen.[23] The regulation of human procreation is an area in which societal stakes are perceived to be high—for women, men, medical professionals, demographers, and religious groups. This is the area of social life where sex and gender matter even to those who would not habitually consider 'women's issues' relevant to the political sphere. Feminists during the 1970s politicized reproduction by denouncing the separation of private and public spheres as false, and by critiquing historical and contemporary interference in women's reproductive bodies and choices. The battle for legal abortion allowed them to crystallize their critique of patriarchy as based crucially on the control of women's reproductive capabilities.

Abortion law in France dated from the 1810 Napoleonic Code, which outlawed it under any circumstances. The debates of the 1970s were focused on the removal of a law introduced in 1920, which reiterated the illegal nature of abortion under any circumstances and allowed for sentences of up to three years in prison. An amendment in 1939 decriminalized abortion only if the woman's life was at risk. Apart from the abolition of the death penalty, the legal framework regulating abortion was not modified after 1945, and it remained a crime even in cases of incest and rape.[24] The official number of illegal abortions was around 850,000 in 1970, although MFPF estimated that the real number was perhaps twice as high. If one had the means, a relatively safe abortion could be obtained by seeking the services of a doctor operating illegally, or by travelling to Britain, Switzerland, or the Netherlands after decriminalization in those countries.[25] Partly as a result of such high numbers, the issue of abortion was permanently at the centre of public debate from the early 1970s, and the health risks were now widely reported in the media. Calls for some form of legal reform grew louder, and not only among feminists, family planners, and leftists. They became all the more urgent as research by the

[23] Susan Gal and Gail Kligman (eds.), *Reproducing Gender: Politics, Publics, and Everyday Life after Socialism* (Princeton, 2000); quotation on p. 10.

[24] On the legal framework see Bibia Pavard, Florence Rochefort, and Michelle Zancarini-Fournel, *Les Lois Veil: contraception 1974, IVG 1975* (Paris, 2012); Bibia Pavard, *Si je veux, quand je veux: contraception et avortement dans la société française (1956–1979)* (Rennes, 2012); Mossuz-Lavau, *Les Lois de l'amour*.

[25] Christabelle Sethna, 'From Heathrow Airport to Harley Street: The ALRA and the Travel of Nonresident Women for Abortion Services in Britain', in ead. and Gayle Davis (eds.) *Abortion across Borders: Transnational Travel and Access to Abortion Services* (Baltimore, 2019), 46–71.

National Demographic Institute (INED) indicated that only around 6 to 7 per cent of women aged between 20 and 44 used the pill in 1970, rising to 25 per cent by 1975.[26] Progressives and feminists argued that the relatively slow uptake of the pill by women after legalization should not be understood as an indication of women's reluctance to engage in premarital or extramarital sex; indeed, the high numbers of illegal abortions supported this view. Rather, the figures regarding contraceptive use strengthened their argument that the only way to confront the problem of illegal abortion was to (partially) legalize it.

The feminist collectives emerging in Western Europe[27] and other parts of the world in the wake of the 1968 student uprisings were motivated above all by a 'politics of the body': a desire to politicize the private sphere, everyday life, family roles, and intimacy. In France as elsewhere, feminist collectives adopted innovative practices, such as holding meetings in small groups, often in private homes, and exclusively for women. They adopted various forms of consciousness-raising aimed at expanding the realms of the political by 'starting from oneself' and at creating a new language with which to narrate the body, sex, and the family. An original feminist agenda was thus articulated, centred on an understanding of the liberation of the gendered self, which relied crucially on the reappropriation of the sexed body.[28] At consciousness-raising meetings, abortion soon emerged as a pivotal theme. In countries including France, Italy, and West Germany, it was the main topic through which the feminist movement gained prominence in the media and was able to have an impact on legislation. It was also the issue on which the various feminist groups and distinct approaches converged and found a degree of strategic unity. To suggest this is not to deny the existence of different approaches across the movement and, increasingly throughout the decade, the loss of a shared vocabulary or agenda. In France, most disputes within the feminist movement were framed by the questions of how gender oppression related to

---

[26] Mossuz-Lavau, *Les Lois de l'amour*, 74.

[27] When discussing European feminism in this essay, I refer primarily to Western Europe. This is not to deny the unique significance of women's activism in Communist Central and Eastern Europe; however, the latter regions are not covered here as women were situated very differently in terms of social conditions and state feminist discourses compared with those in the West.

[28] Bibia Pavard, Florence Rochefort, and Michelle Zancarini-Fournel, *Ne nous libérez pas, on s'en charge: une histoire des féminismes de 1789 à nos jours* (Paris, 2020).

class oppression and how the feminist movement should relate to the
Left. There was open disagreement between Marxist, materialist,
and socialist feminists on the one hand and 'differentialist' feminists
on the other. The latter rejected a politics aimed at equal rights
for men and women, envisaging instead a deeper cultural transformation which would allow women's difference to emerge.[29] These
different agendas included conflicting understandings of women
and their bodies as 'other' and of the implications of this for notions
of equality and citizenship. However, within this landscape, the
gendered reappropriation of the body as a core feminist principle
functioned as a shared agenda in the early to mid 1970s, and
contributed to legal change on abortion.

Between 1972 and 1975 the Mouvement de libération des femmes
(MLF) organized public demonstrations, petitions, and conferences
demanding legal reform on abortion centred on a woman's right to
choose. The MLF's key slogans included: 'Avortement libre' ('Free
abortion', in the double meaning of free choice and free of charge);
'Jouir plutôt que reproduire: laissez-nous choisir' ('Pleasure rather
than reproduction: let us choose'); and 'Aucune loi ne passera sur
nos corps' ('No law at the expense of our bodies').[30] Most feminist
groups adopted the radical position of demanding full liberalization:
a law that would explicitly guarantee a woman's right to choose,
would impose neither conditions nor time limits, and would not
allow doctors to exercise any decision-making power. As was the
case nearly everywhere in Western Europe where liberalization
occurred in this period, France's abortion law of 1975, referred to
as the Loi Veil after Minister for Health Simone Veil, did not give
women full bodily autonomy. It stated that any French adult woman
'in distress' could request an abortion up to ten weeks of gestation,
and authorized by one physician. 'Distress' could be invoked on
several grounds (health risk, mental state, social circumstance) and
need not be evidenced. While in this sense the law came close
to offering abortion on demand, the procedures were explicitly
framed as 'dissuasive', and particularly so in the requirement for an

---

[29] The scholarly discussion of differentialist and materialist feminism in France is
extensive. For an overview of the groups and debates in the long 1970s see Pavard,
Rochefort, and Zancarini-Fournel, *Ne nous libérez pas*, chs. 9–10; Claire Duchen,
Feminism in France: From May '68 to Mitterrand (Abingdon, 2013), 27–47; Françoise Picq,
Libération des femmes: quarante ans de mouvement (Brest, 2011).

[30] CAF, Collection MLAC, Paris, 10 AF, 1, MLAC, 'Présentation de l'association'
[no date].

individual conversation between the woman and her physician and 'reflection time' following the request. Moreover, physicians were allowed to register as conscientious objectors, and were required to inform the woman in a vaguely worded 'timely manner'. Abortions after ten weeks were possible if a commission of doctors established that either the woman's health was at risk or the foetus presented serious problems. After a trial period, the law was passed with minor amendments in 1979.[31] Both in 1975 and in 1979, all feminist organizations, along with the now radicalized MFPF, declared the Loi Veil to be unsatisfactory due to the requirement for medical approval and the conscientious objection clause. Although the new legal framework did not place reproductive agency fully in the woman's hands, the feminist movement had been successful in introducing the principle of full bodily autonomy into public consciousness and the political discourse as a point of reference. This remained the case even as the principle continued to be contested, most strongly by the Catholic Church, the Ordre des médecins—the powerful association of physicians—and the emerging 'anti-choice' movement, which included intense campaigning against the Loi Veil by organizations such as Laissez-les vivre.[32]

In what follows, I illustrate the feminist conceptualization of the embodied political subject by looking at grass-roots abortion activism. I draw on the rich scholarship on twentieth-century feminist theory and its notions of the political subject in relation to the Enlightenment, European rationalism, and citizenship. In a sense, nearly all twentieth-century European feminist theory and politics has pivoted on the question of whether to 'gender and embody' the notion of citizenship articulated in European political thought since the Enlightenment, or to abandon it. However, there is a gap. Sufficient attention has not always been paid to the role played by grass-roots activism in shaping the rich feminist theory on the embodied and gendered citizen during the long 1970s. I reconstruct the ways in which practical campaigning created the impetus behind the new feminist articulation of the embodied, sexed political subject, looking in particular at the Manifesto of the 343, legal activism in the context of the Bobigny trials of 1972, and the abortion work conducted by the Mouvement pour la liberté de l'avortement et de la contraception (MLAC).

A highly provocative and impactful intervention in France was

---

[31] Mossuz-Lavau, *Les Lois de l'amour*, 130–4.   [32] Ibid. 97.

the Manifesto of the 343, published in 1971 in the pages of *Le Nouvel Observateur*. It featured the signatures of Simone de Beauvoir, French Tunisian lawyer Gisèle Halimi, and many women well known in the world of art, literature, and film (including actress Catherine Deneuve, writer Françoise Sagan, film-maker Agnès Varda, and feminist theorist Christine Delphy). The disruptive quality of this text lay in the fact that it boldly revealed deeply personal experiences, while stressing the universal character of abortion. In foregrounding 'we demand legal abortion', and avoiding details on the precise extent of the liberalization demanded, the Manifesto posited nothing less than a new principle—that of women's reproductive autonomy. The Manifesto set the tone for a key characteristic of feminist politics of the body in France: the elevation of women's personal experience into expertise. It involved a radically new questioning of established, patriarchal expertise on women's bodies and women's health, whether on the part of lawmakers, doctors, or scientists, and envisioned medical knowledge as emanating from women's own understanding of their bodies and needs.[33] Further, Halimi went on to lead the organization Choisir la cause des femmes, a high-profile campaigning group on abortion. Its activism was centred on the right of women to choose freely whether to have an abortion—whatever the circumstances, and unconstrained by medical control. Choisir's agenda was threefold: to promote contraception and sex education; to campaign for abortion law reform; and to offer free legal counsel to anyone standing trial for abortion. Choisir's manifesto posited that 'to give life is the freedom of freedoms on which all others depend'.[34]

One of the most eloquent and influential articulations of the demand for bodily self-determination was the defence plea by Gisèle Halimi at the Bobigny trials of 1972. At the first trial, 17-year-old Marie-Claire Chevalier stood accused of having had an illegal abortion; at the second, her mother and three other women stood accused of having facilitated or performed the abortion. The trials became a focal point for the pro-legalization campaign and Chevalier was supported by feminist initiatives across the

---

[33] Jennifer L. Sweatman, '"It is Not your Personal Concern": Challenging Expertise in the Campaign to Legalize Abortion in France', in Shannon Stettner, Katrina Ackerman, Kristin Burnett, et al. (eds.), *Transcending Borders: Abortion in the Past and Present* (Cham, 2017), 103–19.

[34] CAF, Collection Groupe information santé, 44 AF 47/2, Choisir, *A nous de choisir pour nous*, tract, Jan. 1971.

country. Chevalier and two of the women were acquitted, while her mother and the abortion practitioner were found guilty, though the unusually mild sentences were immediately deferred.[35] The victory was a major step towards legal reform in 1975, not least because Halimi, Choisir, and the MLF explicitly mobilized the trial to argue for legalization. Halimi used the universalist language of citizenship, the French republican tradition, and human rights, but explicitly gendered it. Chevalier's fate, she argued, was potentially the fate of any woman in France, and it demonstrated the need for the law to safeguard women's rights, safety, and bodily autonomy. She stressed that Chevalier, like any woman choosing whether to continue a pregnancy or not, had taken a rational and responsible decision, and that, in fact, it was the law which was irrational and irresponsible. Her plea also involved a more fundamental critique of legal concepts rooted in the French Revolution and the Enlightenment, and reminded her audience that the Code Civil had originally described women as 'given' to men 'in order to make children'. Yet she used the language of civil liberties, citizenship, and legal claims (*revendications*) to argue that nothing less than women having full control over their bodies would pull them out of their historical condition of 'serfdom' and alienation. She described the claim to bodily self-determination as 'the most elementary' human right, and the most 'fundamental, intimate' of civil liberties. Halimi saw reproductive rights as a necessary extension to the principles of French citizenship and republicanism, involving a fundamental contract between the citizen and the state which protected the individual's safety and bodily integrity.[36] In her later writing, she was to emphasize the need for a new, gendered, and distinct understanding of citizenship for women ('la citoyenne n'est pas le citoyen', or 'the female citizen is not the male citizen').[37]

Furthermore, at the trial Halimi stressed the need for safe abortions, referencing scientific research and calling Jacques Monod,

[35] CAF, Collection Groupe information santé, 44 AF 47/2, 'Dossier sur Bobigny', *Le Nouvel Observateur*, 20 Nov. 1972. An insightful comparison of the Bobigny trial with the Padua trial of 1973 in Italy, highlighting distinct feminist strategies of politicization, can be found in Lorenza Perini, *Il corpo del reato: Parigi 1972–Padova 1973. Storia di due processi per aborto* (Bologna, 2014).

[36] The full text of the plea can be found at ⟨https://www.lagbd.org/index.php/Le_proces_de_Bobigny_La_cause_des_femmes_La_plaidoirie_de_Me_Gisele_Halimi_(fr)⟩ [accessed 20 Jan. 2022].

[37] Gisèle Halimi, *La Cause des femmes* (Paris, 1992), p. xxii.

biochemist and Nobel laureate in physiology and medicine, as an expert witness. She quite deliberately did not dwell on Chevalier's individual circumstances. Instead, she framed her notion of embodied citizenship and bodily liberty within a wider cultural critique of 'compulsory motherhood', social class, and the lack of sex education. The first point was stressed by Simone de Beauvoir, called as an expert witness, who argued that forcing women into motherhood was the crucial area in which patriarchy oppressed women and denied them their rights to individual freedom and self-determination ('on fabrique à la femme un destin biologique', or 'a biological destiny is constructed for women'). The issue of sex education and sexual knowledge was tackled by another witness, Simone Iff of MFPF. Iff presented an analysis of the lack of sex education at schools and in families both across the board and for girls specifically, whose sexuality continued to be mired in public taboos. Halimi also turned this into a political argument for civil liberties, as she reasoned that by denying young women and men basic knowledge of their own bodies, society was denying them the possibility of exercising full citizenship.[38]

De Beauvoir herself also supported feminist campaigns for reproductive autonomy in the 1970s, including the Manifesto, Choisir, and the materialist feminist collective and periodical *Questions Féministes*.[39] While diverging scholarly interpretations exist on de Beauvoir's relationship with feminist activism in the long 1970s,[40] feminist abortion praxis in many ways revealed the diffuse, long-lasting, but

[38] For the full trial proceedings, see Association Choisir, *Avortement: une loi en procès. L'Affaire de Bobigny. Sténotypie intégrale des débats du Tribunal de Bobigny (8 novembre 1972)* (Paris, 1973).

[39] For de Beauvoir's testimony on her 'conversion' to feminism after 1970, in which she stressed the issue of abortion, see Simone de Beauvoir and Alice Schwarzer, *Simone de Beauvoir aujourd'hui: six entretiens* (Paris, 1984). From 1977, *Questions Féministes* was edited by Christine Delphy, among others, and in 1980 it was refounded as *Nouvelles Questions Féministes* in the context of a conflict within the MLF and a divergence of views between Delphy and Monique Wittig on the issue of political lesbianism. See Duchen, *Feminism in France*, 22–5.

[40] For interpretations stressing her closeness to parts of the feminist movement see Sylvie Chaperon, '*Momone* and the *Bonnes Femmes*; or Beauvoir and the MLF', in Kristina Schulz (ed.), *The Women's Liberation Movement: Impacts and Outcomes* (Oxford, 2017), 73–90; Ursula Tidd, *Simone de Beauvoir* (London, 2004), 77–82; Renate Günther, 'Fifty Years On: The Impact of Simone de Beauvoir's *Le Deuxième Sexe* on Contemporary Feminist Theory', *Modern & Contemporary France*, 6/2 (1998), 177–88. A different view, stressing de Beauvoir's limited influence on French feminists in the long 1970s, can be found in Toril Moi, *Simone de Beauvoir: The Making of an Intellectual Woman* (Oxford, 1994), 180–3.

sometimes ill-acknowledged influence of her thought, primarily as expressed in *Le Deuxième Sexe*, first published in 1949.[41] To argue this is not to minimize the fundamental critiques of de Beauvoir put forward by leading feminist thinkers such as Luce Irigaray and Hélène Cixous, or to ignore the limitations of de Beauvoir's humanism, which, as those critics argued, mistakenly upheld the Enlightenment ideal of a universal, gender-free citizen.[42] De Beauvoir was centrally motivated by the need to bring women into the realm of political subjectivity, making visible their rationalism. For her, feminism aimed to situate women fully as human beings and to create the conditions and the freedom for women to develop fully into 'free and autonomous beings'.[43] While this has been read as a gender-blind neutralism, she also foregrounded the sexed body, and in *Le Deuxième Sexe* posited that the body was the point at which we assume our subjectivity in the world.

De Beauvoir fully valorized the body as foundational both to individual experience and to intersubjectivity and wider social relations. She was inspired by phenomenological philosopher Maurice Merleau-Ponty's idea of the dual nature of bodily experience—a notion which she understood to be specifically relevant to women. Women were alienated from an authentic experience of their bodies by patriarchal society and forced to act and feel in ways that were removed from their bodies' needs and desires. Thus, de Beauvoir identified a fundamental tension between what she called the habitual body of everyday experience and the proper body. Women's bodily experiences, routinely inscribed in patriarchal oppression and exploitation, were separated from their consciousness, which desired liberty and self-expression.[44]

By the late 1970s, many French feminists rejected de Beauvoir's thought in the context of theoretical discussions on equality, difference, and the precise meaning of woman as 'Other'. However, I suggest that feminist praxis of the 1970s, based on the full, principled

[41] Catherine Rodgers, 'Contemporary French Feminism and *Le Deuxième Sexe*', *Simone de Beauvoir Studies*, 13 (1996), 78–88. Simone de Beauvoir, *Le Deuxième Sexe*, 1st edn., 2 vols. (Paris, 1949).

[42] Ursula Fabijancic, '*Le Deuxième Sexe*, 1949–1999: Our Continuing Dialogue with Simone de Beauvoir', *Simone de Beauvoir Studies*, 15 (1998–9), 1–16.

[43] Tidd, *Simone de Beauvoir*, 48–55.

[44] Ibid. 56–9; Marie-Blanche Tahon, 'Maternité, corps et politique dans *Le Deuxième Sexe*', in Cécile Coderre and Marie-Blanche Tahon, *Le Deuxième Sexe: une relecture en trois temps, 1949–1971–1999* (Montreal, 2001), 61–72.

reclaiming of the body, betrayed a proximity to de Beauvoir's key questions on freedom and agency through bodily experience, as well as revealing the continued relevance of her thinking. The question of the embodied citizen and her relationship with the state and the law were at stake at a very practical level in abortion campaigning by the Mouvement pour la liberté de l'avortement et de la contraception. During the 1970s, MLAC was one of the key organizations providing abortion illegally, by setting up neighbourhood clinics and offering the service safely and free of charge. While gender-mixed, it was strongly influenced by the MLF, and initially also by an anarchist ethos that was more interested in community self-help than in legal change. While attracting significant numbers of health professionals as sympathizers, it bypassed medical institutions. Creating alternative medical knowledge, practices, and sites was central to its wider agenda, and it was key in introducing the so-called Karman method in France—a safe and relatively easy abortion procedure.[45] In giving women unconditional access to abortion, MLAC proposed that women should fully reclaim their reproductive agency. MLAC favoured the complete deregulation of abortion and full self-determination, as reflected in its slogans: 'la loi on s'ent fout; pas de loi du tout'; 'c'est aux femmes de décider, pas aux députés' ('we don't care about the law; we want no law whatsoever'; 'women should decide, not MPs'). Its principles centred on the right to motherhood; the right to free contraception, including for minors; sex education at school and beyond; and free abortions for all, including minors, on the basis of the woman's choice only, to be paid for by social security and performed in public hospitals.[46] This practice-based understanding of abortion led MLAC, and the feminist movement more broadly, to critique other, non-feminist actors with which it collaborated in a wider public mobilization for legal reform: far-left groups, the socialist and communist parties, and the trade unions. MLAC and the MLF denounced the supposedly progressive post-1968 milieu for inscribing free abortion in a sexual culture that assumed women's full availability and fed into the deresponsibilization of men. Instead, feminists situated the issue of abortion in relation to wider calls for the dismantling of male domination and privilege ('phallocracy') in the cultures of

---

[45] Leaflet *Oui, nous avortons*, quoted in Mossuz-Lavau, *Les Lois de l'amour*, 107.

[46] CAF, Collection MLAC, 10 AF 15, MLAC, 'Documents législatifs', 'Quelle est la position du MLAC?' [no date].

sex.[47] As the radical group Féministes révolutionnaires stated in 1972 in the key feminist periodical *Le Torchon Brûle*: 'Abortion is not our liberation', and 'Abortion is an aggression', although a necessary one.[48]

MLAC went further than other campaigning groups in questioning the stratified nature of reproductive politics, especially with regard to race and class. It was one of few groups to contrast pronatalism in mainland France with racialized anti-natalism in the overseas departments (*Départements d'Outre-mer*, DOM) of Guadeloupe, Martinique, and, most violently, Réunion. It denounced the French state's population politics and its 'racist and neo-Malthusian' motivations in disseminating contraception earlier than in France, and in allowing the unconsented sterilization of up to 8,000 women in Réunion in the late 1960s.[49] Inscribing this in longer histories of racialized population politics during colonialism and the era of slavery, MLAC called for the right to motherhood as well as the right to refuse it. Herewith, it introduced a more complex perspective into feminist discourse, going beyond the avoidance of pregnancy that was foregrounded by most in the MLF. Moreover, as was also the case for feminist campaigners in Britain and Italy, a class discourse was central to MLAC's abortion work. It pivoted on the argument that wealthy women had always had the opportunity to have safe abortions, while working-class and poor women bore the brunt of oppressive legislation, and that reproductive rights were therefore constrained by one's class position. Before the passing of the Loi Veil, MLAC campaigned in vain for free abortions in state hospitals, and after it was passed, this continued to be a key element of MLAC's mobilization for further legal reform. It demanded that contraception and abortion be financed by the state, and called for society to provide the conditions which would make free choice in reproduction possible: childcare, housing, and income.[50] 'Avortement libre et gratuit' was its key principle, including for minors and non-French citizens. MLAC stood out in the wider abortion

---

[47] Michelle Zancarini-Fournel, 'Histoire(s) du MLAC (1973–1975)', *Clio: Femmes, Genre, Histoire*, 18 (2003), 241–52.

[48] *Le Torchon Brûle*, May 1972, 1.

[49] Bibliothèque Marguerite Durand, Dossier MLAC, 6141 'Mouvement pour la liberté de l'avortement et de la contraception', 1973. On the large-scale reproductive violence inflicted on women in Réunion in the 1960s, see Françoise Vergès, *Le Ventre des femmes: capitalisme, racialisation, féminisme* (Paris, 2017).

[50] Mossuz-Lavau, *Les Lois de l'amour*, 108.

campaign for the attention it paid to social class and the distinct circumstances and needs of immigrant women.

In some respects, MLAC anticipated the notion of reproductive justice. Introduced from the 1980s by US Black feminism including the SisterSong Collective, by indigenous women in North and South America, and by women's organizations in the Global South, this idea is based on intersectional feminist politics.[51] The reproductive justice agenda conceptualizes reproductive rights not only in terms of access to contraception and abortion (which by and large characterized the Western, white feminist agenda of the long 1970s),[52] but more encompassingly in terms of the right to motherhood as well as non-motherhood. It links this with the fight for equality and justice with respect to the conditions in which children are raised. MLAC called for a wider debate and agenda centred on motherhood as a real choice and on the socio-economic conditions of child-rearing.[53] It noted the fundamentally different situations in which women of different social classes, ethnicities, and nationality statuses found themselves in France. MLAC's approach illustrated a practical notion of gendered, embodied, and situated citizenship—that is to say, one which articulated political claims (access to contraception and abortion as well as the right to parent in fair circumstances) on the basis of women's reproductive bodies, and in relation to their social, cultural, and material circumstances.

IV. *Still Only Paradoxes? Feminism and the Critique of Rationalism*

In this section I take a step back from the immediate context of 1970s campaigning and situate the political concepts that emerged from it in a longer historical perspective on embodied citizenship

[51] Loretta J. Ross and Rickie Solinger, *Reproductive Justice: An Introduction* (Oakland, Calif., 2017); Kimala Price, 'What is Reproductive Justice? How Women of Color Activists are Redefining the Pro-Choice Paradigm', *Meridians: Feminism, Race, Transnationalism*, 10/2 (2010), 42–65.

[52] Although this volume has adopted the policy of capitalizing the words 'Black' and 'White' to highlight the fact that race is a social category, not a natural one, I have opted not to follow this practice in order to avoid giving the impression that 'white feminism' was self-consciously and strategically 'white' in a manner analogous to Black feminism. Instead, it refers to a set of majority experiences and perspectives that often remained unquestioned.

[53] CAF, Collection MLAC, 10 AF 3, MLAC, 'Projet de plateforme de lutte' [no date, 1976], and 'Compte-rendu de la coordination nationale des groups femmes du 31 octobre et de l'Assemblée générale ordinaire et extraordinaire du MLAC du 1 novembre' [no date, 1976].

and Enlightenment traditions. The 1970s feminist foregrounding of the body should be read as the proposition of a different rationality rather than as a rejection of the political subject as rational. As Fiammetta Balestracci has argued for Italy, during the long 1970s there was a transformation in the meaning of rationalism in European political discourse: in the context of the sexual revolution, the rational, disembodied subject was rejected, and the deep shifts in sexual practice, moral values, gender roles, and consumer cultures, combined with fundamentally changed legal frameworks in the realms of family and reproductive rights, culminated in the proposition of 'post-rational' values and subjects.[54] To be sure, the body had been foundational to individual political rights in European political thought and praxis since the seventeenth century, and it continued to provide a key principle regulating citizenship throughout European modernity. The English Habeas Corpus Act of 1679 explicitly associated the body with political representation, integrity, and safety. However, the assumption here was that all bodies were equal: the male, heterosexual, able, economically productive, and white European body was universalized, and others were marginalized from political discourse and agency.[55] At the same time, the overriding dynamic throughout European modernity and the development of capitalism, as widely discussed in feminist groups during the 1970s and in feminist theory ever since, was that women's bodies were a site of domination, violence, and the denial of rights. The origin of this domination, as argued by many feminist theorists and especially sharply by Silvia Federici,[56] was sexual difference, which was denied by the language of habeas corpus yet essential to every aspect of social organization—from the economy to the family, religion, and education.

Since the late eighteenth century, European feminists had attempted to think through the implications of sexual and socially gendered difference for the definition of the political subject. Adhering to the principles of rationalism, liberalism, and individual rights, French feminist thinkers of the long nineteenth century faced, as argued by J. W. Scott, the impossible dilemma of reconciling the

[54] Balestracci, *La sessualità degli Italiani*.

[55] Barbara Caine and Glenda Sluga, *Gendering European History, 1780–1920* (Leicester, 2000), 1–6.

[56] Silvia Federici, *Caliban and the Witch: Women, the Body and Primitive Accumulation* (New York, 2004).

rational political subject, defined as male in revolutionary political discourses of the time, with woman's sexual difference and her different social roles. The paradox which lies at the heart of modern European feminist politics—that is to say, the fact that it constitutes a distinct political subject on the basis of sexual difference, while at the same time striving to abolish this difference in social norms, social relations, and law—remained unresolved throughout the nineteenth and early twentieth centuries.[57] While a full discussion of the treatment of the equality/difference paradox during this phase of European feminisms falls beyond the scope of this essay, I wish to point out here, building on Scott's insights, that the paradox of equal and different citizenship was reproposed in a distinct vein by feminists across Western Europe after 1968. The majority of Western European feminist groups and thinkers in the long 1970s placed sexual difference at the centre of political discourse, explicitly aiming to reconstitute the political subject on the basis of this sexual difference, and rejecting the presumed universality of the embodied subject. Indeed, the critique of a politics of equality—claiming equal rights before the law and equal roles in society—lies at the heart of many 1970s feminist projects.[58] I suggest that this foregrounding and claiming of sexual difference was played out crucially on the terrain of reproductive rights. It was in the mobilization for legal abortion that women were endowed with rights not simply as human beings (as had been the case in the granting of suffrage, for example), but as *a type of* human being, and not an exceptional or marginal one (as was the case for much of the labour legislation relative to women workers of the early and mid twentieth century). It was thus the norm of the citizen himself that was put into question, and the universality of the political subject came undone on the basis of the sexed quality of the body. I propose that the presumed universality of the male political subject had never before been challenged so thoroughly or explicitly in the history of Western modernity as it was here. At the same time, the 'obsessive repetitions', as Scott puts it, which have characterized recurring 'waves' of feminist mobilization were not resolved here, as the equality/difference paradox—a seemingly

---

[57] Joan Wallach Scott, *Only Paradoxes to Offer: French Feminists and the Rights of Man* (Cambridge, Mass., 1997), 1–4.

[58] Kristina Schulz, 'A Success without Impact: Cases from the Women's Liberation Movements in Europe', in ead. (ed.), *The Women's Liberation Movement*, 1–14.

never-ending conundrum—continued to provoke conflict between and among feminist groups, not least in France.[59]

Yet feminism in the 1970s, both theoretically and in the form of activism, introduced a different rationality—one that envisaged the political subject as driven by reason as well as by emotions, desires, and the imperative to care. In doing so, it set up a tension between these dimensions of political agency. While situated in the wider socio-cultural changes of the mid twentieth century and responding specifically to the sexual revolution, the 1970s feminist articulation of the embodied political subject built on a field of critical interrogation opened up in previous centuries by feminist Enlightenment thinkers. Even if they did not always acknowledge the significance of earlier feminist traditions, 1970s European feminists stood on the shoulders of Olympe de Gouges and Mary Wollstonecraft, key late eighteenth-century feminist writers. In different ways, both these thinkers' writing centred on their critiques of Enlightenment rationalism and the male-defined notion of citizenship espoused in the French Revolution, and on their ambition to reframe the modern notions of political agency and citizenship through the full inclusion of women. As Barbara Caine and Glenda Sluga argue, a gendered notion of rational man lay at the basis of the eighteenth-century concept of citizenship, which was to inform the European political revolutions of the long nineteenth century. In the context of the French Revolution, the idea of a female citizen became fundamentally problematic, as did women's involvement in public, political, and professional life.[60] The notion of the (male, and therefore universal) citizen that was constructed at this point relied on a cultural model of sexual differentiation that had emerged in the seventeenth and eighteenth centuries, as Thomas Laqueur has argued. In this model, men and women were opposites: the former coded as rational, responsible, and ethical, and therefore suited to public and political life; the latter coded as emotional, irrational, amoral, but suited to providing care and compassion in the private sphere.[61] Whereas the woman *was* her body and her sex—as famously proposed by Simone de Beauvoir—the male, rational political subject was removed from his bodily impulses, desires, and emotions.

[59] Pavard, Rochefort, and Zancarini-Fournel, *Ne nous libérez pas*, chs. 9–10.

[60] Caine and Sluga, *Gendering European History*, 3–7.

[61] Thomas Laqueur, *Making Sex: Body and Gender from the Greeks to Freud* (Cambridge, Mass., 1990).

While a full discussion of women, citizenship, and the French Revolution falls beyond the scope of this essay,[62] I argue that in order to gauge the significance of the 1970s feminist politics of the body, we need to view it in a longer historical perspective and situate it in relation to the fundamental political questions regarding women and citizenship posed in the late eighteenth century. Olympe de Gouges, playwright, author, and advocate of a constitutional monarchy, powerfully disrupted the gendered coding of the new language of citizenship proposed by the revolutionaries, and was executed for it. In her *Declaration of the Rights of Woman and of the Female Citizen* (1791), a direct response to the *Declaration of the Rights of Man and of the Citizen* (1789), she denounced men's 'sovereign right to oppress my sex', and argued that women, too, had natural, inalienable rights on the same basis as did men. She called for women to have equal rights in the public and political realms, including equal access to public offices, professions, and a political voice ('the right to mount the speaker's rostrum'). This text amounted to more than an attempt to include women in a fundamentally hostile notion of citizenship and political agency; it revealed a critical reflection on the idea that citizenship rights were limited to the public sphere only—notably in de Gouges's claim that women had the right to name the father of their children. As Joan W. Scott has argued, this implied a rethinking of the separation and the gendering of private and public spheres, as it pointed to men, rather than women, as sexual and even non-rational, transgressive beings.[63]

Supportive of the French Revolution and the doctrine of citizenship, but inspired by de Gouges to critique it, Mary Wollstonecraft, in her *Vindication of the Rights of Woman* (1792) and other writing, placed women not only into the realm of political agency, but at the centre of the 'City of the Future'. She argued that women were 'reasoning creatures', capable of a harmonious and balanced life and a personhood that would find its fulfilment both in the private sphere and through public agency. This, as Pauline Johnson has proposed, was not a straightforward humanism or the simple extension of the rational subject to include women. In more complex ways, Woll-

---

[62] Among the rich scholarship, see Scott, *Only Paradoxes to Offer*; Olwen H. Hufton, *Women and the Limits of Citizenship in the French Revolution: The Donald G. Creighton Lectures 1989*, rev. edn. (Toronto, 1992); and Caine and Sluga, *Gendering European History*.

[63] Scott, *Only Paradoxes to Offer*, 42–6.

stonecraft's conception of women's rationalism involved notions of care for and duty to others—a rationalized private sphere—as well as participation in the social world. While her thought involved a critique of the gender order of her time, as reflected in her intense dislike of the homebound identity imposed on the bourgeois woman, her views did not challenge the hierarchies that subordinated women and the private sphere to men and the public sphere, and failed to question the sexual division of care work. Nonetheless, it did present a fundamentally different view of the political subject, which was here informed by rationalism as well as driven by the imperative of caring for others.[64]

De Gouges's and Wollstonecraft's unresolved questions opened up the issue of the relationship between rationalism and the body, and that of the gendered citizen, as fundamental political problems of European modernity. Feminists of the long 1970s attempted to work through these questions in various ways, contributing specifically to an emphasis on the body's sexual experiences and reproductive capabilities. The practical and theoretical discourse around reproductive rights pursued by 1970s feminists involved a critique of European Enlightenment traditions and of modern, Western rationalism. The latter had separated body from mind and centred its understanding of citizenship on a rational political agent that it interpreted as removed from the body, emotions, and care. In the 1960s and 1970s, the question of reproduction and the reproductive body provoked a fundamental questioning of the configurations of political agency, citizenship, the rational self, and their gendered underpinnings.

[64] Pauline Johnson, 'Feminism and the Enlightenment', *Radical Philosophy*, 63 (Spring 1993), 3–12. A different view of Wollstonecraft and her ability to challenge gender hierarchies can be found in Timothy J. Reiss, 'Revolution in Bounds: Wollstonecraft, Women, and Reason', in Linda Kauffman (ed.), *Gender and Theory: Dialogues on Feminist Criticism* (Oxford, 1989), 11–50.

11

Body Politics in the *Barrios*: The Long 1970s in Spain

ROSEANNA WEBSTER

On 1 May 1981 in Oviedo, capital of the northern Spanish industrial region of Asturias, Magdalena López Pérez spoke to a crowded room about an underground abortion service in Seville called Los Naranjos. Magdalena was 19 and had grown up in Osuna, a rural town in the province of Seville, before moving to the city. The clinic she was describing had recently been raided and shut down by the new democratic authorities. It was six years after the death of the dictator Francisco Franco, and four years after the official transition to democracy. Magdalena had travelled to Oviedo to discuss Los Naranjos at the First Asturian Feminist Conference.[1] There she explained that a group from Valencia had moved to Seville to establish the clinic in 1979, naming it after the orange trees (*naranjos*) lining the streets of the Andalusian capital. Its members practised the aspiration method, which relied on a suction instrument to perform abortions. Magdalena started working at Los Naranjos in her late teens, when abortion was still a criminal offence in

This essay draws on research funded by the Cambridge Trust and King's College Cambridge. Thanks to archivists at the various sites I consulted, particularly Manuel Bueno Lluch, and, for reading earlier versions, to Rosa Campbell, Lucy Delap, Marta del Moral Vargas, Merve Fejzula, Kostis Kornetis, Julienne Obadia, Nikolaos Papadogiannis, Pedro Ramos Pinto, Hana Sleiman, Jess White, and this volume's editors. Special thanks to my interviewees.

[1] Archivo Histórico de Asturias, Fondo Movimiento Comunista de Asturias, Caja 179.289/8, Balance sobre las 1.ᵃˢ Jornadas Feministas de Asturias, 1981; Magdalena López Pérez, personal interview, Seville, 15 Apr. 2018 (hereafter Magdalena). The interview with Magdalena was one of twenty-two oral history interviews I conducted in 2017 and 2018 in Asturias, Madrid, and Seville, eight of which I draw on in this essay. I use only the interviewees' first names in subsequent references, unless I am reintroducing them in the text after several pages. I also employ interviews from established collections of oral histories, cite interviews within documentaries, and quote from interviews that other historians have conducted and reproduced in their own publications.

Spain. The centre-right coalition legalized contraception in 1978, but it was not until 1983 that the newly elected Spanish Socialist Workers' Party (Partido Socialista Obrero Español) presented a bill in parliament permitting abortion in restricted circumstances. It was finally passed in 1985. Los Naranjos saw its base of staff, users, and support grow while it was open in 1980, and the campaign its members mounted following the clinic's closure attracted local and international backing.

Studies of the twentieth-century politics of reproduction in Europe persistently overlook the part played by working-class people who came from rural areas, like Magdalena. They tend to concentrate either on vocal groups of radical activists based in the universities of major cities, or on healthcare and medical professionals.[2] They do not focus on working-class groups or individuals who lived on the margins of cities or in small towns and who had not received a formal education beyond the age of 14. They often instead depict such people as the recipients of change, not as active instigators. Scholarship on Spain is no exception. Work on reproductive health and abortion activism under Franco by Teresa Ortiz-Gómez and Agata Ignaciuk helped challenge a major assumption: that the history of reproductive change in postwar Europe was divided along the fault lines of dictatorship and democracy, Catholicism and secularism. But Ortiz-Gómez and Ignaciuk still stress the role of middle-class professionals, students, and graduates.[3] They argue

[2] For an exception, although one that still focuses more on groups who settled in communities than on the residents themselves, see Maud Anne Bracke, 'Our Bodies, Ourselves: The Transnational Connections of 1970s Italian and Roman Feminism', *Journal of Contemporary History*, 50/3 (2015), 560–80.

[3] Teresa Ortiz-Gómez and Agata Ignaciuk, 'The Fight for Family Planning in Spain during Late Francoism and the Transition to Democracy, 1965–1979', *Journal of Women's History*, 30/2 (2018), 38–62; Agata Ignaciuk, 'Love in the Time of El Generalísimo: Debates about the Pill in Spain before and after *Humanae Vitae*', in Alana Harris (ed.), *The Schism of '68: Catholicism, Contraception and* Humanae Vitae *in Europe, 1945–1975* (Cham, 2018), 229–50; Agata Ignaciuk and Christabelle Sethna, 'Charters for Choice: Abortion Travel, Abortion Referral Networks and Spanish Women's Transnational Reproductive Agency, 1975–1985', *Gender & History*, 32/2 (2020), 286–303. See also Kostis Kornetis, '"Let's get laid because it's the end of the world!": Sexuality, Gender and the Spanish Left in Late Francoism and the *Transición*', *European Review of History/Revue Européenne d'Histoire*, 22/1 (2015), 176–98; Soraya Gahete Muñoz, 'Las luchas feministas: las principales campañas del movimiento feminista español (1976–1981)', *Revista de Investigaciones Feministas*, 8/2 (2017), 583–601; Nuria Capdevila-Argüelles, *El regreso de las modernas* (Valencia, 2021); Ana M. Aguado, 'Mujeres y participación política entre la transición y la democracia en España', *Estudios de derecho judicial*, 142 (2007), 165–80; Pamela Beth Radcliff, 'Imagining Female Citizenship in the

that the fight for family planning was led by health professionals and Catholic intellectuals operating in medical circles in the mid 1960s, and that educated feminist groups pioneered abortion rights activism a decade later.[4] The cases I explore paint a different picture.

I argue that groups of working-class activists on the fringes of urban spaces and in industrial towns led efforts to change Spain's reproductive politics from the late 1960s. I focus on groups based in mining towns in Asturias and on the outskirts of Seville, and the Asturian cities of Oviedo, Gijón, and Avilés. These distinct and contrasting locations are often overlooked in the focus on major cities such as Madrid, Barcelona, and Bilbao. In this essay, by combining an analysis of oral history interviews with archival material, I demonstrate that the activism which developed in these underexplored areas helped shape the movements for reproductive justice that emerged in Spain in the 1970s.[5]

Spanish movements for reproductive control and abortion included tens of thousands of people by the end of the decade. But I show that the reproductive politics that emerged by the end

"New Spain": Gendering the Democratic Transition, 1975–1978', *Gender & History*, 13/3 (2001), 498–523; Daniela Melo, 'Women's Movements in Portugal and Spain: Democratic Processes and Policy Outcomes', *Journal of Women, Politics & Policy*, 38/3 (2017), 251–75; Maria Ángeles Larumbe, *Las que dijeron no: palabra y acción del feminismo en la Transición* (Zaragoza, 2004). For exceptions, see Mónica Moreno Seco, 'Sexo, Marx y Nova Cançó: género, política y vida privada en la juventud comunista de los años setenta', *Historia Contemporánea*, 54 (2017), 47–84; David Beorlegui Zarranz, "Detrás de lo que quieren que seamos, está lo que somos': revolución sexual y políticas sexuales feministas durante las décadas de los setenta y de los ochenta. Una aproximación al caso del País Vasco', *Feminismo/s*, 33 (2019), 199–223. For a survey of recent work on movements led by sexual minorities, a topic not explored in this essay, see Javier Fernández Galeano, 'Las cartas al Institut Lambda: narrativas íntimas de liberación homosexual en la España de la Transición (1976–1983)', *Bulletin of Spanish Studies: First View*, 17 Jan. 2023, 1–28 ⟨https://doi.org/10.1080/14753820.2022.2155381⟩; see also Claudia Hinojosa, 'Gritos y susurros: una historia sobre la presencia pública de las feministas lesbianas', *Desacatos*, 6 (2001), 177–86; Abel Díaz. 'Afeminados de vida ociosa: sexualidad, género y clase social durante el franquismo', *Historia Contemporánea*, 65 (2021), 131–62. For relevant recent work charting cultural change less rooted in activism, see Mónica García Fernández, *Dos en una sola carne: matrimonio, amor y sexualidad en la España franquista (1939–1975)* (Granada, 2022).

[4] Ortiz-Gómez and Ignaciuk, 'The Fight for Family Planning in Spain', 39–40.

[5] The people involved in these movements did not use phrases like 'reproductive politics' or 'reproductive justice', instead framing issues relating to reproductive health and bodies in a variety of ways. I am sensitive to the activists' own terms throughout this essay, but I see the use of terms such as 'reproductive politics' as contributing to histories of reproductive justice and employ them while recognizing their anachronistic character.

of the 1970s was built on practices which had been developing in Spain's marginal places for decades, and that we cannot understand the transformation of values that occurred in the 1970s without considering that these values were also rooted in continuity.

The three sections of the essay trace the evolution of a reproductive politics in some of Spain's coalfields and *barrios* (neighbourhoods) throughout the long 1970s. The first examines grass-roots associations of women from the Asturian mining towns that started providing access to abortion from the late 1960s, and considers how they drew on networks of gossip and hearsay that had long functioned as a way of airing concerns relating to sex and the body. The second explores the arrival of feminist students in these areas from the mid 1970s. It considers how they planned to proselytize local residents, but found they learnt as much as they taught. The third compares how campaigns around abortion trials unfolded in Asturias and Seville in the late 1970s and early 1980s. In the early 1970s a group in Madrid had tried to initiate a campaign against similar prosecutions, but with scant success.[6] By the late 1970s, however, local and student activists had merged their resources and laid the groundwork for more extensive protests, and the cases of the Bilbao Eleven and Los Naranjos generated support from tens of thousands of people across Spain.

The essay ends in 1982, when the Spanish Socialist Workers' Party won a general election after promising to decriminalize abortion in its electoral programme. Many of the groups and people who form the subject of this essay continued to organize thereafter. Yet by 1982 it was clear that Asturias and Seville had witnessed the emergence and development of new forms of reproductive politics led by grass-roots groups which were largely based on the outskirts of metropolitan areas. I conclude that Seville became a particularly important international hub for reproductive justice activism, thanks to how groups in the *barrios* blended influences from long-standing political collectives and practices with the newer networks they were helping to form. A history of reproductive politics that begins in working-class towns and *barrios* provides a framework for analysing how processes and events at the edges of the metropolitan heartlands were key to shaping what we often see

---

[6] Mary Salas and Mercedes Comabella, 'Asociaciones de mujeres y movimiento feminista', in *Españolas en la transición: de excluidas a protagonistas (1973–1982)* (Madrid, 1999), 25–125, at 96.

as the most far-reaching set of value changes in the 1970s: shifts relating to sex, childbirth, and the body.

I. Curiosas, *Menstruation, the Pill*

By the middle of the twentieth century, clandestine abortions had long been common in Spain. Recent data show that an estimated 125,000 abortions were carried out annually throughout Franco's dictatorship, even though abortion was illegal.[7] In almost every town, village, and neighbourhood in Spain there was a woman known to help with unwanted pregnancies. In Asturias such individuals were called *curiosas*. A *curiosa* could be an illegal back-street abortionist who received payment or simply someone famed for her knowledge of reproductive health. *Curiosas* acquired their knowledge not through formal education, but from older female relatives. Aida Concheso was an activist in her twenties in the Asturian mining town of Barredos whose grandmother had been a *curiosa* in her village. In an oral history interview, Aida recalled: 'She'd always help women with babies, this was typical of Asturian villages, you see? They often had a *curiosa*'.[8] Aida said her grandmother did not perform abortions but had the resources to help in such circumstances. People in Seville did not have an equivalent term for this role, but the former activist Julia Campos Benítez described such a figure in a working-class part of Seville. 'In fact, there was this woman in Triana who was famous for performing abortions, you see? She used some safeguards, not all of them but at least some minimal safeguards, she wasn't a doctor but a woman who'd done loads of abortions.'[9]

Abortions carried out under these circumstances were widely held to be dangerous in mid-century Spain, and to lie in the purview of women. Julia described the practice of the Triana abortionist as 'bestial' and recounts: 'It could well be that the lives of some women ended there—on the [operating] table.'[10] She describes other women using something like a cactus needle or inserting bay leaves and parsley into their vaginas to terminate their pregnancies.

---

[7] Ignaciuk, 'Love in the Time of El Generalísimo', 234.

[8] Aida Fuentes Concheso and Maricusa Argüelles Pérez, personal interview (second interview), Pola de Laviana, Asturias, 7 Nov. 2017 (hereafter Aida and Maricusa II).

[9] Archivo Histórico de CCOO de Andalucía (hereafter AHCCOOA), Seville, Colección Oral, Julia Campos Benítez, interview with Inmaculada García Escribano, 3 June 2008.　　　　　　　　　　　　　　　　　　　　　　[10] Ibid.

Julia explained that the aim of the herbs was 'to ferment the foetus', and according to her, 'some succeeded while others died, you follow me? Others died.'[11] These methods had been 'passed down from generation to generation—you'd have heard it from your mother, who'd have heard it from your grandmother'.[12] Both Aida and Julia suggested that there could be no question about who was responsible for all the work involved in undergoing and performing abortions: it was women.

Asturian activists started organizing around the issue of abortion from the late 1960s. Aida and her friend Maricusa were in their twenties and belonged to a mixed-sex neighbourhood association that formed after many local women had led a march for better water services.[13] Aida and Maricusa explained that their leading roles in neighbourhood activism caused women from the coalfield town of Barredos to start asking for their assistance with unwanted pregnancies. Aida recalled, 'many women came to us for help because they could see we had a different kind of outlook, you see?'[14] Aida and Maricusa helped the women who approached them by divulging information about which *curiosas* were based nearby—information gleaned by gossiping with their neighbours while organizing over other resources such as electricity services or green spaces. The pair fused practices prevailing among women, namely of spreading information about bodily concerns orally, with newer ways of acting—demanding *cosas básicas* (basic things)—to form a network of abortion activism.

By organizing abortions, Aida and Maricusa gained authority within their mixed-sex association. Maricusa's husband Gustavo was well known in the area for having previously fled the Francoist authorities to live abroad. She recalls that he was devastated by his experience of visiting a *curiosa* after he agreed to cover for her on one occasion. 'He accompanied a young woman, a—a neighbour to one of these uh—abortions. And so he arrived home, well, white as a sheet, from the young woman's suffering and—and from her screams. "Send me wherever you like, but don't you ever send me to something like that again," he said to me.'[15] Maricusa was in charge

[11] Ibid.   [12] Ibid.

[13] See Roseanna Webster, 'Women and the Fight for Urban Change in Late Francoist Spain', *Past & Present*, 17 Oct. 2022 ⟨https://doi.org/10.1093/pastj/gtac016⟩.

[14] Aida and Maricusa II.

[15] Aida Fuentes Concheso and Maricusa Argüelles Pérez, personal interview (first interview), Pola de Laviana, Asturias, 3 Nov. 2017 (hereafter Aida and Maricusa I).

of deciding whether or not to 'send' Gustavo to the *curiosas*. As the female activists introduced these activities into their association, male members started to appreciate how hard they were to carry out. Seville did not have a tradition of women mobilizing politically on the scale of Asturias. Asturian women had begun organizing during the solidarity movements that accompanied strikes undertaken by the region's miners in 1962.

Along with addressing abortion in local politics, Asturian women also raised the topic of menstruation. Fabiola Quiroga grew up in Mieres, a mining town famous for its role in the Asturian rebellion of 1934. Her parents were leading members of the local branch of the Communist Party, and she belonged to the associated youth club linked to this branch. 'I've got my period, Marilu, do you have a sanitary pad?', Fabiola recalled asking a fellow female member in the early 1970s.[16] Discussing these topics 'felt political' as there was 'such a taboo around menstruation'.[17] They were also speaking in front of the male members of their group, and Fabiola found that this brought her and other young women a certain cachet within their circles, as it allowed them to exclude male members who felt uncomfortable.

Obtaining the pill also felt subversive. Fabiola recalled that she and others in her youth club informally shared information among themselves about a chemist in Gijón known to sell the pill to anyone who asked. 'So me and my sister went there and bought the contraceptive pill, which was strictly prohibited!'[18] Fabiola and her sister hid the packets they had acquired from the chemist by concealing them inside their clothes until they returned home. Asturian factory workers also swapped secrets about the pill in their lunch breaks at a textile plant in the Gijón *barrio* El Coto in the mid 1970s. Teresa Sanjurjo González worked at the factory in her twenties and remembered that she and her female workmates swapped information about the two or three doctors in the city known to 'help you get a prescription [for the pill]'.[19]

Teresa and Fabiola would not have faced legal consequences had they been found with the pill, but still emphasized that they

[16] Fabiola Quiroga, personal interview, Gijón, 27 Sept. 2017 (hereafter Fabiola). For a related point see Beorlegui Zarranz, 'Detrás de lo que quieren que seamos', 207.

[17] Ibid. [18] Ibid.

[19] Teresa Sanjurjo González, interviewed in 2017 for a documentary by Alberto Vázquez García and Benjamín Gutiérrez Huerta, *La lucha de las mujeres obreras en los barrios de Gijón en el final de la dictadura: años 60 y 70 del siglo XX*, Gijon, 2017.

were acting unlawfully. The legislation on contraception was never used to prosecute anyone, and Ignaciuk argues that the police did not prioritize measures to prevent women using the pill under the Franco regime.[20] She also notes that sales of blister packs of the pill reached nearly 2 million by 1969, suggesting widespread use.[21] Yet Fabiola and Teresa still stressed the pill's proscribed status in their retrospective accounts. They did so because it was a contested topic within their own counter-cultural circles, while defying the regime was not. Teresa remembered male members of her trade union berating women for raising any topic they did not deem specifically anti-Francoist.

Meanwhile, the tensions Fabiola faced were intergenerational: Fabiola's mother argued that focusing on anything related to the body was a distraction from anti-Francoist causes. She resisted her daughter using the pill, as Fabiola explained: 'For my mother the topic of the contraceptive pill was, like it was dangerous . . . She thought that taking the pill meant you wanted to sleep with the first person you met and . . . so what if that were the case?'[22] Fabiola also recalled her mother telling her 'not to go out every night, or you'll get a reputation'. Fabiola chafed against the unfairness she perceived, as her parents allowed her brother to come and go at will. She described arguing against her mother on the grounds that to obtain the pill was to challenge Francoist laws, and by pointing out that her mother was being hypocritical by encouraging her children to demand equality while treating them according to different standards: 'And I'm talking about a Communist mother.'[23] Fabiola's mother may not have recalled acting in the way Fabiola describes, and methodological questions relating to memory lie beyond the scope of this essay, but intergenerational tensions are certainly prominent in Fabiola's account of obtaining the pill.

By the mid 1970s, Asturian women such as Fabiola, Aida, and Maricusa had started to politicize issues associated with reproduction, abortion, and the body. They did this partly by drawing on the webs of hearsay that had long existed in their localities, and by weaving them into the political groups in which they mobilized in the late 1960s and early 1970s. Doing so encouraged wider

---

[20] Agata Ignaciuk, 'Anticoncepción hormonal en España y Polonia: discursos, debates y prácticas entre 1960 y 1980' (Ph.D. thesis, University of Granada, 2015), 97–8.

[21] Ignaciuk, 'Love in the Time of El Generalísimo', 234.   [22] Fabiola.

[23] Ibid.

discussions related to reproductive health, sex, and the body, but these conversations were frequently marked by tensions, as from the outset many people disagreed about the appropriateness of such issues for local politics.

II. *Students Arrive in the* Barrios

Women living on the outskirts of Asturias and Seville started receiving visits from female students wanting to discuss matters relating to sexuality in the early 1970s. Alicia Rodríguez described this happening in her *barrio*, La Calzada, on the outskirts of Gijón. She helped lead La Calzada's neighbourhood association and was a mother and a homemaker in her early thirties. Alicia recalled that at some point in the mid 1970s she was approached by two 'very young women' asking if she could help them to convene a meeting in the association with other homemakers in the area on the topic of 'sexual relations'. Alicia agreed and arranged a discussion with women from the neighbourhood, most of whom were older than her. During the meeting, the two students embarked on some role-play. According to Alicia they were trying to show the homemakers how to 'sleep with your husband in bed'. She implied that the students were demonstrating acts to the homemakers that they thought would enhance their sexual pleasure. The meeting proceeded smoothly until the students raised the topic of 'free love'. Alicia said: 'And that was it, they [the students] were ushered out, with the homemakers saying "you can take your free love with you!"'[24]

The homemakers were not, however, reacting to the ideology of free love out of ignorance or unworldliness, but because this concept had particular connotations in popular discourse. It first gained ground in Spain in the 1920s and 1930s through anarchist movements with international links and an accompanying print culture. Anarchist periodicals in Spain used the term 'free love', drawn from movements in the United States, to cover a variety of things: premarital sex, polygamy, open relationships, or group sex.[25] Often free love was invoked simply to separate sex from

[24] Alicia Rodríguez Trapiello, personal interview, Gijón, 31 Oct 2017.

[25] Sophie Turbutt, 'Sexual Revolution and the Spanish Anarchist Press: Bodies, Birth Control, and Free Love in the 1930s Advice Columns of *La Revista Blanca*', *Contemporary European History: First View*, 7 July 2022, 1–19 ⟨https://doi.org/10.1017/S0960777322000315⟩. See also Luz Sanfeliu, 'Educando y viviendo en la "libertad sexual": "Mujeres Libres" y Lucía Sánchez Saornil', in Raquel Osborne (ed.) *Mujeres bajo sospecha: memoria y sexualidad, 1930–1980* (Madrid, 2012), 331–46.

its reproductive function, although generally with an emphasis on heterosexuality.[26] Yet many conservative Spaniards were concerned that the more extreme practices associated with the term 'free love' would prevail. These fears deepened after Federica Montseny, as Minister of Health and Social Policy under the Republic, passed laws legalizing abortion, divorce, sex education, and contraception. After the war, the regime weaponized this legislation to claim that the Republic had tried to undermine Spain's 'core values': the family and Catholicism.[27] The term 'free love' was part of its rhetorical ammunition, as the dictatorship promoted the narrative that all Republicans had campaigned to abolish traditional familial relations, and in Francoist discourse, 'free love' was contrasted with all things Spanish. While the homemakers in Gijón were dismissive of the students, their views were equally informed by a cultural discourse that used terms drawn from abroad. There was intergenerational tension between some of the older homemakers and the students, but the arrival of the latter group did not catalyse this alone; intergenerational friction was already a feature of the *barrios* and coalfields.

Another Asturian activist also remembered several female students arriving to discuss sex at the factory in which she worked. Lola de Llano was employed by a textile plant in Gijón. She also helped lead the factory's branch of a clandestine trades union, the Workers' Commissions (Comisiones Obreras). In 1974 young women visited the factory and introduced themselves as members of a feminist group based at the nearby university. They wanted to hold a meeting with the female employees on the topic of sex and the body, which Lola helped to convene by gathering her co-workers. Lola described the students trying to teach them 'things about masturbating with your little finger'.[28] She remembered leaving the meeting thinking the students were 'a little bit crazy'.[29] Although

[26] For an investigation into changing attitudes to and experiences of male homosexuality in this period, see Richard Cleminson and Francisco Vázquez García (eds.), '*Los Invisibles*': *A History of Male Homosexuality in Spain, 1850–1939* (Cardiff, 2007), esp. 254–6.

[27] Aurora G. Morcillo, *True Catholic Womanhood: Gender Ideology in Franco's Spain* (DeKalb, Ill., 2000); Shirley Mangini, *Memories of Resistance: Women's Voices from the Spanish Civil War* (New Haven, 1995).

[28] Archivo de Fuentes Orales para la Historia Social de Asturias, (hereafter AFOHSA) Oviedo, Serie: Movimiento obrero en Asturias, B23/7, María Dolores Menéndez del Llano López (Lola), interview with Claudia Cabrero Blanco, Oviedo, 2011.

[29] Ibid.

the students left contact details inviting the workers to join their group and learn more about the meeting's subject matter, Lola was unimpressed.

The students arriving in the *barrios* of Gijón came from the University of Oviedo, where groups dedicated to organizing around sexual concerns were emerging in parallel with those in the *barrios* and coalfields of Asturias in the early 1970s. The student collectives formed through sharing insights gleaned from translated texts. *Hablan las women's lib (Women's Lib Speaks)* was one such publication.[30] It arrived at the University of Oviedo in 1972 and was based on a collection of American feminist essays compiled and translated by the Valencian feminist writer María José Ragué Arias on her return from California. The most popular essays among the students in Oviedo were translations of Anne Koedt's 'The Myth of the Vaginal Orgasm' and 'Liberation of Women: Sexual Repression and the Family' by Laurel Limpus. The former student and activist Teresa Meana remembered eagerly swapping these texts in seminars and reading groups at university when she was in her late teens. She recalled that 'in talks and classes we'd swear that the vaginal orgasm didn't exist'.[31]

Teresa's fellow students Amelia Valcárcel and Olivia Blanco decided to emulate the American practices they were reading about in 1973 by establishing the university's first group for 'reflection and self-knowledge'.[32] The discourse on self-help, which Spanish activists translated as 'self-knowledge', had originally stemmed from women's liberation groups in Los Angeles, Boston, and New York.[33] Maud Bracke defines it as 'a series of practices that allowed women to explore their bodies and sexuality, based on the notion that political liberation was to be rooted in a new relationship to one's body'.[34] The self-knowledge group at the University of Oviedo provided the foundations for an official organization, the

---

[30] María José Ragué Arias (ed.), *Hablan las women's lib (movimiento de liberación de la mujer)* (Barcelona, 1972).

[31] Teresa Meana, interview with Carmen Suárez Suárez, Oviedo, 2 Jan. 2002, cited from Carmen Suárez Suárez, *Feministas en la transición asturiana (1975–1983): la Asociación Feminista de Asturias* (Oviedo, 2003), 131.

[32] 'Reflexión y autoconciencia', ibid. 120.

[33] For a discussion of the translation of feminist terms see Hannah Kaarina Yoken, 'Nordic Transnational Feminist Activism: The New Women's Movements in Finland, Sweden and Denmark, 1960s–1990s' (Ph.D. thesis, University of Glasgow, 2020), 48–52.

[34] Bracke, 'Our Bodies, Ourselves', 562.

Asturian Feminist Association (Asociación Feminista de Asturias, AFA).[35]

AFA members started going to the *barrios* of Gijón and Asturian towns to share insights about sexuality they had gleaned from their reading groups in the mid 1970s. In doing so, they were following entryist practices that had become widespread among left-wing organizations in Spain and internationally. A police report on AFA from 1976 notes that the feminist association's members were deploying 'a well-known strategy of subversion' and 'infiltrating all manner of organizations', and suggests that the group was 'nothing more than a cover for Maoist parties'.[36] Its author assumed that AFA's main agenda was to promote the ideology of the New Left groups with which they were linked. Yet AFA members explained that their main purpose in entering organizations was to spread information about sexuality and the body. Emilia Vázquez, who co-founded AFA at the university, remembered that in the early 1970s she and other students started travelling to Asturian *pueblos* (villages) 'to evangelize about sexual matters'.[37]

Asturian school students also travelled to Gijón's outskirts to talk about sexuality and the body. At the age of 14, Dulce Gallego Canteli helped establish a female-only reading group in her school. She and her classmates swapped photocopies of Betty Friedan's *The Feminine Mystique* (1963), which had been translated into Spanish in 1965 with a prologue by the Catholic feminist writer and international sportswoman Lilí Álvarez.[38] Reading Friedan prompted Dulce and her friend Lourdes Pérez 'to bring the housewives out of their homes'.[39] Dulce, who also belonged to her school's local branch of the Trotskyist group the Red Flag, decided to approach homemakers in El Llano, a working-class and peripheral *barrio* near her school. She advertised the meeting in El Llano as a knitting workshop, but in reality, she 'was using it to convey the idea that sexuality

---

[35] At this time the organization was called Asociación Feminista Democrática de Asturias (AFDA), although it would lose the D in 1977. I use 'AFA' throughout.

[36] Bibliotéca de Ciencias Jurídico-Sociales, University of Oviedo, Colección Archivo de Feministas Asturianas, box 2, Jefe Superior, 'Nota informativa asunto Asociación Feminista Democrática de Asturias', Oviedo, 12 July 1976.

[37] Emilia Vázquez interview with Carmen Suárez Suárez, Asturias, 17 Jan. 2003, cited from Suárez Suárez, *Feministas en la transición asturiana*, 273–4.

[38] Pilar Godayol, 'Feminism and Translation in the 1960s: The Reception in Catalunya of Betty Friedan's *The Feminine Mystique*', *Translation Studies*, 7/3 (2014), 267–83, at 276.

[39] Dulce Gallego Canteli, personal interview, Gijón, 29 Nov. 2017 (hereafter Dulce).

isn't simply reproduction, that it's one thing to have children and another to have emotional and sexual relations'.[40]

The Asturian students stressed the secretive nature of their actions in the mid 1970s, in a similar way to how the *barrio* and coalfield activists had behaved furtively about the pill. Dulce says that they had to be 'very clandestine'.[41] Marisa Castro, who had moved to Gijón on finishing secondary school in Madrid, convened meetings about sex and the body in the *barrios* and advertised them as 'talks on the sexuality of beetles, because the police might have come at any moment'. She added: 'We were very closely surveilled.'[42] Dulce and Marisa suggested that the politics of anti-Francoism and reproductive justice were often mutually reinforcing, and that they were motivated to educate others about these topics by the frisson of possibly getting caught.

Students in Seville also travelled to the city's outskirts in 1975 to educate female residents about sex and the body. Translated texts had started circulating in the University of Seville in the early 1970s. In 1975 the psychology student Margarita Laviana rallied others to meet and discuss what they were reading, and they formed a branch of the Andalusian Women's Democratic Association (Asociación Democrática de la Mujer Andaluza, ADMA), an organization linked to the Spanish arm of the Trotskyist group El Partido de Trabajo (Workers' Party). Members of Seville's ADMA named their branch Mariana de la Pineda (Mariana) after a nineteenth-century Andalusian liberal thinker. Unlike the Asturian activists, members of Mariana did not try to hide what they were doing in Seville. Franco had died in December 1975 and King Juan Carlos I was nominally governing Spain with the Francoist prime minister Carlos Arias Navarro. The Seville students did not feel the need to act surreptitiously, nor did they think it would aid their cause.

In early 1976 members of Mariana started planning a citywide campaign on contraceptive methods.[43] One Mariana member wrote in a 1976 article that starting the project demonstrated to them that they 'lacked direct contact' with ordinary women, and that they 'needed to go to the *barrios*. So that's what we decided to

---

[40] Ibid. [41] Ibid.

[42] AFOHSA, Serie: Juanín, llabraor de llibertaes, B21/9, Marisa Castro Fonseco, interview with Claudia Cabrero Blanco, Madrid, 2006.

[43] Margarita Laviana Cuertos, interview with Mercedes Liranzo Hernández, cited from Mercedes Liranzo Hernández, *Mujeres antifranquistas: testimonio de mujeres sevillanas* (Seville, 2018), 281–301.

do!'[44] They prepared information stands in three of Seville's then most economically deprived neighbourhoods: Macarena, Nervión, and Distrito VII. They also prepared accompanying round-table discussions that would include a psychologist, a doctor, a priest, a biologist, and a social worker, and to which they invited women from the *barrios* to ask questions. Just before Mariana went ahead with their plans, however, the local authorities cancelled them.

Mariana members reacted with scorn. They criticized what they deemed the hypocrisy of the decision, much as Fabiola chastised her mother for demanding freedom and equality but not applying these beliefs to how she raised her children. The students claimed they had been 'gagged' for trying to discuss the 'oh so subversive topic of contraceptives'.[45] Everywhere in Spain people were discussing the likelihood of an imminent transition to democracy, and Mariana members highlighted this context to deride what had happened to them. One member, 'Isabel', wrote in an article about the suspension:

And in the newspapers [all we hear is] 'talk, talk, the people must talk!' I wonder if women are not included in 'the people'? I wonder . . . what television understands as talk, because that's exactly what women in Macarena, Nervión, and Distrito VII wanted to do—talk loudly and clearly about problems directly concerning us. But it's clear that the 'telly' is talking about different people, those who can talk, because women aren't allowed to.[46]

Isabel disparaged a discourse that encouraged people to engage in dialogue, but only on certain terms.

The more time students spent in these marginal sites, the more they learnt from the *barrio* activists. Back in Gijón, Dulce and Lourdes started emulating the neighbourhood activists' use of local spaces by holding meetings in churches instead of neighbourhood associations. The gatherings consequently grew more popular. Dulce said: 'It was really interesting for me because the women really opened up. They'd tell us very personal things . . . we began learning about what it was like for women who got pregnant and didn't want to be.' Dulce learnt that many of the local women had already used

[44] AHCCOOA, Colección hemerográfica, Isabel (surname unknown), 'Las compañeras opinan: A las mujeres sevillanas no nos dejan hablar', *La Voz de la Mujer*, 3 (Jan. 1976), 2.
[45] AHCCOOA, Colección hemerográfica del AHCCOOA, Carmen (surname unknown), 'La lucha feminista en Seville', *La Voz de la Mujer*, 3 (Jan. 1976), 4.
[46] 'Isabel' (no surname provided), 'Las comañeras opinan'.

knitting needles or parsley stems to abort. By the age of 15, she had been in school for longer than the women she was meeting in the *barrios*. Dulce described them exchanging knowledge. She started to gather information about the local *curiosas* through the webs of neighbourhood activism, just as Aida and Maricusa had done. With the availability of these data, more of the women based in these peripheral neighbourhoods 'came to us for help with what to do . . . We sent them to the people we knew who would terminate the pregnancy, who were illegal then.'[47] Dulce joined AFA in 1976 and passed on information about the *curiosas* to other Asturian students.

Left-wing expatriates also started settling in Seville's *barrios* in the late 1970s, bringing with them texts and discourses on sexuality and the body. Such figures were particularly attracted to Seville for its perceived exoticism, linked to the region's relatively established flamenco culture. Mireya was a Swiss activist who moved into the city's run-down *barrios* soon after Franco's death, seeking to 'bring on a revolution', she said while laughing.[48] A group of Germans also moved into a run-down *barrio* called San Bernardo and established a commune with several Andalusians. One of these was a young woman named Claudia, who moved into La Comuna in the late 1970s. She brought with her a vaginal speculum, and held 'self-knowledge workshops'.[49] Attendees discussed the contents of a book which had recently arrived in Seville: *Cuaderno feminista: introducción al self-help*. This was a translation of *Our Bodies, Ourselves*, written by the Boston Women's Health Book Collective in 1971.[50] Leonor Taboada, originally from Argentina, had translated it into Spanish after living in Boston and then moving to Valencia, and it was published by the Valencian press Las Desobedientes. Residents of La Comuna had links with activists in Valencia, who sent them *Cuaderno feminista* in the late 1970s.

La Comuna promoted bodily autonomy, which diverged from, but coexisted alongside, other discourses stressing the dangers of back-street abortions. Magdalena López, whom I discussed at the start of this essay, was a teenager who moved into the Seville commune in 1978. In her home town of Osuna, where she was one of four women to mobilize in solidarity with strikes by *jornaleros* (agricultural day

---

[47] Dulce.   [48] Mireya Forel, personal interview, Seville, 29 Mar. 2017.

[49] Magdalena.

[50] Ignaciuk and Sethna, 'Charters for Choice', 294; Kathy Davis, *The Making of Our Bodies, Ourselves: How Feminism Travels across Borders* (Durham, NC, 2007).

labourers) in 1976. Within months of moving to La Comuna, Magdalena fell pregnant. She visited a back-street abortionist, who terminated the pregnancy using a needle. Magdalena said she 'became a convert' to abortion activism during this period for two reasons: first, because her experience of having an abortion 'made her aware of how many women were dying', and second, 'because of the speculum'. Attending Claudia's self-knowledge classes also made her think about 'the right to your own body and to your reproductive cycle'.[51] These two ways of framing abortion rights indicate increasingly diverse modes of talking about concerns relating to sex and the body, but different perspectives had marked the reproductive politics of the *barrios* from the start.

The students who arrived in marginal spaces in Asturias and Seville contributed to, but did not completely alter, the reproductive politics that had already started to emerge at the local level. Often the students acted like the *barrio* activists, and faced equivalent challenges. They also emulated the methods local activists had established for mobilizing other women, such as using church spaces, acting secretively, or pointing out hypocrisy. And they learnt from the women they met, whom they had expected only to teach. Instead, their exchanges were reciprocal, which would prove key to how this politics continued to develop throughout the late 1970s and early 1980s. This convergence of old and new dynamics is important for explaining why a reproductive politics reached large sections of Spanish society and became one of the main factors mobilizing people by the late 1970s.

III. *The Bilbao Eleven and Los Naranjos Campaign Trials*

Asturian activists started to build on existing networks in the towns and *barrios* so as to expand into more visible and public terrain in the late 1970s, and to align themselves with feminist groups in other Spanish regions. This shift was driven by a national campaign related to the trial of the Bilbao Eleven. In October 1976 a middle-aged woman, her daughter, and nine other people were arrested for performing or having abortions in Bassauri, an industrial town on the edge of Bilbao in the Basque Country.[52] The abortions were

---

[51] Magdalena.

[52] Salas and Comabella, 'Asociaciones de mujeres y movimiento feminista', 113.

carried out using soap and a pear.[53] Following the arrest of the eleven individuals implicated, members of the Women's Assembly of Biscay (Asamblea de Mujeres de Bizkaia) asked the National Feminist Network (La Coordinadora Feminista Estatal, known as La Coordinadora) to initiate a cross-regional solidarity campaign for the Bilbao Eleven. La Coordinadora did so in 1977, encouraging people to denounce themselves by entering their local courtroom to declare: 'I too have had an abortion.' The aim of the campaign was to overwhelm the judicial system and to communicate the need for legislative change.[54] Spanish feminist groups had first used this method in a smaller campaign—'I too am an adulterer'—which had successfully helped to abolish discriminatory adultery laws in 1978.[55]

In encouraging people to state that they had had illegal abortions, La Coordinadora copied campaigns held in France and Italy earlier in the 1970s. In 1971 Simone de Beauvoir was among more than three hundred public figures who signed the *Manifeste des 343*, declaring that they had undergone an abortion in defiance of the law and demanding that the procedure be legalized.[56] Bracke has described how Italian activists subsequently used the practice of 'turning abortion trials into politically charged media events'.[57] During a trial at the High Court in Padua in 1973, at which Gigliola Pierobon stood accused of having had an abortion and was in the dock along with two friends who had helped her, dozens of Italian activists declared that they too had had abortions. Groups belonging to Spain's La Coordinadora had connections with these organizations in France and Italy, including AFA, and sought their advice in setting up the Bilbao Eleven campaign.

Asturian activists began more publicly to politicize their demands for greater access to abortions after joining the Bilbao Eleven campaign. In October 1979 they targeted the outskirts of Asturian cities and the coalfields, as well as wealthier neighbourhoods and towns, collecting the signatures of those in favour of legalizing abortion. They then attempted to present these petitions to Oviedo's central court, but were denied entry. This prompted them to storm

[53] 'Once mujeres van a ser juzgadas por abortar', *Egin* (Bizkaia, 19 Aug. 1979), 3.
[54] Maud Anne Bracke, *Women and the Reinvention of the Political: Feminism in Italy, 1968–1983* (Abingdon, 2014).
[55] Giuliana Di Febo, *Resistencia y movimiento de mujeres en España: 1936–1976* (Barcelona, 1979), 203.   [56] Bracke, 'Our Bodies, Ourselves', 576.
[57] Ibid.

and occupy the building until the local authorities forcibly removed them the next day.[58] Two months later, AFA members sabotaged a major local newspaper. Teresa Meana said: 'We arrived [at the kiosk] at six in the morning, one of us would get out to grab a bundle of the newspapers, *La Nueva España*. We'd put the bundle in the car and attach a false cover reading: "Spain Legalizes Abortion", and we'd run out of the car and leave them at the kiosk.'[59] Teresa saw the Bilbao Eleven campaign as 'marking a before and after' in her organization's trajectory.[60]

The demand for reproductive justice reached a peak in Asturias in the early 1980s. Groups from across the region joined forces on multiple occasions in 1980 and 1981 to protest and march through Oviedo, urging the government to make abortion *libre y gratuito* (free from regulation and free of charge). Women in local neighbourhood associations also painted murals encouraging people to join the struggle for access to abortion. Elena Solís, an activist in the housing estate La Luz on the outskirts of the Asturian city of Avilés, remembered her association painting one that read: 'Women, unshackle yourselves.' Her association also led demands for a family planning clinic.[61] The Asturian authorities first responded to similar claims being made in Gijón, where such a centre was set up in 1981. More of these services were established in other parts of Asturias after actions by women in neighbourhood associations, such as the protests led by Aida, Maricusa, and other women in the mining town of Barredos. On 1, 2, and 3 May 1981 AFA held the first Asturian feminist conference in Oviedo. It was attended by about five hundred people from across the region and Magdalena was invited to speak about the situation in Seville.

Movements for reproductive justice in Seville in the late 1970s and early 1980s were less public than those in Asturias. This difference owed much to the group of activists who had arrived in Seville's *barrios* from Valencia in 1979, seeking to establish an illegal feminist

---

[58] *La Nueva España*, 21 Oct. 1979, 10.

[59] 'Encuentro de Llanuces (Quirós) de Begoña Sánchez, Teresa Meana, Maria José del Río, Maria José Olay y Margarita Riera', 24 Nov. 2001, in Suárez Suárez, *Feministas en la transición asturiana*, 215–16.

[60] Teresa Meana interview with Carmen Suárez Suárez, Oviedo, 2 Jan. 2002, in Suárez Suárez, *Feministas en la transición asturiana*, 279.

[61] 'Elena Solís', personal interview, el Barrio de La Luz, Avilés, 2 Nov. 2017. Elena Solís is a pseudonym chosen by her. The other interviewees chose not to use pseudonyms.

abortion clinic in the city. The Valencia collective included two women, Rosalía and Elisa, and two men, José Ángel and Jaime.[62] The group offered abortions for pregnancies of up to twelve weeks using the Karman method, named after the American psychologist who helped invent it, Harvey Karman. This method was based on a process of aspiration that required a vacuum suction instrument, and it had first become popular among groups and abortion centres in California in the 1960s, where it was used by the 'legendary underground abortion service' Jane.[63]

The Karman method gained ground internationally in the late 1960s and early 1970s. It was adopted by a French feminist group, the Movement for the Freedom of Abortion and Contraception (Mouvement pour la liberté de l'avortement et de la contraception, MLAC).[64] MLAC encouraged its members to perform illegal terminations in order to pressure the state into legalizing abortion. The organization established numerous underground clinics throughout France, as captured in a scene from the 1977 film *L'une chante, l'autre pas* (*One Sings and the Other Doesn't*) by Agnès Varda.[65] After the French government passed the law decriminalizing abortion in 1975, MLAC member Françoise (surname unknown) moved to Valencia to teach the Karman method to people demanding reproductive justice in the Catalan city. Among others, Françoise taught Rosalía, Elisa, José Ángel, and Jaime.

The four activists were prompted to share the method with activists beyond Valencia by the Bilbao Eleven campaign advancing throughout Spain. Valencia already had several underground abortion clinics, but the group wanted 'to create a unique place' which would also serve as a feminist space where people could 'learn about sexuality'.[66] By then it was legal to establish family planning clinics, but the activists did not want to call it a 'family planning' centre as they 'did not understand why family was linked to sexuality'.[67] As they were also performing abortions, they wanted to establish

---

[62] José Ángel Lozoya Gómez, *El aborto: historias de combate y resistencia. El caso de la clínica 'Los Naranjos'* (Seville, 2014), 45.

[63] Laura Kaplan, *The Story of Jane: The Legendary Underground Feminist Abortion Service* (Chicago, 2019).

[64] Lucile Ruault, 'Une fête pour l'avortement libre: la mobilisation autour du procès des militantes du MLAC d'Aix (1976–1977)', *Genèses: Sciences Sociales et Histoire*, 2/107 (2017), 32–55.

[65] Agnès Varda, *L'une chante, l'autre pas*, Ciné-tamaris, Institut national de l'audiovisuel, 1977.   [66] Lozoya Gómez, *El aborto*, 39–44.

[67] Ibid. 58.

the planning centre in a place where they could 'pass unnoticed for a while until we'd gathered a local support base'.[68] Their choice fell on Seville because they thought it would have a lower police presence than sites such as Madrid or Bilbao, particularly in the light of recent activities organized by the militant nationalist group Euskadi Ta Askatasuna (ETA).

The Valencia group drew on networks that had formed over decades as they established themselves in Seville. Before moving there, they visited the city in December 1979 and 'spoke to anyone who would listen' about their intention to start a clinic.[69] They contacted members of Mariana, other feminist groups which had recently emerged, such as the radical Primula, a feminist bookshop called María Fulmen, and the Organization for Women's Liberation (Organización para la Liberación de la Mujer, OLM), and alerted neighbourhood and housewives' associations, trade unions, branches of the local Communist Party, and New Left groups before briefly going back to Catalonia. In January they returned to Seville, this time permanently. Within days they found a flat to rent, which would serve as their home and the base for the 'planning centre'. The flat was in Seville's city centre, 'up the road from the cathedral and the archbishop's palace'.[70]

Despite the central location of Los Naranjos, its members advertised that it was an abortion clinic via existing counter-cultural channels. They recalled that women and couples started booking abortions at the clinic from the middle of January. Those running Los Naranjos preferred not to perform the operations within the clinic for fear of police surveillance, instead choosing the homes of the women seeking abortions. Members of Los Naranjos 'visited all of the city's *barrios*' to perform abortions in 1980. José Ángel recalls that one of the 'most rewarding' abortions was performed in one of Triana's working-class *corrales de vecinos* (tenements with central courtyards). José Ángel recalled: 'I'd never seen so many flowerpots in such a small space, nor so many langoustines to celebrate us finishing.'[71]

Los Naranjos also developed ties with residents of La Comuna such as Claudia and Magdalena López. In the spring of 1980 Magdalena heard about Los Naranjos and decided to start working at the clinic along with Eloísa Galindo, another young activist from Osuna who had joined Magdalena in solidarity actions with

[68] Ibid. 46.   [69] Ibid. 47.   [70] Ibid. 54.   [71] Ibid. 104.

the *jornaleros*. Magdalena remembered that she and others from the commune demonstrated the self-knowledge practices they had adopted and developed through Claudia's workshops. They describe providing those who attended the clinic at Los Naranjos 'with a mirror and a speculum before the procedure, to show them how to look at their vaginas'.[72] After someone attending the clinic had undergone one of these self-knowledge sessions, she would receive information about the Karman method and then, with the clinicians, travel either to her own home or to that of another client for the procedure. Magdalena remembered that the women coming to Los Naranjos 'would get there so afraid, imagining we were going to butcher them'. She explained that 'it did hurt, but when it's done, so is the pain . . . and afterwards they'd even invite us to have some tapas, you see? "Let's have some tapas, let's have a chat," and we'd get to know them.'[73]

By the autumn, Los Naranjos had grown in popularity among the residents of Seville, and more than four hundred women had received abortions through the clinic. Magdalena recalled that one of them was a young woman from Granada, a city in the east of Andalusia. She explained that, unbeknownst to the clinicians, this woman had felt pressured into attending by her partner and had subsequently informed the police, who told a judge in Granada, who in turn alerted Seville's authorities. Within weeks, on 21 October 1980, the police raided the clinic and detained all those present, including clients. Later that day they also arrested anyone implicated in the clinic and all of La Comuna's residents, including some who had played no part in Los Naranjos. In total, twenty people were held in custody for seventy-two hours. The case trial notes written by the defence lawyer state that the police physically tortured two of the men they had arrested: they forced one man to do pull-ups while they beat his feet, and they directed homophobic insults at a man named Juan Pedro who lived at La Comuna but had never been involved in Los Naranjos. The notes also state that the police threw a typewriter at Juan Pedro's head 'when they eventually freed him, deciding they had nothing to charge him with'.[74] All of the accused were released on bail.[75]

---

[72] Magdalena. [73] Ibid.

[74] AHCCOOA, Fondo Temas Varias, box 526, 'Informe del sumario por delito de aborto contra los trabajadores del centro de planificación "Los Naranjos"', 19 Feb. 1989, fos. 1ʳ–5ᵛ, at 3ʳ. [75] Ibid., fo. 2ᵛ.

'Expressions of solidarity' for the people arrested 'were immediate'.[76] News of what had happened prompted hundreds of people to protest outside the police station.[77] The crowds consisted of coalitions of men and women from the various groups, associations, organizations, and trade unions that Los Naranjos had been connected with during the previous year, as well as people who had used the clinic. The crowd raised money to cover the cost of bail for the accused. When let out on bail, several of those who were awaiting trial decided to leave Seville, including Rosalía and Elisa, who had formed the original Valencia group. Magdalena, José Ángel, Jaime, and Eloísa, however, began gathering support and resources for their defence, and to mount a wider campaign about abortion rights.

From 1981, Magdalena and other campaigners for Los Naranjos increasingly formed links with organizations abroad. Magdalena said she also contacted groups belonging to La Coordinadora and travelled to Madrid, but found these interactions more difficult: 'They spent the whole time fighting, and the truth was I couldn't stop to debate whether abortion should be decriminalized or legalized because I had a trial coming up.'[78] Magdalena turned instead to a group based in London called the International Campaign for Abortion Rights, which later changed its name to the International Contraception, Abortion, and Sterilization Campaign (ICASC). In April 1981 Magdalena visited London, where she helped organize a protest about Los Naranjos outside the Spanish Embassy. On her return, she also contacted the Women's Global Network on Reproductive Rights. This organization prompted its members to write letters and postcards in solidarity with those awaiting trial in the Los Naranjos case, and to contact their own Spanish embassies or the Spanish government demanding acquittals. During the next decade, hundreds of groups and individuals from all over the world wrote such letters.

The Seville activists organized the International Feminist Conference for the Legalization of Abortion, held on 27 and 28 June 1982 in a municipal sports centre in a *barrio* on the outskirts of Seville called Pino Montano.[79] The event was the first feminist conference

---

[76] Ibid., fo. 4[v].   [77] Ibid., fos. 1[r]–5[v].
[78] Magdalena.
[79] Los Naranjos Private Archive, box 5, 'Jornadas Internacionales de la Mujer', 1 June 1981.

in Spain to include substantial representation from abroad. Over two hundred people attended the conference, including activists from Italy, France, Germany, Holland, Britain, and Ireland. It had a particularly strong Italian presence, and was attended by Adele Faccio, deputy of the Radical Party (Partito Radicale) and founder of the Information Centre on Sterilization and Abortion (Centro d'informazione sulla sterilizzazione e sull'aborto). People from Spain were also present at the conference, including a coach-load of activists from Zaragoza and the well-known Basque abortion rights campaigner based in Madrid, Empar Pineda. Conference delegates later protested outside the city's courtrooms when they were denied access to present the six thousand signatures they had collected in solidarity with those accused. The protests ended on the evening of 28 June, with the police charging and beating the campaigners for blocking the road. José Ángel recalled his friend Consuelo Catalá, who had come from Valencia for the conference, returning that evening 'covered in bruises'.[80]

By the early 1980s, northern Spanish activists were inviting their counterparts in Seville to the Asturian feminist conference. Seville had become one of Europe's focal points for abortion activism, and Magdalena was asked to talk about the movements developing in the southern city and to share ideas with the Asturian activists about how to develop a global centre. Magdalena stood up and described how the clinic and subsequent campaign had successfully galvanized— and was continuing to galvanize—the reproductive politics that had been developing in Seville for decades. Although Los Naranjos had combined this politics with newer groups, networks, and practices, it had originally been shaped by grass-roots activists based on the geographical and political margins.

IV. *Conclusion*

The struggles for reproductive justice that started quietly in the late 1960s and early 1970s had culminated in a significant level of militancy by the early 1980s. Between 1979 and 1982, an estimated 25,000 men and women in Spain notified magistrates that 'I too have had an abortion', or that they had helped terminate a pregnancy.[81]

[80] Lozoya Gómez, *El aborto*, 191.

[81] Antonio Tiedra, 'Recogida de firmas a favor del derecho al aborto', *El País*, 7 June 1981.

The campaign forced the Bilbao Eleven trial to be suspended several times, and all but two of the individuals accused were acquitted in 1982.[82] Local activism also compelled municipal governments to provide more family planning facilities throughout Spain in the early 1980s.[83]

The movements that emerged in Spain encouraged the Spanish Socialist Workers' Party to promise to reform the abortion law in its programme for the 1982 election, which it won by a sizeable margin.[84] The legal reform decriminalized abortion in three limited cases: where there was a risk to the physical or mental health of the pregnant woman; where conception followed rape; and where there were 'documented foetal deformities'. Despite these changes, organizations within and beyond Spain criticized the law for not recognizing a woman's right to choose. Groups including AFA, OLM (which by then included members of Mariana, which had disbanded), Los Naranjos, and many neighbourhood associations continued to agitate over the provision of abortion access, which they argued remained unavailable to many. The manner in which these movements evolved and mutated throughout the 1980s is a topic deserving further study, but it is clear that grass-roots groups on the margins of political power had helped lay the groundwork for this later mobilization.

The reproductive politics of the *barrios* emerged in the late 1960s and early 1970s, before students arrived and before the official transition to democracy in Spain. This politics relied on activists framing issues relating to sex, reproductive health, and bodies in a variety of ways. Some depicted it as continuing the kinds of organizing they were already using to demand resources, while others stressed the illegal nature of politicizing reproductive and body issues to gain credibility within their counter-cultural circles. Networks of gossip and hearsay were critical to both varieties of campaigning for reproductive justice in peripheral urban spaces.

[82] 'Fortalecer el movimiento abortista', *Combate*, 211 (20–7 Nov. 1980); 'La campaña de solidaridad con las once mujeres acusadas de abortar se intensifica', *El País*, 14 June 1981, 8.

[83] Balance sobre las 1.ᵃˢ Jornadas Feministas de Asturias, 1981; see also Eugenia Gil García, Teresa Ortiz Gómez, and Agata Ignaciuk, 'El movimiento de planificación familiar en la ciudad de Sevilla durante la transición democrática (1975–1983)', *Congreso Universitario Nacional Investigación y Género*, 3 (2011), 726–36, at 729.

[84] Belén Cambronero-Saiz, María Teresa Ruiz Cantero, Carmen Vives-Cases, et al., 'Abortion in Democratic Spain: The Parliamentary Political Agenda 1979–2004', *Reproductive Health Matters*, 15/29 (2007), 85–96.

Students arriving in these marginal areas introduced new concepts from abroad, added to the nascent intergenerational tensions, and promoted reproductive justice. Yet elements of the original politics prevalent in these neighbourhoods continued to manifest themselves, as many groups still acted clandestinely and merged these demands with anti-Francoist organizing. The confluence of values, both established and new, local and international, helps to explain the rising tide of grass-roots activism by both men and women in the late 1970s.

12

Vamps, Wives, and (Im?)Potent Socialist Heroes: An Explorative Study of Sex and Power in Polish TV Series from the 1970s

KINGA S. BLOCH

In her popular book *Why Women Have Better Sex under Socialism*,[1] Kristen Ghodsee claims that women in the Soviet bloc had more fulfilling sex lives than housewives and stay-at-home mothers in capitalist nations because of the liberties inherent in their economic independence. The following essay takes a closer look at the presentation of 'better sex' on television in a socialist state in which norms about sexuality evolved within a very specific, normative framework: the People's Republic of Poland (1947–89). In socialist Poland, citizens had to navigate conceptions of 'good sex' in a public space that was influenced simultaneously by the politics of a socialist government, the Catholic Church, and gender ideals that were deeply rooted in nationalism. What position did the state-controlled Polish public television broadcasting network (Telewizja Polska, TVP) take in the complex negotiations about 'good' and 'bad sex' in television series produced and screened during and after the global sexual revolution of the 1960s and 1970s? The key question pursued in the following is whether the makers of Polish TV programmes presented their audiences with a conservative concept of sexuality, or whether they can be seen as 'catalysts of change'[2] within the global

I would like to thank the staff of the archives of Telewizja Polska and of the Filmoteka Narodowa as well as the German Historical Institute Warsaw for its generous financial support. Translations are my own unless stated otherwise.

[1] Kristen R. Ghodsee, *Why Women Have Better Sex under Socialism, and Other Arguments for Economic Independence* (London, 2019; first pub. 2018).

[2] Christina von Hodenberg, *Television's Moment: Sitcom Audiences and the Sixties Cultural Revolution* (New York, 2015), argues that Johnny Speight's popular British TV sitcom *Till Death Us Do Part* and its German and American adaptations catalysed a milder version of the radical sexual liberation claimed by the 1968ers, turning it into the mainstream.

framework of the 'sexual revolution'.[3] Did the negotiations about sexual morals that had dominated public discourse in capitalist countries in the West since the 1960s[4] transfer into Polish TV series about everyday life?

I. *Why Does Sex on TV Matter?*

Normative ideas about sexuality are deeply entangled with the moral values and gender stereotypes in any given historical and societal constellation. Ideas about 'good sex' are debated in many spaces, including the family, local communities, the religious sphere, scientific discourse, political debates, and last but certainly not least, the media. Since the mid twentieth century, television has increasingly manifested itself as a discursive sphere in which societies negotiate moral values via narratives and images. In accordance with Foucault's notion of sexuality and power, the former is perceived as a culturally constructed categorization of appropriate and inappropriate behaviour. The following argument therefore does not engage with actual sex, but will instead explore an instance of discursive production in a specific socio-historical context: the contemporary representation of sexuality in Polish TV series set in everyday life from the mid 1960s to 1981. Televised fiction is read as a space that produces power by providing the audience with narratives and images of 'normal sexuality'.[5]

TV series are known both as carriers of knowledge and as catalysts of value change.[6] Aspects of sexuality, such as prostitution, abortion, and homosexuality, that are taboo[7] in a specific historical constellation might be omitted on screen, or can become a trigger for debates about these issues. Scholars across disciplines such as

---

[3] Dagmar Herzog, *Sexuality in Europe: A Twentieth-Century History* (Cambridge, 2011), ch. 4.

[4] Ibid. For the USA and Britain see Linda Grant, *Sexing the Millennium: A Political History of the Sexual Revolution* (London, 1993), ch. 5.

[5] Michel Foucault, *The History of Sexuality*, trans. Robert Hurley, 4 vols. (New York, 1990), i: *An Introduction*, 33–4.

[6] On *Lindenstraße* and homosexuality see Georg Uecker, *Ich mach' dann mal weiter!* (Frankfurt a.M., 2018), 135–55; on the influence of the American miniseries *Holocaust* (1978) on West German Holocaust memory and historiography see Frank Bösch, 'Film, NS-Vergangenheit und Geschichtswissenschaft: Von "Holocaust" zu "Der Untergang"', *Vierteljahrshefte für Zeitgeschichte*, 55/1 (2007), 1–32.

[7] Barbara Klich-Kluczewska, *Rodzina, tabu i komunizm w Polsce 1956–1989* (Cracow, 2015).

media studies, psychology, and sociology argue that the permeation of TV series through society provides a space in which normative discourse that is firmly embedded in the rituals of everyday life can resonate.[8] One of the key factors that establish the impact of a television programme is its reach in society.[9] Katarzyna Pokorna-Ignatowicz and Patryk Pleskot trace the increasing prominence of television in the quotidian experience of the Polish People's Republic from the 1960s.[10] Even though the two public television stations in socialist Poland (TVP1 and TVP2) were controlled by the authorities,[11] fiction programmes were popular with the national audience as writers for Polish TV often pushed the boundaries of what could be said by humorously critiquing the challenges inherent in everyday life under real socialism.[12] By the mid 1970s, television had reached 92 per cent of all Polish households, increasing to 98 per cent in 1980.[13] The series examined in this essay and others like them enjoyed extremely high viewing rates and were widely discussed privately and in the press.[14] Televised narratives about human relations can therefore be seen as a significant part of societal reflective practices in Poland. These often entail lifelong emotional attachments to the characters, as expressed in Joshua Meyrowitz's concept of 'media friends'.[15] In a Western context, he shows how

[8] The following studies show that TV families' impact on societal discourse was a global phenomenon in the twentieth century: James Lull (ed.), *World Families Watch Television* (London, 1988); David Morley, *Family Television: Cultural Power and Domestic Leisure* (London, 1986); Lothar Mikos, *Es wird dein Leben! Familienserien im Fernsehen und im Alltag der Zuschauer* (Münster, 1994); and Anikó Imre, *TV Socialism* (Durham, NC, 2016).

[9] Christina von Hodenberg, 'Expeditionen in den Methodendschungel: Herausforderungen der Zeitgeschichtsforschung im Fernsehzeitalter', *Journal of Modern European History*, 10/1 (2012), 24–48, at 25 and 43.

[10] Katarzyna Pokorna-Ignatowicz, *Telewizja w systemie politycznym i medialnym PRL: między polityką a widzem* (Cracow, 2003); Patryk Pleskot, *Wielki mały ekran: telewizja a codzienność Polaków w latach sześćdziesiątych* (Warsaw, 2007).

[11] Pokorna-Ignatowicz, *Telewizja w systemie politycznym*, 66–79 and 107–34.

[12] In 'Telewizyjny Alfabet Wspomnień Jerzego Gruzy', *Gazeta Wyborcza*, 30 June 2000, director Jerzy Gruza claims that *Wojna Domowa* (*Domestic War*) was censored and thus discontinued because the dog Lejek urinated on the magazine *Kultura*. For similar issues in 1980s Poland see Dorota Ostrowska, 'The Carnival of the Absurd: Stanisław Bareja's Alternatywy 4', in Anikó Imre, Timothy Havens, and Katalin Lustyik (eds.), *Popular Television in Eastern Europe during and since Socialism* (London, 2013), 65–80.

[13] Pokorna-Ignatowicz, *Telewizja w systemie politycznym*, 365.

[14] All the participants in my oral history project recalled lively discussions about the series, while large newspaper article collections (1960s–1970s) at the Filmoteka Narodowa and the TVP archives illustrate high media attention.

[15] Joshua Meyrowitz, 'The Life and Death of Media Friends: New Genres of Intimacy

audience members develop unilateral relationships with celebrities and fictional characters that become a fixed part of the emotional and social spheres in which people live their lives and negotiate their identities. This concept took a specific form in Poland, where socialist media friends remained a frame of reference after the fall of the Iron Curtain and can therefore be seen as bearers of a lasting cultural identity.[16]

The notion that popular Polish TV series were, and still are, perceived as part of Poland's cultural heritage is corroborated by the adoption in colloquial language of punchlines from the series, the recent publication of remastered versions of the programmes, museums and events dedicated to TV neighbours,[17] and the naming of public spaces after the protagonists.[18] All this suggests that socialist TV neighbours do indeed impact on perceptions of the past and therefore, according to Emily Keightley and Michael Pickering's concept of mnemonic imagination,[19] also on Polish identity.[20] The mnemonic imagination entails mediated narratives being enmeshed with personal and collective memory by a creative, imaginative process. It could therefore be argued that the reception of normative gender roles shown on television forms part of one's personal memory. According to the mnemonic imagination, television's normative view on appropriate and inappropriate behaviour is considered to be a valid representation of the past if it encompasses an acceptable version of one's past self in the present while simultaneously matching the concept of a desired future identity. With regard to gender roles represented by Polish TV neighbours, such mnemonic processes were confirmed in nineteen oral history interviews that I conducted in the early 2010s with a geographically and generationally diverse group of

and Mourning', in Susan J. Drucker and Robert S. Cathcart (eds.), *American Heroes in a Media Age* (Cresskill, NJ, 1994), 62–81.

[16] Kinga S. Bloch, 'The Life and Afterlife of a Socialist Media Friend: On the Longterm Cultural Relevance of the Polish TV Series *Czterdziestolatek*', *VIEW: Journal of European Television History and Culture*, 2/3 (2013), 88–98.

[17] The term is used to describe the characters in TV series because they can be seen as an entire nation's neighbours in an 'era of limited choice' (von Hodenberg, 'Expeditionen in den Methodenschungel', 40–7).

[18] Explored in detail in my Ph.D. thesis, 'European Television Families in Cold War Europe' (University College London, 2023).

[19] Emily Keightley and Michael Pickering, *The Mnemonic Imagination: Remembering as Creative Practice* (Basingstoke, 2012).

[20] See Bloch, 'The Life and Afterlife'.

participants.[21] Without exception, my interviewees knew all the popular TV series broadcast in socialist Poland; most importantly, however, they considered them to be realistic representations of Polish family life. Familiarity with the series' settings and with the characters finds further expression in popular publications such as Piotr Piotrowski's *Kultowe Seriale*,[22] fan sites, and recent influencer videos.[23] There is good reason, therefore, to suggest that televised ideas about 'good' and 'bad' sex present issues that have been part of Polish societal discourse about sexuality since the 1960s and 1970s.

Historians have only recently started to explore the impact of television on societal value change.[24] For this study, Christina von Hodenberg's suggestion to understand televised fiction as a 'catalyst of change' is of particular relevance.[25] Looking at the popular British sitcom *Till Death Us Do Part* and comparing it with its two Western adaptations, in the USA and West Germany, von Hodenberg shows that the crude, humorous interpretation of the post-1968 clash of generations presented in the series eased societal acceptance of a milder version of the sexual revolution's demands for liberalization. A similar approach is applied here to fictional television's influence on public and private discourse about gender ideals in socialist TV series, a genre that has not yet received much academic attention.[26] More precisely, the question is whether and, if so, how Polish TV neighbours contributed to the catalysation of the global shift in normative ideas about sexuality like their Western peers, or whether they fostered an adherence to a culturally specific model of gendered behaviour that was, to an extent, rooted in the nineteenth-century national ideal of the *Matka Polka* (the Polish

---

[21] In 2012 I interviewed a gender-balanced group of individuals (born 1939–77) from Słupsk, Warsaw, Gdańsk, Lubomierz, and villages in the county of Wałcz.

[22] Piotr K. Piotrowki, *Kultowe Seriale* (Warsaw, 2011).

[23] For example, the Facebook site *Czterdziestolatek — wielbiciele serialu* is three years old and has over 12,000 followers: ⟨https://www.facebook.com/groups/1371706889596862/about⟩ [accessed 10 Sept. 2021]. For *Daleko od Szosy* there is a similar group with 16,000 followers: ⟨https://www.facebook.com/groups/1687631458149990⟩ [accessed 10 Sept. 2021]. Videos about 1970s TV series by influencers such as Paula Rodak have been watched over 200,000 times. See ⟨https://www.youtube.com/watch?v=2LMTnMFTe-Q⟩ [accessed 10 Sept. 2021].

[24] Examples are Heather L. Gumbert, *Envisioning Socialism: Television and the Cold War in the German Democratic Republic* (Ann Arbor, 2014); and Reinhold Viehoff (ed.), *'Die Liebenswürdigkeit des Alltags': Die Familienserie 'Rentner haben niemals Zeit'* (Leipzig, 2004).

[25] Von Hodenberg, *Television's Moment*.

[26] For societal issues see Ostrowska, 'The Carnival of the Absurd'; gender issues on socialist television have merely been touched upon so far by Imre, *TV Socialism*.

Mother).[27] My focus on this particular stereotype stems from the fact that it is explicitly mentioned in a pioneering study on Polish film and gender.[28] Furthermore, the *Matka Polka* also occurs across several sources in connection with Polish TV series of the 1960s and 1970s, including my oral history study and various newspaper articles.[29] Originally, the concept ennobled motherly sacrifice in the context of the preservation of the nation.[30] The *Matka Polka* contributes to her husband's struggle for the freedom of the Polish nation at home: she ensures the continuity of Polish culture by raising and educating the next generation. Offering her sons to Poland's fight for freedom resonates with the deep veneration of the selfless sacrifice made by Mary, mother of Jesus, that is as central to understanding Polish history and culture as it is to analysing the nation's gender stereotypes. My thesis is that the nationalist veneration of the *Matka Polka* establishes a normative difference between the moral evaluation of male and female sexual desire that reverberates both in expert knowledge about sex and in televised storytelling in socialist Poland.

Given the constraints of space, I here examine four TV series dating from the mid 1960s to the early 1980s with regard to the representation of male and female sexuality.[31] The programmes, almost exclusively written by men, are Jerzy Gruza's *Wojna Domowa* (*Domestic War*, 1965–66), the first Polish family series in a contemporary setting,[32] and his *40-Latek* (*The 40-Year-Old*, 1974–7);[33] Zbigniew

[27] Brian Porter, '*Hetmanka* and Mother: Representing the Virgin Mary in Modern Poland', *Contemporary European History*, 14/2 (2005), 151–70. See also Brian Porter-Szűcs, *Faith and Fatherland: Catholicism, Modernity, and Poland* (New York, 2011), ch. 10: 'Mary, Militant and Maternal', 360–90.

[28] Joanna Szwajcowska, 'The Myth of the Polish Mother', in ead., Ewa Mazierska, and Elżbieta Ostrowska, *Women in Polish Cinema* (New York, 2006), 15–36.

[29] e.g. 'Wojna Domowa dziś', *Gazeta Wyborcza*, 27 Sept. 1997, and 'Wojna po latach', *Kurier Polski*, 15 Sept. 1997.

[30] See Porter, '*Hetmanka* and Mother'; and Szwajcowska, 'The Myth of the Polish Mother'.

[31] TV series produced after the lifting of martial law in Poland, such as *Alternatywy 4* (produced 1983; censored release 1986), *Zmiennicy* (1987), and Kieslowski's *Dekalog* (1989–90), have not been considered here as they no longer tell stories about one nuclear family. While *Dom* (1980–2000), produced in the 1980s, does present a narrative about Polish family life, the historical perspective of the early episodes excludes it from a sample of series that explore contemporary sexuality as part of Polish family life.

[32] For *Wojna Domowa* see ⟨https://www.filmpolski.pl/fp/index.php?film=123751⟩ [accessed 24 Aug. 2021]; TVP/Galapagos Film (ed.), *Wojna Domowa* (Warsaw, 2010).

[33] For *40-Latek* see ⟨https://www.filmpolski.pl/fp/index.php?film=123482⟩ [accessed 24 Aug. 2021]; TVP/Galapagos Film (ed.), *40-Latek* (Warsaw, 2009).

Chmielewski's *Daleko od Szosy* (*Far from the Country Lane*, 1976);[34] and Radosław Piwowarski's *Jan Serce* (*Jan Heart*, 1982).[35] These series were chosen for their popularity and because they were frequently mentioned in my oral history study.[36] Another important aspect is that these TV neighbourhoods portray everyday family life in socialist Poland. Their settings foster a cultural and temporal proximity between the TV neighbours and their audience.[37] Furthermore, a diverse sample allows the discourse on sexuality to be probed across a set of stories that illuminate different phases of life. *Wojna Domowa* humorously engages with urban teenagers and their parents in the mid 1960s, while *Daleko od Szosy* follows a peasant boy's challenging path of personal and professional development in the 1970s. Meanwhile, *40-Latek* and *Jan Serce* present men in a personal crisis. The former accompanies construction engineer Stefan Karwowski and his family through his mid-life crisis, and *Jan Serce* depicts a chivalrous 40-year-old bachelor who lives with his elderly mother while searching for his true love—that is, a wife to build a home with. In one way or another, the exclusively male lead characters are both Polish and socialist heroes. In *Wojna Domowa* and *Daleko od Szosy*, Paweł and Leszek embody the confident, modern generation of Poles growing up under socialism; Stefan Karwowski in *40-Latek* oversees some of the nation's most prestigious building projects; and Jan Serce leads a brigade maintaining Warsaw's sewers, which have highly symbolic connotations in Polish history as a key site in the Warsaw Uprising during the Second World War. In the 'fight' for the nation's prestige that lies at the heart of each story, every male protagonist has a female character at his side who embodies a socialist manifestation of the *Matka Polka*. Finally, the programmes represent a diverse range of genres. While *40-Latek* and *Wojna Domowa* are comedies, *Jan Serce* and *Daleko od Szosy* can be regarded as melodramas.

[34] For *Daleko od Szosy* see ⟨https://www.filmpolski.pl/fp/index.php?film=123417⟩ [accessed 24 Aug. 2021]; TVP (ed.), *Daleko od Szosy* (Warsaw, 2005).

[35] For *Jan Serce* see ⟨https://www.filmpolski.pl/fp/index.php?film=123578⟩ [accessed 24 Aug. 2021]; TVP (ed.), *Jan Serce* (Warsaw, 2008).

[36] All four series are featured in Piotrowski, *Kultowe Seriale*, and are available on TVP's streaming service. Jerzy Gruza's series were mentioned spontaneously by my nineteen interviewees when asked to recall TV series from the socialist era. The other programmes were known to all interviewees, too; however, they were named by only a third of the participants.

[37] Kinga S. Bloch, 'Realism Bites! The Impact of a Fictional Teen Suicide on West German Public Debates in the 1980s', *Opticon1826*, 13 (2012), 45–55, at 51.

Methodologically, I approach the series' normative position on sexuality from several angles. First, the plots are screened for the presence of sexual encounters. These are then scrutinized in a structured content analysis to identify distinct patterns of gendered behaviour. As TV series tell their stories visually, the presentation of male and female bodies on screen is addressed via reflections on characteristic camera angles used to depict sexual tension and attraction. Following Joan W. Scott,[38] the linchpin of my approach is a relational analysis of televised sexuality. My engagement with both genders is particularly relevant as studies of masculinity in Polish gender history are rare.[39] Before I proceed to engage with televised discourse on sexuality, I shall briefly establish what sexologists and other normative agents such as the socialist state and the Catholic Church considered to be appropriate behaviour in 1960s and 1970s Poland.

Public discourse on sexuality in Poland in the 1960s and 1970s was laden with contradictions and ambiguities. On the one hand, the state fostered a climate of gender equality rooted in communist ideas about society.[40] On the other, pornography was prohibited,[41] while patriarchal gender roles persisted alongside a remarkably progressive perspective on sexuality.[42] Women were offered opportunities for education and professional careers,[43] and sexual liberties were

---

[38] Joan W. Scott, 'Gender: A Useful Category of Historical Analysis', *American Historical Review*, 91/5 (1986), 1053–75.

[39] See Krzysztof Arcimowicz, 'Przemiany męskosci w kulturze wspołczesnej', in Małgorzata Fuszara (ed.), *Nowi mężczyźni? Zmieniające się modele męskości we współczesnej Polsce* (Warsaw, 2008), 23–7; and Ewa Mazierska, *Masculinities in Polish, Czech and Slovak Cinema: Black Peters and Men of Marble* (New York, 2010), 1–6.

[40] For postwar developments see Małgorzata Fidelis, *Women, Communism, and Industrialization in Postwar Poland* (Cambridge, 2010). For a comprehensive overview see Katarzyna Stańczak-Wiślicz, Piotr Perkowski, Małgorzata Fidelis, and Barbara Klich-Kluczewska, *Kobiety w Polsce 1945–1989: nowoczesność, równouprawnienie, komunizm* (Cracow, 2020).

[41] See Agata Chałupnik, 'Wychowanie seksuale: "sztuka kochania"', in Małgorzata Szpakowska (ed.), *Obyczaje Polskie: wiek XX w krótkich hasłach* (Warsaw, 2008), 420–28, at 427.

[42] Agnieszka Kościańska, *Gender, Pleasure, and Violence: The Construction of Expert Knowledge of Sexuality in Poland* (Bloomington, Ind., 2021), 41; and ead., 'Beyond Viagra: Sex Therapy in Poland', in *Health and Medicine: Post-Socialist Perspectives*, special issue of *Sociologický Časopis/Czech Sociological Review*, 50/6 (2014), 919–38.

[43] For the experience of female labour see Andrzej Szwarc and Anna Żarnowska (eds.), *Kobieta i praca: wiek XIX i XX. Zbiór studiów* (Warsaw, 2000), in particular the contributions by A. Kurzynowski, 'Przemiany wzorów karier zawodowych kobiet w latach 1950–1989', 189–215, and D. Jarosz, 'Kobiety a praca zawodowa w Polsce w latach 1944–1956: główne problemy w świetle nowych badań źródłowych', 217–41.

fostered via wide-ranging reproductive rights and permissive divorce legislation. In practice, divorce cases did not necessarily align with the permissive legislation and often resulted in social issues.[44] The 1956 abortion law legalized the termination of pregnancy for both medical and socio-economic reasons, giving women significant control over their bodies.[45] Conscious family planning was encouraged by the state and contraceptives were both subsidized and increasingly popular; however, it must be noted that the supply never met the demand.[46] Instead, abortion, coitus interruptus, and calendar control were commonly used as methods of birth control.[47] The socialist state's liberal stance towards sexuality also manifested itself in a wide range of institutions, such as the Towarzystwo Świadomego Macierzyństwa (Society for Conscious Motherhood), later renamed Towarzystwo Planowania Rodziny (Family Planning Institute). Such institutions aimed to disseminate knowledge about family planning and addressed a wide range of issues ranging from infertility to gender reassignment.[48] They were founded and run by scholars in the emerging field of Polish sexology, the most renowned being Kazimierz Imieliński (1929–2010), Michalina Wisłocka (1921–2005), and Zbigniew Lew-Starowicz (born 1943). Unlike their US peers, progressive Polish sexologists approached sexual issues in a holistic manner rather than from a purely biomedical perspective. Based on experience in the field, their therapeutic methods took entanglements between biological and many other factors into consideration. Culture, working life, psychology, and the social environment—to give just a few examples—were seen to influence problems such as impotence, premature ejaculation, low libido, and infertility.[49] By means of advisory columns responding to letters from the readers of

For further insights see Małgorzata Fidelis, 'Równouprawnienie czy konserwatywna nowoczesność? Kobiety pracujące', in Stańczak-Wiślicz, Perkowski, Fidelis, et al., *Kobiety w Polsce*, 103–64.

[44] See Klich-Kluczewska, *Rodzina, tabu i komunizm*, 121–78; also ead., 'Prawo: równość, świeckość, partnerstwo', in Stańczak-Wiślicz, Perkowski, Fidelis, et al., *Kobiety w Polsce*, 299–306.

[45] Agnieszka Wochna-Tymińska, 'O dopuszczalności przerywania ciąży: ustawa z dnia 27 kwietnia 1956 r. i towarzyszące jej dyskusje', in Marcin Kula (ed.), *Kłopoty z seksem w PRL: rodzenie nie całkiem po ludzku, aborcja, choroby, odmienności* (Warsaw, 2012), 99–186.

[46] Renata Ingbrant, 'Michalina Wisłocka's *The Art of Loving* and the Legacy of Polish Sexology', *Sexuality and Culture*, 24 (2020), 371–88.

[47] Klich-Kluczewska, *Rodzina, tabu i komunizm*, 233–60.

[48] Kościańska, 'Beyond Viagra', 927   [49] Ead., *Gender, Pleasure, and Violence*, 42.

magazines, such as Imieliński's sex column in the student magazine
itd. (etc.), therapeutic advice on 'good sex' was accessible to a wide
range of people outside clinical settings.[50] Sexologists also published
popular literature, one of the best-known titles being Wisłocka's
Sztuka Kochania (The Art of Loving, 1978).[51] Their advice was eagerly
sought and their publications sold out swiftly.[52]

Experts' ideas about male and female sexuality, however, tended
to entail patriarchal role models, and from today's point of view this
appears to contradict the modernity of their therapeutic approach.[53]
Wisłocka's book is a case in point. On the one hand, she disseminated
detailed knowledge about sexuality, including illustrated guidelines
for enhancing pleasure. On the other, she suggested women should
not voice their erotic desires directly, as that might irritate their
partners. Instead, *Sztuka Kochania* recommends that women should
manipulate their husbands in 'the female way' to achieve what they
want. By no means should the husband's confidence be 'undermined' by emancipation.[54] Furthermore, wives were warned not to
touch upon 'ugly' quotidian issues at bedtime, such as problems with
the children, household issues, or their work, as this might quench
their partners' sex drive. According to Wisłocka, responsibility for
a satisfactory sex life lay mainly with women. Male sexuality, particularly in youths, was seen to be subject to strong physical urges
that superseded female lust and desire. This perception led to the
bewildering notion that rape was 'an aberrant form of discharging
[male] sexual tension'.[55] Morally and emotionally 'good sex', also
referred to as 'cultured sex' that satisfied both partners, was seen to
be exclusive to heterosexual matrimony.

Disparate perceptions of male and female sexuality also informed
sex education.[56] Since 1969, information about family planning
had been a compulsory part of the Polish school curriculum by

---

[50] Ibid. 40–61.

[51] Ingbrant, 'Michalina Wisłocka's *The Art of Loving*'. I quote from the recent new
edition: Michalina Wisłocka, *Sztuka Kochania* (Warsaw, 2016), 114; published in English
as *A Practical Guide to Marital Bliss* (Worcester, 1987).

[52] Ingbrant, 'Michalina Wisłocka's *The Art of Loving*', 379.

[53] Kościańska, *Gender, Pleasure, and Violence*, 47; and Barbara Klich-Kluczewska
and Piotr Perkowski, 'Objekty biopolityki? Zdrowie, reprodukcja i przemoc', in
Stańczak-Wiślicz, Perkowski, Fidelis, et al., *Kobiety w Polsce*, 384.

[54] Wisłocka, *Sztuka Kochania*, 114.

[55] Ingbrant, 'Michalina Wisłocka's *The Art of Loving*', 382.

[56] Agnieszka Kościańska, *To See a Moose: The History of Polish Sex Education* (New
York, 2021).

law.[57] Earlier publications addressing parents and young people had been in circulation since the beginning of the 1960s.[58] The ambiguous nature of sexologists' advice can be traced in pamphlets written for adolescents. These booklets vaguely presented 'good sex' as part of mature relationships.[59] Only young women were threatened with dire stories about the hardship of single parenthood that awaited them should they engage in promiscuous behaviour. They were expected to restrain themselves,[60] while adolescent male sexuality was seen as a natural part of masculine coming of age.[61] Ultimately, the booklets fostered the notion that women had sole responsibility for guarding themselves against young men chasing sexual adventures without any emotional involvement. It was assumed that young men would not face up to the consequences of sex with a girl who 'lost control'. Women who simply enjoyed sex without wanting to marry their partner right away did not exist in sex education pedagogy. The advice literature emphasized that 'good sex' should be postponed until marriage.[62]

This perspective also resonated in religious debates. The Catholic Church was another important normative agent when it came to matters of the flesh.[63] From a Catholic point of view, the sacrament of matrimony is the only space in which sex should occur, as the central purpose of marriage is procreation. Therefore 'good sex' is confined to a heterosexual couple and bound to a result: conception. From the early 1960s, Rome classified abortion as murder by defining human life as beginning at conception in 1962. The pope rejected birth control as being opposed to the 'sole and sacred' purpose of sex: procreation. Polish Catholics were subject to

[57] Maria Woźniak, 'Sexuality Education in Polish Schools', *Przegląd Socjologiczny/ Sociological Review*, 64 (2015), 121–35, at 127.

[58] References to contraception in the context of future matrimony and subject to maturity and independence occur in publications such as Halina Chatys-Skirzyńska's pamphlet for girls, *Okres dojrzewania dziewcząt*, 5th edn. (Warsaw, 1968), 74–8. Janusz Łopuski's publication for boys, *Co chce wiedzieć każdy chłopiec*, 4th edn. (Warsaw, 1961), addresses the negative consequences of promiscuity, prostitution, and venereal disease.

[59] Kościańska, *To See a Moose*, 95 ff.

[60] Ibid. 44. See also Elżbieta Jackiewicz, *O czym chcą wiedzieć dziewczęta* (Warsaw, 1958), 22–7.   [61] Kościańska, *To See a Moose*, 81–3.

[62] Ibid. 95–6.

[63] Ibid. 248–75; and Joanna Z. Mishtal, 'How the Church Became the State: The Catholic Regime and Reproductive Rights in State Socialist Poland', in Shana Penn and Jill Massino (eds.), *Gender Politics and Everyday Life in State Socialist Eastern and Central Europe* (New York, 2009), 133–49. For Catholic discourse see Grant, *Sexing the Millennium*, 63–77.

moral appeals from local clergy, after-school catechism classes, and the Catholic press.[64] Reproductive rights and masturbation were condemned and contraception was considered sinful as it dissociated sex from procreation and potentially served as a means of concealing sinful extramarital sex.[65] While the ideological clash between the Catholic Church and political officials about reproductive rights was clear, the relative lack of a public confrontation between these two normative entities under socialism fostered a false impression of the Polish episcopate's tolerance in these matters.[66] Here it must be noted that the Catholic Church held a unique position of respect in Poland, rooted in 'age-long influence' as a 'keeper of Polish identity, culture and traditional Christian moral values, as well as its social influence through its sacraments, charities, custodianship of records', and the education of the young.[67] A common perception was that the Catholic Church was a sanctuary for Polishness at times of oppression and need, such as during the Partitions and the Nazi occupation, as well as taking the role of an adversary of the socialist state. The notion of the Catholic Church's subversive position and its entanglement with the preservation of the Polish nation in periods of hardship reverberates in the nineteenth-century stereotype of the *Matka Polka*, as mentioned above.[68] This ideal of femininity tied women's sacred task of reproduction to the survival of the nation and ennobled motherly sacrifice by aligning it with Mary's suffering. Catholic sexual morality in Poland was therefore expanded by a nationalistic dimension that implicitly subordinated women's reproductive rights to the 'higher' cause of preserving the nation and giving birth to sons who would continue the fight for Poland's freedom and glory.

To sum up, all agents involved in public discourse about sexuality in Poland normatively differentiated between men's and women's sexuality. Men were seen as subject to greater biological urges than women, who were considered more emotionally mature and able to restrain their erotic urges. The Christian and nationalist ennoblement of motherhood, matrimony, and the family heightened the moral value of conception. Women's sexuality was thus a matter of national relevance that demanded mature responsibility,

---

[64] Kościańska, *To See a Moose*, 255–71.

[65] Mishtal, 'How the Church Became the State', 140–1.   [66] Ibid. 142–5.

[67] Ingbrant, 'Michalina Wisłocka's *The Art of Loving*', 374.

[68] Porter, '*Hetmanka* and Mother'.

superseding the desire for personal pleasure. Meanwhile, the male sex drive was seen as a natural urge inherent in a concept of virility that shunned any responsibility for potential conception outside wedlock.

II. *Sex in Socialist TV Neighbourhoods*

The following analysis explores how the ambiguities and normative patterns inherent in Polish public discourse about sexuality in the 1960s and 1970s translated to the television screen. As in Western TV series,[69] sex was embedded into narratives about family life in an increasingly casual manner in Poland in the 1960s and 1970s. Can the presence of sexuality in Polish TV neighbourhoods be read as promoting liberalism and an egalitarian perspective on sexual agency? I shall argue that Polish TV series tended to make a highly gendered moral differentiation between premarital sex and sexuality within and outside matrimony, thus creating a moral hierarchy between men, the (future) wife—the *Matka Polka*—and the figure of the 'vamp'. Here, I use the term 'vamp' to describe a woman who uses her charm and her looks to manipulate and seduce men for fun, without any interest in a lasting relationship or concern for the man's marital status. This section will start with a quantitative overview of sex in Polish TV series and move on to explore the visual representation of sex on the small screen. I shall then briefly touch upon the expert discourse of sexologists in TV neighbourhoods before presenting a case study from *40-Latek*.

From a quantitative point of view, Polish television casually presented sexuality as a significant part of everyday life. If all direct and indirect references to erotic encounters are counted, my sample features at least twenty sexually active individuals.[70] It must be noted, though, that TV neighbours in Poland explicitly engaged in pre- and extramarital sex only from the 1970s, and that any prior references to sexuality in family series remained vague. There are

[69] For discourse about sex triggered by the British sitcom *Till Death Us Do Part* and its adaptations see von Hodenberg, *Television's Moment*, and my Ph.D. thesis 'European Television Families'.

[70] The following protagonists are either shown to be sexually active or talk about sexual experiences: *Wojna Domowa*: Paweł's parents; *40-Latek*: Magda, Stefan, Krysia, Mariola; *Daleko od Szosy*: Leszek, Bronka, Irena, sadownik Wieczorek, Ania, Lola, Mietek, three of Mietek's girlfriends, and a couple at a party; *Jan Serce*: Jan, Danusia, Piotr, Małgosia, Matylda, Gabi, Tycjan, Basia, Aleksander. I have not counted the numerous women listed in Tycjan's notebook.

almost twice as many sexually active women as sexually active men (17 women; 9 men), but these female characters are predominantly in supporting roles, meaning that their side of the story is rarely told in detail. Evidently, sexuality in the Polish TV neighbourhood was not confined to matrimony. All married couples have a sex life that was referred to verbally from the 1960s and visually from the 1970s. Male adultery occurs in all TV families from the 1970s.[71] Every TV husband is subjected to temptation at least once, and there is always a woman available who is interested in 'an adventure'. Wives, however, with one exception, never have extramarital sex.[72] The clearly gendered allocation of televised sexual encounters can be seen as echoing Polish sexologists' normative ideas about gendered differences in sex drive. The number of sexual encounters points to narrative patterns that underline the wife's fidelity, and to a televised concept of virility that suggests adultery is a trait of 'normal' masculinity. Throughout the sample, adultery never leads to divorce or a permanent separation of the spouses, a pattern that normalizes male adultery and emphasizes the sanctity of matrimony.

Despite the prohibition of pornography in socialist Poland, erotic tension was depicted both verbally and visually in Polish TV neighbourhoods. Kissing, passionate embraces, and erotic glances occur in different spaces, such as the marital bed, a party, the forest, an orchard, and even the basement under a public swimming pool. All these erotic scenes are highly suggestive of the upcoming sexual encounter, but full nudity was not present in Polish TV neighbourhoods until the early 1980s. Instead, sex scenes were cut before the act, leaving it to the spectator to guess what would happen next. In this respect, the 1970s can be seen as a transitional phase, gradually loosening the restrained references to sexuality in 1960s TV series.[73] In episode 11, 'Co każdy chłopiec' ('What Every Boy . . .'), the 1965

---

[71] There might already have been a hidden reference to adultery in the 1960s series *Wojna Domowa*, where the father travels for work regularly. There is often talk about going out or seeing a film with 'some ladies' on business trips. These brief remarks can be read as suggestive passages that point to sexual adventures. Male adultery and the temptation to have extramarital sex occur in *40-Latek* (episode 3), twice in *Daleko od Szosy* (Leszek has sex with the prostitute Lola in episode 2 and is exposed to erotic temptation by the landlady's daughter, episode 6), and in *Jan Serce* (Danusia's husband Aleksander talks about another relationship that he had after running away from his marriage; the second case is Piotr's affair with Matylda).

[72] The only exception is single mother Danusia in *Jan Serce*, whose husband left her without explanation years ago.

[73] While Paweł from *Wojna Domowa* was dating, sex was explicitly not part of that, as Paweł's friend Anula explains to his parents in episode 11 (34:38–38:00).

series *Wojna Domowa* humorously explores generational differences in sex education. The title itself is a reference to Janusz Łopuski's sex education pamphlet *Co chce wiedzieć każdy chłopiec* (*What Every Boy Wants to Know*, 1961), but the concept of teenage sexuality is merely addressed verbally. What stands out here is the parents' highly gendered reaction to Paweł Jankowski's 'erotic' awakening. The boy himself is merely shown going on a walk to the park with a girl, ending up on a bench talking about the weather. Meanwhile, his mother, Zofia Jankowska, reads this innocent encounter with the utmost alarm and rallies the reluctant father to get involved.[74] Two of *Wojna Domowa*'s characteristic song and dance sequences underline profound differences in the father's and the mother's perception of their son's blossoming sexuality. Zofia imagines plump twin babies in a sequence featuring her and her husband happily doing a huge load of laundry manually, in an old-fashioned washtub, while proudly entertaining their grandchildren.[75] The mother's hopes and worries are revealed in an impassioned attempt to motivate her husband Kazimierz to have 'the talk' with their son; after all, the girl might very well be their future daughter-in-law.[76] To his own great relief, the father's inept approach to his son's sex education ultimately results in the news that Paweł has already learnt everything about sex at school.[77]

The parents' acceptance of Paweł's buoyant social life culminates in a scene at the end of the episode in which they evaluate all the girls he has dated by ranking ten photographs on their coffee table. The episode closes with another music video to a song sung by Paweł's father: 'Oni mają teraz życie!' ('They Have Such a Great Life Now!'). The lyrics and the images contrast his own rather dreary youth with the lives of young people in Poland now, who receive sex education and have a great deal of time for leisure activities. It is notable that the second music clip takes a clearly masculine view of the pleasure to be had: shots of the table with pictures of Paweł's collection of girlfriends are blended with images of girls in bikinis, female silhouettes, couples kissing in public, and young men pursuing daring sports such as parachuting and high-diving. The difference between male and female readings of the merits of sex education is emphasized again when Kazimierz ends his musical

---

[74] *Wojna Domowa*, episode 11 (1:35–6:11).
[75] Ibid. (06:32–7:37).
[76] Ibid. (09:25–12:00). [77] Ibid. (29:20–31:20 and 38:40–39:33).

reflections. Zofia looks up in bewilderment when his song ends with the words 'They have such a great life now . . . in the category of "S"', immediately scolding him: 'Kazio! What are you talking about?' The episode closes with Kazimierz's embarrassed stammer: 'What? No, I mean, because schools are free of charge now.' The parents' song sequences differentiate clearly between female and male views of teenage sexuality. While the mother eventually opens up to her son's interest in girls, marriage and children are, in her view, the final goal of his sex life. At the same time, the father expresses envy and appreciation of the pleasures now available to young men. One profound difference between male and female sexuality familiar from contemporary sexology can therefore be traced in *Wojna Domowa*'s androcentric tribute to sex education: it is presented as 'normal' that the male protagonist explores girls as a coming of age ritual, while the girls themselves remain relatively anonymous and voiceless. Girls are objectified and evaluated via images of their bodies and their outward appearance—by the father, the son, and ultimately also by the mother.[78]

While this androcentric pattern persists, sexuality is addressed in a more direct and increasingly visual manner in the 1970s, and the visual restraint on eroticized nudity ends in the early 1980s. *Jan Serce* can be seen as a turning point, as this series features both the first striptease to reveal breasts in a Polish TV series[79] and erotic scenes between Jan and the single mother Danusia.[80] The couple engages in a passionate conversation praising the beauty of Danusia's body. Accompanied by her aroused moaning, the camera traces her body, starting at her toes and moving up her back to her face. The light in the bedroom is tinted red in both scenes that display nudity, visually underlining erotic tension with the colours of the boudoir. While the camera does not record the protagonists sleeping together, physical intimacy is nevertheless depicted directly. The camera and the couple's dialogue objectify the woman's naked body. Ever since, images of women resembling those of the 1960s

---

[78] The experiences of teenage girls are not narrated fully here, but the views of young men on dating multiple girls as a coming of age ritual were picked up again in episode 10, 'Zagraniczny gość' ('A Guest from Abroad'), in which Paweł and his British cousin Richard bond over common ideas about dating and the use of animal terms to describe girls, such as 'ptaszki' (birds) and 'kociaki' (kittens) (17:51–19:53).

[79] *Jan Serce*, episode 3 (28:21–29:56).

[80] *Jan Serce*, episode 4 (4:47–7:43 and 45:14–46:13). Jan and Danusia also have sex in the bathroom at their friends' house (51:39–52:21).

Western commercial sex wave,[81] involving striptease, erotic dance, and full or partial nudity, have prevailed.[82] It is therefore safe to say that the erotic objectification of the female body was one of the elements adapted by Polish TV directors from Western film and television.[83]

The androcentric perspective on sexuality in Polish TV series directly translates into their visual language. Erotic imagery of bodies is casually embedded in the series from the mid 1960s, but it is notable that in the fifty-three episodes (forty-five hours) of film material examined for this essay there are only three scenes that display erotic footage of male bodies: muscular swimmers, a high-diver jumping into a pool,[84] and two bodybuilders, the latter being examined with great interest by the female protagonist Danusia.[85] At the same time, the camera persistently casts an invasive gaze on female bodies. Even though pornography was forbidden in Poland, state-censored TV programmes allowed slow close-ups of cleavage accompanied by shots panning up actresses' legs and under their skirts.[86] These camera movements also underline the differentiation between the wife and the vamp. While the wife's physique is rarely exposed, every vamp's body is subjected to close scrutiny, often starting with the legs, slowly wandering upwards, and finally skimming the woman's bosom in slow-motion sequences. In *40-Latek*, for example, a short scene of the naked nurse Krysia peeking out of a bathroom is included in the series' opening sequence, underlined by the lyrics: 'As the world puts its attractions your way, you just have to help yourself!', suggesting that an attractive female body is one of life's pleasures that is 'up for grabs'. Stefan's wife Magda is also shown rolling around in bed with him in the opening scene; however, unlike Krysia, she is fully dressed. While both scenes

---

[81] Herzog, *Sexuality in Europe*, 134.

[82] e.g. Ewa Majewska's appearance as a stripper in episode 8 of *Alternatywy 4* (1983); and the prostitute Maria 'Mariola' Grzybianka in *Zmiennicy* (1987).

[83] For West Germany, see e.g. Dagmar Herzog, *Sex after Fascism: Memory and Morality in Twentieth-Century Germany* (Princeton, 2005), 145–8.

[84] *Wojna Domowa*, episode 11 (44:46).   [85] *Jan Serce*, episode 5 (13:39–13:59).

[86] In *Daleko od Szosy* the camera peeks up the skirt of a girl picking fruit; Wieczorek's wife's legs and breasts are exposed to the viewer, as is the prostitute Lola's body. Jadzia, the landlady's daughter, is also filmed in an erotic manner. In *40-Latek* Krysia's body is scrutinized by the camera repeatedly: for example, when she crawls over her bed searching for a packet of tea, the camera is fully focused on her rear. Instances of the objectification of female bodies in *Jan Serce* are provided by Danusia, the stripper at the lonely hearts ball, teenager Gabi dancing, and Matylda, Piotr's girlfriend.

suggest physical intimacy, there is a stark visual difference. Stefan and Magda are focused on each other, expressing their affection at eye level, while the naked Krysia looks seductively at the viewer (Stefan).

The expectation of a high level of personal grooming for women, as expressed in the advice of sexologists and in the contemporary press,[87] is also reflected in the series. With a few exceptions, the wives and fiancées, as well as the vamps, are dressed attractively, have modern haircuts, and always wear make-up—even in bed. The lead actresses' physiques mostly adhere to the contemporary ideal of a slim silhouette, while some of the 'vamps' are played by busty women with curvy bodies, thus embodying the stereotype of a 'sex bomb'.[88] The vamps, who do not matter in the male lead's life in the long term, are presented in a way that underlines features of the female body considered to be sexually attractive to heterosexual men. Cleavages, women in bikinis, and busty chests are casually integrated into all four series from 1965 onwards, the camera thus providing the audience with a male perspective that objectifies voiceless female bodies in an eroticized manner. Meanwhile, male physical beauty in a classical sense is marginalized in, if not almost entirely absent from, Polish TV series. Men are predominantly shown fully dressed and the protagonists do not illustrate a distinct aesthetic or physique. Unlike femininity, virility is not established by any distinct visual markers. The lead actors present a wide range of body types, from the old-world elegance of slender Kazimierz (*Wojna Domowa*) to short and wiry Leszek Górecki (*Daleko od Szosy*) and the slightly stocky Jan Serce.

Meanwhile, any attention to men's physique tends to be ridiculed, such as Stefan's concern about hair loss or about what to wear at a photo shoot at work in *40-Latek*; Leszek's attempt to improve his hygiene by washing his feet and spraying them with eau de cologne before a date; or Jan Serce's post-coital appearance in his girlfriend's embroidered nightgown. As long as a man is educated, chivalrous, has a minimum level of culture or confidence, and can put on a nice suit and shirt to mark an occasion, he is deemed to be attractive on

---

[87] The prescriptive reflections on women's personal grooming in Wisłocka, *Sztuka Kochania*, 80–93, are a striking example.

[88] Lola and the orchard owner's wife from *Daleko od Szosy* in particular embody this stereotype. So far, the Polish appropriation of the 'sex bomb' in popular culture has been addressed in only one publication, Krzysztof Tomasik, *Seksbomby PRL-u* (Warsaw, 2014).

Polish television. Formal dress is presented as an important attribute of the 'attractive man' across all four series.[89] The socialist ideal type of the muscular physical worker, though, is completely absent from Polish TV neighbourhoods. In summary, the disparity in normative ideas about sexual attractiveness in Polish public discourse in the 1960s and 1970s is expressed in the series' visual language.[90] While women's bodies had to conform to a rigid ideal of beauty, there were few visual benchmarks for male attractiveness on TV. At a visual level, there is a strong resemblance between the presentation of women's bodies in Polish TV neighbourhoods and the Western trend towards displaying eroticized women's bodies in the media.[91]

The episode of *Wojna Domowa* mentioned above also pays tribute to the increasing public presence of sex advice literature in Poland from the 1960s. In three-quarters of the series analysed, the protagonist seeks sex advice in a bookshop. Kazimierz Jankowski, the father in *Wojna Domowa*, purchases a pile of sex education literature to prepare for the 'big conversation' with his son.[92] Both parents admire the abundance of expert knowledge available to modern adolescents while regretting that they themselves were educated merely by reading entries in an encyclopaedia. In a humorous scene, Zofia Jankowska says to her husband that the books are 'crazy interesting' and that she 'didn't have an inkling about any of this'. Both agree that there is a lot to learn from the literature, but perhaps not all of it is suitable for children. The couple decide to give Paweł and his friend Anula pamphlets directed at boys and girls respectively, so that 'they can talk to each other on the same level'.[93] While *Wojna Domowa* thus presents the most extensive references to sex education publications, Stefan Karwowski in *40-Latek* also rushes to a bookshop when his sex drive falters. He merely peeks through the

---

[89] Further examples: Paweł wears a suit and white shirt for his date; in *40-Latek* an entire episode focuses on the correct outfit for a photo shoot; Leszek Górecki initially borrows and then buys formal clothes to impress his family and his girlfriend in the village; and Jan Serce dresses in his suit when accompanying his mother to meet a potential wife, Lusia.

[90] Małgorzata Fidelis and Katarzyna Stańczak-Wiślicz, 'Piękne i zaradne: rytuały ciała, moda i uroda', in Stańczak-Wiślicz, Perkowski, Fidelis, et al., *Kobiety w Polsce*, 407–55.   [91] Herzog, *Sexuality in Europe*, 134–46.

[92] Kazimierz agrees to buy books about sex education before talking to his son in *Wojna Domowa*, episode 11 (11:55, 16:08–18:53). Zofia Jankowska hands Anula a copy of Halina Chatys-Skirzyńska's *Okres dojrzewania dziewcząt* (33:52). The other book seen on screen in this episode is Łopuski, *Co chce wiedzieć każdy chłopiec* (22:35–25:34).

[93] *Wojna Domowa*, episode 11 (22:35–25:34).

window, however, before fleeing.[94] Finally, middle-aged bachelor Jan Serce walks into a bookshop asking for a guide to explain love to him.[95] Read against the grain, the presence of sex education publications in Polish pop culture suggests that TV series referenced a widely known source of information and, probably most effectively from the mid 1960s, promoted this modern way of learning about sex to a national audience. In this respect, TV series enhanced the reach of popular science publications about sexuality. Nevertheless, the androcentricity of the narratives persists in these instances. Whenever books about sex and love are referenced, they appear in relation to male issues, suggesting that sex troubles bother only men. Meanwhile, all references but one to contemporary Western discourse about female pleasure are negative, taking the focus away from women's erotic fulfilment.[96]

I shall explore this issue further by turning to a relational analysis of erotic experiences and sexual agency. For the sake of legibility, the following reflections examine structural elements from the entire sample, concentrating mainly on two representative episodes from the series *40-Latek* and on the sex life of its leading couple, Magda and Stefan Karwowski, as a case in point. Evidence from the remainder of the sample is provided in the references. The family in *40-Latek*, the Karwowskis, consists of a middle-aged, working couple who live in a modern high-rise in Warsaw with their two teenage children, Jagoda and Marek. While Magda works in the city's waterworks laboratory, engineer Stefan supervises construction sites for Poland's prestige projects, such as Warsaw's Central Station or the Trasa Łazienkowska, a highly modern city motorway, that were actually being built at the time.[97] The couple embodies an average, educated urban family which lives in the modest prosperity of a modern flat and owns a car (a small red Polski Fiat), modern furniture, a TV set, and a telephone. Stefan has just turned 40 and his mid-life crisis provides the linchpin of each episode, addressing issues such as hair loss, physical fitness, nicotine addiction, career problems, and, last but not least, sexuality.[98] In the following, two

---

[94] *40-Latek*, episode 3 (04:53–05:20).   [95] *Jan Serce*, episode 1 (25:36–27:04).

[96] Grant, *Sexing the Millennium*, 109–26. The scene is the conversation between Stefan and Karol in *40-Latek*, episode 3 (05:21–08:52).

[97] See Kazimierz Kunicki and Tomasz Ławecki, *Budujemy Drugą Polskę: wielkie inwestycje PRL-u* (Łódź, 2018), 105–16.

[98] For episode summaries see ⟨https://www.filmpolski.pl/fp/index.php?film=123482⟩ [accessed 10 Sept. 2021].

erotic encounters from this series will be compared. Episode 3, 'Wpadnij, kiedy zechcesz, czyli bodźce stępione' ('Pop in Whenever You Like, or Blunted Stimuli'), tells the story of Stefan's affair with the attractive nurse Krysia, while episode 10, 'Pocztówka ze Spitsbergenu, czyli oczarowanie' ('A Postcard from Spitzbergen, or The Enchantment'), explores the repercussions of a romantic encounter between Magda and Professor Koziełło at a hydrology conference. I shall here demonstrate that both male and female sexual agency is narrated from a masculine perspective.

Married couples in Polish TV neighbourhoods are explicitly or implicitly shown to have a sex life that follows a fixed routine. Intimacy between spouses, however, is never accompanied by erotic visuals entailing nudity.[99] When Stefan displays signs of restlessness and suggests sleeping on the balcony instead of in the marital bed, for example, Magda responds by trying to seduce him. She engages in a well-rehearsed routine of erotic moves such as ruffling her hair and adopting a provocative pose. However, her efforts backfire and are highly comical because she is wearing a long, bulky nightgown. Stefan escapes to the toilet while Magda utters the affectionate diminutive 'Stefciu!' in wide-eyed bewilderment.[100] Deeply worried about his lack of erotic desire, Stefan talks about his ailment in a medical consultation with his friend Dr Karol Stelmach. While Stefan emphasizes that he loves his wife, Karol is convinced that he is a victim of contemporary 'sex propaganda' and modern women's heightened erotic expectations. Stefan is not sure about this interpretation; ultimately, he insists on a prescription to help with his feelings of being obliged to respond adequately to his wife's sexual advances.[101] On the one hand, the desire to please his spouse sexually is firmly established in the husband's mind. Stefan's concern about Magda's pleasure embeds contemporary theories about the importance of a cultured matrimonial sex life into the narrative. On the other, marital sex is presented from a male perspective: as a safe, pleasant, albeit often boring, routine.

---

[99] Further examples of references to marital sex: in *Wojna Domowa*, Paweł's parents discuss whether they should consider some of the advice from the publications they bought for their son. In *Daleko od Szosy*, Jan and Ania are shown having sexual encounters while courting and after getting married. The scenes at home always follow the same routine, including gentle kissing and romantic expressions of affection while fully clothed. In *Jan Serce*, Małgosia and Piotr exchange flirtatious glances at a party.

[100] *40-Latek*, episode 3 (02:36–04:49).

[101] Ibid. (05:21–08:52).

Meanwhile, both spouses are exposed to erotic tension outside their relationships. But these encounters differ profoundly between the genders. Men are exposed to temptation,[102] or chase after a woman,[103] but the socialist *Matka Polka* receives attention from admirers who need to be fended off by the husband.[104] In the case of Magda and Stefan, this pattern materializes as follows. Once Stefan holds the prescription for solving his sex issues in his hands, the pretty young nurse Krysia enters the scene.[105] He picks her up at the bus stop and offers to drive her home. After a flirtatious ramble in a department store, they end up at her home. When Krysia enquires about Stefan's medical issues, she throws his prescription in the air, laughing loudly, and they embrace passionately.[106] Stefan's impotence appears to be cured instantly. Magda, however, becomes an object of interest for internationally renowned Professor Koziełło while attending a conference for work. Before the first sessions, she goes for a walk in a wintry park where an attractive, sporty man is doing laps in a tracksuit. The youthful stranger flirts with Magda, rolls on the ground, and confidently grabs her hand to twirl across the frozen lake with her.[107] While she is clearly flattered, she instantly refers to her husband, making it clear that she is a married woman. The central difference between the husband's and the wife's encounters with attractive people outside their relationship lies in their agency. Whereas the husband actively pursues an erotic adventure, the wife becomes the untouchable object of another man's desire. Furthermore, her marital status is immediately disclosed, while her husband does not refer to his at

---

[102] In *Daleko od Szosy* there are scenes with girls in the orchard, Wieczorek's wife, the landlady's daughter, and Lola the prostitute. *Jan Serce* features Danusia, Matylda (who has an affair with Piotr), and Jan's female boss at work.

[103] In *Wojna Domowa*, Paweł tries to impress his date with formal attire and gentlemanly demeanour. Leszek works hard to win both his first girlfriend Bronka and his future wife Ania, flirting and showing off his skills as a mechanic and later as a student. The entire series of *Jan Serce* is dedicated to Jan's search for a *Matka Polka* to complete his life. The journey of this chivalrous, entertaining, and honest mature bachelor involves experiences with a range of women and is so exhausting that he ends up in a sanatorium with a 'broken heart' before he finds his destiny with Kalina.

[104] Suitors who need to be chased away in *Daleko od Szosy* are: Bronka's neighbour Staszek; Ania's urban friends and her admirer at the sanatorium. *40-Latek* constantly features Magda's enamoured boss, Mieczysław Gajny. In *Jan Serce*, Danusia's 'lost and found' husband ousts Jan, who himself steps aside for Piotr when he reclaims his wife Małgosia after leaving her for Matylda. Finally, Lusia's memories of her late true love prevent her from marrying Jan.   [105] *40-Latek*, episode 3 (05:21–08:52).

[106] Ibid. (09:44–20:38).   [107] *40-Latek*, episode 10 (14:31–17:27).

all. This divergence establishes a patriarchal perspective within a sexually permissive constellation.

The background of supporting characters interfering in the protagonist's sex life underlines gendered variations of sexual demeanour and morality. While male suitors are educated or highly chivalrous,[108] husbands have affairs with women who are less well educated.[109] Krysia, for example, is a nurse, while Magda has a university degree. The woman with whom the adulterous husband has an affair does not have to be his intellectual equal because all he wants from her is an erotic adventure. His personal and professional growth, however, is constantly supported by his wife in every episode. By contrast, Magda's suitors—her boss and the distinguished, attractive Professor Koziełło—are both her professional equals and are better suited to her than her husband, and are constantly referred to as benchmarks for him. Yet again, the series takes a male perspective on the issue. Rather than considering the wife's desires and feelings, her erotic encounter is presented from her husband's point of view as a threat to his matrimonial authority.

While both spouses experience erotic tension and flirtations, the clearest dichotomy in the stories lies in their references to sex. No socialist *Matka Polka* is shown to engage in extramarital sex, while most husbands and fiancés commit adultery. Krysia's relationship with Stefan does not have any deeper emotional meaning for either of them, and it ultimately has a positive effect on his marriage. After the camera cuts away from the erotic scene, Stefan is shown skipping home merrily with flowers for his wife. In the evening, he lies in bed half-naked and seductively invites Magda, who is hoovering a bathroom carpet, to join him.[110] All his confidence issues appear to have been solved by his sexual adventure. Here the series implies that the husband's extramarital sex is 'good sex' in the sense that it restores the protagonist's confidence and virility. Thus, the TV series underlines and normalizes the gender-specific concept of sexuality that

---

[108] *40-Latek*: Mieczysław Gajny is head of the Warsaw waterworks laboratory and Magda's boss. *Daleko od Szosy*: Ania's rich friends from Łódź; intellectuals at university; a suitor at the sanatorium. *Jan Serce*: chivalrous, sensitive Jan in pursuit of Małgosia, Danusia, Gabi, and Lusia.

[109] Women involved in affairs with married or engaged men are a prostitute and a middle-aged married woman (*Daleko od Szosy*), a hairdresser and a barmaid (*Jan Serce*), and Mariola, a junior lab girl from *40-Latek* who constantly brings up her affairs, including those with married men.

[110] *40-Latek*, episode 3 (21:25–22:59).

was evident in scientific and public discourse in Poland. Permissive sexuality is a privilege of the male protagonist. Only the adulterous husband's experiences matter in the long term, while the vamp is merely a vehicle for boosting his confidence, the embodiment of an ephemeral male erotic fantasy. This constellation is presented without reference to Western feminist discourse that criticized the objectification of women for the sake of male pleasure.[111]

Magda's extramarital adventure follows a profoundly different pattern. After their flirtation in the park, Professor Koziełło asks her to take notes during his opening address. Meanwhile, her boss, Mieczysław Gajny, grows jealous and warns his employee against liaising with 'the wrong people'. Instead of following this advice, Magda calls Stefan to ask him for her fashionable wig so that she can look attractive to the professor, lying that she needs it because it is cold at the venue. When Stefan gives the wig to Gajny, the latter expresses his concern that Magda has joined a crowd of pseudo-scientists. Subsequently, she is shown entering Koziełło's room at night to discuss her notes, wearing her fashionable wig. The professor praises her handwriting, saying it indicates her focus and organization, and Magda is flattered. Yet their intimate flirtation is ended abruptly by a call from Stefan, who criticizes Magda for risking her career by liaising with dubious scientists. Magda becomes very protective of Koziełło, defending him against her husband and her boss, and she actively fosters an atmosphere of mutual attraction by dressing up and by flattering him. Her proximity to her suitor, however, remains verbal only. The wife's unwavering fidelity castrates the suitor of the socialist *Matka Polka*. Even though the narrative presents Magda as flirtatious, the perspective taken on the issue is centred on the men who claim a stake in her life. First and foremost, her husband is unsettled by her admiration for another man. While Magda enjoys the professor's attention, it is always clear that there will be no sex between her and Koziełło, even though he would evidently be interested in such relations, seeking physical contact with her from their first encounter. It is Magda who draws a red line from the start. In a way, the interest of a romantic admirer can be read as ennobling the socialist *Matka Polka*. Her refusal to give in to temptation establishes that there is only one kind of 'good sex' for the wife: a physical relationship with her husband. Both

---

[111] Herzog, *Sex after Fascism*, 231–4.

she and her suitor, who is subjected to this structural castration, are entangled in an idealized concept of chastity.[112]

Meanwhile, her husband's punishment appears to be inevitable, suggesting that the adulterous man's potency is, to a certain extent, limited. Stefan's brief purgatory manifests itself on three levels: humiliation, ridicule, and the threat of losing his family. First, he is humiliated at work when his colleagues eavesdrop on a conversation about Krysia.[113] Second, his reignited confidence is undermined when another admirer, Benek, casually answers her door. He forces Stefan to walk Krysia's dog Agatka and insults him by insinuating that Stefan does not own a car. Stefan's discomfort increases when he is spotted walking the ridiculous poodle Agatka by his wife's boss.[114] Finally, his humiliation peaks when Magda finds out about the betrayal as Mieczysław Gajny 'innocently' enquires about her 'lovely new dog' in a team meeting. In the episode's final scene, further shame is inflicted as Stefan and Krysia break up in a café. When Stefan says that he might start to cry, his former lover laughs at him and suggests calling an ambulance. After she leaves, a homosexual man approaches Stefan in a flirtatious manner. Stefan, visibly irritated, flees the scene while the gay man mutters 'dziwak' (weirdo) to the camera.[115] In conclusion, the moral lesson is that 'good sex' in an affair is not entirely good, as it ultimately entails some sort of humiliation.

Extramarital sexuality and erotic attraction, however, inevitably result in reconciliation. The husband has to actively win his spouse back, and the wife accepts her husband's betrayal if it is disclosed to her. The difference between the narratives' moral stance and the characters' agency in relation to sex outside marriage is clearly tangible in the voice of Kobieta Pracująca (the Working Woman), who gives Magda and Stefan counselling. This character advises the Karwowskis in a monologue in every episode. Based on a parody of Stalinist propaganda, the Working Woman has done so many jobs in her life that she has expert knowledge on everything from the right

---

[112] Examples of men trying to have sex with *Matka Polka* in *Daleko od Szosy* are Ania's rich friend who is embarrassed by Leszek's knowledge of cars, and her suitor at the sanatorium who is put off by Leszek's surprise visit. At the New Year's Eve ball Leszek 'fights' a rival with words instead of fists. Furthermore, Jan Serce is disappointed when Małgosia, Gabi, and Danusia return to their husbands or boyfriends. Jan has sex with Danusia only while her husband is missing.

[113] *40-Latek*, episode 3 (23:18–25:52).   [114] Ibid. (26:22).

[115] Ibid. (44:35–46:47).

glasses for serving cognac to plumbing and marital issues. When she encounters Magda crying about Stefan's affair, the Working Woman explains how wonderful it is that Stefan has regained his virility and his confidence. She emphasizes that whatever makes a husband happy contributes to his wife's happiness too, adding that men need female admiration as a space in which their actions can resonate, as an affirmation of their masculinity. Female attention makes men feel young, intelligent, and entertaining—even if they are none of these. This has been achieved by Stefan's other woman, so the Working Woman advises Magda to turn Stefan's adultery into a 'historical event', encouraging her to close this unpleasant chapter in their relationship in order to move on as a couple.[116] The Working Woman thus makes Stefan an object of analysis who can easily be manipulated if the right toolkit is available, and Magda applies the advice straight away. When Stefan bounces into the flat happily proclaiming that he is ravenous and asking Magda to make a meal for 'the awesome leader of two building sites', Magda quenches his enthusiasm by drily disclosing her knowledge of the poodle Agatka. Stefan is shocked. Magda announces that she is moving out with the children (who enter the scene in winter clothes and carrying bags overflowing with their belongings) so that Stefan can enjoy some peace and quiet and live up to his potential. Stefan helps Magda into her coat, but suddenly declares passionately that nobody is leaving. On the way out, the suitcase drops open and Magda's clothes scatter on the floor. The couple kneel down together and pick up the garments, but Stefan suddenly throws everything, including the suitcase, into the air and shouts 'I love you!' six times in a crescendo of words amid a flurry of colourful blouses. Magda hugs him, starts crying, and sobs: 'And I will cook that lunch for you!'[117] Marital bliss à la polonaise is restored. Magda not only immediately forgives the intermezzo with Krysia, but seamlessly reverts to the role of the homemaker. The instant return to normality suggests that adultery is something that men simply do every now and then. The exchange with the promiscuous vamp benefits both partners for a limited period of time and is shown ultimately to stabilize their marriage and their enduring attachment to their family.

Marital reconciliation following Magda's adventure takes a different turn. On her return, Stefan and Magda quarrel about her admiration for the professor. Stefan references Gajny's dismissive

---

[116] Ibid. (35:50–41:11).   [117] Ibid. (40:59–44:04).

evaluation of the 'pseudo-scientist', while Magda fiercely defends Koziełło's academic achievements and his flexible working style. The confrontation escalates and Stefan bellows that he would love to give Koziełło a beating, rushes out of the room, and slams the door. Magda yells that he is behaving like a simpleton before leaving the flat.[118] In the next scene she is shown in a café ordering four desserts that she wolfs down in a bout of emotional eating.[119] Meanwhile, it has turned dark outside and Stefan is waiting for her impatiently. The Working Woman enters the scene to collect payment for a plumbing bill. Stefan confesses to her that Magda has met some 'little professor', and as a result she is no longer happy with him. The Working Woman explains to Stefan that Magda is subject to an 'enchantment', and that if treated properly, this state will pass after two weeks. She also recommends that Stefan do something eccentric to reignite his wife's interest in him.[120] When Magda comes home, Stefan is ready. He sings 'My Bonnie Lies over the Ocean' while accompanying himself on the guitar. Magda is astonished to hear him singing in English. Stefan casually responds that he likes singing in different languages and starts a Polish song. Then he suddenly jumps up, puts the guitar aside, and records instructions for his team on tape. Magda is so impressed that she drops her teacup on the floor and drinks from the teapot's spout.[121] The husband thus restores his matrimonial position of power by being better than his rival.

Superficially, it could be argued that Polish TV series from the 1960s on are set in a sexually liberated world that allows for promiscuous behaviour by both men and women. But the women who enjoy sexual freedom have no lasting presence in the storylines, which are each centred on a male protagonist's experiences and emotions. The vamp's path is briefly entangled with his life, but her episodic existence does not allow her to become a realistic character with feelings of her own. Instead, seductive vamps embody male fantasies of attractive women who want sex with no strings attached.[122] Another narrative pattern

---

[118] *40-Latek*, episode 10 (43:46–46:16).   [119] *40-Latek*, episode 10 (46:17–47:17).

[120] *40-Latek*, episode 10 (47:46–51:45).   [121] *40-Latek*, episode 10 (51:46–53:50).

[122] Such as Krysia and Mariola from *40-Latek*; Lola and her friend at the bar, Mietek's girlfriends, and the orchard owner's wife from *Daleko od Szosy*. In *Jan Serce*, Basia from the bar and the girls in Tycjan's notebook exhibit these characteristics, but Matylda and, to an extent, Danusia present a hybrid form of the stereotype as they are briefly interested in a longer relationship.

surrounding male sexuality lies in minor punishments for adultery that establish a sense of impotence: ridicule,[123] humiliation, and, in one case, venereal disease.[124] These mishaps underline the idea of male weakness in facing sexual temptation. According to televised narratives in Poland, having extramarital sex is good to a certain extent as it boosts male confidence; yet at the same time, that kind of sex is always rather humiliating. Meanwhile, the male sinner is invariably forgiven by his wife, making her the morally superior character.

In the long term, the socialist *Matka Polka* always wins out against the vamp because she is the mother of her adulterous husband's children and bound to him by matrimony. Her presence is eternal, while the vamp only briefly appears on the stage. Thus, narratives about male adultery on Polish television adhere to a double standard of femininity. On the one hand, there are women who satisfy sexual desires and are objectified in an erotic manner, similar to the Western objectification of women in the sex wave of the 1960s.[125] They are briefly necessary to establish virility, but irrelevant to the family's story. On the other hand, there is the *Matka Polka*, who provides the lasting framework that the lead male character needs in order to be a successful member of society. She moulds him, constantly works to better him, gives him a home, and ultimately is his long-term sexual partner and mother to his children. On Polish television from the mid 1960s to the early 1980s, the 'other woman', the seductive vamp, never poses a serious threat to the integrity of the adulterous husband's family. In a way, the *Matka Polka*'s idealized fidelity and devotion to the family persist in an increasingly permissive setting that allows the husband to pursue his sexual desires without any consequences for his marriage. Divorce and illegitimate children

---

[123] Male sexuality is frequently ridiculed in *Daleko od Szosy*. Lola laughs hysterically at Leszek's lorry and his naivety and lack of experience. His girlfriend Bronka visits him right after he contracts a venereal disease, resulting in ridiculous scenes with Leszek desperately avoiding being alone with her. He is also forced to discuss his embarrassing ailment with a female doctor. When he tries to be responsible and warns Lola, she slaps him in public. His future wife Ania also initially makes fun of Leszek's shy attempts to flirt with her.

[124] Several male characters are dropped by the women they have affairs with. In *Jan Serce* Matylda leaves Piotr, Danusia returns to her husband, and Małgosia takes Piotr back after his fling instead of staying with Jan. In *Daleko od Szosy* Lola slaps Leszek when he tries to warn her about her venereal disease, and Leszek is beaten up by young men from the village when he tries to return to his old girlfriend Bronka.

[125] See Krzysztof Tomasik, *Seksbomby PRL-u*, for Polish actresses' appropriation of Western trends in erotic attire and behaviour.

are not part of Poland's TV neighbourhoods until the late 1980s. The second narrative pattern, the wife's erotic encounter, is one of temptation, desire, and rivalry, and the *Matka Polka* is not an active agent in these relationships. She is subjected to the interest and flattery of another man. While there is certainly an erotic element to these encounters, the socialist *Matka Polka* is attractive to educated, cultured men based on her intellect as well as her physical beauty. Her education, professional life, and engagement in cultural activities such as playing the piano or going to the theatre elevate her value in the eyes of the suitor and the husband alike. It is her sophistication, not her physical attractiveness alone, that triggers male desire. Ultimately, televised stories about attraction to the socialist *Matka Polka* are about male rivalry and the affirmation provided by the fidelity of a 'good' wife, despite the attentions of other men.

III. *Conclusion*

Was Kristen Ghodsee's thesis that women had better sex under socialism true for Poland's TV neighbourhoods?[126] Polish television series from the mid 1960s to the early 1980s presented their audiences with a highly gendered take on sexual liberation. Far from being egalitarian, the predominantly male screenwriters behind the shows differentiated morally between the socialist *Matka Polka* and promiscuous vamps. The feelings and issues experienced by sexually liberated women were not included in their narratives. Instead, TV neighbourhoods were androcentric discursive spaces that objectified the honourable *Matka Polka* and the promiscuous vamp equally. Both categories of female characters were defined from a male perspective. While women did have sex within this highly normative framework, Polish TV series paid little attention to female pleasure. Female bodies, especially those of the 'vamps', were presented in a highly eroticized manner, while male bodies were not exposed to the erotic gaze of the camera. This selective objectification occurred alongside a differentiation between the morally superior wife and the promiscuous vamp that resonated with the gender roles inherent in the Catholic–nationalist stereotype of the *Matka Polka*. This constellation translated on to the small screen an ambiguous and highly gendered sexual morality that

[126] Ghodsee, *Why Women Have Better Sex under Socialism.*

was also present in Poland's progressive contemporary sexology. Visually, the reduction of women's sexuality, seen through a male lens, borrowed elements from the eroticization of the female body in Western media.

The tacit dichotomy between tradition and modernity in Polish narratives about permissive sexuality represents a central difference from the role of British or US television programmes as discursive spaces in propelling the sexual revolution into the mainstream, as von Hodenberg argues. Polish television's strictly androcentric perspective and its increasingly permissive visual language about sex did not give way to the confrontational plots found on Western television from the mid 1960s. I argue that the quality of sex for women was only marginally relevant to the makers of Polish television series between 1965 and 1982. For them, women's sexuality was merely a vehicle for negotiating masculinity, as the socialist *Matka Polka* established the male protagonist's identity. Having sex with her meant that he became a husband, a father, and a hero of the Polish People's Republic. Matrimonial sex thus resonated with Catholic and Polish nationalist ideals. The vamp, by contrast, was a vehicle for granting men greater sexual freedom in line with global developments. It appears that the only stories about the sexual revolution's impact on Polish society worth telling on national television under socialism were those taking a male point of view. Considering the unfaltering popularity of Polish television series from the socialist era, these programmes can be seen as a part of Poland's cultural heritage that resonates with an androcentric view of female sexuality. To use Polish feminist Agnieszka Graff's pointed description of Poland's public sphere in her book *Świat bez kobiet* (*A World without Women*),[127] fictional TV neighbourhoods presented normative ideas about sexuality that entailed a conservative view of femininity embodied by the wife, alongside a crude objectification of the female body (the vamp).

[127] Agnieszka Graff, *Świat bez kobiet: płec w Polskim życiu publicznym* (Warsaw, 2001).

Notes on Contributors

FIAMMETTA BALESTRACCI is a historian specializing in the history of Germany, the history of the Italian Communist Party, and the history of sexuality. She obtained her Ph.D. at the University of Milan and was recently awarded her habilitation in Italy. She has worked at many Italian and European universities, and in 2011 she founded the Italian Society for the Contemporary History of the German Language Area (SISCALT). Her next book will be published in 2024 by Giulio Einaudi.

KINGA S. BLOCH is a Teaching Fellow at Queen Mary University of London and Deputy Director of the Leo Baeck Institute London, where she is involved in developing innovative web-based formats for education on German Jewish history and culture. Her research focuses on television's impact on memory and societal discourse, including her upcoming comparative Ph.D. on televising gender in the Cold War (UCL).

MAUD ANNE BRACKE is Professor of Modern European History at the University of Glasgow. She holds a Ph.D. from the European University Institute. She is the author of two monographs, three edited collections, and over thirty articles on the gender, social, and political history of post-1945 Europe. Her forthcoming monograph *Reproductive Rights in Modern France: Feminism, Contraception, and Abortion, 1950–1980* will be published by OUP.

MARTIN DEUERLEIN is Assistant Professor of Contemporary History at the University of Tübingen. He has published on the interconnections of globalization discourse and international politics in the long 1970s in *Das Zeitalter der Interdependenz* (2020). His research interests include intellectual history, the history of the Cold War, and transnational relations. He is currently working on a book on 'strategies of indigeneity' in the nineteenth and twentieth centuries.

LISA DITTRICH was a Research Fellow at the LMU Munich. Her Ph.D. thesis on nineteenth-century anticlericalism in Europe was awarded the Max Weber Prize of the Bavarian Academy of Science in 2012. Her habilitation project looked at social transformations in East and West Germany from 1945 to 1990 through the prism of married and unmarried couple relationships.

JULIANE FÜRST is Head of the Department 'Communism and Society' at the Leibniz Centre for Contemporary History, Potsdam, and Professor of Modern

History at the Central European University. Her publications include *Flowers through Concrete: Explorations in Soviet Hippieland* (2021), *Stalin's Last Generation: Soviet Post-War Youth and the Emergence of Late Socialism* (2010), and, as editor, *Dropping Out of Socialism: The Creation of Alternative Spheres in the Soviet Bloc* (2016).

PASCAL GERMANN is a senior researcher at the Institute for the History of Medicine at the University of Bern. He is currently working on a research project on the transnational history of quality of life knowledge since the 1970s.

NORBERT GÖTZ holds the Chair of Contemporary History at Södertörn University, Stockholm. His current research focuses on humanitarianism, moral economy, global civil society, and civil society–state relations. His latest book is *Humanitarianism in the Modern World: The Moral Economy of Famine Relief*, co-authored with Georgina Brewis and Steffen Werther (Cambridge University Press, 2020; open access).

PATRICIA HERTEL is a historian of nineteenth- and twentieth-century Europe. She is a researcher at the Centre Marc Bloch Berlin and a Visiting Professor at the FU Berlin in 2023/24, and teaches modern and contemporary history at the University of Basel. Her second book, *Europe's Favourite Dictatorships*, is forthcoming with De Gruyter.

CHRISTINA VON HODENBERG is the Director of the German Historical Institute London (GHIL) and a Professor in European History at Queen Mary University of London. She has written five monographs in the fields of media history, social protest, and gender history. Her revisionist account of the late 1960s protest movements, *The Other 1968: Social History of a West German Revolt*, will be published in 2024.

KRISTOFF KERL is a cultural and social historian. He received his Ph.D. at the University of Cologne in 2015. His research interests include the history of bodies and emotions, gender history, the history of antisemitism, the history of the 1960s, and the history of counter-cultures. His current research project examines the politics of ecstasy in the United States, the United Kingdom, and Western Germany during the 1960s and 1970s.

ISABEL RICHTER is a Deputy Director at the German Historical Institute Washington DC and Head of the GHI Pacific Office at UC Berkeley. She received her Ph.D. in modern history from the TU Berlin and her habilitation from the Ruhr University Bochum. Her research interests include German cultural history (late eighteenth century to the present), National Socialism and its aftermath, resistance and counter-cultures in the twentieth century, the global 1960s, and the history of life stages.

Roseanna Webster is a junior research fellow at Trinity College, Cambridge and an associate lecturer in twentieth-century European history at the University of St Andrews. She was previously a visiting fellow at the European University Institute in Florence and in 2023 an article she published won the RHS Alexander Prize.

Index